Leveraging Visual Basic® with ActiveX™ Controls

How to Order:

For information on quantity discounts contact the publisher: Prima Publishing, P.O. Box 1260BK, Rocklin, CA 95677-1260; (916) 632-4400. On your letterhead include information concerning the intended use of the books and the number of books you wish to purchase. For individual orders, turn to the back of this book for more information.

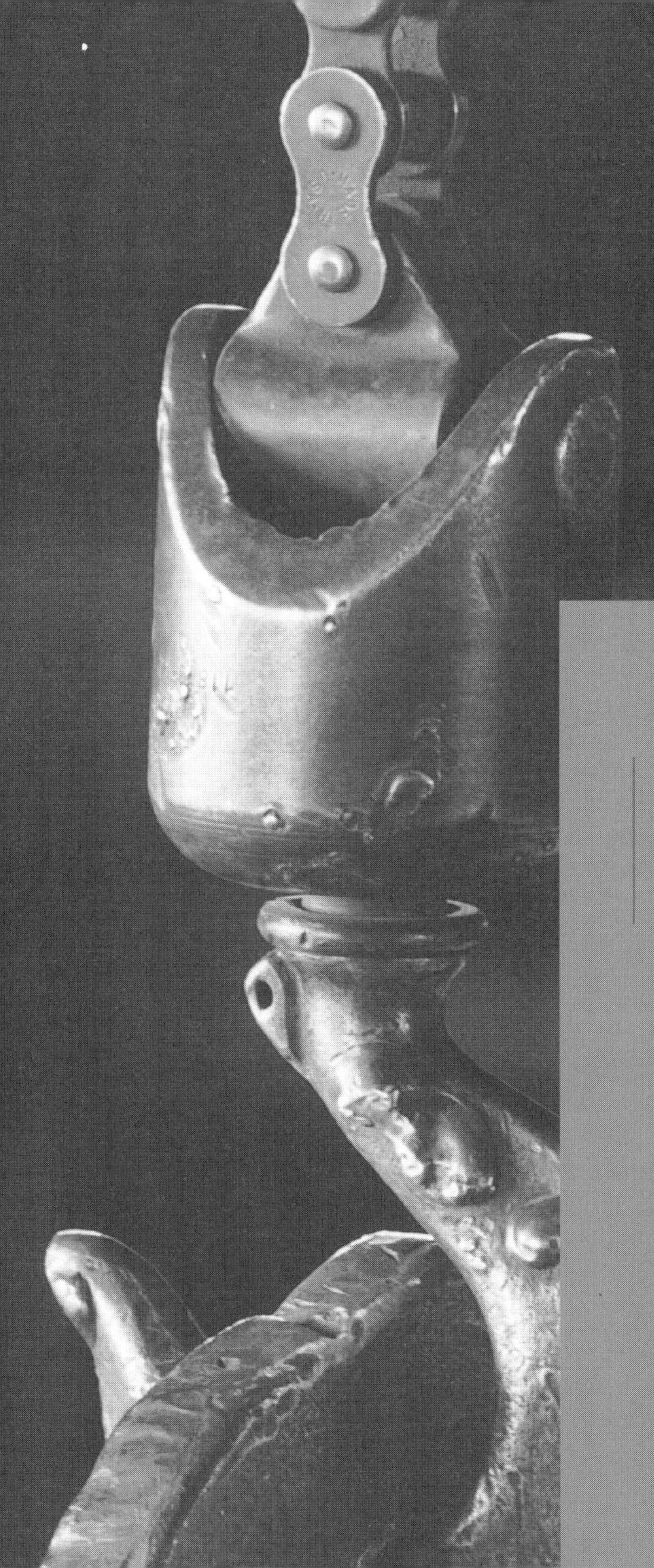

Leveraging Visual Basic® with ActiveX™ Controls

Wayne S. Freeze

Prima Publishing

P

PRIMA is a trademark of Prima Publishing, a division of Prima Communications, Inc. Prima Publishing, Rocklin, California 95677.

Prima Publishing® is a registered trademark of Prima Communications, Inc.

ISBN: 0-7615-0901-1

Library of Congress Catalog Card Number: 95-72671

Printed in the United States of America

96 97 98 99 DD 10 9 8 7 6 5 4 3 2 1

Publisher Don Roche, Jr.
Associate Publisher Ray Robinson
Acquisitions Manager Alan Harris
Managing Editor Tad Ringo
Product Marketing Specialist Julie Barton

Acquisitions Editor
Ian Sheeler

Development Editor
Angelique Brittingham

Project Editor
Heather Kaufman Urschel

Technical Reviewer
Sundar Rajan

Indexer
Sharon Hilgenberg

Cover Designer
Rick Wong

Acknowledgments

To Bill Adler, Jr., thank you for posting your note on the Internet newsgroup comp.lang.basic.visual.misc. Little did I realize it would eventually lead to my first book. I also want to thank you for the answers to all of my stupid questions and for reassuring me that things will work out in the end. I'm sure this will be the start of a long relationship.

To my new friends at Prima, Julie Barton, Angelique Brittingham, and Heather Urschel, thank you for your comments and suggestions, and also thank you for your patience and assistance while I learn about how to write a book for a real publishing company. Because of your efforts, I can't wait to start my next book!

To Steve Edwards and Butch Reinke, thank you for your understanding and cooperation, without which this book would never have been written.

To Walter Smith, thank you for the challenge you laid at my feet: because if you can write a book, so can I!

To Rick, Shaun, Elwyn, Ian, Kyle, Michelle, and Wanda, thank you for believing that I could write this book, even when I thought I couldn't.

To Bucky and Goose, thank you for your wonderful daughter, without whom I couldn't (and probably wouldn't) have written this book.

To my Mother and Father, see how a little technology can turn someone who hated taking English classes in school into a published author.

To Christopher and Samantha, thank you for understanding that Daddy can't always play with you while I'm writing. Because you are only 3 and 2 years old, you may not understand what this means to me now, but someday you will.

And finally to my wife, Jill, thank you for being yourself. I doubt that I would have ever given this project a second thought except for your interest in writing. I know that your book will be the next one published. Thank you for all the hard work (and commas) you put into this book, even though your name is not listed on the cover it probably should be. Also I want to know that I appreciate all of the sacrifices you made and the support and encouragement you gave me while I was working on this book. Finally there is one last thing I want to say, I love you.

About the Author

Born and raised in Baltimore, Maryland, **Wayne S. Freeze** is currently the Technical Support Manager for the University of Maryland at College Park's Administrative Computing Center. He is responsible for a large-scale IBM mainframe as well as developing client-server architectures and advising high-level administrators on technical issues. He is also the author of the popular shareware program Car Collector (http://www.JustPC.com/cc.html), which is written in Visual Basic and incorporates the ActiveX technology.

When Wayne is not playing with computers, you can find him reading science fiction, photographing WWII aircraft at air shows, watching NASCAR races, or playing with his two children, Christopher and Samantha.

Contents at a Glance

Contents

Part III Reading News with NNTP 157

11 NNTP Protocols and Functions 163

19 The POP Client Control 331

25 The HTML Client Control 441

28 NetRunner—Part Four 499

29 NetRunner—Part Five 515

30 Now It's Your Turn 535

PART I

Fundamental Concepts

Welcome

Do you know what the hardest part of writing a book is? Well, you're reading it! In just a few short words, I am supposed to grab your interest and keep it for the next 500 pages. (If you think it is that easy, just try it sometime!) Sometimes the material I discuss is pretty monotonous (after all, how interesting can you make a property that sets the background color of an HTML document), while others are very interesting (just wait for the Five-Minute Web Browser). But on the whole, I think you will find many parts of the book very interesting. I also hope that you will be inspired to take the sample programs and add your own improvements or take portions of the code and add new functions to your existing programs. In either case, I hope you will enjoy your experiments with the Internet.

One of your first questions might be: Who is this Freeze character anyway? Well, I currently work for the University of Maryland at College Park where I am responsible for technical support of the Administrative Computer Center. I also advise the University's management on new computer technology. I have worked with computers ranging in size from one of the original Altair personal computers (the first available build-it-yourself computer) to large IBM mainframes (with more main memory than you find on most PCs' hard disks) and everything in between for the last 20 years. I started working with computers by programming in Basic on a teletype many years ago. Since then I've used nearly every popular programming language available (and a few not so popular ones, too) and have returned to using Basic because I believe that Visual Basic is the best way to write Windows programs.

This is my first book, so please go easy on me for a while. I promise to try my best to be informative and at the same time interesting to read. Then again if it was entertainment you were after, you'd be reading a Dave Barry humor book or a Tom Clancy techno-thriller now, wouldn't you? But I bet neither of them could show you how to build a Web browser in five minutes or less! Hang in there!

A Window onto the Information Superhighway

The Internet has been experiencing rapid growth since it was first formed years ago. Originally designed to facilitate communication among researchers working for the Department of Defense, the Internet has grown far beyond its original expectations.

When some of the Internet's inner workings are closely examined, we can see that many of the most commonly used features were designed to be easily extended. This makes it easier to adapt new features to the existing infrastructure without changing how the existing applications work. This flexibility means a lot to people who develop Internet applications because it means that their applications will continue to run while new functions are added over time.

Such flexibility often comes from a clean and simple design. This makes it easy to develop programs that take advantage of the available Internet services. Because it is difficult to find a program that does not contain at least a passing reference to the Internet, the ease of implementation is very important. Even if a program is designed to be totally independent of any other computer, the company that is offering the program probably has a presence on the Internet for advertising and technical support.

With tens of millions of copies of Windows 95 installed on computers, it is important for Microsoft to offer the best available tools for application programmers. Visual Basic is one of those tools and so are the new ActiveX controls found in the Internet Control Pack. The combined power of the two means that programmers like you can easily build Internet applications so that you, too, can open a Window onto the Information Superhighway.

Where We Are Going

This book is organized into seven parts. The first part covers such background material as client-server computing, TCP/IP applications, Windows 95's TCP/IP implementation, and how to install TCP/IP support and the ActiveX controls onto your system. The next four parts each discuss the protocols used by the high-level ActiveX controls, provide references to the controls, and then build sample programs that demonstrate how to use the controls. We also begin building a do-everything program in these parts. In part six, we take the do-everything program and add several interesting features that are not normally found in Internet programs. Finally, we conclude the book by reviewing what we accomplished and talk about some ideas you can use to improve the programs in this book.

Chapter 1—Introduction

This chapter introduces the reader to the book by identifying the skills the reader should already know, describing the material that the book will cover, listing the programs that will be written, and discussing the type of hardware and software that should be available on the reader's system. It also presents general notation and conventions used throughout the book.

- Overview
- Microsoft Declares War
- Goals
- Audience
- Software and hardware requirements
- Notation
- Programs
- Summary

Chapter 2—TCP/IP Concepts

This chapter introduces the reader to the Internet, TCP/IP, and client-server processing, and then discusses some of the key technical concepts that are necessary to use the Internet ActiveX controls from Visual Basic.

- Overview
- The Internet
- TCP/IP
- Clients and servers
- Domain names and IP addresses
- Port numbers
- Summary

Chapter 3—TCP/IP Applications

This chapter introduces the reader to the various applications available as part of the Internet ActiveX controls and how they work the Internet. Some other Internet applications are briefly discussed as well.

- Overview
- Applications
- FTP

- NNTP
- SMTP
- POP
- HTTP
- Other protocols: Telnet, Gopher, Talk, Finger
- Summary

Chapter 4—TCP/IP and Windows 95

This chapter introduces the reader to the how TCP/IP is implemented on Windows 95. It covers how to connect to the Internet, including SLIP and PPP. WinSock, VBXs, and OCXs are also briefly discussed. The chapter also presents information about the new ActiveX technology and identifies some Windows 95 applications that are included with the system, but not well known.

- Overview
- Connecting to the Internet
- WinSock, VBX, and OCX
- Windows 95 and ActiveX
- Windows 95 TCP/IP Applications
- Summary

Chapter 5—Installing the ActiveX Controls and Sample Programs

This chapter explains how to load the Active controls and sample programs from the CD-ROM onto their computer.

- Overview
- Installation of TCP/IP in Windows 95
- Installation of the ActiveX Internet Control Pack
- Installation of the ActiveX controls in Visual Basic
- Installation of the sample programs
- Summary

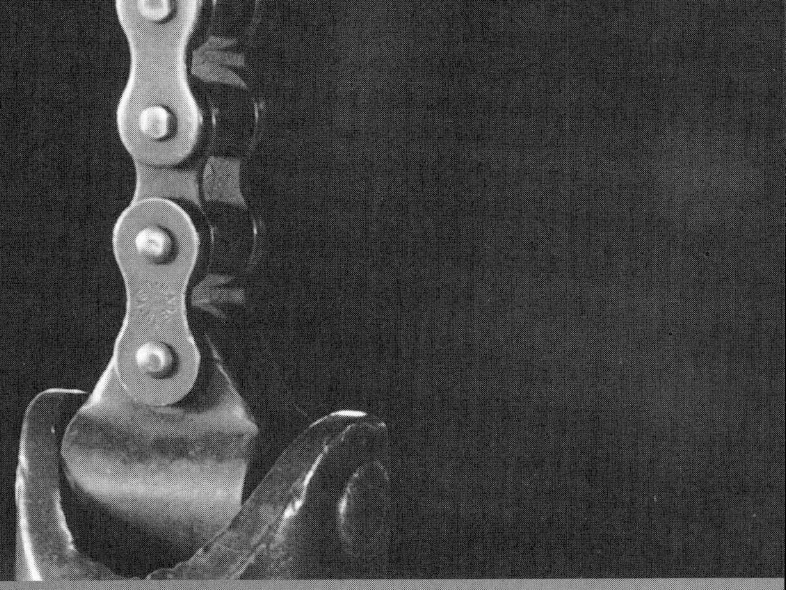

Chapter 1

Introduction

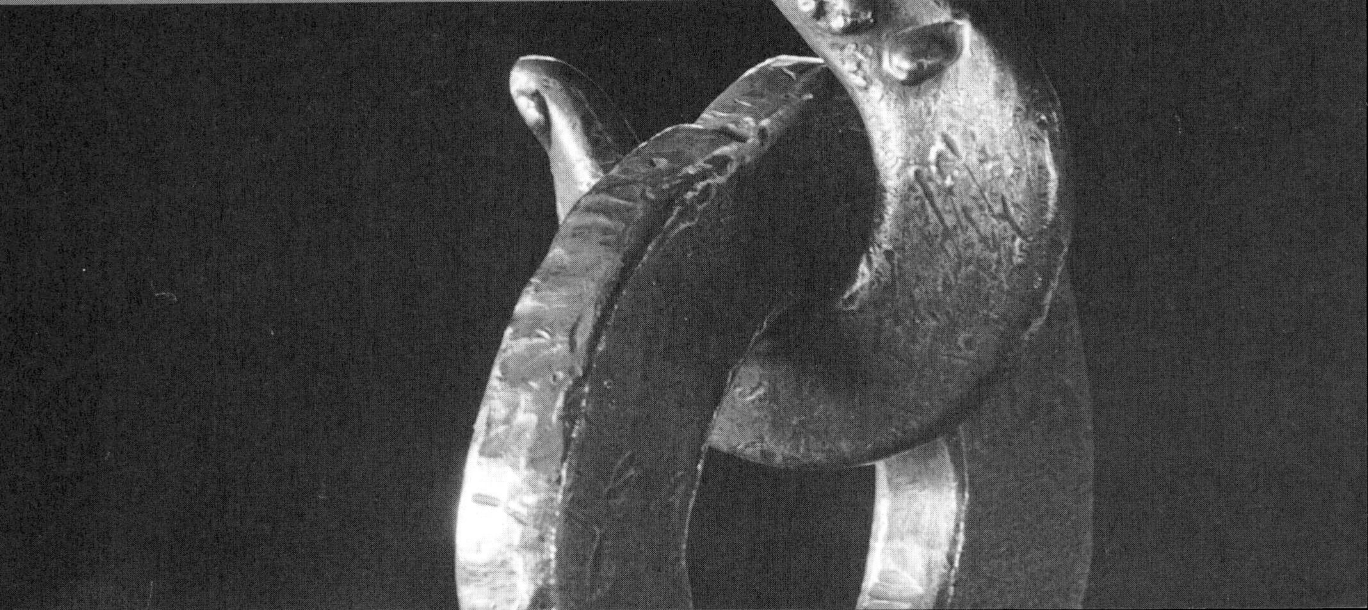

Overview

In this chapter I discuss the programs we are going to develop throughout this book, as well as some of the included reference material. I also identify the skills you should have to read this book, and the hardware and software that are required to use the Internet Control Pack.

By the end of this chapter, you should be able to answer the following questions:

- What skills should you have before starting this book?
- What kind of computer system should you have?
- What software should be installed on your computer system?

Microsoft Declares War

Welcome to the future and Web War III. On March 16, 1996, Microsoft launched yet another attack in the battle for computing dominance. This time the battlefield has shifted from the desktop to the Internet. With Netscape's Navigator dominating the marketplace, Microsoft chose to respond to this challenge with a new version of the Internet Explorer and something called *ActiveX controls*.

ActiveX controls are essentially the old Object Linking and Embedding (OLE) controls with a new name and some new features. There are essentially two flavors of the controls: those designed to be called from the within the Internet Explorer, and those designed to be called from their conventional programming languages like Visual Basic, Visual C++, and Visual FoxPro.

The ActiveX controls that are called from Visual Basic Script programs running inside the Internet Explorer correspond to the JavaScript programs and Java applets that are common for Netscape's Navigator. In addition to this capability, Microsoft has also provided viewers that let people view Word, Excel, and PowerPoint documents over the Internet and has made them available to the public at no charge.

The other flavor of ActiveX controls is very interesting because they are designed to be called from a conventional programming language like Visual Basic and Visual C++. One of the first ActiveX packages is the ActiveX Internet Control Package, which is designed to add Internet capabilities to existing applications. The ActiveX controls are designed to be easy to use (just wait until you build your own Web browser in less than five minutes) and well-integrated into Windows 95. This lets you focus on meeting the needs of the user and leaves the grungy details of the Internet protocols to Microsoft's development engineers.

Many people remember "war is hell," but it is important to remember that technology change occurs most rapidly during times of war. Most of us depend on new technology to make our applications appealing to our customers, so while the battle over the Internet may leave some victims, it also brings us new tools like the ActiveX Internet Control Package. When tools like that help us make our applications better while making our job much easier, maybe war (in the computing industry, at least) isn't so bad after all.

Goals

The primary goal of this book is to provide sufficient information so that you can build your own programs using the ActiveX Internet Control Pack. Because these controls are relatively new and Microsoft's documentation alone is not sufficient for the average programmer to build a working program, I believe that this book will be extremely helpful to anyone who wants to build an Internet-capable application. I intend to accomplish this goal in three ways.

First, I am going to discuss the protocols that each control uses. This provides a little background to help you understand what the controls are doing on your behalf. The relevant standards documents that these chapters were written from are included on the CD-ROM that comes with this book.

Second, I provide some basic documentation that talks about each of the controls. While I do not expect you to read these chapters straight through, you will find them useful as a reference while writing your own programs. Occasionally the documentation supplied by Microsoft glosses over some of the problem areas or does not supply sufficient information with respect to the specific control that is being discussed. That is why I feel these documentation chapters are so valuable.

Finally, I provide sample programs that focus on how to use the controls. Using these controls is not always as simple as it may seem (sometimes due to bugs in the control itself, other times it is because of the limitations the ActiveX implementation). These programs are not intended to replace their commercial counterparts, but rather to show how they work. You can then expand and/or integrate them into your personal applications. Finally, as a bonus, I have created a do-everything program that incorporates all the

ActiveX controls into a single program. This program includes all the functions included in the stand-alone programs plus a few interesting features that are not generally included with these types of programs.

To help you understand how the controls work, I have provided some background material on TCP/IP, some common TCP/IP applications, and on Windows 95, which you may find useful while getting started with the controls. I also included some Visual Basic programming tricks that you may find useful.

Audience

This book is aimed at the person who is familiar with Visual Basic, Windows 95, and the Internet. How familiar should you be? If you have problems booting Windows 95, I suggest that you try another book. However, if you already understand how to write Visual Basic programs (or even Delphi or PowerBuilder programs) and have done a little surfing on the Internet, you should be very comfortable with the material in this book. If you understand how to write 32-bit Windows drivers or if you prefer to write programs in binary rather than bothering with compilers, you may want to skip this book and go to work for Microsoft.

This book assumes that you already know how to use Visual Basic. While do you not need to be an expert Visual Basic programmer, you should understand how to create a program, add controls to a form, and how to declare variables. Understanding how to use Visual Basic's debug facility is a plus. This level of experience lets me show (and explain) fragments of code rather than entire programs. (The complete source code is on the CD-ROM, however.)

Of all the programming languages I have used over the years, Visual Basic is one of the best (especially when you compare it with writing Windows programs in C or C++). It is relatively easy to learn to build meaningful programs quickly. While these programs tend to use more resources than their C and C++ counterparts, remember that right now memory is dirt cheap and our friendly Intel salesman is always willing to sell you a faster processor for the right money.

For Windows 95, you should be familiar with how to change settings and add software to your system. I give you a little help with setting up your system to talk to the Internet and installing the controls. I guess it goes without saying that you know how to run programs and browse files.

Because we are going to build an FTP program, a newsreader, a mail program, and a Web browser, you should be familiar with those types of programs. Specifically, you should understand how to use them so you can compare what you know with the sample programs we build. I'm also going to provide a few examples of how some of the functions work using Windows' Telnet program. If you would like to try them on your own, knowing a little bit about how Telnet works may be useful.

Software and Hardware Requirements

All the programs in this book were written using Windows 95 and Visual Basic Professional 4.0. No updates, other than the Internet Control Pack, were made to Windows or Visual Basic on any of the systems that I used to test the programs.

Visual Basic 4.0 Professional Edition is required to run the sample programs from this book. While it might be possible to use the Standard Edition, some of the programs use the Rich Text Box control, which is included only with the Professional Edition. (Note that Microsoft also requires the Professional Edition to run its sample programs.) By using the Rich Text Box, I avoid the 64KB limit of a regular text box. There may be a few additional controls from the Professional Edition simply because they look better than the Standard Edition counterparts. I see no reason why the Standard Edition should not work, but I simply have not tried it.

Obviously you need Windows 95 to run these programs. Visual Basic requires Windows 95 (or at least the 32-bit version of Visual Basic requires it). You also need to install the software necessary to have a working Internet connection.

The programs in this book were developed using both dial-up PPP connections and full-time Ethernet network connections. Some kind of real attachment to the Internet is required because without one, the ActiveX controls are going to be pretty much useless. Also, I do not consider connections from such services as AOL or CompuServe to be acceptable because they do not give you a real IP address. Unless your machine has a real IP address (if you do not understand this, keep reading and you will shortly), none of the ActiveX controls will work nor will any of the programs.

The computers I used while working on this book ranged in speed from a Pentium 75 to a Pentium 133. I have not tested these programs on any 486 systems, but as long as your machine runs Internet Explorer or Netscape Navigator well, you probably will not have any problems. However, I suspect that any system slower than a 486DX/2 66 will be too slow, and even a 486/DX2 66 may be too slow under some circumstances.

I believe that the amount of memory you have is far more critical than the speed of the processor. If you have only 8MB or less of RAM, expect serious problems. You may be able to squeak by with 12MB, but I strongly recommend that you have at least 16MB of RAM. If you can afford it, 24 or 32MB are desirable; Visual Basic seems to run better with a lot of memory.

For testing these programs, it is desirable that you have access to various servers on the Internet. To test the FTP program, you can use any anonymous FTP server, but your best bet is to have a general purpose account on a UNIX host system somewhere on the Net. That way you can test uploading and downloading files. To test the news program, you need access to a news server. To test the mail program, you need access to an SMTP mail server (for outgoing mail) and a POP3 mail server (for incoming mail). To test the Web browser, you need a general-purpose Web site (for example, www.microsoft.com). If you cannot find one of these, you are in for a rough ride for the rest of this book!

I have accessed a number of different servers for the various controls and have had good luck testing the programs with one exception. The FTP program prefers to get its directory listings from UNIX- or NT-based systems. You can forget trying to access other operating systems like IBM's MVS. (I'm hoping that Microsoft fixes this problem in a future release of the ActiveX controls.)

When the programs in this book were written, the most current version of the Internet Control Pack was Beta 2. While much of the code worked well, there were significant problems with some of the controls. Hopefully by the time you read this, Microsoft will have released a new version of the Internet Control Pack. The version of the Internet Control Pack on the CD-ROM that accompanies this book is Beta 2. If you have already experimented with the Beta 1 control, you must deinstall the Beta 1 controls before you install the Beta 2 controls. You also need to run the conversion utility on any programs you may have written using the Beta 1 controls. Remember you can always download the latest version from Microsoft's Web site at http://www.microsoft.com/icp. Just note that the size of the controls themselves is about 2.5MB.

Notation

When describing various aspects of the protocols and the ActiveX controls, I use a few symbols that you should be somewhat familiar with. For the most part the symbols are very straightforward. I use square brackets ([ ]) to identify when something is optional or not required. For example, if I show something as "Hello [World]", either "Hello" or "Hello World" would be acceptable. "World" would not be acceptable.

The square brackets can also be nested. So in this example, "Hello [World [Again]]", "Hello", "Hello World", and "Hello World Again" would be acceptable. "Hello Again" and "World Again" and simply "Again" would be unacceptable.

Another symbol that I occasionally use is "::=". For those of you who are familiar with Backus Normal Form (BNF) notation, you should be very comfortable with this symbol. For those who aren't, this symbol represents the phrase "is defined as." So in the following example, "<hello> ::= Hello [World]", the symbol "<hello>" can mean either "Hello" or "Hello World".

These symbols can be combined to form a more complex description. Let us consider a more complex example:

<hello-goodbye> ::= <hello> <dash> <goodbye>

<hello> ::= Hello [World]

<dash> ::= "-"

<goodbye> ::= [Good] Bye

Any of the following values would be acceptable: "Hello-Bye", "Hello World-Bye", "Hello-Good Bye", and "Hello World-Good Bye".

Note that computer scientists will probably object to the way I am using the BNF notation. (But then those same computer scientists would probably object to Visual Basic also!) It is my intention to help you understand what is happening with the controls and how to use them (after all, when was the last time a computer scientist wrote an application?), not to design a new programming language.

Programs

In this book, we are going to build five different programs: FTPRunner, NewsRunner, MailRunner, WebRunner, and NetRunner. (Actually there is a sixth program, called the Five-Minute Web Browser, but I hesitate to count that one because it consists of only one line of code.) The first four programs are used to discuss how the controls work. NetRunner, on the other hand, is an attempt to build a complex integrated do-it-all Internet product.

In all cases the programs are not commercial quality. The user interface needs a lot of improvement, and many more features need to be added before the program could be sold in the marketplace. In fact some of the limitations of these programs are not strictly limitations of the code that I have written, but limitations of the ActiveX controls themselves.

For example, the HTML control that is used to display Web pages currently does not support frames. Because both Internet Explorer and Navigator both support frames, this is a serious limitation for a commercial Web browser. While I expect Microsoft to expand the capabilities of this control in the future, there is not much you can do about it right now.

NetRunner combines all the functions included in the individual programs into one big program. This program will be built in several stages, with each stage adding several new enhancements to the individual programs. Finally, we create some brand new functions for NetRunner that take advantage of the work we have already done, but are not normally found in commercial applications.

Summary

In this chapter, I discussed the skills needed for this book and what kind of hardware and software you should have access to. I have also identified the programs we are going to write and talked about the goals of this book. In the next chapter, we begin our discussion of the ActiveX controls by reviewing some basic TCP/IP networking concepts.

In case you want to check your answers to the questions in the Overview section, here are the answers:

- *What skills should you have before starting this book?*

  You should have a working knowledge of Visual Basic, Windows 95, and the Internet.

- *What kind of computer system should you have?*

  You should have at least a 486DX/66 or faster with a minimum of 12MB of memory. It is strongly recommended that you have a Pentium 75 or faster with 16MB of RAM. The computer should also have a connection to the Internet. Usually this will be a dial-up connection using a V.34 (28,800 baud) modem.

- *What software should be installed on this computer system?*

  The system should have Windows 95 and Visual Basic. Everything else that you will need is on the CD-ROM included with this book.

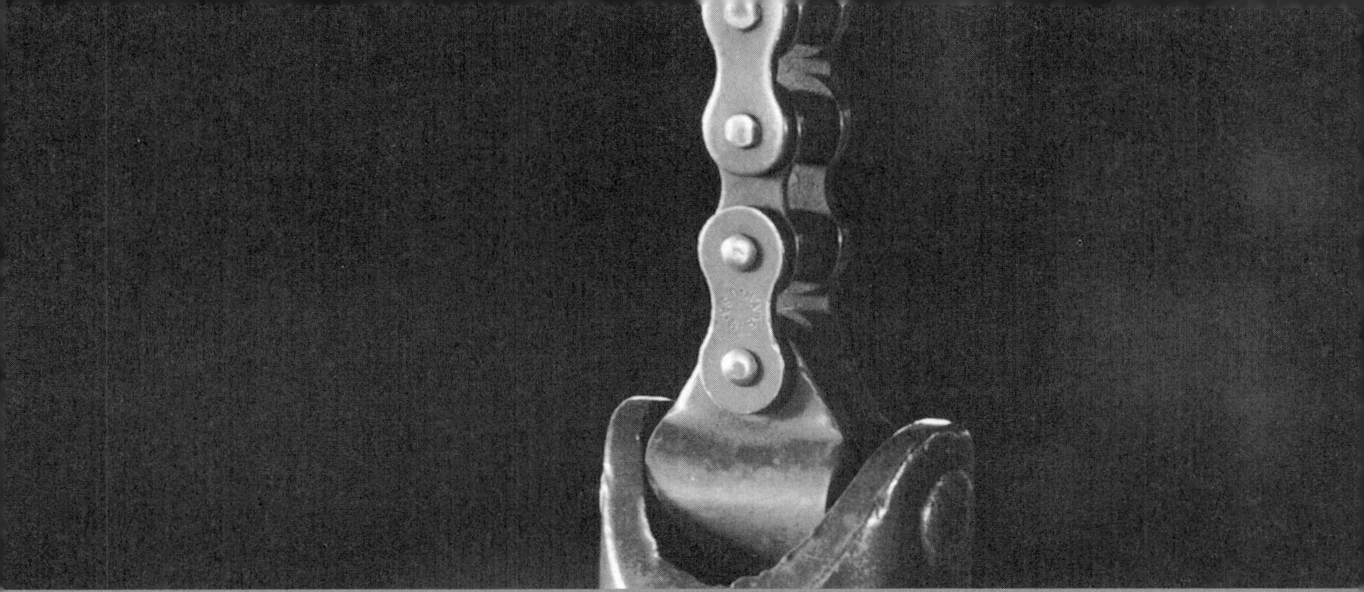

Chapter 2

TCP/IP Concepts

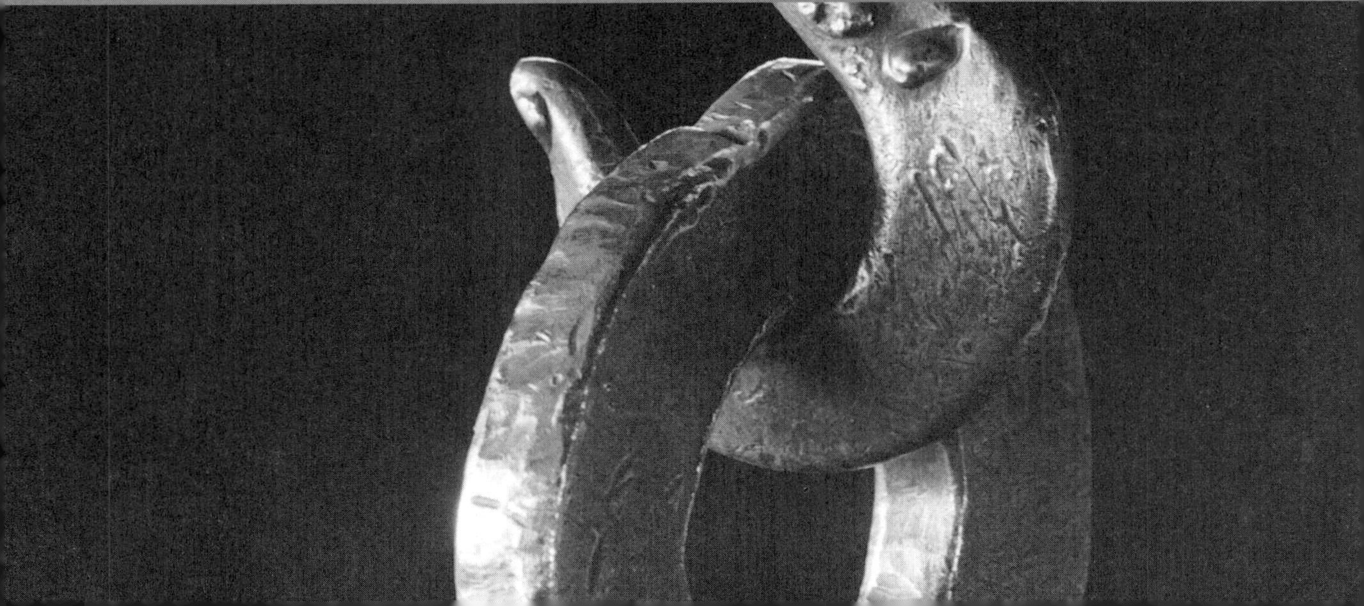

Overview

In this chapter, we explore some of the basic concepts about TCP/IP and the Internet. While a complete study of TCP/IP is beyond the scope of this book, this section is intended to you give a flavor of some of the more important concepts necessary to understand how to use the ActiveX controls.

By the end of this chapter, you should be able to answer the following questions:

- What is the difference between the Internet and an intranet?
- What is a client?
- What is a server?
- What is a host name?
- What is a domain?
- What is an IP address?
- What is a name server?
- What is a port number?
- What is a socket?

The Internet

In the late 1960s, the Department of Defense's Advanced Projects Agency (then known as ARPA and later known as DARPA) began funding research into computer networks that was being done by several university computer science departments and a few private companies. In December 1969, four different computers were connected together, thus forming a network that eventually became known as the ARPANET. Throughout the 1970s and early 1980s, ARPA encouraged more and more of its research organizations to connect to this network. In 1983, DARPA split the ARPANET into two pieces: the research part, which retained the name ARPANET; and the military part, which became known as MILNET.

In 1985, the National Science Foundation established a high-speed network to facilitate communication among researchers and to link NSF's six supercomputer centers. This network became known as NSFNET. When this network was tied into the existing ARPANET, they jointly became known as the Internet. Since then, the growth of the Internet has been phenomenal. In 1987, there were approximately 20,000 computers attached to the Internet. Just three short years later, in 1990, the number of computers attached to the Internet increased tenfold to over 200,000. In January 1996, one source estimated that more than 37 million people over the age of 16 in the U.S. and Canada alone have access to the Internet.

Despite the enormous size of the Internet, it operates using the same principals as any other computer network. So whether the computer network has only two or three computers connected together or the millions found on the Internet, they all have to work together to perform common tasks.

Recently the term *intranet* has begun to appear all over the news media. The technology used to support the Internet is exactly the same for intranets. While there is not a widely accepted definition for an intranet, the main difference between the Internet and an intranet is that an intranet is intended to provide information to a select group of people rather than provide information to everyone on the Internet. Its primary purpose is to take advantage of Internet tools without running the security risks of using the Internet.

Intranets are very popular with the business community because they can provide information such as policy and procedures manuals and personnel handbooks electronically by using Web technology. Both types of documents are frequently updated, and it is costly to distribute paper updates. Users are happy because they can use familiar Web browsers to access the information.

In many cases, intranets are implemented on private networks. This ensures that the information cannot be accessed by normal Internet users because the two networks are not interconnected. In other cases, an intranet can be attached to the Internet using a device called a *firewall*, which permits only authorized connections to pass through it. Finally, in some other implementations, secure Web browsers and Web servers are used to encrypt all data that is transmitted between the client and the server. While the last two approaches permit access from Internet users, only those users that have been specifically authorized by the intranet's manager can access the intranet's facilities.

TCP/IP

To understand the tasks required in a computer network, let us begin by defining computer network. A *computer network* is a collection of computers that have connections between them. These computers are also known as *nodes*. The simplest case is one in which two computers are connected by a single link (see figure 2-1). The network can grow more complex by adding another computer with a path to one of the computers already in the network (see figure 2-2). It can also grow more complex by adding a second path between any two existing computers in the network (see figure 2-3).

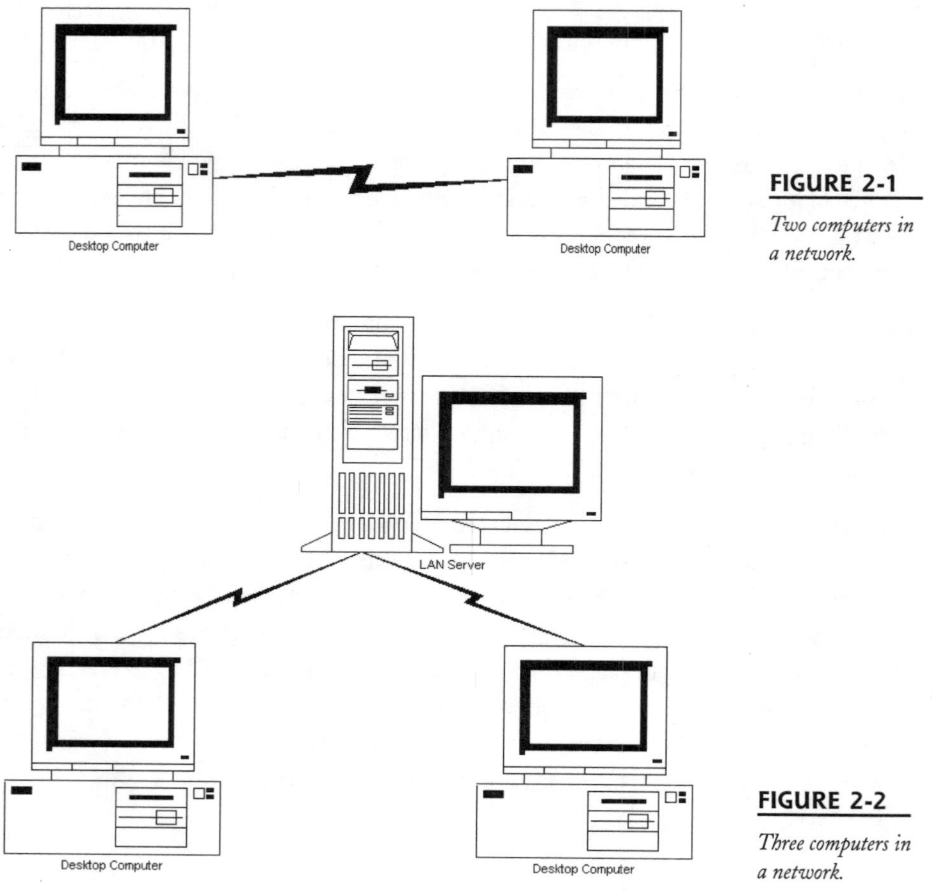

FIGURE 2-1

Two computers in a network.

FIGURE 2-2

Three computers in a network.

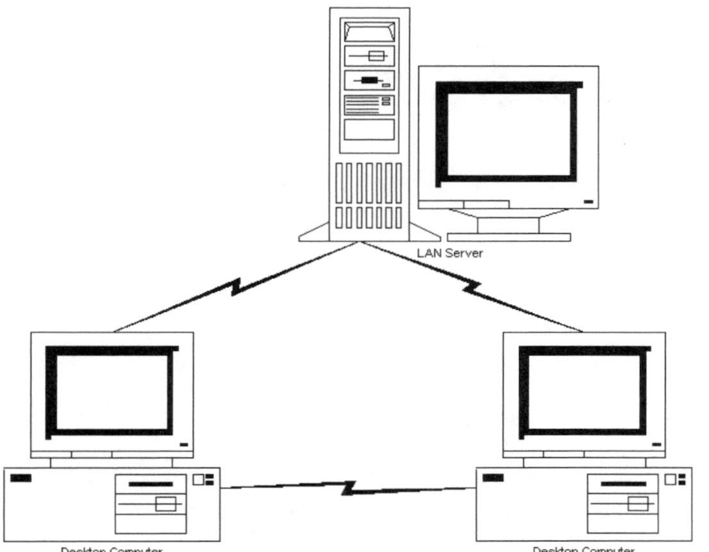

FIGURE 2-3

Many computers in a network.

Notice that each computer attached to the network is not directly attached to all the other computers. To pass information between computers that are not directly attached, the first computer examines each of the computers that are directly connected to it, determines the one that is closest to the destination computer, and passes the information on to it. This process repeats on each computer until the information eventually reaches its destination.

Passing the information from one node to another requires that one computer talk to the next in a common language. One of the most common languages in use today is *TCP/IP* (*Transmission Control Protocol/Internet Protocol*). Formally known as TCP/IP Internet Protocol Suite, this language defines a series of protocols that standardize how computers talk to each other in order to exchange information.

The protocols in TCP/IP are arranged in a series of layers known as a *protocol stack* (see figure 2-4). What happens within a layer is isolated from the layer above it or below it. There is a physical layer that deals with the actual communications hardware (modems, Ethernet cards, etc.). Above this layer is the Internet Protocol (IP) layer that handles moving data from one node in the network to the next. Above the Internet Protocol layer is a third layer called the Transmission Control Protocol (TCP) that deals with how to move

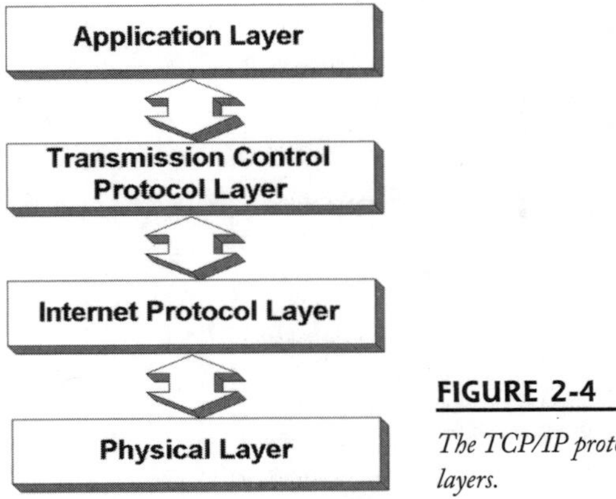

FIGURE 2-4

The TCP/IP protocol layers.

data from the source to the destination, ignoring any of the nodes in between. Above this layer is the application layer, which deals with functions we are more familiar with, such as FTP and HTTP.

Clients and Servers

When two computers work together, they generally operate as a client and a server. Basically, the *client* generates requests and sends them to the server. The *server* then processes the request and sends its response back to the client.

For example, imagine two computer systems called Chris and Sam. Assume that Chris does not have a way to tell time, but Sam does. The following exchange could occur when Chris wants to know the time.

> Chris: "What time is it?"
>
> Sam: "It is 11:15am."

In this case, Chris is the client and Sam is the server. Chris sends a request to Sam ("What time is it?"), which Sam must receive and translate into the functions required to get the time and return it back to Chris ("It is 11:15am"). Finally, Chris must be able to translate the response back into something useful.

While this seems simple, remember that a number of things must exist for this exchange of information to occur. A common language or protocol must be in place so that Sam can understand Chris's request and so Chris can understand Sam's answer. Second, if Sam is busy and does not hear Chris's request, Chris needs a way to recognize that Sam did not hear him so he can repeat the request. The same applies for Sam's response to Chris. Also, methods are needed to handle the situation in which Chris says, "What time is it?" and Sam hears "What mumble mumble mumble."

A more complete example would be:

Chris: "Sam, can you help me?"

Sam: no response

Chris: "Sam, can you help me?"

Sam: "Yes I can, Chris."

Chris: "What time is it?"

Sam: "You want to know what time it is?"

Chris: "Yes"

Sam: "It is 11:15am."

Chris: "Thank you for telling me it is 11:15am."

Sam: "You are welcome."

As you can see, this exchange is much more complicated than the first one, yet no additional information was really exchanged. While this example is still somewhat simplistic, this concept forms the basis for nearly all client-server-based computing programs.

Domain Names and IP addresses

The preceding example is somewhat simplistic from yet another angle: it was implied that Chris and Sam knew how to reach each other. With millions of computers attached to the Internet, this is not as easy as it may seem. For example, what happens if two people want to name their computer Chris or Sam? A solution to this problem, which has evolved over time, is a naming concept called the *Domain Naming System*.

In general, all computers attached to the Internet have a unique hierarchical domain name associated with them. Consider the name WWW.JustPC.COM (pronounced W-W-W dot JustPC dot COM). The name consists of three parts, WWW, JustPC, and COM. Working from the right, *com* is known as the top-level domain. In this case COM indicates that the site belongs to a commercial organization. Other valid top-level domain names are EDU for educational institutions, GOV for government organizations, MIL for military organizations, NET for major network support centers, and ORG for other types of organizations. You can also use a country code in place of the top-level domain. Thus, US, UK, and CA are valid top-level domain names for places in the United States, United Kingdom (England), and Canada, respectively.

The second-level domain name, JustPC in this case, indicates the name of a business, organization, or institution. Unlike top-level domain names, the second-level domain name has no real format other than being limited to 22 characters in length. I should also point out that the names are case insensitive; JustPC is the same as justpc and JUSTPC. Usually, companies like IBM and Toyota tend to use their corporate name as the second-level domain. Other organizations may choose names that relate to particular projects or products.

Country codes are generally used for organizations that exist outside of the United States. However, all state governments, libraries, and elementary and secondary schools use .US as their top-level domain. For example, the Baltimore County Public Library's computer system used for mail would be known as mail.bcpl.lib.md.us.

The lowest level of the domain name is often referred to as the *host name*. In the case of WWW.JustPC.COM, WWW is the host name of a specific computer system that is operated by JustPC.COM. The host name can be one level as in this example, or multiple levels as determined by the organization. Some host names are very common based on the function provided by the computer. WWW indicates a machine that has information that can be used by a Web browser. FTP indicates a computer that operates an FTP server. Mail may simply be directed to JustPC.COM. Notice that a third-level name is not necessary; however, only one machine connected to the Internet may be labeled JustPC.COM.

While domain names are easy to understand by humans, they are difficult to use by computers. Computers translate the domain name into something known as an *IP address*. The

IP address consists of four sets of numbers. In the case of WWW.JustPC.COM, the IP address is 206.153.49.129. Each of the numbers can range in value from 0 to 255 (or 2 to the 8th power, the largest value you can store in 8 bits). Just like the domain name must be unique within the Internet, so must the IP address; and just like the domain names, there are organizations that are responsible for ensuring that IP addresses do not overlap.

Why is having an IP address easier to use by a computer? Consider the case of your telephone number. You have a three digit area code, followed by a three digit exchange, followed by a four digit number. When someone dials your telephone number, there is information about exactly where you are located in the telephone network. Dialing the area code directs the call to your state (or area inside of a state when there is more than one area code in a state). Dialing the exchange directs the call to your community within your state. Finally the last part of the number directs the call to your home. The same process is followed by the computers that pass information around the Internet.

Because the lower layers of TCP/IP only move information around using IP addresses, a facility known as a *Domain Name Server* (DNS), or name server for short, is used to translate the domain name into an IP address. Each domain name has a unique IP address associated with it. However, the reverse is not always true. It is possible to have multiple domain names point to the same IP address. Consider the case of a company that provides information to people on the Internet. They may have a World Wide Web site called WWW.JustPC.COM, an FTP site called FTP.JustPC.COM, and may receive electronic mail at JustPC.COM. While these represent three different types of services, there may be no reason for them to reside on different computers. Thus the three different domain names all point to the same computer system. This also gives the organization that is responsible for the domain names the flexibility to move various functions to a different machine without having to notify everyone who may access that service.

Port Numbers and Sockets

By using domain names and IP addresses, you can find any computer on the Internet. But that does not mean that we have all the information necessary to have a client and server talk to one another. Most computers today have the capability of running more than one program at a time. The clients and servers we have talked about previously are really computer programs that run on a particular computer. Therefore, we need a method that not only uniquely identifies a computer, but also the particular program running on that computer. This is done through the use of a *port*.

A port is simply another number. Consider it an extension of the IP address. This value can range from 0 to 65,535 ($2^{16}-1$, the largest value you can store in 16 bits). Port numbers are used to uniquely identify a message box on the computer. For standard Internet servers, there is a set of well-known port numbers. For example, FTP always uses port 21 for communication and port 20 for data transfer, and World Wide Web HTTP servers usually use port 80. Table 2-1 lists some values for well-known port numbers. You can check RFC-1700 for a complete list. (A copy of this RFC can be found on the CD-ROM in the back of this book.)

Table 2-1 Selected Well-Known Port Numbers

Name	Port Number	Description
daytime	13	Daytime
ftp-data	20	File transfer [default data]
ftp	21	File transfer [control]
telnet	23	Telnet terminal emulation
smtp	25	Simple mail transfer
time	37	Time
domain	53	Domain Name Server
gopher	70	Gopher
finger	79	Finger
www-http	80	World Wide Web HTTP
pop3	110	Post Office Protocol
nntp	119	Network News Protocol
ntp	123	Network Time Protocol
irc	194	Internet Relay Chat Protocol
ldap	389	Lightweight Directory Access Protocol
imsp	406	Interactive Mail Support Protocol
talk	517	Talk
doom	666	Doom (ID Software)

Rather than require each program to have its own version of the code to access the communications network, most operating systems provide a programming interface to access the communications subsystem. This interface is called a *socket*.

A server program periodically checks for messages in its assigned message box. When it finds a message, the server program removes the message from the message box, and then either processes it directly or starts another program to process the message. Finally, the server program goes back to periodically checking for messages.

A client program prepares and sends a message using an IP address and port number of the desired server. As part of the message, the client tells the server to send its response back to a specific port. Then, like the server program, the client program waits until it receives a message before continuing to process.

Starting with our previous example and adding the new information we just learned, we arrive at this:

> Chris: "Calling Domain Name Server, port 53. Where is Sam? Respond to 128.128.128.001, port 888"
>
> Domain Name Server: "Calling 128.128.128.001, port 888. Chris, you can reach Sam at 128.128.128.002."
>
> Chris: "Calling 128.128.128.002, port 999. Sam, can you help me? Respond to 128.128.128.001, port 888."
>
> Sam: no response
>
> Chris: "Calling 128.128.128.002, port 999. Sam, can you help me? Respond to 128.128.128.001, port 888."
>
> Sam: "Calling 128.128.128.001, port 888. Yes I can, Chris."
>
> Chris: "Calling 128.128.128.002, port 999. What time is it?"
>
> Sam: "Calling 128.128.128.001, port 888. You want to know what time it is?"
>
> Chris: "Calling 128.128.128.002, port 999. Yes"
>
> Sam: "Calling 128.128.128.001, port 888. It is 11:15am"
>
> Chris: "Calling 128.128.128.002, port 999. Thank you for telling me it is 11:15am."
>
> Sam: "Calling 128.128.128.001, port 888. You are welcome."

This time, before Chris can talk to Sam he must first talk to the Domain Name Server. Unlike most other computers on the network, Chris knows the IP address for the Domain Name Server because that was defined in Windows 95 (or any other system) when the TCP/IP software was first configured. Also, in this example, the IP addresses and ports are now included as part of the communication.

Summary

In this chapter, we briefly discussed a little history and some of the basic concepts of TCP/IP and the Internet. We developed an example of how a client and a server cooperate to perform a task. In the next chapter, we continue to explore the TCP/IP, clients, and servers by looking at some of the "standard" clients and servers available on the Internet.

In case you want to check your answers to the questions in the Overview section, here are the answers:

- *What is a client?*

  A client is a computer program that makes requests of another computer program.

- *What is a server?*

  A server is a computer program that receives requests from another computer program, and then processes the request and returns the result to the original computer.

- *What is a host name?*

  A host name is the name of computer.

- *What is a domain name?*

  A domain name is a hierarchical name that uniquely describes a computer on the Internet.

- *What is an IP address?*

  An IP address is a series of four numbers, each ranging from 0 to 255 in value, that uniquely identifies a computer on the Internet.

- *What is a name server?*

  A name server is used to translate a domain name into an IP address.

- *What is a port number?*

  A port number is a value ranging from 0 to 65,535 that uniquely identifies a program running on a computer.
- *What is a socket?*

  A socket is a programming language interface between an applications program and a communications facility.

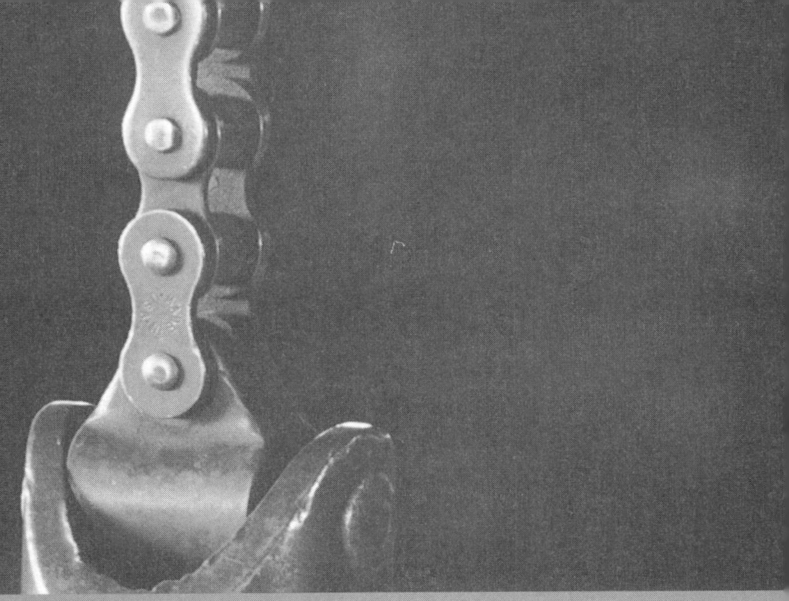

Chapter 3

TCP/IP Applications

Overview

In this chapter, we discuss some of the common TCP/IP applications that are available on the Internet. These applications are named after the protocol they use to communicate between the client and the server. These protocols are usually described by a document called a request for comments or RFC, which is issued by a group known as the Internet Engineering Task Force. Each RFC is assigned a sequential number. (Remember: Applicable RFC text is available for reference on this book's CD.)

By the end of this chapter, you should be able to answer the following questions:

- What is FTP?
- What is NNTP?
- What is SMTP?
- What is POP?
- What is HTTP?
- What are some other TCP/IP applications?

Applications

At this point you hopefully understand how clients and servers work, so why do we need them? In a single word, applications. Applications are programs designed to help a user perform useful work. While some may argue that little or no useful work is done on the Internet, I disagree. Without the services of the Internet, I would not have been able to write this book. Almost all the research I did for this book was done using a Web browser. I have communicated with my editor (including sending copies of each chapter as they were written) using an e-mail application. I also used the Usenet news and e-mail to talk to some of my peers who are using the new ActiveX controls. All of this was possible because of the applications available on the Internet.

Unlike many applications that are developed for other environments, the Internet applications are based on standards. Well, sort of. It is very easy to develop a standard for a computer like IBM's mainframes. Because IBM provides the hardware and software, IBM has total control of the standards used on the mainframes. On the other hand, the Internet is best pictured as a cloud with all different brands of computers attached (see figure 3-1). This makes the job of the developing standards a far more complicated process.

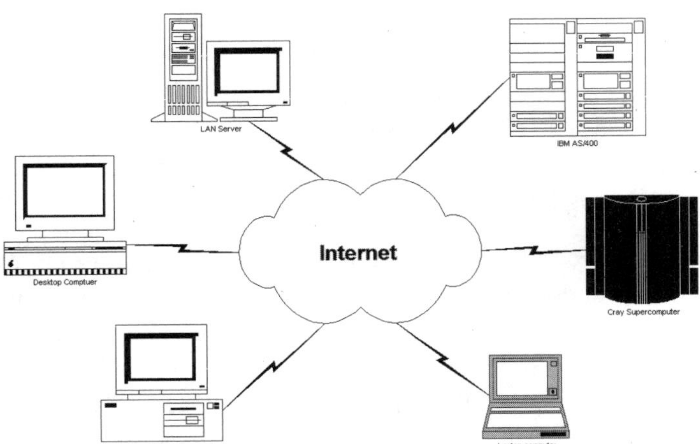

FIGURE 3-1

The Internet.

On the Internet, standards are developed by individuals or organizations and then submitted to the entire Internet community. There is an organization known as the *Internet Engineering Task Force* (*IETF*) that is charged with overseeing the standards development process for the Internet. An important part of this process is the *Request for Comments* (*RFC*) process.

The RFC process is used to distribute proposals for new standards for the Internet and solicit comments from the Internet community. A wide range of standards are available that cover everything from how e-mail messages are formed to details about the very lowest levels of the TCP/IP protocol stack. There is even one RFC (RFC-1700) that lists all the numbers used in the Internet, including the well-known port numbers (even some not so well-known port numbers). It is nearly half a megabyte in size! Often these documents themselves become the standards for various Internet applications.

In this book, most of the protocols we discuss are based on various RFC documents. In many cases these documents serve as the sole source of information about the protocol. But without these standards, it would be impossible for two computers on the Internet to work together. With them, it is possible to copy a file from an IBM mainframe and receive it on your Windows 95-based PC and have it look the same as it did on the mainframe. That is the real power and flexibility of the Internet.

FTP

When the need arises to move files between computers on the Internet, most people rely on FTP. *FTP*, which stands for *File Transfer Protocol*, is one of the oldest applications available on the Internet. You can trace its origins all the way back to 1971. The last time the protocol was revised was back in 1985 under RFC-959.

FTP was developed to provide an easy method of exchanging files between multiple computer systems reliably and efficiently while shielding the user from variations in file storage systems. Consider the problems of copying a text file from an MVS system to a UNIX system. The MVS file is stored as a series of 80-character records with EBCDIC characters. UNIX systems store a text file as a stream of ASCII characters with lines separated by line feeds. FTP handles this situation properly without any special prompting by the user.

Security is handled by requiring the client to identify himself to the server by supplying a user ID and password. Assuming that the user ID and password are valid, the client program is permitted to list file names on the remote host, to retrieve files from the server, and to send files to the server.

Many FTP servers also support the use of a special user ID known as *anonymous*. This user ID is permitted to retrieve selected files from the server. These files generally contain information that people want to make public, such as the IETF's RFCs and other useful information. Shareware programs like Doom were also made available via anonymous FTP. (To give some idea of the impact of anonymous FTP, the Internet was saturated for several days after the release of Doom while people all over the world downloaded demo copies of the program.) To track who has accessed the FTP server, most servers ask the users to enter their e-mail address as the password.

NNTP

One of the most popular functions on the Internet is *Usenet news*. Usenet news was developed by graduate students at the University of North Carolina—Chapel Hill and Duke University in 1979. In fact, Usenet actually preceded the Internet by a few years. Usenet news was designed to address the need to disseminate information to a large number of people quickly and efficiently, and to allow others to share their comments on it.

If you have ever used a Bulletin Board System (BBS), you know the value of having a chat group. It allows you to consult with a number of experts in a particular area and gain their advice on various issues. It also puts you in touch with individuals with similar interests and desires. However, one of the biggest problems with BBS systems is that they are usually limited to a particular geographic area.

Usenet news operates much like a BBS system, but on an international level. You can find places to talk about such obscure topics as: What was the best piston powered fighter aircraft in World War II?; When is Mattel going to release its latest Barbie doll?; Where is the best place to stay at Disney World?; or What has more caffeine, Mountain Dew or Jolt? Of course there are more conventional groups that discuss everything from programming issues related to Visual Basic to jobs available in the Research Triangle area of North Carolina. In general, with over 10,000 newsgroups available (depending on your Internet provider), nearly anyone can find a group of people with similar interests.

Usenet consists of a series of *newsgroups*. Newsgroups are named in a hierarchical fashion to make it easier to find interesting newsgroups. For example, one of the most common newsgroups for Visual Basic is comp.lang.basic.visual.misc. *Comp* is short for computer, which is the root of the computer hierarchy. *Lang* is short for programming language. *Basic* refers to the programming language that we are all familiar with (at least I assume that anyone reading this book has used it at least once in their life). *Visual* (in combination with Basic) refers to Microsoft's Visual Basic product. Finally, *misc* means that the group is intended for miscellaneous discussions. Other groups in the comp.lang.basic.visual subtree are 3rdparty, announce, and database.

A newsgroup consists of a collection of articles that a person must connect to a news server to read. First, an article is posted to a newsgroup on a server. Then this article, which was posted on one server, is forwarded to other servers so that multiple users may download it. The *NNTP protocol* is used to communicate between the news server and the client programs (in this case your newsreader). It can also be used to send articles between servers. While the NNTP protocol is discussed in RFC-977, there are a number of extensions that are not part of the standard. Most NNTP servers support at least some of these extensions.

SMTP

One of the most basic functions on the Internet is the capability to exchange electronic mail. The entire idea of electronic mail is a revolutionary concept. Essentially, a person can type a letter into a computer and the computer sends it to the recipient(s). No postage is required, and there's relatively little waiting for the mail carrier because electronic mail generally arrives within minutes after it was sent.

Consider the impact that electronic mail has on a large multinational business. Electronic mail can replace long-distance telephone calls in many cases. Also, electronic mail can help when people need to communicate across many time zones as it is very easy to send a message to someone in another country and have it available for them when they arrive at work. It also helps eliminate the telephone tag that often occurs even in a small business. And naturally, response time between messages can be a lot quicker than with standard mail delivery (or snailmail, as it is often called).

Electronic mail is not a total replacement for regular mail because the messages are not necessarily secure. Someone else could possibly read them, and it is possible for someone to send a false message. But, for the most part, these problems are so unlikely that for routine communications the benefits of electronic mail still far outweigh the liabilities. These limitations, however, are being addressed by new extensions to the standards. Some of these extensions have already been implemented in the ability to transport images, zip files, and word processing documents along with a note, with more to come in the future.

The *Simple Mail Transport Procotol* (*SMTP*) was developed in order to transport mail from one computer to another. Sending mail is not quite as easy as it sounds. Even if the host computer has a full-time connection to the Internet, network problems or system problems may make the host unavailable to receive mail from time to time; therefore, SMTP servers may have to try to send a message several times over a period of a few minutes, hours, or even days. SMTP servers also verify addresses in the electronic messages to ensure that they can be delivered. If they cannot be delivered, the server has to return the mail to the sender as undeliverable.

POP

While SMTP offers a great solution for sending electronic mail between host systems that have a full-time connection to the Internet, computers that have a part-time connection to the Internet have a real problem. Because they are attached to the Internet only occasionally, it is likely that they will not be online when they need to receive a piece of mail. While SMTP servers try to deliver mail several times before giving up, they do not try constantly. They may try once an hour for a few hours, and then once a day for a few days. If the machine is not online when the server attempts to send the mail, it will never receive it.

One solution to the problem is to create a mail server that has an SMTP server to send and receive mail and assign users electronic mail addresses on it. Then all you need is a way to access the mail on the mail server. This solution resulted in yet another TCP/IP protocol (surprise) that allows a remote client to access mail on the remote mail server. This protocol is known as the *Post Office Protocol* (*POP*). Because the client requests the mail from the mail server, there is no need for a full-time Internet connection. POP Version 3 (also known as POP3) is the most current version of the protocol, and is designed to be a simple and easy-to-implement technique to allow a client program to download mail files from a host server.

HTTP

As more and more people became able to access the Internet, there arose a desire to make information easily available. While anonymous FTP lets people download files, this can be a difficult process for the novice user. Also, files that are retrieved from an FTP server are relatively static. What Tim Berners-Lee (known as the father of the World Wide Web) proposed in 1989 was a solution to this problem that used a hypertext retrieval system.

A *hypertext retrieval system* displays a document and throughout the document are words or phrases that a user can click on and be transferred to another document. In his role as a physicist at CERN (Conseil Européan pour la Rechérche Nucleaire, a research laboratory for particle physics near Geneva in Switzerland and France), Berners-Lee wanted a method that allowed research papers to be presented with hypertext links to simplify data lookup and to provide a common interface to access this information.

In 1991, the first line mode browser was made available to permit people to access Web information. In 1993, the first graphical-based browser, Mosaic, was made available. In 1994, the World Wide Web began its rapid growth, surpassing Gopher as the primary method used to access information on the Internet. In 1995, the term Information Superhighway was coined and the term Internet became a household word. In 1996, corporate America began to embrace the Internet.

Much like Visicalc and Lotus 1-2-3 helped to establish the personal computer as a necessary business tool, the World Wide Web has helped to establish the Internet as a necessary business tool. (Here is an interesting game to play: watch prime time television one evening and watch the commercials to see how many refer to a Web site. Also count the number of commercials with an 800 telephone number. See which is greater; you may be surprised.)

Without the *HyperText Transport Protocol* (*HTTP*), none of this would have been possible. This procotol and *HyperText Markup Language* (*HTML*) are the standards at the core of the World Wide Web. The HTTP protocol provides a low overhead method of retrieving information from remote servers, while the HTML language provides a rich method in which to write complex documents.

Other Applications: Telnet, Gopher, Finger, Talk

A number of other applications are used on the Internet. This list is nowhere near complete because many other protocols exist. Most are special-purpose protocols that are used with specialized application software. Others are obsolete and no longer used. But of the remaining applications, some are still very popular, but these functions are not included as part of the ActiveX Internet Control Pack. These include applications like Telnet, Gopher, Finger, and Talk.

Telnet dates back to the earliest days of the Internet when most users accessed computers using dumb terminals. It lets a user on one computer access another computer just like they had a dumb terminal directly attached to the remote computer. We use this application from time to time to manually access some of the servers. Usually all the communications between client and server are based on understandable test commands with text result codes.

Before the World Wide Web sprang into being, another technique called *Gopher* was in use. Developed in 1991 by the University of Minnesota, Gopher provides the capability to transmit text documents and images over the Internet without the complexity of using FTP. Unlike the newer World Wide Web clients, Gopher is unable to dynamically format text or mix text and graphic images on the same display. While it was extremely popular a couple of years ago, it has been eclipsed by the modern World Wide Web clients.

One of the more informative applications on the Internet is *Finger*. Finger is used to find out information about other computer systems on the Internet. It will list all of the users who are signed on to a remote computer or list of useful information about any one user on the remote computer, including things like their real name, e-mail address, and other information the user chooses to make public.

Another of the older applications in use over the Internet is a *talk* program. Basically a talk program permits two computer users to communicate with each by typing and displaying text. It works by using two windows on your screen. In the first window, everything you type is displayed and sent to the other user. In the second window, everything the other user types is displayed. Unlike most of the other applications where a client runs on one computer and the server on another, each computer must run both a client and a server for the two-way communication to work.

Summary

In this chapter, we discussed some of the common TCP/IP applications that are available today on the Internet. The ActiveX Internet Control Pack provides easy access to some of the most common applications. These include FTP, NNTP, SMTP, POP, and HTTP.

In case you want to check your answers to the questions in the Overview section, here are the answers:

- *What is FTP?*

  FTP stands for File Transfer Protocol. This protocol is used to transport files between two different computers on the Internet.

- *What is NNTP?*

  NNTP stands for Network News Transport Procotol. This protocol is used to move Usenet news messages from one system to another.

- *What is SMTP?*

  SMTP stands for Simple Mail Transport Procotol. This protocol is used to move mail messages from one host system to another.

- *What is POP?*

  POP stands for Post Office Protocol. This protocol is used to permit part-time Internet clients to access mail on a full-time host system.

- *What is HTTP?*

  HTTP stands for HyperText Transport Protocol. This protocol is used to transfer World Wide Web documents across the Internet.

- *What are some other Internet applications?*

  Telnet is used to access a remote computer system as a dumb terminal.

  Gopher is an application that was intended to provide easy access to information on the Internet. It has been largely replaced by the World Wide Web.

  Finger is an application that provides information about the users on a remote system.

  Talk is an application that allows two users to exchange text messages in real time.

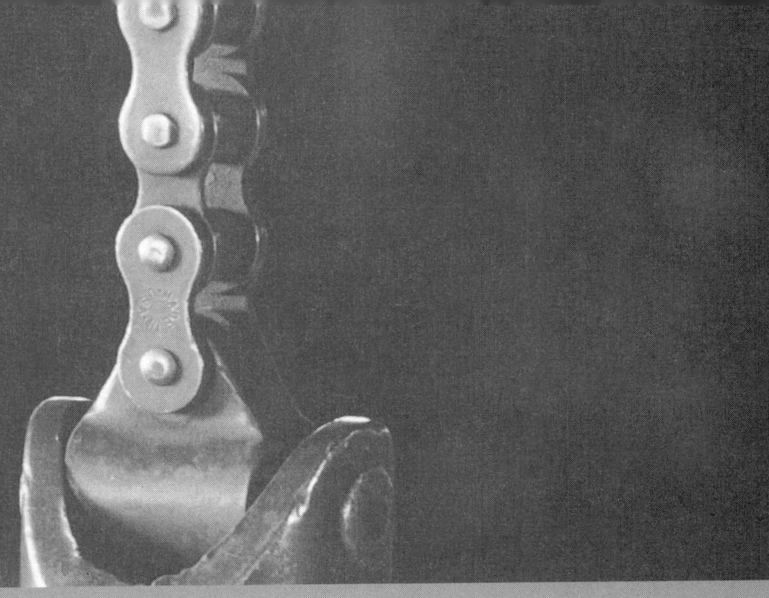

Chapter 4

TCP/IP and Windows 95

Overview

In this chapter, we discuss how TCP/IP functions are implemented in Windows 95, including how SLIP and PPP work, and we touch briefly on WinSock, VBXs, OCXs, and the ActiveX controls. Finally, we discuss some not-so-well documented Internet tools included with Windows 95.

By the end of this chapter, you should be able to answer the following questions:

- What protocol is most commonly used to connect to the Internet using Windows 95?
- What is the difference between a DLL and an OCX?
- What Internet tools are included with Windows 95?

Connecting to the Internet

There are many ways to connect to the Internet. In general, the more money you are willing to spend, the faster the connection you can get. Because a T-1 (1.544Mb per second) connection to the Internet costs about $4,000 per month, I chose to spend $200 on a V.34 modem and connect to the Internet through a local Internet provider. Net cost (pun intended) for the V.34 connection is about $25 per month. Of course, your costs will vary depending on which provider you select and your geographic location.

The V.34 modem lets you transfer data at speeds up to about 3,000 bytes per second, which means that a Web page with 90,000 bytes of data would take about 30 seconds to display. Of course, because a T-1 lets you download at speeds approaching 200,000 bytes per second, displaying the same Web page would theoretically take less than one second. Practically speaking, it is rare that you can actually transfer data that fast due to congestion on the Internet and overworked Web servers. I have a PC at work with an Ethernet connection to a local FDDI ring that is attached to a T-3 link (30 times faster than a T-1) to the rest of the Internet. I rarely see speeds over 10,000 bytes per second when downloading a file from outside our local network, and I often see speeds below 3,000 bytes per second.

Connecting to the Internet over a modem poses a set of problems that are normally not found with other types of connections. Until just recently, the Internet consisted primarily of full-time connections. If people wanted to access the Internet from home, they merely dialed into their local host computer and from that system they were able to access all the functions they needed. However, as personal computers became more powerful, it became desirable to allow them to connect directly to the Internet. Connecting a PC to the Internet was not a real problem; it was simply a matter of loading the proper software and configuring the adapter and, boom, you could Telnet or FTP to your local host system.

Part-time connections were hard to implement because each PC that dialed into the system needed an IP address and a host name. A protocol called *Serial Line Internet Protocol* (*SLIP*) was developed to permit a computer to connect to the Internet using a serial data port. The fact that a modem is in the line is irrelevant because the serial port of the PC connects to a modem that is connected to another modem and finally connected to the serial port of a remote computer (or a specialized network device called a *terminal adapter*).

SLIP is not a perfect solution, though, because the protocol does not communicate the IP address to the PC. While this does not sound like a problem, consider the typical situation of an Internet provider. Rather than having just one modem line, they have many modem lines that are reached by calling a single telephone number. As the calls reach the provider, they are assigned to the next available modem. Because the IP address is assigned to the modem that is actually used, the bottom line is that a new IP address will be used each time the user calls the service. This also ignores the problem of how to get information about name servers and other things that are needed for an Internet connection.

This brings us to the *Point-to-Point Protocol* (*PPP*). This protocol addresses the limitations we have just discussed and is now probably the most common technique used to remotely connect to the Internet. I should also point out that while the SLIP protocol does not provide these functions, it is possible to get this information after the connection is established. It just requires a little special programming. But because PPP handles this condition, it is probably easier just to use PPP.

WinSock, VBX, and OCX

We saw in Chapter 2 how sockets are used to communicate between multiple computers. However, this specification exists only for the data packets that are sent between the computers, not how an application program generates these packets. A few years ago a standard was developed that identified how application programs should interact with Windows to access Internet services. This standard is known as *WinSock*.

WinSock is a standard maintained by Microsoft that basically defines the a set of subroutine definitions that reside in a *Dynamic Link Library* (*DLL*) file. The WinSock DLL, in turn, uses the appropriate drivers to talk to the specific hardware in the PC. A number of third-party vendors developed Internet packages for Windows 3.0 and 3.1. These typically included an FTP program, a Telnet program, the WinSock DLL, and the drivers for the most popular hardware cards. When Microsoft released Windows 95, it chose to include WinSock and the related drivers on the system. In fact, Microsoft did this for a number of other networking products, including Novell's and Microsoft's own proprietary networking systems.

While the WinSock library provides a standard way for Windows to communicate with the Internet, it is difficult for the average programmer to use. A number of companies have provided easier methods for Visual Basic programmers, which are known as VBXs and OCXs.

VBXs and OCXs contain common libraries of routines similar to DLLs. Unlike DLLs, VBXs and OCXs provide an easier way to access the functions. In a DLL you must explicitly declare the functions before you can use them. A VBX or OCX exploits some of the aspects of object-oriented programming by providing standard techniques for interacting with the functions. These techniques are called *properties*, *methods*, and *events*, which should be familiar to all Visual Basic programmers.

While VBXs and OCXs are very similar externally, their internal differences are significant. The largest difference between the two is that VBXs are limited to 16-bit code, while the OCXs are limited to 32-bit code. This means that an OCX should run faster than the equivalent VBX. (This is a hotly debated topic and one that I really want to avoid here. Suffice it to say Microsoft's position is that the 32-bit code is the way of the future so it really does not matter in the long run.) The other significant difference is that the OCXs are based on OLE (Object Linking and Embedding) technology, which provides a better foundation than what is used for VBXs.

The 16-bit version of Visual Basic 4.0 and all prior versions of Visual Basic can only use VBX controls in their programs. The 32-bit version of Visual Basic 4.0 can only use OCXs. Is this a real problem? Probably not, unless you are using the 16-bit version of Visual Basic and you really need to access a new OCX, or you are using the 32-bit version of Visual Basic and the functions only exist an a VBX.

Windows 95 and ActiveX

Now that we have covered OCXs and VBXs, Microsoft has thrown a monkey wrench into the works. Faced with increased competition in the marketplace, Microsoft is following the time-honored practice used by many companies in this business of taking an old product and giving it a few new features along with a new name. (This is especially true of IBM, whose premier operating system has been called OS/360, MFT, MVT, OS/VS, OS/VS II, MVS, MVS/XA, MVS/ESA, and now OS/390.) Thus ActiveX was born. ActiveX still uses the OLE technology used to create OCXs. While there have been some changes to the specifications, they probably do not justify the new name.

ActiveX is being used in two different places. First and probably most visible, Microsoft is working hard at improving Internet Explorer and adding new features that are designed to compete with Netscape's Navigator. These new features include a special version of Visual Basic called VBScript (which was derived from Visual Basic for Applications) to compete with Netscape's JavaScript. It has also included the capability to call ActiveX functions from Internet Explorer, which is designed to compete with Sun's Java. Microsoft has also released special editions of Word and Excel that can only display Word and Excel documents. This lets users include Word and Excel documents as part of their Web pages and have them automatically displayed by Internet Explorer.

This means that version 3.0 of Internet Explorer can access a Web page that references a Word or Excel document and have those documents automatically displayed when the user clicks on the hypertext link. It also lets Visual Basic programmers leverage their expertise on the Internet.

Along with the Internet Explorer ActiveX functions, Microsoft has released the Internet Control Pack, which is another set of ActiveX functions designed to allow the Visual Basic, Visual Foxpro, and Visual C++ programmer easier access to Internet functions. Users of other programming tools, such as Borland's Delphi, should also be able to take advantage of these tools. These ActiveX functions are the ones covered in this book. The main reason for this discussion is so you will understand that while both types of controls are called ActiveX, there is a significant difference between the two. One is intended for use by conventional programming languages, and the other is designed to be called from Internet Explorer.

Windows 95 TCP/IP Applications

Windows 95 is the first real version of Windows that is equipped to handle TCP/IP connections. But simply connecting to the Internet is not sufficient. You need applications that can take advantage of the connections. We have talked about Internet Explorer, which is Microsoft's Web browser. Microsoft also includes an electronic mail client in Windows 95 called Microsoft Exchange. But as a standard part of Windows 95 a few other less-documented Internet utilities that may be of some interest are included.

PING

Perhaps the simplest Internet program is known as *Packet InterNet Groper* (*PING*). PING simply sends a message to a remote computer system and waits for an acknowledgment (see figure 4-1). PING is an MS-DOS command found in the \Windows directory. It is extremely useful when you want to know if a system is up and running. For example, one day while I was working on this book, I tried to read my e-mail but my e-mail program could not reach the server. Because I was not sure what was happening, I used the PING command to see if the computer was up. The PING command waited a while and then gave me an error message saying that nothing was received from the host. I later found out that someone was moving the computer that day and did not expect anyone to use it.

The point behind this story is that the PING command can be useful to determine if the system is online or offline. Another use of the PING command is to quickly test if your network connection is working properly. When I make changes to the network configuration on my PC, the first test I use is to PING a system that I know is up. If that fails, I try a couple of other systems just to be sure. If all of them refuse to respond to the PING, I go back and double-check my network configuration because something is probably wrong.

Trace Route

Another MS-DOS-based command is the TRACERT, or trace route, command (see figure 4-2). This command is useful to see all the intermediate steps between your local computer and a specified remote host. This command provides similar information to the PING command (i.e., is the remote host up?), but because this command provides details of each node that the packets must pass through, it can be useful to detect network

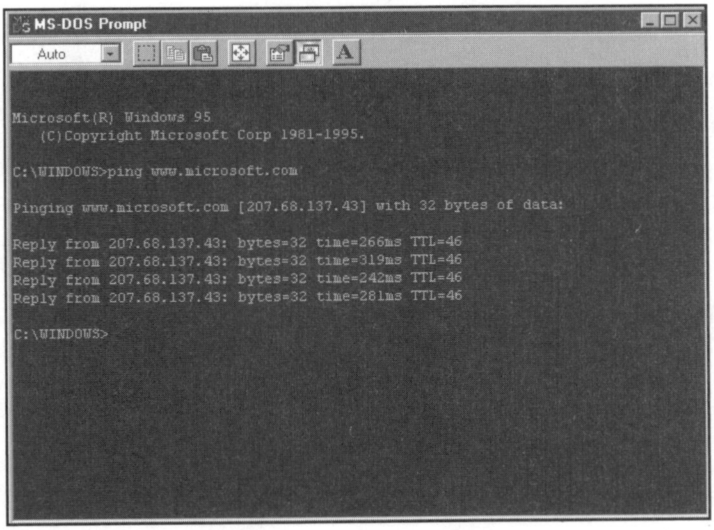

```
MS-DOS Prompt

Microsoft(R) Windows 95
   (C)Copyright Microsoft Corp 1981-1995.

C:\WINDOWS>ping www.microsoft.com

Pinging www.microsoft.com [207.68.137.43] with 32 bytes of data:

Reply from 207.68.137.43: bytes=32 time=266ms TTL=46
Reply from 207.68.137.43: bytes=32 time=319ms TTL=46
Reply from 207.68.137.43: bytes=32 time=242ms TTL=46
Reply from 207.68.137.43: bytes=32 time=281ms TTL=46

C:\WINDOWS>
```

FIGURE 4-1

PINGing www.microsoft.com.

```
MS-DOS Prompt

C:\WINDOWS>tracert www.microsoft.com

Tracing route to www.microsoft.com [207.68.137.34]
over a maximum of 30 hops:

  1   154 ms   145 ms   143 ms  annex13.umd.edu [128.8.10.113]
  2   144 ms   144 ms   152 ms  csc2gw-fddi4/0.umd.edu [128.8.10.1]
  3   145 ms   148 ms   148 ms  csc0gw-f0.umd.edu [128.8.1.228]
  4   151 ms   147 ms   157 ms  dca3-core1-h4-0-2.atlas.digex.net [206.205.243.1
]
  5   152 ms   151 ms   149 ms  iad1-core1-h0-0.atlas.digex.net [206.205.246.2]

  6   159 ms   149 ms   164 ms  vienna1.va.alter.net [192.41.177.249]
  7   165 ms   152 ms   162 ms  Hssi1-0.CR2.DCA1.Alter.Net [137.39.100.22]
  8   362 ms   291 ms   228 ms  101.Hssi4-0.CR2.SCL1.Alter.Net [137.39.58.86]
  9   228 ms   224 ms   224 ms  Fddi0-0.Cisco1.Santa-Clara.CA.MS.UU.Net [137.39.
19.2]
 10   281 ms   239 ms   239 ms  Dist1-SCL.MOSWEST.MSN.NET [137.39.100.58]
 11   353 ms   304 ms   238 ms  msft1-f0.moswest.msn.net [207.68.145.46]
 12   283 ms   245 ms   244 ms  www.microsoft.com [207.68.137.34]

Trace complete.

C:\WINDOWS>
```

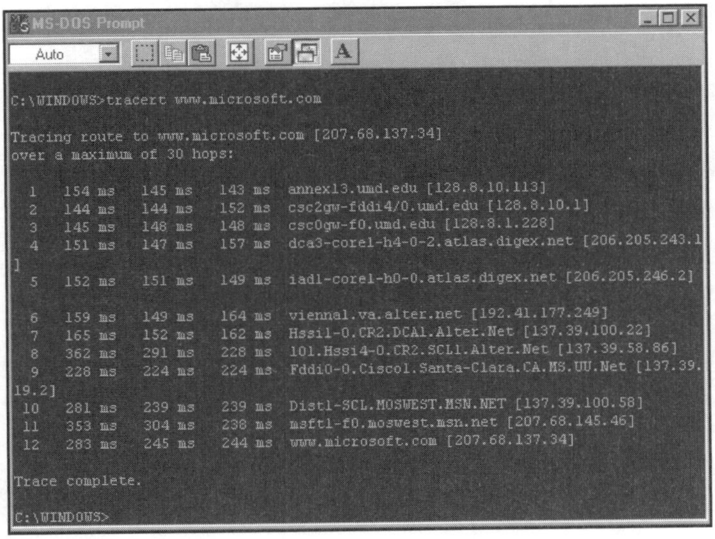

FIGURE 4-2

TRACERT to www.microsoft.com.

failures. Another situation I ran across one day at work was when someone complained that they could not reach the department's mainframe. I knew that the mainframe was working because I was using it at the time. I was able to use the trace route command and found that I could not reach the user's computer. There was a failure in part of the network between his computer and mainframe that prevented access to the major part of the local network. When the failure was corrected, everything went back to normal.

FTP

Because we are talking about MS-DOS-based Internet tools, there is one last tool that is worth mentioning: FTP. Having cruised the Information Superhighway since it was an old winding dirt road, I grew very familiar with command-driven FTP programs (see figure 4-3). This implementation of the FTP program is not really different from any of the other ones I have used over the years. In fact, I often find it comforting to have this old friend around.

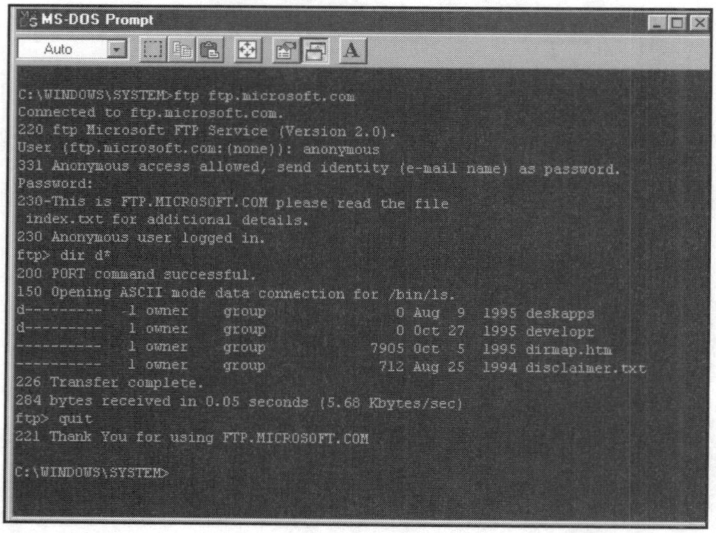

MS-DOS Prompt

Auto

```
C:\WINDOWS\SYSTEM>ftp ftp.microsoft.com
Connected to ftp.microsoft.com.
220 ftp Microsoft FTP Service (Version 2.0).
User (ftp.microsoft.com:(none)): anonymous
331 Anonymous access allowed, send identity (e-mail name) as password.
Password:
230-This is FTP.MICROSOFT.COM please read the file
 index.txt for additional details.
230 Anonymous user logged in.
ftp> dir d*
200 PORT command successful.
150 Opening ASCII mode data connection for /bin/ls.
d---------   1 owner    group               0 Aug  9  1995 deskapps
d---------   1 owner    group               0 Oct 27  1995 developr
----------   1 owner    group            7905 Oct  5  1995 dirmap.htm
----------   1 owner    group             712 Aug 25  1994 disclaimer.txt
226 Transfer complete.
284 bytes received in 0.05 seconds (5.68 Kbytes/sec)
ftp> quit
221 Thank You for using FTP.MICROSOFT.COM

C:\WINDOWS\SYSTEM>
```

FIGURE 4-3

FTP to ftp.microsoft.com.

Telnet

There is one last Internet application I want to talk about: *Telnet*. While Microsoft's implementation of Telnet is not very fancy, it provides all the basic functions that let you emulate a terminal into another computer system. This is a fairly standard function that is handy to have around. We find this useful later in the book when we experiment with the various protocols.

FIGURE 4-4

Telnet.

Summary

In this chapter we discussed how TCP/IP is implemented on Windows 95. This included such topics as how to connect to the Internet, what are SLIP and PPP, what is WinSock, and how VBX controls, OCX controls, and ActiveX controls differ. Then we went through some useful (but not well-known) Internet applications that are included in Windows 95.

In the next chapter, we discuss how to set up your machine to access the Internet, how to install the ActiveX controls, and how to set up the sample programs.

In case you want to check your answers to the questions at the front of the chapter, here are the answers:

- *What protocol is most commonly used to connect to the Internet using Windows 95?*

  PPP is the most commonly used protocol to connect to the Internet using a modem.

- *What is the difference between a DLL and an OCX?*

  An OCX is a collection of properties, methods, and events that work together to provide a solution to a programming need. A DLL includes only a set of subroutines that correspond to methods of an OCX.

- *What Internet tools are included with Windows 95?*

  Internet Explorer—a Windows application that is used for accessing the World Wide Web.

  Microsoft Exchange—a Windows application that is used to accessing e-mail and faxes.

  PING—an MS-DOS command that is used to see if a computer is online and reachable via the Internet.

  TRACERT (Trace Route)—an MS-DOS command that is used to check each of the intermediate nodes between the local computer and the specified computer on the Internet.

  FTP—an MS-DOS command that is used to move files around the Internet.

  Telnet—a Windows program that is used to access a remote host system as a dumb terminal.

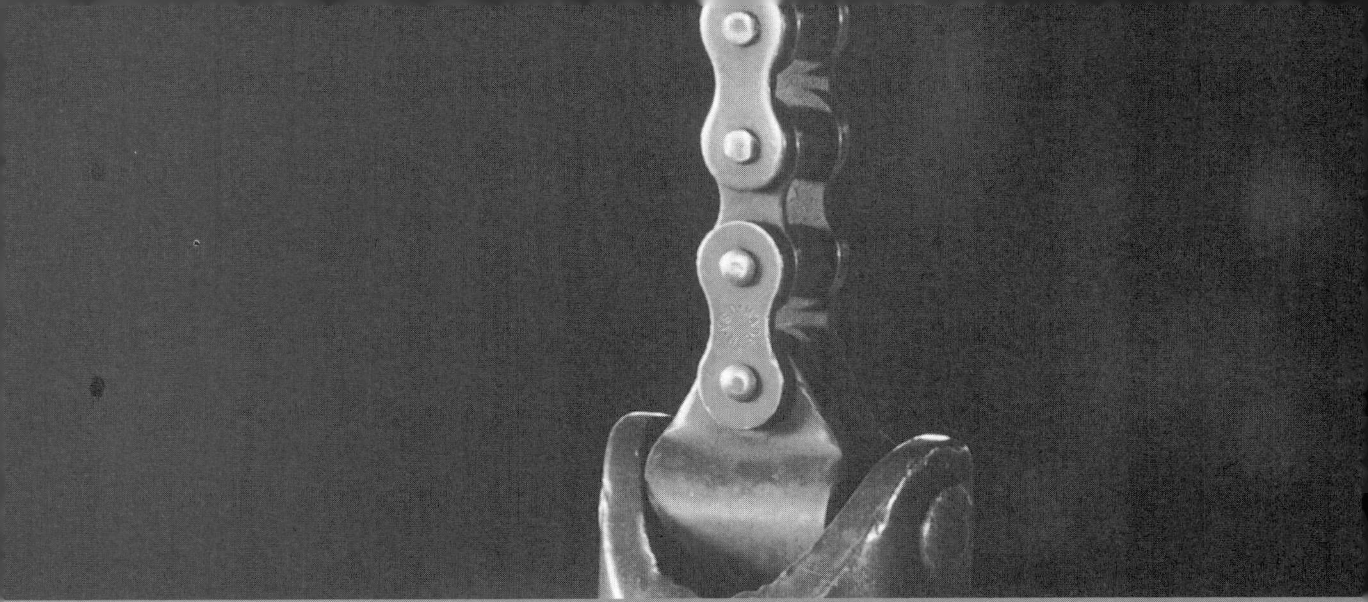

Chapter 5

Installing the ActiveX Controls and Sample Programs

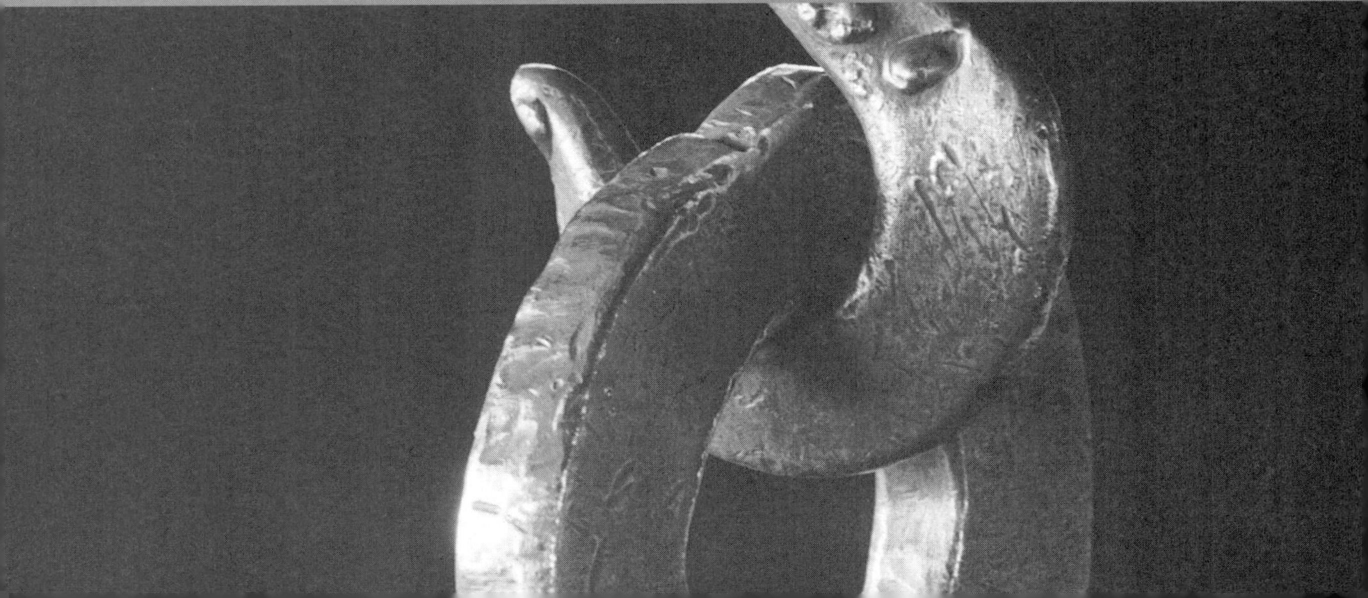

Overview

In this chapter, I help you set up your system so you can use the Internet Control Pack. First, we walk through an installation and setup of Windows 95 TCP/IP. Then I show you how to install the Internet Control Pack and add the controls and their support objects to Visual Basic.

By the end of this chapter, you should be able to answer the following questions:

- What information do you need from your Internet service provider to complete the Internet setup process?
- How do you include the ActiveX controls into a Visual Basic program?

Installation of TCP/IP in Windows 95

Installing TCP/IP support on Windows 95 is not a hard process when you know what you are doing. You need some information from your Internet service provider, though. Figure 5-1 lists the most important information you need from the provider. If you already have a working Internet connection, you can skip this section and continue with the installation of the ActiveX Internet Control Pack.

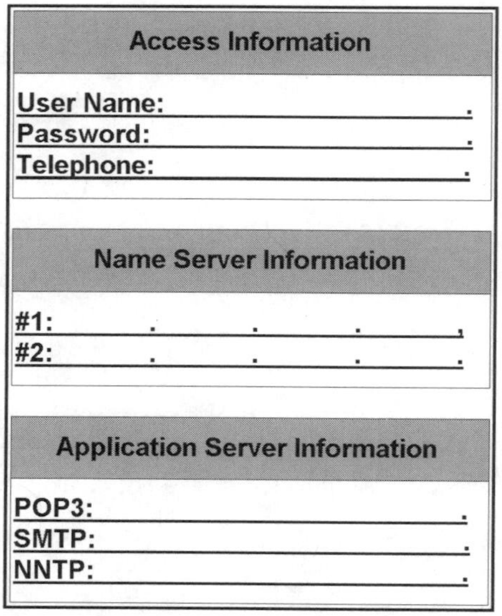

Access Information

User Name: ________________.
Password: ________________.
Telephone: ________________.

Name Server Information

#1: ____ . ____ . ____ . ____
#2: ____ . ____ . ____ . ____

Application Server Information

POP3: ________________.
SMTP: ________________.
NNTP: ________________.

FIGURE 5-1

Information from the Internet service provider.

The access information and name server information are used to create a working PPP connection. (There is an update available from Microsoft, called DSCRIPT, that adds support for SLIP. See the CD-ROM in the back of this book for a copy of this utility.) The application server information is used later in this book while testing the various ActiveX programs we create.

Installing Dial-Up Networking

To start the installation process, insert the Windows 95 installation CD-ROM into the computer and wait for the display in figure 5-2 to appear.

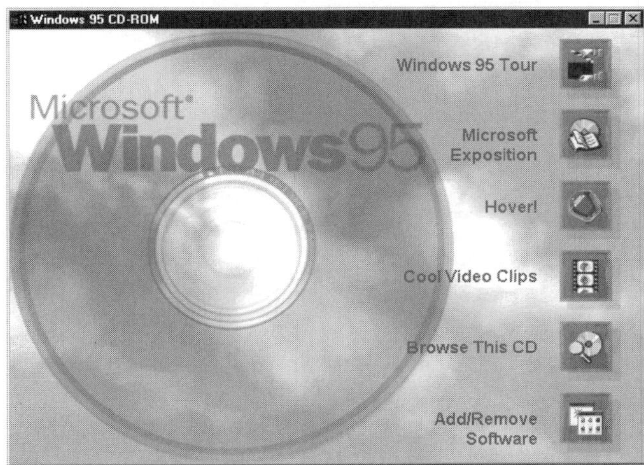

FIGURE 5-2

Windows 95 CD-ROM.

From this window, click the Add/Remove Software button (see figure 5-3). (You can also go through the Start | Settings | Add/Remove Software path to get to the same place).

In the Add/Remove Software window, select the Windows Setup tab and double-click Communications in the Components window. This displays the information as shown in figure 5-4.

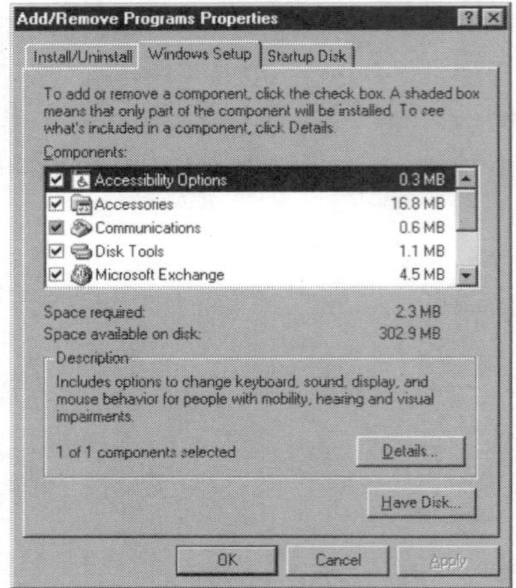

FIGURE 5-3

Add/Remove Software.

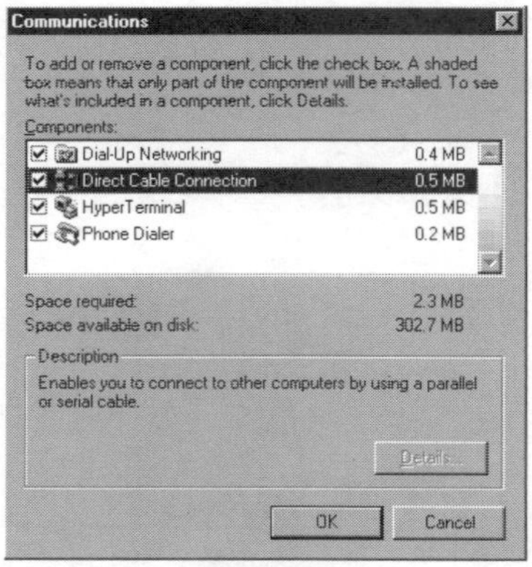

FIGURE 5-4

Communications.

Be sure that there is a check mark in the box next to Dial-Up Networking, and then click OK. The system loads some software and lets you know that you need to reboot the system when the process is complete because some system settings have changed. Finally, you receive the message box shown in figure 5-5.

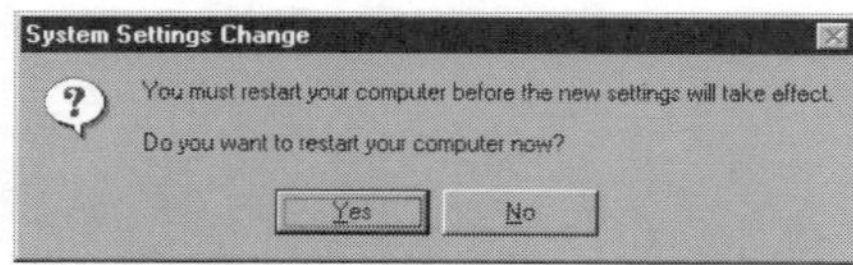

FIGURE 5-5

Restart your system.

Make sure that you do not have any floppy disks in the system and click Yes. Windows 95 restarts and does a few extra things during the restart process to complete the installation process. When this finishes, you are half-way there. All you need to do is to run the Internet Setup Wizard and you are finished.

Using the Internet Setup Wizard

Now that we have loaded the drivers necessary to access the Internet, we need to finish the installation by defining an Internet connection. To start this process, select Start | Programs | Accessories | Internet Tools | Internet Setup Wizard. This starts the Internet Setup Wizard and displays the window seen in figure 5-6.

FIGURE 5-6

Internet Setup Wizard.

The Internet Setup Wizard leads you through a bunch of questions and creates a dial-up connection based on your responses. The first question the wizard asks is whether you are using The Microsoft Network or a different service provider (see figure 5-7). Because I do not have an account on The Microsoft Network, I selected the different service provider and pressed Next.

The next form asks if you want to use Microsoft Exchange to send and receive mail (see figure 5-8). Because we will be working on our own mail program later in this book, select No and press Next.

At this point, the wizard has sufficient information to begin installing files and creating the icons that you need to access the Internet (see figure 5-9).

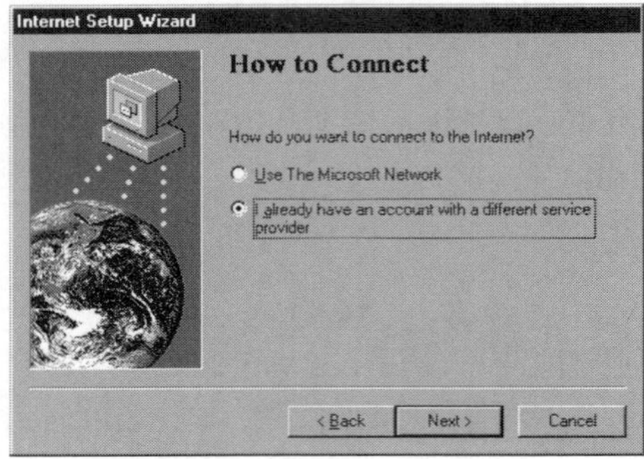

FIGURE 5-7

How to connect.

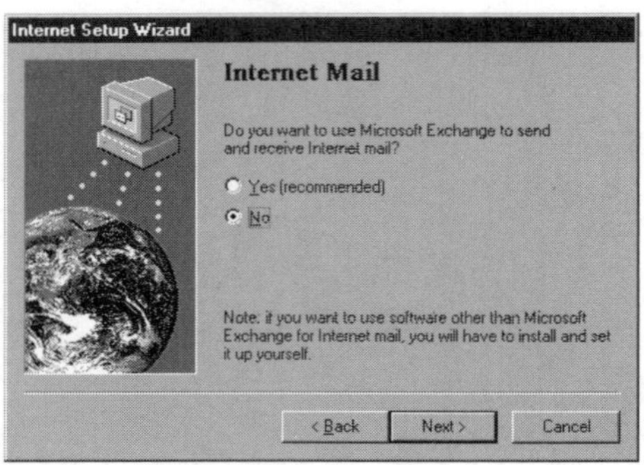

FIGURE 5-8

Internet Mail.

FIGURE 5-9

Installing files.

To begin the second half of the process, the wizard asks you for the name of your Internet service provider (see figure 5-10). You can enter any name that you want. This is used to create the button that you click on to make the connection. If wizard determines that you need additional files, it will prompt you to load the CD-ROM so it can copy the files.

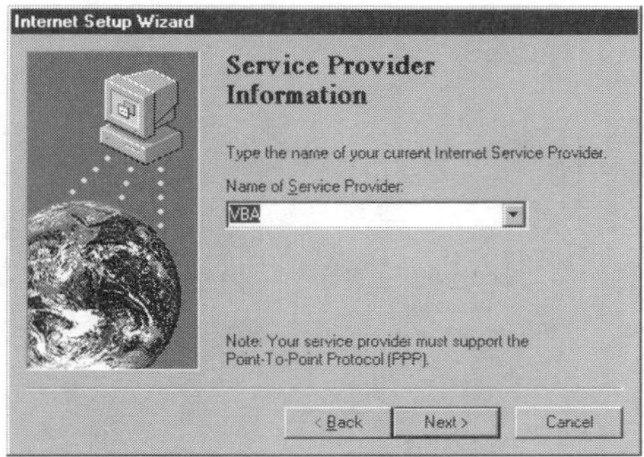

FIGURE 5-10

Service provider information.

The next step is to enter the telephone information (see figure 5-11). This is the telephone number that you filled in earlier in figure 5-1. It also asks for the country code where the Internet provider's telephone number is located. Finally, there is a check box that asks if Windows should bring up the terminal window after dialing. Because most Internet providers need a username and password to gain access and Windows 95 is not equipped out of the box to handle other Internet providers, you have to manually enter this information. Or you can install the DSCRPT fix from Microsoft, which allows you to build a logon script and also adds support for SLIP connections. This file is also included on the CD-ROM for your convenience.

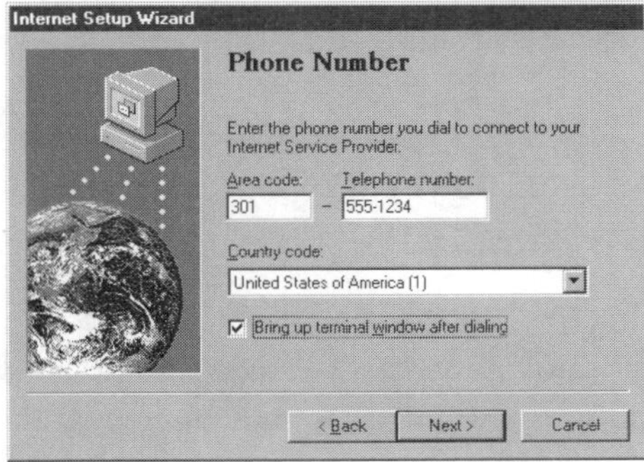

FIGURE 5-11

Phone number.

The next screen displayed by the wizard asks for your username and password for the Internet service provider (see figure 5-12). Because we manually enter this information, you may or may not want to enter it here. (If you want to install the DSCRPT update, you will want to enter this information because the script uses this information.)

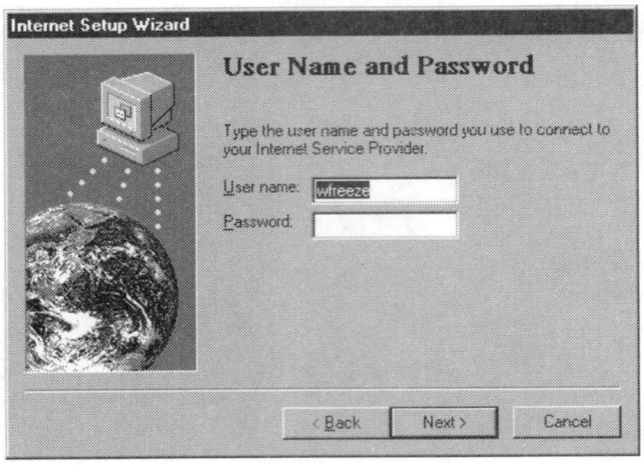

FIGURE 5-12

Username and password.

The IP Address screen lets you either use a static IP address that was assigned by the Internet provider, or lets you receive an IP address at the time the connection is made (see figure 5-13). The later option is probably the better of the two because it works even if you have been assigned a static IP address; however, you may want to check with your Internet service provider to be sure.

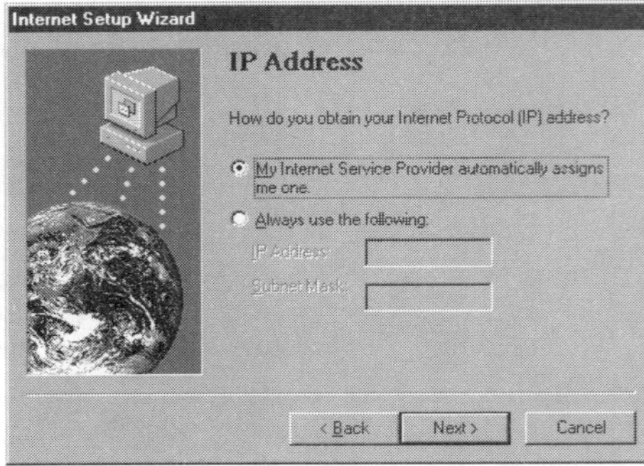

FIGURE 5-13

IP address.

One last piece of information that is needed to set up the PPP connection is the IP addresses of the Domain Name Server (DNS). This information is entered on the DNS Server Address form as shown in figure 5-14. Without the domain name server IP addresses, you are unable to translate a domain name into an IP address. The reason for specifying two addresses is that if one of the servers is unavailable, the other server is used automatically. While losing a name server is not a very likely event, it does happen from time to time and having a second address may make the difference between being able to use your Internet connection or not.

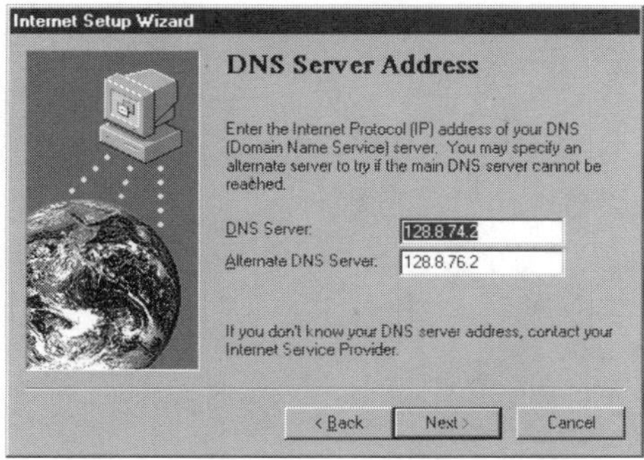

FIGURE 5-14

DNS server address.

Figure 5-15 shows that the setup process is finished. In the next section, I show you how to link up to the Internet using the definitions we just created.

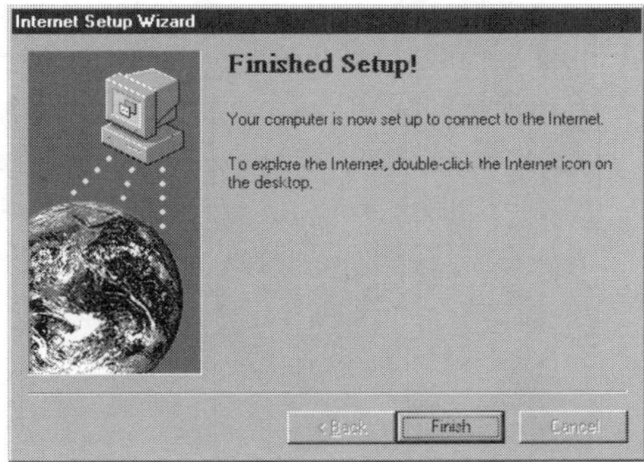

FIGURE 5-15

Finished setup.

Testing the Connection

Now that we have created a connection to the Internet, let's go and test it. Find the Dial-Up Networking window by clicking Start | Programs | Accessories | Dial-Up Networking (see figure 5-16). From this window, click the VBA button to begin the connection process.

Notice that there are a number of other connections shown in the Dial-Up Networking window in figure 5-16. That is because I have defined a number of connections over time. I am currently using three different providers and some of those providers have alternate numbers in different area codes. You can easily create additional connections by double-clicking the Make New Connection button.

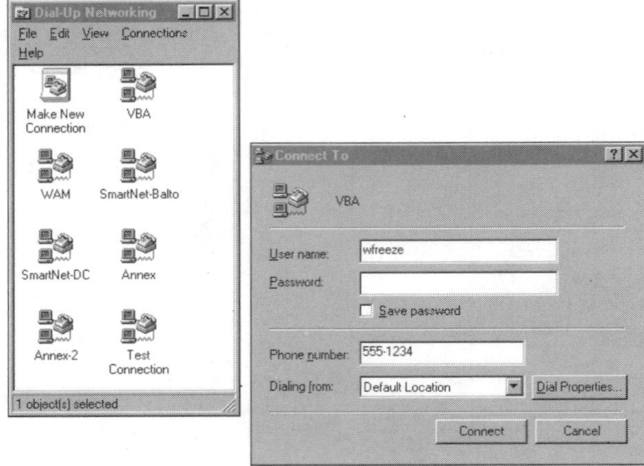

FIGURE 5-16

Connect to VBA.

When you click the Connect button, Windows dials the telephone number supplied on the VBA form. (By the way, the phone number supplied on this form will not work. I put in the working number between figures 5-16 and 5-17.) When the modem on the other end answers and finishes its initial setup work, the terminal screen in figure 5-17 appears. The exact information on this screen varies from one Internet provider to another, but in general all require you to enter a username, password, and possibly an option to connect using a PPP connection.

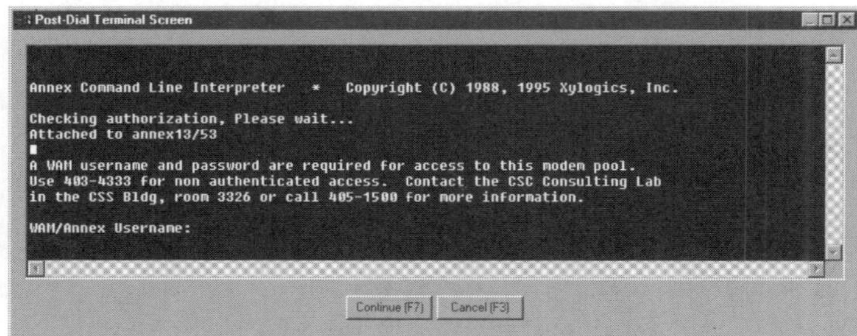

FIGURE 5-17

Terminal screen.

After entering your username, password, and selecting a PPP connection, the PC and remote host begin to communicate with each other. This is the line of "garbage" that you see at the bottom of the terminal screen in figure 5-18. When you see this information, press the F7 key to continue with the connection.

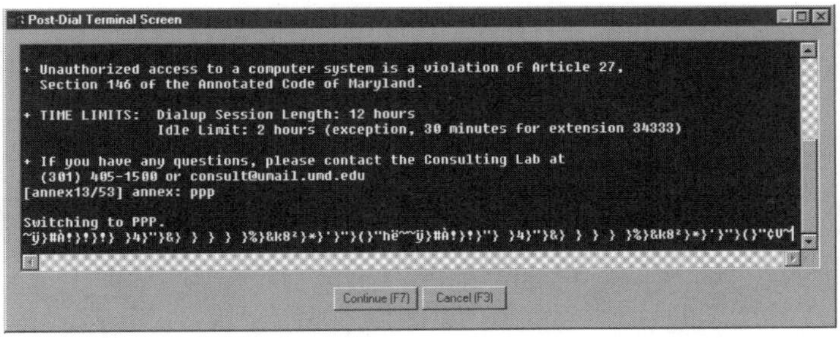

FIGURE 5-18

Terminal screen revisited.

Assuming that everything has worked properly, you see a window similar to the one shown in figure 5-19.

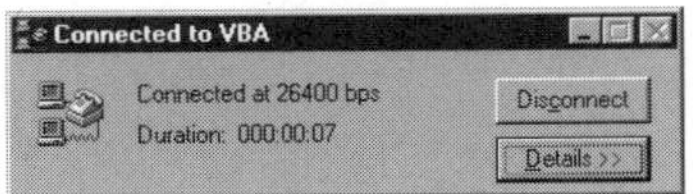

FIGURE 5-19

Connected to VBA.

Installation of the ActiveX Internet Control Pack

Now that we have a working Internet connection, it is time to install the ActiveX Internet Control Pack. The first step is to select Start | Run from the task bar. Then enter the location of the installation program. For installation from the CD-ROM in the back of this book, enter **D:\MS\MSICPB.EXE** (replace D: with the address of your CD-ROM drive) and then click OK. The installation program loads and begins execution by displaying the window shown in figure 5-20.

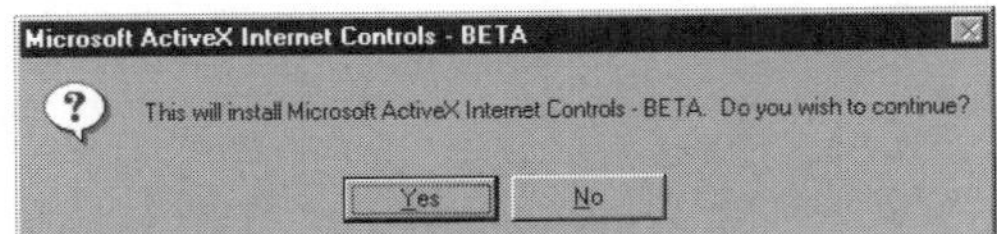

FIGURE 5-20

Install Microsoft Internet Controls.

As usual, the lawyers have to have their say, so take a moment and review the terms of the License agreement (see figure 5.21). If you agree, click the Yes button.

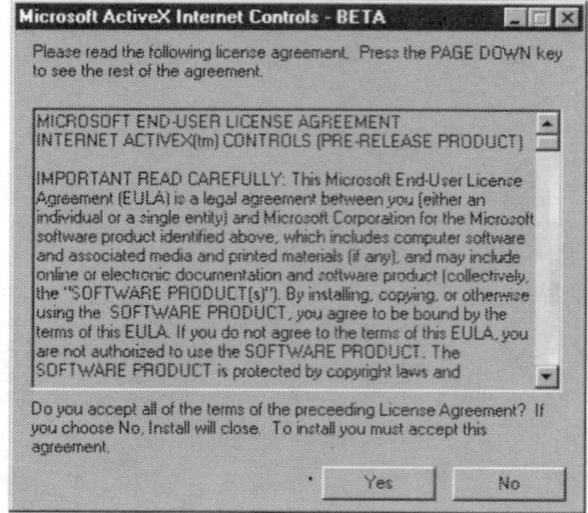

FIGURE 5-21

License agreement.

The installation program begins the installation process by extracting the files needed to run the installation program as shown in figure 5-22.

FIGURE 5-22

Install setup materials.

After these files have been extracted, the installation program begins by telling you to exit all other running programs (see figure 5-23).

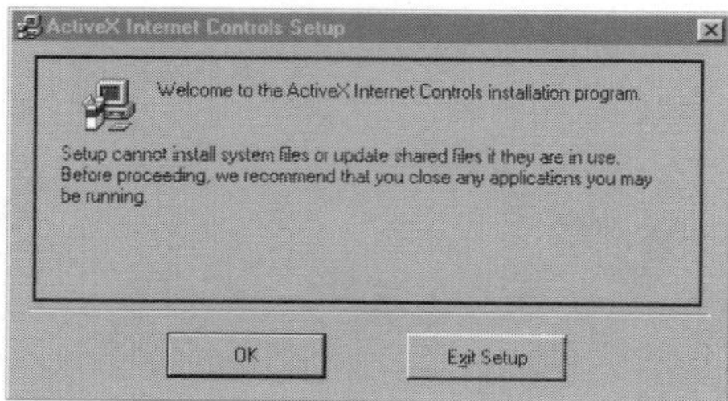

FIGURE 5-23

Exit all programs.

As shown in figure 5-24, the setup program instructs you to change the location of where the files are stored, and then to start the installation. Only a few files are actually installed into this directory. The bulk of the files are installed into the \Windows and \Windows\System directories.

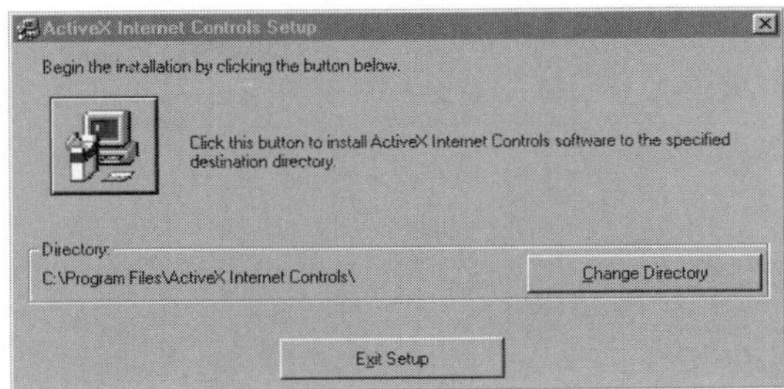

FIGURE 5-24

ActiveX Internet Controls setup.

After clicking the installation button, the necessary files are copied into their proper destinations (see figure 5-25).

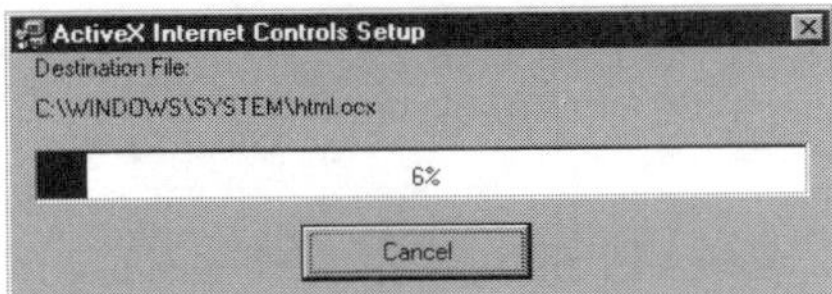

FIGURE 5-25

ActiveX Internet Controls setup—copying files.

When the last file has been installed, the window shown in figure 5-26 appears. Clicking OK is the last step in the process.

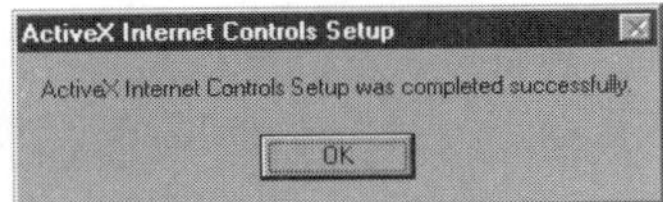

FIGURE 5-26

ActiveX Internet Controls setup—finished.

Installation of the ActiveX Controls in Visual Basic

Installing the controls into Visual Basic is a relatively straightforward task. Using the Visual Basic menu, choose Tools, Custom Controls. This displays the window shown in figure 5-27. All you need to do is put an X in the boxes next to the controls that you want to have available to you while writing your program. When you click OK, the controls appear in the toolbox, ready to use.

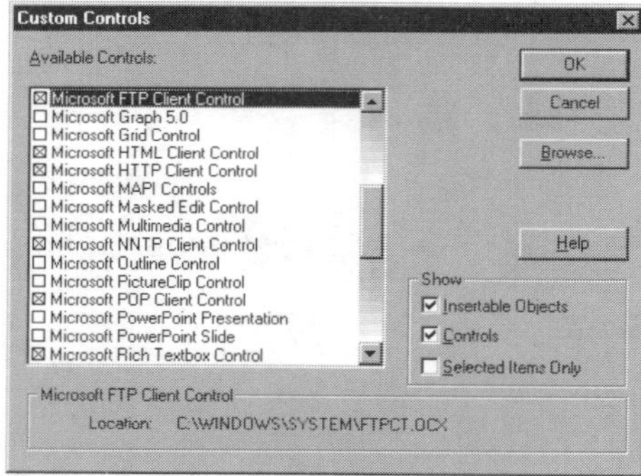

FIGURE 5-27

Visual Basic—Selecting ActiveX Controls.

Simply adding the controls to the toolbox, however, is not sufficient. There are some support objects that the controls use. These are added to your program by going to the Visual Basic Tools menu and selecting Tools, References. This displays the window shown in figure 5-28. Clicking the box next to Microsoft Internet Support Objects and then clicking OK includes them in your program.

Installation of the Sample Programs

While I am on the topic of installing various things, I thought I should cover the sample programs. On the CD-ROM are two sets of sample programs. One set includes the programs we create later in this book. The remaining programs are the ones supplied by Microsoft.

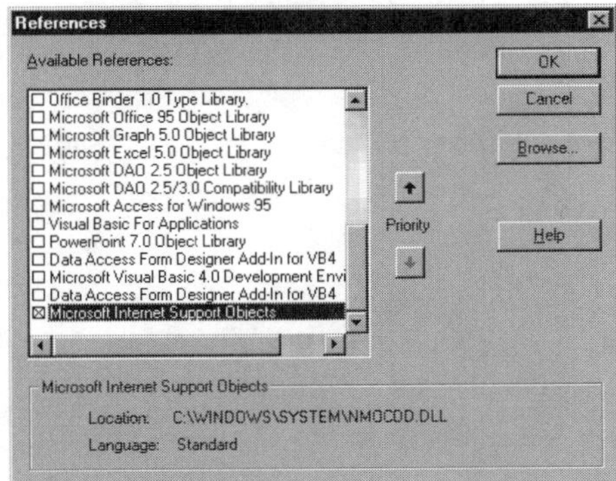

FIGURE 5-28

Visual Basic—selecting the Internet Support Objects.

The programs that we discuss later in this book are stored in individual directories as normal Visual Basic projects. You can open the programs directly from the CD-ROM in Visual Basic and run them without changes. If you want to make some changes (something I highly recommend), all you have to do is save the project in Visual Basic into a directory on your hard disk.

In addition to the programs we develop in this book, I also include the sample programs from Microsoft. Microsoft's programs are stored as self-extracting EXE files. They are stored in the MS directory where the Internet Control Pack is stored. To install any of these programs, simply create a folder, copy the program to the folder, and then run the copy. The program extracts all the individual files into the folder, and then the sample program is ready to use.

Summary

In this chapter we learned how to install and configure a connection to an Internet provider. We also walked through the installation of the ActiveX Internet Control Pack onto a Windows 95 system and how to enable the ActiveX controls in Visual Basic. Finally, we discussed how install the sample programs that we discuss later in this book.

This concludes the introduction part of the book. In the next part, we discuss the FTP protocol and the FTP ActiveX control, and then go through how to write an FTP program using the ActiveX control.

In case you want to check your answers to the questions at the front of the chapter, here are the answers:

- *What information will you need from you Internet service provider to complete the Internet setup process?*

  You need the following:

  The telephone number for the provider's modems.

  A valid username and password.

  The IP addresses for two Domain Name Servers.

  Any special instructions for starting a PPP connection after you have logged onto the network.

  Also, while not specifically needed for the connection, you should have the names of the POP3 mail server, SMTP mail server, and NNTP news server. These are used later in the book when we test the MailRunner and the NewsRunner programs.

- *How do you include the ActiveX controls into a Visual Basic program?*

  You can add the controls to the Toolbox by using the Tools | Custom Controls menu item, but then you must add the support objects by using the Tools | References command.

PART II

Transferring Files with FTP

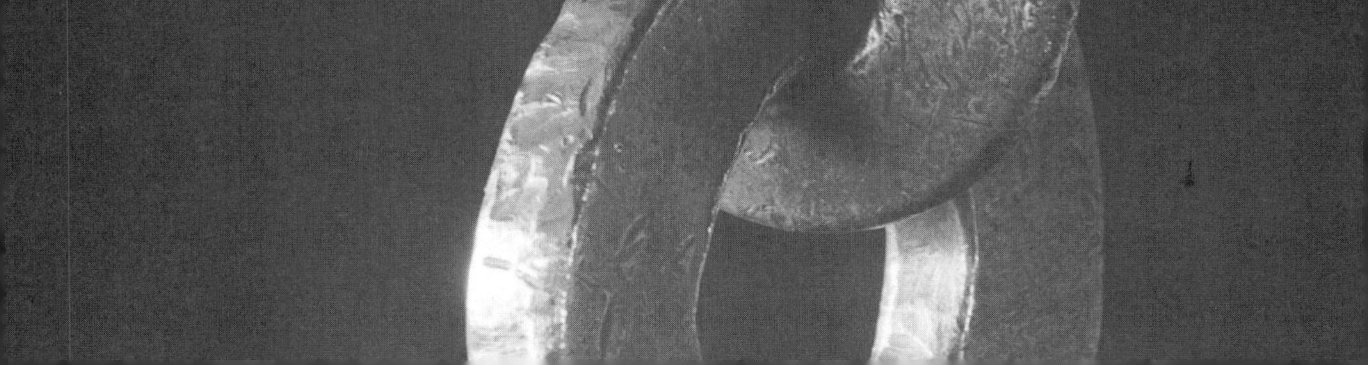

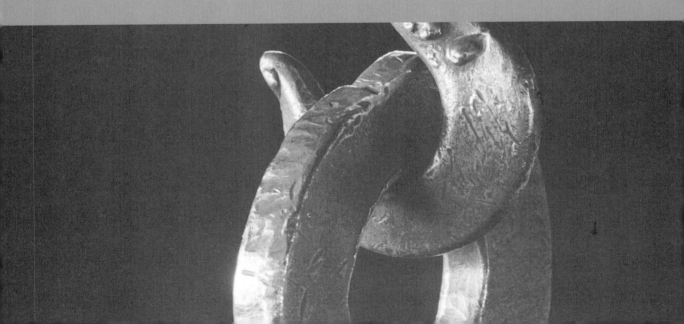

What Is the FTP Client Control

The FTP client control simplifies the job of transferring files over the Internet. Not all programs benefit from this capability, but some do. FTP is a widely used and accepted method of transferring files. With servers available for nearly all types of computer systems, FTP provides a near universal method for transporting data files.

Unlike some other Internet protocols, FTP permits both authenticated and anonymous access to files.

- *Authenticated access* requires that the client supply a valid userid and password to access the server. This is useful when you want to permit only an authorized user to access files on the server.
- *Anonymous access* means that no special permissions are required to access the server. This useful when you want to make files available for public access.

Where Would I Use the FTP Client Control?

Because the FTP client control deals with the transferring of files between the local machine and a remote server (hence the name File Transfer Protocol), it can be used in a number of ways.

Consider the case of a chain of fast food restaurants. Each restaurant operates independently each day, but at night it needs to upload financial and inventory information to the corporate mainframe for processing. A Visual Basic program could be started each night after closing that collects the appropriate information from the local databases into a set of files to be uploaded. Then it contacts the mainframe and uploads the data for that night's batch processing cycle and downloads data from the previous night's cycle.

Another possibility is a case where a user can request an application to determine if an updated version is available. If one is available, the application could then download the updated module and install it without any effort required by the user. Because FTP supports authenticated user access, this would ensure that only an authorized user could gain access to the update.

Yet another situation occurs when a user wants to archive infrequently used data. By incorporating a menu selection component in the application, you could permit the user to retrieve any piece of information from the remote machine and make it available without the user having to know a lot of technical details.

One final example is the situation where a user wants to create offsite backups of his critical data. By placing a copy of the critical data away from the local facility, it should be possible to recover from a disaster where the local facility was destroyed. This example makes auditors very happy, and is good common sense.

Summary

The FTP client control offers a lot of capabilities that are easy to include in Visual Basic programs. It is best used in those situations where you want to shield the user from all of the details of how the files are transferred. In the following chapters, we explore in more depth how FTP actually works across the Internet, discuss the ActiveX controls that assist with the FTP process, and go through a sample program that shows how to incorporate the FTP client control into a real program.

Chapter 6—FTP Protocols and Functions

This chapter discusses in detail how FTP works from a functional level and the protocols that are used to communicate between the client and the server. This serves as background material for understanding the FTP client control, the `FTPDirItem` object, and the FTP sample program discussed later in this part of the book.

- Overview
- The FTP Model
- FTP Protocol Commands
- FTP Reply Codes and Messages
- Accessing the Server
- Directory Information

- Setting Options
- Transferring Files
- Other Facilities
- Example
- Summary

Chapter 7—The FTP Client Control

This chapter discusses all of the programming aspects (properties, methods, and events) provided by the FTP client control. The control allows high level access to an FTP server.

- Overview
- Properties
- Methods
- Events
- Summary

Chapter 8—FTPDirItem Object

This chapter discusses all the programming properties provided by the `FTPDirItem` object. This object contains information about a file or directory on a remote FTP server.

- Overview
- Properties
- Example
- Summary

Chapter 9—icError Object and the icErrors Collection

This chapter discusses all the programming properties and methods provided by the `icError` object and the `icErrors` collection. These objects contain information about errors encountered by the FTP client control while connected to a remote FTP server.

- Overview
- Properties—icErrors
- Methods—icErrors
- Properties—icError
- Example
- Summary

Chapter 10—FTPRunner

This chapter walks the reader through the design and implementation of a simple FTP client program using the ActiveX FTP client control.

- Overview
- How to Use FTPRunner
- The Program Structure
- Connecting to the Server
- Disconnecting from the Server
- Listing a Directory
- Changing Directory
- Sending a File
- Receiving a File
- Transferring Multiple Files
- Summary

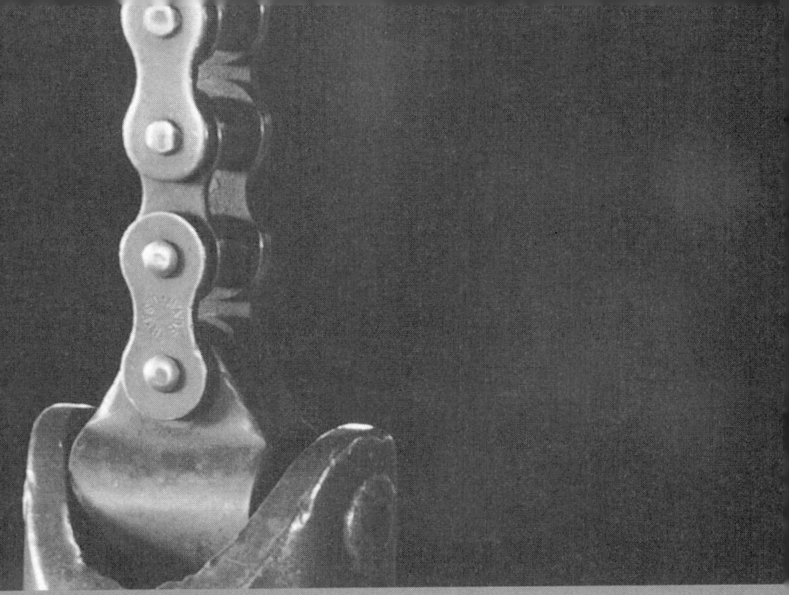

Chapter 6

FTP Protocols and Functions

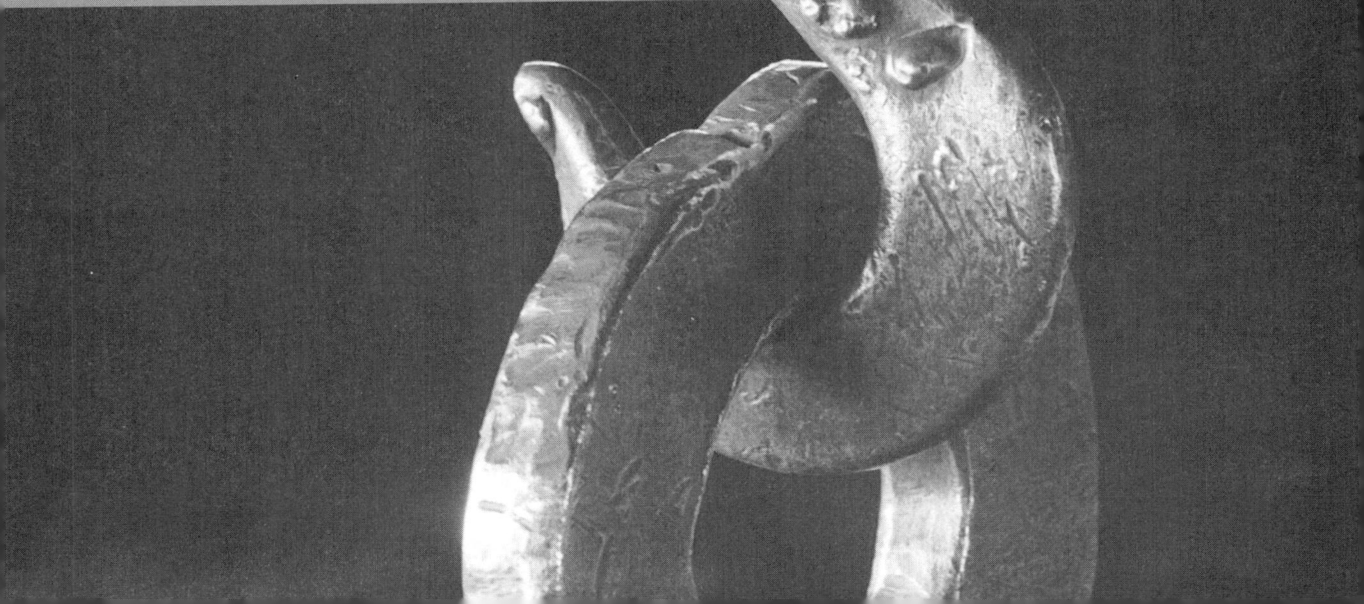

Overview

In this chapter we discuss how FTP works from a functional level and learn about the protocols that are used to communicate between the client and the server. These protocols are discussed in much greater detail in RFC-959. (A copy is provided on the CD-ROM if you are really interested in all the details.) If you really want to understand all the details about the FTP protocol, take some time to read the document. It is a good source of information about how FTP operates at the lowest level.

By the end of this chapter, you should be able to answer the following questions:

- How do you access the server?
- What commands can be used to retrieve directory information?
- What command instructs the server to send binary data?
- What commands are used to transfer data?

The FTP Model

The FTP protocol operates as a pair of client-server processes (see figure 6-1). The first client-server process is the *Protocol Interface* (*PI*). This is the process that the user interacts with. On the client side, this process takes commands from the user and passes them to the server. The server, in turn, receives the commands and generates replies back to the client.

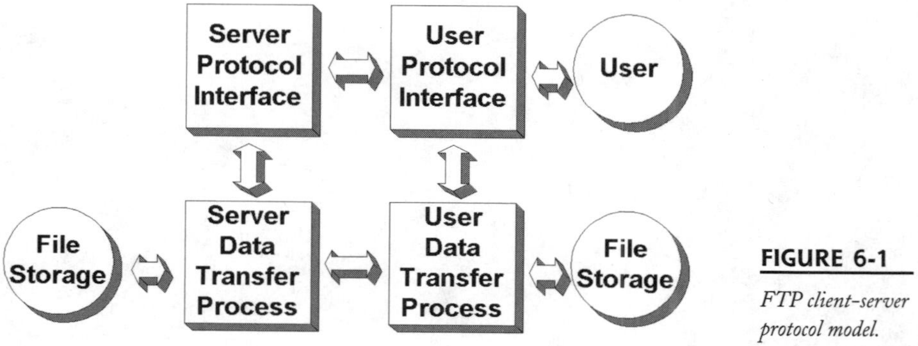

FIGURE 6-1

FTP client-server protocol model.

The other client-server process is the *Data Transfer Process* (*DTP*), which is used to move files between the client and server systems. The client side of this process is managed by the client side's PI, while the server side's PI manages the server's DTP.

FTP Protocol Commands

Commands are sent from the client PI to the server PI as standard ASCII text followed by a carriage return and a line feed. Responses are sent from the server the same way. Some commands also start a data transfer between the DTPs.

Generally, commands take the form of a one- to four-character command name, followed by an optional set of parameters, followed by a carriage return and line feed. (A carriage return is an ASCII character that is used to move the cursor to the first position of the current line. A line feed is an ASCII character that is used to begin a new line and scroll the previous line up one position. Together they are typically used to signal the end of a command or other input in a character-based system such as UNIX or MS-DOS.)

Table 6-1 lists the FTP protocol commands and their syntax; Table 6-2 shows the syntax of the parameters.

Table 6-1 FTP Protocol Commands

Command	Syntax
Abort	ABOR <crlf>
Account	ACCT <space> <account-information> <crlf>
Allocate	ALLO <space> <decimal-integer> [<space> <space> <decimal-integer>] <crlf>
Append	APPE <space> <pathname> <crlf>
Change Directory Up	CDUP <crlf>
Change Working Directory	CWD <space> <pathname> <crlf>
Delete	DELE <space> <pathname> <crlf>
Help	HELP [<space> <string>] <crlf>
List	LIST [<space> <pathname>] <crlf>
Make Directory	MKD <space> <pathname> <crlf>
Mode	MODE <space> <mode-code> <crlf>

continues

Table 6-1 Continued

Command	Syntax
Name List	NLST [<space> <pathname>] <crlf>
NOOP	NOOP <crlf>
Password	PASS <space> <password> <crlf>
Passive	PASV <crlf>
Port	PORT <space> <host-port> <crlf>
Print Working Directory	PWD <crlf>
Reinitialize	REIN <crlf>
Remove Directory	RMD <space> <pathname> <crlf>
Rename From	RNFR <space> <pathname> <crlf>
Rename To	RNTO <space> <pathname> <crlf>
Restart Marker	REST <space> <marker> <crlf>
Retrieve	RETR <space> <pathname> <crlf>
Quit	QUIT <crlf>
Site	SITE <space> <string> <crlf>
Statistics	STAT [<space> <pathname>] <crlf>
Store	STOR <space> <pathname> <crlf>
Store Unique	STOU <crlf>
Structure	STRU <space> <structure-code> <crlf>
Structure Mount	SMNT <space> <pathname> <crlf>
System	SYST <crlf>
Type	TYPE <space> <type-code> <crlf>
User Name	USER <space> <username> <crlf>

Table 6-2 FTP Command Parameter Syntax

Parameter	Syntax
<account-information>	::= <string>
<byte-size>	::= <number>
<char>	::= any of the 128 ASCII characters except <cr> and <lf>
<decimal-integer>	::= any decimal integer
<form-code>	::= N | T | C
<host-number>	::= <number>,<number>,<number>,<number>
<host-port>	::= <host-number>,<port-number>

Parameter	Syntax
<marker>	::= <pr-string>
<mode-code>	::= S | B | C
<number>	::= any decimal integer 1 through 255
<password>	::= <string>
<pathname>	::= <string>
<port-number>	::= <number>,<number>
<pr-char>	::= printable characters, any ASCII code 33 through 126
<pr-string>	::= <pr-char> | <pr-char><pr-string>
<string>	::= <char> | <char><string>
<structure-code>	::= F | R | P
<type-code>	::= A [<space> <form-code>] | E [<space> <form-code>] | I | L <space> <byte-size>
<username>	::= <string>

Responses take the form of a three-digit reply code number followed by a reply message, followed by a carriage return and line feed. The number is intended to be interpreted by the client PI, and the text is designed to be understandable by a user. However, not all messages need to be passed to the user directly. For example, a client PI may simply prompt the user for a password when it receives a message that says a password is required for access.

FTP Reply Codes and Messages

Messages returned by the server PI consist of two parts: the first is a *reply code*, and the second is a *reply string*. The reply code is a highly structured three-digit number. The first digit indicates whether or not the command was successful. The first digit numbers are:

1 Means that the command has been accepted and is being processed, but wait for another reply code before issuing another command.

2 Means that the command was completed successfully and the server is ready for additional commands.

3 Means that the command is being processed, but additional information is needed before the command can be completed. An example of this would be the server accepting a User Name command and needing a Password command before granting access to the system.

4 Means that the command was rejected because the system was down or the file was busy. The same command could be sent back to the server later and may be accepted.

5 Means some kind of permanent error, such as a syntax error or that an action is not permitted.

The second digit of the reply code further refines the type of information returned.

0 Refers to a syntax error.

1 Means the message contains information such as the response to a Help or status command.

2 Refers to the control and data connections.

3 Relates that the reply code contains authentication and accounting information.

4 Reserved for future use.

5 Means the reply code contains file system information.

The text associated with the reply code often depends on the exact situation that generated the code. For example, a reply code of 501 may have a more descriptive response like `Invalid value for type-code` rather than simply saying `Syntax error`. Table 6-3 lists the reply codes with the standard reply text.

Table 6-3 FTP Reply Codes and Reply Text

Reply Code	Reply Text
110	`Restart marker reply.`
120	`Service ready in nnn minutes.`
125	`Data connection already open; transfer starting.`
150	`File status okay; about to open data connection.`
200	`Command okay.`
202	`Command not implemented, superfluous at this site.`
211	`System status, or system help reply.`
212	`Directory status.`
213	`File status.`
214	`Help message.`
215	`NAME system type.`
220	`Service ready for new user.`
221	`Service closing control connection. Logged out if appropriate.`
225	`Data connection open; no transfer in progress.`
226	`Closing data connection.`

Reply Code	Reply Text
227	Entering Passive Mode (h1,h2,h3,h4,p1,p2).
230	User logged in, proceed.
250	Requested file action okay, completed.
257	"PATHNAME" created.
331	User name okay, need password.
332	Need account for login.
350	Requested file action pending further information.
421	Service not available, closing control connection.
425	Can't open data connection.
426	Connection closed; transfer aborted.
450	Requested file action not taken.
451	Requested action aborted: local error in processing.
452	Requested action not taken.
500	Syntax error, command unrecognized.
501	Syntax error in parameters or arguments.
502	Command not implemented.
503	Bad sequence of commands.
504	Command not implemented for that parameter.
530	Not logged in.
532	Need account for storing files.
550	Requested action not taken.
551	Requested action aborted: page type unknown.
552	Requested file action aborted.
553	Requested action not taken.

Accessing the Server

The FTP server PI waits for a connection to be established from a client process. When the connection is established, the server PI then waits for a requests. Because all FTP servers require users to identify themselves before any functions can be processed, the User Name command follows next, and is generally followed by a Password command. These two commands generally provide sufficient information for someone to gain access to an FTP server. Occasionally the Account command is required to provide additional security information to the server. If the account information is needed, the server responds with a reply code of 332.

When the session has been established, the server responds with a reply code of 220, indicating that it is ready for the user to sign on. Then the client can respond with the User Name command and Password command to gain access to the server.

Two other commands are also useful when managing a connection. The first is the Reinitialize command, which places the FTP server back to the state in which the connection was first established and waits for a User Name command to be sent. The other is the Logout command. Executing this command terminates all activity and closes the connection.

User Name

My user ID on atlantis.umd.edu is wfreeze, so the User Name command the client PI would send to the server PI is `USER wfreeze`. (I use this example throughout the rest of the chapter.) If the user ID is acceptable to the system, the server responds with a reply code of 230. If the user ID is not valid, the server responds with a 530 reply code. If a password is required, the reply code of 331 is returned. If a password is not required but some account information is required, a reply code of 332 is returned.

Password

If the password is not needed by the FTP server, it responds with a reply code of 202. (This code is used by the server to indicate that the command was accepted, but ignored.) If the password is acceptable, it returns a 230. If an account code is required, a code 332 is returned.

Account

This command may be needed after processing the User Name and Password commands or when other commands are processed. Basically this is another way to send a second password to the computer. If it is included as part of the logon process, a code of 230 is returned if it is acceptable, or 530 if it is not. If account information is needed later in the session, the FTP server sends either a 332 or a 532 depending on how the FTP server was written.

Reinitialize

If it is successful, the FTP server responds with a code of 220.

Logout

If the FTP server accepts the command, it responds with a code of 221.

Directory Information

Directories are highly dependent on the FTP server host system. Many host systems, such as Windows NT, Novell's Netware, and most Posix compliant systems, use a UNIX-like directory path even if they don't have an underlying UNIX file system. Some notable exceptions are IBM's MVS and Digital's VMS systems where slashes are replaced with periods, and IBM's VM, where directories correspond to mini-disks. IBM's VM system is also one of the few machines that I've seen that uses the Account command. It uses the account information to supply a new mini-disk password when changing directories.

Change Working Directory

If the server accepts the change, 250 is returned as the reply code. A 550 is returned if the server cannot change to the new directory.

Change to Parent Directory

This command is useful on those machines that have a non-UNIX directory structure. If the command is successful, the server returns a code of 200 or a code of 500 if the change could not be made.

Print Working Directory

This command asks the server to return the current directory path. A reply code of 257 is returned with the current directory path.

Make Directory

A reply code of 257 is returned with the directory name if the command is successful, otherwise one of the standard error codes is returned.

Remove Directory

A reply code of 250 is returned if the command worked properly.

List

This command causes the FTP DTP to send a directory listing to the client's DTP. This listing usually includes detailed information about each file in the directory. Usually this information comes directly from the host system's list directory command. If successful, a series of messages is sent from the server: 150 for successfully retrieving the directory information, and 125 and 226 for the transfer of the directory information.

Name List

This command operates identically to the LIST command with the exception of the data that is sent between the DTPs. The Name List command requires that the data be transferred as a list of file names with only one name per line. The primary use of this function is to implement a multiple get or put operation. Therefore it is important the file names be returned in a format that can easily be passed back to the server.

Setting Options

There are a number of options that can be set during an FTP file transfer, including the Type command, which is used to determine the translations that occur during the file transfer and the number of data ports to which the file will be sent. The type information is necessary to ensure that the data in the file is readable in the remote system. The data port is also important because the actual file transfer may not be able to use the standard FTP data port.

Type

File transfers can either be text oriented or binary. Text transfers are generally assumed to be ASCII. If the client or server is a machine that is not ASCII based, the characters are translated to their equivalent. Thus, if you happen to download a text file from an IBM MVS computer system (which uses EBCDIC instead of ASCII) to a Windows-based PC (which I do all the time), FTP handles the character translation process. (If you have never worked on an IBM mainframe, consider yourself lucky. This incompatibility occurs frequently when exchanging data between an IBM mainframe and nearly any other brand of computer system.) Also, FTP text transfers properly handle translating end of line markers from Windows where the end of a line is stored as a carriage return and a line feed, and UNIX systems where it is stored as a single line feed.

Another issue in transferring text files is how to handle printer control information. While the default is to ignore printer control information, it is often necessary to perform the proper translation. IBM mainframes (and several other systems) store printer control information as the character before the first character in the line called the carriage control character. A space in this position means that the printer will move to the next line before printing this line. A `1` in this position means to go to the top of the page before printing. FTP automatically translates the form feed character (Ctrl+L) to a `1` in the carriage control character when transferring a print file from a UNIX system to MVS.

The type code is one of the following: `A` for ASCII; `E` for EBCDIC; or `I` for Image. The form code is `N` for non-print; `T` for Telnet format; or `C` for carriage control. An alternate form is `TYPE` followed by a space, an `L`, a space, and a decimal integer with the number of bits in a byte. (Remember that not all computers use 8-bit bytes. For example, the Univac 1100 computer systems have bytes that are 9 bits wide.) A reply code of 200 is returned if the command is successful, otherwise one of the standard error reply codes is returned.

To do normal transfers, the client can request either ASCII or EBCDIC data from the server by selecting either ASCII or EBCDIC in the TYPE command. To handle binary transfers (like the latest version of Doom or that cool JPEG of your dream car), use the TYPE Image command. Note that if you are using compatible systems, it is possible to transfer text files as TYPE images. However, transferring a file from a Windows system to a UNIX system using TYPE image results in the file on the UNIX system having extra Ctrl+M characters in the file at the end of each line. This drives UNIX editors like vi and emacs crazy.

Handling carriage control properly is done by selecting carriage control for the data transfer. Otherwise, non-print should be selected for ASCII, EBCDIC, or IMAGE transfers.

Data Port

The first four numbers of `<host-port>` contain the IP address where the data is to be sent (usually your local machine). The last two sets of digits are the port address where the DTP receives the information. Often the FTP server changes the data port from the well-known value of 20 to another value. This prevents problems in which file transfers may be running concurrently. With each transfer having its own port, there is no possibility of confusion about which packet belongs to which transfer.

Transferring Files

After accessing the FTP server, checking the remote directory, and setting options, it is time to begin transferring files. Essentially all the file transfer protocol commands assume that the action is being taken against the server. Files are stored to the server, retrieved from the server, or you can append data to the end of an existing file on the server. However, the protocol does not discuss anything about how local files are handled. All the FTP protocol specifies is that a stream of characters is sent to or from the local machine and it is up to the implementor as to how the files are accessed on the local machine.

The FTP protocol specifies four basic commands to manage files on the remote server. They are the Delete command, which deletes a file on the server; the Retrieve command, which starts a file transfer from the server to the local machine; the Store command starts a file transfer from the local machine and creates a new file on the remote machine; and the Append command works similarly to the Store command, but the transferred file is appended to an existing file on the server.

Delete

If the file exists and is successfully deleted, a reply code of 250 is sent. Otherwise one of the standard error codes is sent.

Retrieve

If the file exists, a series of messages is sent from the server: 150 for successfully finding the file; and 125 and 226 for starting and ending the transfer process without error.

Store

If the file exists, a series of messages is sent from the server: 150 for successfully creating the new file; and 125 and 226 for starting and ending the transfer process without error.

Append

If the file exists, a series of messages is sent from the server: 150 for successfully finding the file; and 125 and 226 for starting and ending the transfer process without error.

Other Facilities

There are a couple of other commands that are worth mentioning: Abort, Help, and Site.

Abort

This command is used to stop the data transfer process between DTPs. If successful, it returns either a 226 reply code if no data transfer was in progress or a 426 reply code if a data transfer was in progress.

Help

The Help command is used to retrieve help information from the remote FTP server. If the command is successful, a reply code of 211 or 214 is returned. This is one of the cases where the reply text should be closely examined—it contains the help information.

Site

The Site command is used to handle situations between the FTP client and server that are highly host-dependent. For example, files on MVS are allocated in a rather complicated fashion. By using the site command, a client can pass information to the MVS FTP server to override the default values for creating files. If the command is successful, a reply code of 200 or 202 is returned or one of the standard error codes.

Example

In the following example, I use a DOS session in Windows 95 to run the DOS-based FTP program. From the `C:>` prompt, I use the FTP command with the `-d` option to place the program in debug mode. This shows all the commands that are sent to the server and the server's responses. User commands are entered at the `ftp>` prompt, commands sent to the server are prefixed by `--->`, and responses from the server begin with the three-digit reply code that we previously discussed.

```
C:\>ftp -d
ftp> open atlantis.umd.edu
Connected to dbserva.acc.UMD.EDU.
220 dbserva.acc.umd.edu FTP server (Version 4.14 Fri Aug 5 13:39:22 CDT 1994) ready.
User (dbserva.acc.UMD.EDU:(none)): wfreeze
---> USER wfreeze
331 Password required for wfreeze.
Password:
---> PASS porsche
230 User wfreeze logged in.
ftp> dir
---> PORT 128,8,24,37,4,25
200 PORT command successful.
---> LIST
150 Opening data connection for /bin/ls.
total 192
drwxrwxrwx  6 wfreeze users1   2560 May 24 08:56 docs
drwx------  2 wfreeze users1    512 Dec 09 1995 mail
-rw-r-----  1 wfreeze users1  61049 Jun 25 1995 news.all
-rw-r-----  1 wfreeze users1    1462 Jun 25 1995  news.grp
-rw-r-----   1 wfreeze  users1        13 Jun 11 21:11 news.jil
-rw-r-----   1 wfreeze  users1      1510 Jun 25 1995  news.sav
-rw-r-----   1 wfreeze  users1        13 Jun 25 1995  news.tim
-rw-r-----   1 wfreeze  users1      2457 Jun 25 1995  nr2.ini
drwxr-xr-x   2 wfreeze  users1      2048 Nov 27 1995  pub-html
-rw-r-----   1 wfreeze  users1      1375 Apr 12 14:13 test1.pl
```

```
226 Transfer complete.
642 bytes received in 0.11 seconds (5.84 Kbytes/sec)
ftp> get news.all
---> PORT 128,8,24,37,4,26
200 PORT command successful.
---> RETR news.all
150 Opening data connection for news.all (61049 bytes).
226 Transfer complete.
61088 bytes received in 10.82 seconds (5.65 Kbytes/sec)
ftp>quit
---> QUIT
221 Goodbye.
```

Notice that opening the connection with the open command results in the server returning a reply code of 220, to which the client program prompted the user for a user ID. I entered a user ID that was then sent to the server with the USER command. The server responded with a reply code of 331, which meant a password was required to log onto the server. The client then prompted me for my password and responded to the server with the PASS command. A reply code of 230 was returned, indicating that I had successfully signed on.

At this point, the client prompted me for a command, using `ftp>` as a prompt. When I entered `dir` to list the files on the remote system, the client did two things. First, it told the server to talk to the DTP at a different port using the PORT command, and then it sent the `LIST` command to transfer the directory listing. This resulted in a reply code of 150, indicating the start of the transfer, followed by the directory data, and finally a reply code of 226 was sent indicating that the transfer was complete. Note that while the directory appears in the middle of this example, it was transferred between the client and server DTPs, not the PIs.

After the `LIST` command was finished, I entered `get news.all`. As with the directory listing, the client program told the server to transfer the data to a different port. Notice that this port is different than the previous one. Most FTP client programs choose to receive data on a different port for each transfer to minimize problems. After the port command was accepted by the server, the retrieve command was given. Again, the server responded with a reply code of 150, then the data was transferred and a reply code of 226 was sent when the data transfer was complete.

To end this example, I entered `quit` at the next `ftp>` prompt. The client then sent the `QUIT` command to the server. When the server responded with a reply code of 221, the client program terminated.

Summary

In this chapter, we briefly discussed the protocols used by the FTP client and server and reviewed a sample FTP session. This information is derived from the RFC-959 document "File Transfer Protocol." We discussed the protocols related to accessing the server, changing directories, listing files, setting options, and transferring files. In terms of the total scope of the protocol, we have covered about half of the options and commands available. Most of the remaining commands and options are used to cover unusual situations. (The Account command is a good example.) While the protocol needs to cover these topics, most users will never encounter a situation where they would be needed.

In the next chapter, we continue to explore FTP by looking at the FTP ActiveX client control. While much of the protocol handling we have just discussed is hidden by the control, this knowledge will be useful when debugging programs.

In case you want to check your answers to the questions in the Overview section, here are the answers:

- *How do you access the server?*

  You access the server by first establishing a session with the server and then executing the User Name command, followed by the Password and Account commands if needed.
- *What commands can be used to retrieve directory information?*

  The `List` and `Name List` commands retrieve directory information from the remote system. `Name List` retrieves only the file names (one per line), while `List` returns a more detailed listing.
- *What command instructs the server to send binary data?*

  The `TYPE I N` command sets Image data type and non-print file type, which prevent the server from performing any translation on the data as it is sent.
- *What commands are used to transfer data?*

  The `Store` command is used to copy a file to the server, while the retrieve is used to get a file from the server.

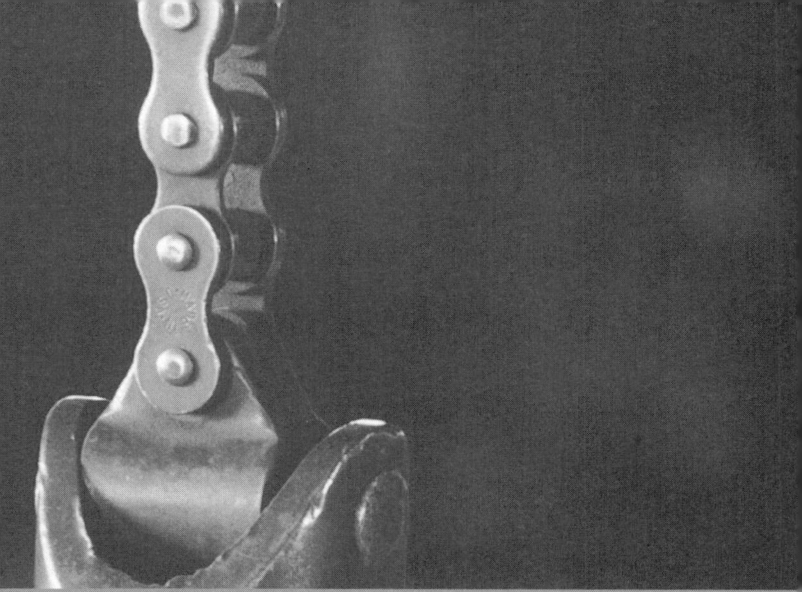

Chapter 7

The FTP Client Control

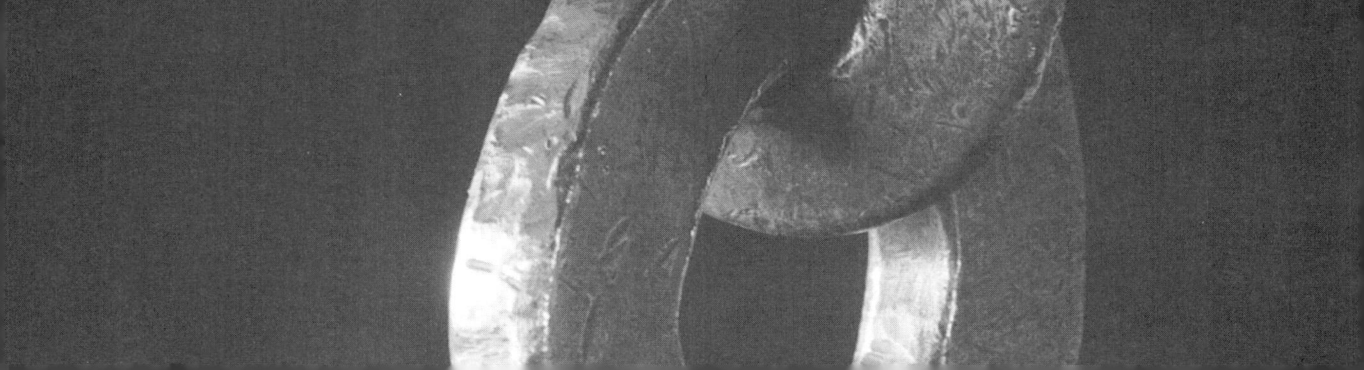

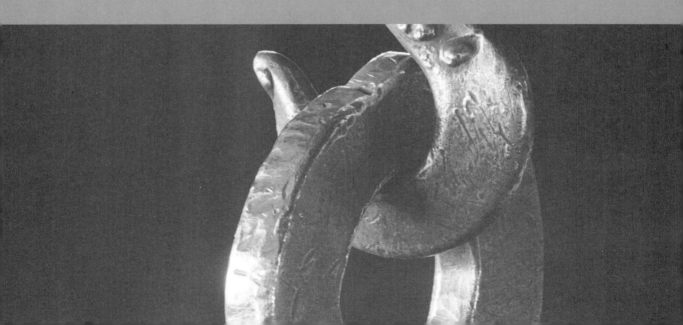

Overview

In this chapter, we discuss the properties, events, and methods of the FTP client control. This control handles the protocol interaction with the remote FTP server and provides a high-level method of performing FTP file transfers. While this is primarily a reference chapter and may not be very interesting to read, it is probably worth the time to scan through it to familiarize yourself with the basic properties, methods, and events before you begin writing a program using the FTP control. Also, you will probably want to refer to this chapter from time to time while you are developing a program that uses this control.

By the end of this chapter, you should be able to answer the following questions:

- What other objects are used by this control?
- What methods are used to transfer files and retrieve directory information?
- What methods are used to manage a connection?

Properties

The FTP ActiveX control contains a number of properties that make it easy to write programs that include FTP functions. Many of these properties are used to set default values for many of the operations performed by the control. Other properties allow the program to inquire about the status of the control, thus making it possible to monitor the control while it performs various tasks.

AppendToFile

Format: `FTPObject.AppendToFile [= boolean]`

The `AppendToFile` property returns or sets a flag that indicates whether a file that is transferred should be appended to an existing file or replace an existing file. The default is to replace the existing file.

Table 7-1 ***AppendToFile*** **Values**

AppendToFile Value	Description
True	The contents of the source file will be appended to the destination file.
False	The contents of the source file will not be appended to the destination file. (Default)

Busy

Format: `FTPObject.Busy`

The `Busy` property returns `true` if the FTP client control is executing a command. Most commands cannot be started until the current command has finished. One exception to this is the `Abort` command, which is used to stop the processing of a command.

Table 7-2 ***Busy*** **Values**

Busy Value	Description
True	The FTP client control is executing a command.
False	The FTP client control is not executing a command.

DocInput

Format: `FTPObject.DocInput`

The `DocInput` property returns a reference to the `DocInput` object associated with the control. It is used primarily to access the various properties of the `DocInput` object.

DocOutput

Format: `FTPObject.DocOutput`

The `DocOutut` property returns a reference to the `DocOutput` object associated with the control. It is used primarily to access the various properties of the `DocOutput` object.

EnableTimer

Format: `FTPObject.EnableTimer(event) [= boolean]`

The `EnableTimer` property sets or returns a flag that controls one of several different timers.

Table 7-3 *EnableTimer* Events

EnableTimer	Event Name	Description
`prcConnectTimeout`	1	If a connection is not made within the timeout period, the `TimeOut` event is triggered.
`prcReceiveTimeout`	2	If no data arrives for a receive process within the timeout period, the `TimeOut` event is triggered.
`prcUserTimeout`	65	User defined timeout event.

Table 7-4 *Timeout* Values

Timeout Value	Description
`True`	The timer for this event is enabled.
`False`	The timer for this event is not enabled.

Errors

Format: `FTPObject.Errors`

The `Errors` property returns a `icErrors` collection that contains information about the last error that occurred. It is used primarily to access the properties of the `icErrors` object. (For more information about the `icErrors` and `icError` objects, see Chapter 9, "icError Object and the icErrors Collection.")

ListItemNotify

Format: `FTPObject.ListItemNotify [= boolean]`

The `ListItemNotify` property returns or sets a flag that indicates whether the output from a `List` method is sent to the `DocOutput` event (`false`) or the `ListItem` event (`true`).

Table 7-5 *ListItemNotify* Values

ListItemNofity Value	Description
`True`	The output from the `List` and `NameList` methods should be sent to the `ListItem` event.
`False`	The output from the `List` and `NameList` methods should be sent to the `DocOutput` event.

NotificationMode

Format: `FTPObject.NotifictionMode [= integer]`

The `NotificationMode` property returns or sets a value that indicates when notification should be provided for incoming data. This is most useful when working with the `DocInput` and `DocOutput` objects.

Table 7-6 *NotificationMode* Values

NotificationMode Value	Description
`0`	**Complete:** Notification is given when the response is complete.
`1`	**Continuous:** Notification is given as new data is received.

Operation

Format: `FTPObject.Operation`

The `Operation` property is used to determine the last operation to transfer data. This is used in conjunction with the `DocInput` and `DocOutput` routines to determine the source of the information.

Table 7-7 *Operation* Values

Operation Value Name	*Operation* Value	Description
`ftpFile`	0	The `GetFile` method was used to retrieve data.
`ftpList`	1	The `List` method was used to retrieve data.
`ftpNameList`	2	The `NameList` method was used to retrieve data.

Password

Format: `FTPObject.Password [= string]`

The `Password` property holds the password used to connect to the remote host. This property is useful when you do not want to specify the password as part of the `Authentication` method.

ProtocolState

Format: `FTPObject.ProtocolState`

The `ProtocolState` property is used to determine which state the protocol is in: Base State, Authorization State, or Transaction State.

Table 7-8 *ProtocolState* Values

ProtocolState Value Name	*ProtocolState* Value	Description
`ftpBase`	0	**Base state**: Before a connection is established with the server.
`ftpAuthorization`	1	**Authorization state**: After connection is established and before the user has been granted access to the server.
`ftpTransaction`	2	**Transaction state**: After the user has been granted access to the server. The client can now interact with the server.

RemoteDir

Format: `FTPObject.RemoteDir`

The `RemoteDir` property is a string that has the value of the current directory on the remote host. It is read-only and can only be changed by using the `ChangeDir` or `PrintDir` methods.

RemoteFile

Format: `FTPObject.RemoteFile`

The `RemoteFile` property is a string that has the value of the current file on the remote host. It is used with the `GetFile` and `PutFile` methods.

RemoteHost

Format: `FTPObject.RemoteHost [= string]`

The `RemoteHost` property is a string that contains the host name or IP address of the remote host. It is used with the `Connect` method to establish a connection to the remote computer.

RemotePort

Format: `FTPObject.RemotePort [= long]`

The `RemotePort` property contains a long value that contains the port number that the FTP server is listening to; usually this value is 21.

ReplyCode

Format: `FTPObject.ReplyCode`

The `ReplyCode` property contains a long value that contains the reply code of the most recent message generated by the FTP server. (Refer to Table 6-3 for a list of valid reply codes and sample messages.)

ReplyString

Format: `FTPObject.RemoteString`

The `ReplyString` property is a string that contains the text of the message last received from the FTP server. (Refer to Table 6-3 for a list of valid reply codes and sample messages.)

State

Format: `FTPObject.State`

The `State` property returns an integer and is used to determine which state the connection is in.

Table 7-9 *State* Values

State Value Name	*State* Value	Description
`prcConnecting`	1	**Connecting state**: A connection has been requested and is waiting for an acknowledgment.

State **Value Name**	***State*** **Value**	**Description**
`prcResolvingHost`	2	**Resolving Host state**: Waiting for a host name to be translated into its IP address. (Not entered if an IP address was supplied as the `RemoteHost` property.)
`prcHostResolved`	3	**Host Resolved state**: After the host name has successfully translated into an IP address. (Not entered if an IP address was supplied as the `RemoteHost` property.)
`prcConnected`	4	**Connected state**: A connection has successfully been established.
`PrcDisconnecting`	5	**Disconnecting state**: A request to disconnect has been requested.
`prcDisconnected`	6	**Disconnected state**: Before a connection is requested and after a connection has been closed.

TimeOut

Format: `FTPObject.TimeOut(event) [= long]`

The `TimeOut` property sets or returns a flag that controls how much time must pass before a `TimeOut` event.

Table 7-10 ***TimeOut*** **Events**

TimeOut **Event Name**	***TimeOut*** **Event Value**	**Description**
`prcConnectTimeout`	1	If a connection is not made within the timeout period, the `TimeOut` event is triggered.
`prcReceiveTimeout`	2	If no data arrives for a receive process within the timeout period, the `TimeOut` event is triggered.
`prcUserTimeout`	65	User defined `TimeOut` event.

URL

Format: `FTPObject.URL [= string]`

The `URL` property is a string that holds the name of the current document being transferred. The URL may be set before using the `SendDoc` or `GetDoc` methods. This property is used primarily to support the `DocInput` and `DocOutput` objects.

Userid

Format: `FTPObject.UserId [= string]`

The `UserId` property is a string that contains the user ID to log on to the FTP server. It can be specified before using the `Authenticate` method, or will be set if it is passed as a parameter to the `Authenticate` method.

Methods

The methods available for the FTP ActiveX control are used to activate various functions within the control. For the most part, you can think of these methods as subroutines that can be called to perform standard tasks.

Abort

Format: `FTPObject.Abort`

The `Abort` method is used to send a message to the FTP server to stop the last data transfer request. It generates an RCF-959 `Abort` command. Notice that even though the `Abort` command may have been sent to the server, a few seconds may be necessary for the transfer process to be stopped. After this method is finished, the `Abort` event is triggered.

Account

Format: `FTPObject.Account [account]`

The `Account` method is used to pass account information to the remote FTP server using the RFC-959 `Account` command. If the account is not passed as an argument, the current value of the `Account` property is sent. After this method is finished, the `Account` event is triggered.

Table 7-11 ***Account*** **Method Arguments**

Argument Name	Argument Type	Description
`account`	string	RFC-959 account-information

Authenticate

Format: `FTPObject.Authenticate [userid] [,password]`

The `Authenticate` method is used to gain access to the FTP server using the RCF-959 `User Name` and `Password` commands. If the userid and password arguments are not specified, the `Userid` and `Password` properties are used. After this method has finished, the `Authenticate` event is triggered.

Table 7-12 ***Authenticate*** **Method Arguments**

Argument Name	Argument Type	Description
`userid`	string	RFC-959 user ID
`password`	string	RFC-959 password

Cancel

Format: `FTPObject.Cancel`

The `Cancel` method is used to cancel a pending request. After this method has finished, the `Cancel` event is triggered.

ChangeDir

Format: `FTPObject.ChangeDir directory`

The `ChangeDir` method is used to tell the FTP server to change the current directory to the specified directory using the RCF-959 `Change Working Directory` command. The `directory` argument must be specified or an error will occur. Also, it is not possible to change the value of the `RemoteDir` property because that property is read-only. After this method is finished, the `ChangeDir` event is triggered.

Table 7-13 *ChangeDir* Method Arguments

Argument Name	Argument Type	Description
`directory`	string	RFC-959 directory-path

Connect

Format: `FTPObject.Connect [remotehost] [,remoteport]`

The `Connect` method is used to establish a connection to a remote FTP server. Both parameters are optional but if they are not specified, the values from the `RemoteHost` and the `RemotePort` properties are used. After this method is finished, the `Connect` event is triggered.

Table 7-14 *Connect* Method Arguments

Argument Name	Argument Type	Description
`remotehost`	variant	Either a remote host name or an IP address.
`remoteport`	variant	Numeric port value.

CreateDir

Format: `FTPObject.CreateDir directory`

The `CreateDir` method is used to create a new directory on the FTP server using the RCF-959 `Make Directory` command. The `directory` argument must be specified. Notice that the userid must have the appropriate privileges to delete the directory. After this method is finished, the `CreateDir` event is triggered.

Table 7-15 ***CreateDir*** **Method Arguments**

Argument Name	Argument Type	Description
`directory`	string	Name of the new directory to be created.

DeleteDir

Format: `FTPObject.DeleteDir directory`

The `DeleteDir` method is used to delete an existing directory on the FTP server using the RCF-959 `Remove Directory` command. The `directory` argument must be specified. Notice that the userid must have the appropriate privileges to delete the directory. After this method is finished, the `DelDir` event is triggered.

Table 7-16 ***DeleteDir*** **Method Arguments**

Argument Name	Argument Type	Description
`directory`	string	Name of the directory to be deleted.

DeleteFile

Format: `FTPObject.DeleteFile filename`

The `DeleteFile` method is used to delete an existing file on the FTP server using the RCF-959 `Delete` command. The `filename` argument must be specified. Notice that the userid must have the appropriate privileges to delete the directory. After this method is finished, the `DelFile` event is triggered.

Table 7-17 *DeleteFile* Method Arguments

Argument Name	Argument Type	Description
`filename`	string	Name of the file to be deleted.

Execute

Format: `FTPObject.Execute command`

The `Execute` method passes a command to the remote FTP server for execution using the RCF-959 `Quote` command. The `command` argument must be specified. After this method is executed, the `Execute` event is triggered.

Note that this method bypasses the FTP client control's normal processing. The program must examine the reply code and take the appropriate action.

Table 7-18 *Execute* Method Arguments

Argument Name	Argument Type	Description
`command`	string	Command to be executed.

GetDoc

Format: `FTPObject.GetDoc [url] [,[headers] [,outputfile]]`

The `GetDoc` method works with the `DocOutput` object to transfer a file from the remote FTP server to the local machine. All three arguments are optional and if not specified, the appropriate values from the `DocOutput` object are used.

The URL, if specified, should be of the form `FTP://remotehost/filename`

where

> `FTP:` is optional when used with the FTP client control
>
> `remotehost` is optional and assumed to be the current machine
>
> `filename` is required and is the fully qualified name of the file on the remote FTP server.

The headers argument should not be specified for FTP transfers. It is included as an argument to maintain compatibility without other client controls.

Table 7-19 *GetDoc* Method Arguments

Argument Name	Argument Type	Description
`url`	string	Name of the file on the remote system to be retrieved in URL format.
`Headers`	DocHeaders	Not used with the FTP client control.
`outputfile`	string	Name of the output file on the local machine.

GetFile

Format: `FTPObject.GetFile remotefile, localfile`

The `GetFile` method issues an RFC-959 `Retrieve` command to get a file from the remote FTP server. Both arguments are required.

Table 7-20 *GetFile* Method Arguments

Argument Name	Argument Type	Description
`remotefile`	string	Name of the file on the remote system to be retrieved.
`localfile`	string	Name of the file on the local machine.

Help

Format: `FTPObject.Help helpinfo`

The `Help` method requests information from the remote FTP server based on RFC-959's Help command. The information returned is in the argument `helpinfo`. After this command is issued, the `Help` event occurs. The information returned is intended to be viewed by the user and has information about the specific implementation of the FTP server.

Table 7-21 ***Help* Method Arguments**

Argument Name	Argument Type	Description
`helpinfo`	string	Help information from the remote FTP server.

List

Format: `FTPObject.List directory`

The `List` method requests information on the files in the specified directory by issuing an RFC-959 `List` command. The directory listing is returned through the `DocOutput` object if the `ListItemNotify` property is false, or through the `ListItem` event if the `ListItemNotify` property is true.

Table 7-22 ***List* Method Arguments**

Argument Name	Argument Type	Description
`directory`	string	Directory on the remote FTP server to be listed.

Mode

Format: `FTPObject.Mode mode`

The `Mode` method implements the RFC-959 `Mode` command, which allows the user to select Stream, Block, or Compressed for the transmission. After this command is issued, the `Mode` event occurs.

Table 7-23 *Mode* Method Arguments

Argument Name	Argument Type	Description
`mode`	string	First character is used to specify the transfer mode.

Table 7-24 Mode Values

Mode Name	Mode Value	Description
`ftpStream`	0	Transmit data in stream mode.
`ftpBlock`	1	Transmit data in block mode.
`ftpCompressed`	2	Transmit data in compressed mode.

NameList

Format: `FTPObject.NameList directory`

The `NameList` method requests information on the files in the specified directory by issuing an RFC-959 `Name List` command. The directory listing is returned through the `DocOutput` object if the `ListItemNotify` property is false, or through the `ListItem` event if the `ListItemNotify` property is true.

Table 7-25 *NameList* Method Arguments

Argument Name	Argument Type	Description
`directory`	string	Directory on the remote FTP server to be listed.

NOOP

Format: `FTPObject.NOOP`

The `NOOP` method requests that the server respond with a reply code of 200. This method issues an RFC-959 `NOOP` command. (*NOOP* actually stands for *No Operation*.) This command is useful to let you know if the FTP server is still running. You need to check the reply code for the results of this call. If this is successful, the `NOOP` event is triggered.

ParentDir

Format: `FTPObject.ParentDir`

The `ParentDir` method requests that the server change the current directory to its parent directory. This basically issues the RFC-959 `Change Directory Up` command. If this is successful, the `ParentDir` event is triggered. The new directory is listed in the `FTPObject.RemoteDir` property.

PrintDir

Format: `FTPObject.PrintDir`

The `PrintDir` method requests the FTP server to return the current directory. This method basically issues the RCF-959 `Print Working Directory` command. If this is successful, the `PrintDir` event is triggered. This sets the `FTPobject.RemoteDir` property.

PutFile

Format: `FTPObject.PutFile remotefile, localfile`

The `PutFile` method issues an RFC-959 `Store` command to transmit a file from the local system to the remote FTP server. Both arguments are required.

Table 7-26 *PutFile* Method Arguments

Argument Name	Argument Type	Description
`remotefile`	string	Name of the file on the remote system to be retrieved.
`localfile`	string	Name of the file on the local machine.

ReInitialize

Format: `FTPObject.ReInitialize`

The `ReInitialize` method sends the RFC-959 `REIN` command to the FTP server, which leaves the FTP server in the same state it would be after an `open` command is executed, but before any user ID, password, or account information has been sent. Thus you should probably follow this method with an `Authenticate` method. A `ReInitialize` method is triggered after this method finishes.

SendDoc

Format: `FTPObject.SendDoc [url] [,[headers] [,[inputdata] [,[inputfile] [,outputfile]]]]`

The `SendDoc` method works with the `DocInput` object to transfer a file to the remote FTP server from the local machine. All five arguments are optional and if not specified, the appropriate values from the `DocInput` object are used.

The URL, if specified, should be of the form *`FTP://remotehost/filename`*

where

`FTP:` is optional when used with the FTP client control

`remotehost` is optional and assumed to be the current machine

`filename` is required and is the fully qualified name of the file on the remote machine.

The headers argument should not be specified for FTP transfers. It is included as an argument to maintain compatibility without other client controls.

Table 7-27 *SendDoc* Method Arguments

Argument Name	Argument Type	Description
`url`	string	Name of the file on the remote system to be retrieved in URL format.

continues

Table 7-27 Continued

Argument Name	Argument Type	Description
`headers`	DocHeaders	Not used with the FTP client control.
`inputdata`	variant	Optional data buffer containing the document to be sent.
`Inputfile`	variant	Optional file containing the document to be sent.
`outputfile`	string	Name of the output file on the local machine to which the reply document is written.

Site

Format: `FTPObject.Site command`

The `Site` method passes a command to the remote FTP server for execution using the RCF-959 `Site` command. The `command` argument must be specified. After this method is executed, the `Site` event is triggered. This method is typically used to execute commands on the remote FTP server that are very specific to that type of machine. For example, the `Site` command is used with the MVS FTP server to allocate space for a file. Because space for a file is always preallocated, the default values for file space on the FTP server may not always be appropriate.

Table 7-28 *Site* Method Arguments

Argument Name	Argument Type	Description
`command`	string	Command to be executed.

Status

Format: `FTPObject.Status status`

The `Status` method is used to determine information about a file or directory on the remote system. It issues an RCF-959 `Status` command. The `status` argument must be specified. After this method is executed, the `Status` event is triggered. While the information returned may be similar to the `List` command, the information is returned using reply codes 211, 212, and 213 along with the related message text.

Table 7-29 *Status* Method Arguments

Argument Name	Argument Type	Description
`status`	string	Name of file or directory on the remote system.

System

Format: `FTPObject.System`

The `System` method is used to request information about the FTP server's operating system using the RFC-959 `System` command. The server returns to the client information about its operating system with the reply message. This method triggers the `System` event after it is finished.

Type

Format: `FTPObject.Type value`

The `Type` method implements the RFC-959 `Type` command, which enables the user to set ASCII, EBCDIC, Image, or Binary type for the transmission of the files. After this command is issued, the `Mode` event occurs.

Table 7-30 *Type* Method Arguments

Argument Name	Argument Type	Description
`value`	integer	Transfer type

Table 7-31 ***Type* Values**

Type Name	Type Value	Description
`ftpASCII`	0	Transmit data in ASCII mode.
`ftpEBCDIC`	1	Transmit data in EBCDIC mode.
`ftpImage`	2	transmit data in image mode.
`ftpBinary`	3	Transmit data in binary mode.

Events

Now that we have seen how to set default values and monitor the control's activity through its properties and how to invoke the control's various functions through the supplied methods, it is now time to look at the events for this control. The events are subroutines that are called by the FTP control in response to various conditions the control encounters. Note that it may not be necessary to provide code for all of these events, because in many cases the default processing for the control is sufficent.

Abort

Format: `FTPObject_Abort`

The `Abort` event occurs after the `Abort` method is invoked, or in response to an `ABORT` command.

Account

Format: `FTPObject_Account`

The `Account` event occurs after the `Account` method is invoked, or in response to the `ACCT` command.

Authenticate

Format: `FTPObject_Authenticate`

The `Authenticate` event occurs after the `Authenticate` method is invoked.

Busy

Format: `FTPObject_Busy(ByVal isBusy As Boolean)`

The `Busy` event occurs when the `FTPObject.Busy` property changes state. This event occurs when a command begins or finishes execution.

Table 7-32 *Busy* Event Parameters

Parameter Name	Argument Type	Description
`isBusy`	boolean	Indicates when a command is being executed.

Table 7-33 *isBusy* Values

isBusy Value	Description
`True`	A command is being executed.
`False`	A command is not being executed.

Cancel

Format: `FTPObject_Cancel`

The `Cancel` event occurs after the `Cancel` method is invoked.

ChangeDir

Format: `FTPObject_ChangeDir`

The `ChangeDir` event occurs after the `ChangeDir` method is invoked, or in response to the `CWD` command.

Connect

Format: `FTPObject_Connect`

The `Connect` event occurs after the `Connect` method is invoked.

CreateDir

Format: `FTPObject_CreateDir`

The `CreateDir` event occurs after the `CreateDir` method is invoked, or in response to the `MKD` command.

DelDir

Format: `FTPObject_DelDir`

The `DelDir` event occurs after the `DeleteDir` method is invoked, or in response to the `RMD` command.

DelFile

Format: `FTPObject_DelFile`

The `DelFile` event occurs after the `DelFile` method is invoked, or in response to the `DEL` command.

DocInput

Format: `FTPObject_DocInput(ByVal docinput as DocInput)`

The `DocInput` event occurs when data has been transferred to this control.

Table 7-34 ***DocInput* Event Parameters**

Parameter Name	Argument Type	Description
`docinput`	DocInput	Object that describes the current input data for this transfer.

DocOutput

Format: `FTPObject_DocOutput(ByVal docinput as DocInput)`

The `DocOutput` event occurs when data has been transferred from this control.

Table 7-35 ***DocOutput* Event Parameters**

Parameter Name	Argument Type	Description
`docoutput`	DocOutput	Object that describes the current output data for this transfer.

Execute

Format: `FTPObject_Execute`

The `Execute` event occurs after an `Execute` method is invoked, which enables you to check the ReplyString for errors.

Help

Format: `FTPObject_Help`

The `Help` event occurs after a `Help` method is invoked. The `ListItem` event occurs after a `List` or `NameList` method is invoked when the `ListItemNotify` property is set to true. An `FTPDirItem` is passed to this routine that contains information about the file or directory to be returned. This routine is executed once for each file or directory returned.

ListItem

Format: `FTPObject_ListItem(item as FtpDirItem)`

The `ListItem` event occurs when directory information is sent from a remote FTP server in response to a `List` or `NameList` method. Note that the `ListItemNotify` property must be set to true.

Table 7-36 *ListItem* Event Parameters

Parameter Name	Argument Type	Description
`item`	FtpDirItem	Object that holds information about a directory entry.

Mode

Format: `FTPObject_Mode`

The `Mode` event occurs after a `Mode` method is invoked or an RFC-959 `MODE` command is issued.

NOOP

Format: `FTPObject_NOOP`

The `NOOP` event occurs after a `NOOP` method is invoked or an RFC-959 `NOOP` command is issued.

ParentDir

Format: `FTPObject_ParentDir`

The `ParentDir` event occurs after a `ParentDir` method is invoked or an RFC-959 `CDUP` command is issued.

PrintDir

Format: `FTPObject_PrintDir`

The `PrintDir` event occurs after a `PrintDir` method is invoked or an RFC-959 `PWD` command is issued.

ProtocolStateChanged

Format: `FTPObject_ProtocolStateChanged(ByVal protocolstate as integer)`

The `ProtocolStateChanged` event occurs whenever the protocol state is changed.

Table 7-37 *ProtocolStateChanged* Event Parameters

Parameter Name	Argument Type	Description
`protocolstate`	integer	The value of the protocol state.

Table 7-38 *protocolstate* Values

ProtocolState Value Name	*ProtocolState* Value	Description
`ftpBase`	0	**Base state**: Before a connection is established with the server.
`ftpAuthorization`	1	**Authorization state**: After connection is established and before the user has been granted access to the server.
`FtpTransaction`	2	**Transaction state**: After the user has been granted access to the server. The client can now interact with the server.

Quit

Format: `FTPObject_Quit`

The `ParentDir` event occurs after the `Quit` method is invoked.

ReInitialize

Format: `FTPObject_ReInitialize`

The `ReInitialize` event occurs after a `ReInitialize` method is invoked or an RFC-959 `REIN` command is issued.

Site

Format: `FTPObject_Site`

The `Site` event occurs after a `Site` method is invoked.

StateChanged

Format: `FTPObject_StateChanged(ByVal state as integer)`

The `StateChanged` event occurs whenever the transport state is changed.

Table 7-39 *StateChanged* Event Parameters

Parameter Name	Argument Type	Description
`state`	integer	The value of the transport state.

Table 7-40 *state* Values

state Value Name	*state* Value	Description
`prcConnecting`	1	**Connecting state**: A connection has been requested and is waiting for an acknowledgment.
`prcResolvingHost`	2	**Resolving Host state**: Waiting for a host name to be translated into its IP address. (Not entered if an IP address was supplied as the `RemoteHost` property.)
`prcHostResolved`	3	**Host Resolved state**: After the host name has successfully translated into an IP address. (Not entered if an IP address was supplied as the `RemoteHost` property.)
`prcConnected`	4	**Connected state**: A connection has successfully been established.
`prcDisconnecting`	5	**Disconnecting state**: A request to disconnect has been requested.
`prcDisconnected`	6	**Disconnected state**: Before a connection is requested and after a connection has been closed.

Status

Format: `FTPObject_Status`

The `Status` event occurs after a `Status` method is invoked or an RFC-959 `STAT` command is issued.

System

Format: `FTPObject_System`

The `System` event occurs after a `System` method is invoked or an RCF-959 `SYST` command is issued.

TimeOut

Format: `FTPObject_TimeOut(ByVal event as integer, continue as boolean)`

The `TimeOut` event occurs when the specified event does not occur within the interval defined in the `TimeOut` property for that event.

Table 7-41 *TimeOut* Event Parameters

Parameter Name	Argument Type	Description
`event`	integer	Event to which the timer interval applies.
`continue`	boolean	Determines whether the timer will remain active.

Table 7-42 *event* Values

event Name	*event* Value	Description
`prcConnectTimeout`	1	If a connection is not made within the timeout period, the `TimeOut` event is triggered.
`prcReceiveTimeout`	2	If no data arrives for a receive process within the timeout period, the `TimeOut` event is triggered.
`prcUserTimeout`	65	User defined `TimeOut` event.

Table 7-43 *continue* Values

continue Value	Description
`True`	The timer continues to run.
`False`	The timer is stopped.

Type

Format: `FTPObject_Type`

The `Type` event occurs after a `Type` method is invoked or an RFC-959 `TYPE` command is issued.

Summary

In this chapter we discussed the properties, methods, and events of the FTP client control, which work together to provide the Visual Basic programmer with an easy way to perform FTP file transfers from within their programs.

In case you want to check your answers to the questions in the Overview section, here are my answers:

- *What other objects are used by this control?*

  `DocInput` is used to information coming to this control.

  `DocOutput` is used for information leaving this control.

  `FtpDirItem` is used to contain information about an entry from the remote system's directory.

  `icErrors` is used to hold error information.

- *What methods are used to transfer files and retrieve directory information?*

  `GetDoc` is used with `DocOutput` objects.

  `SendDoc` is used with `DocInput` objects.

  `GetFile` is used with regular files.

  `PutFile` is used with regular files.

  The following methods access directory information.

  `List` is used to retrieve detailed information.

  `NameList` is used to retrieve only filenames.

- *What methods are used to manage a connection?*

  `Connect` is used to connect to the remote to the remote server.

  `Authenticate` is used to sign on to the remote server.

  `Quit` is used to disconnect from the remote server.

Chapter 8

FTPDirItem Object

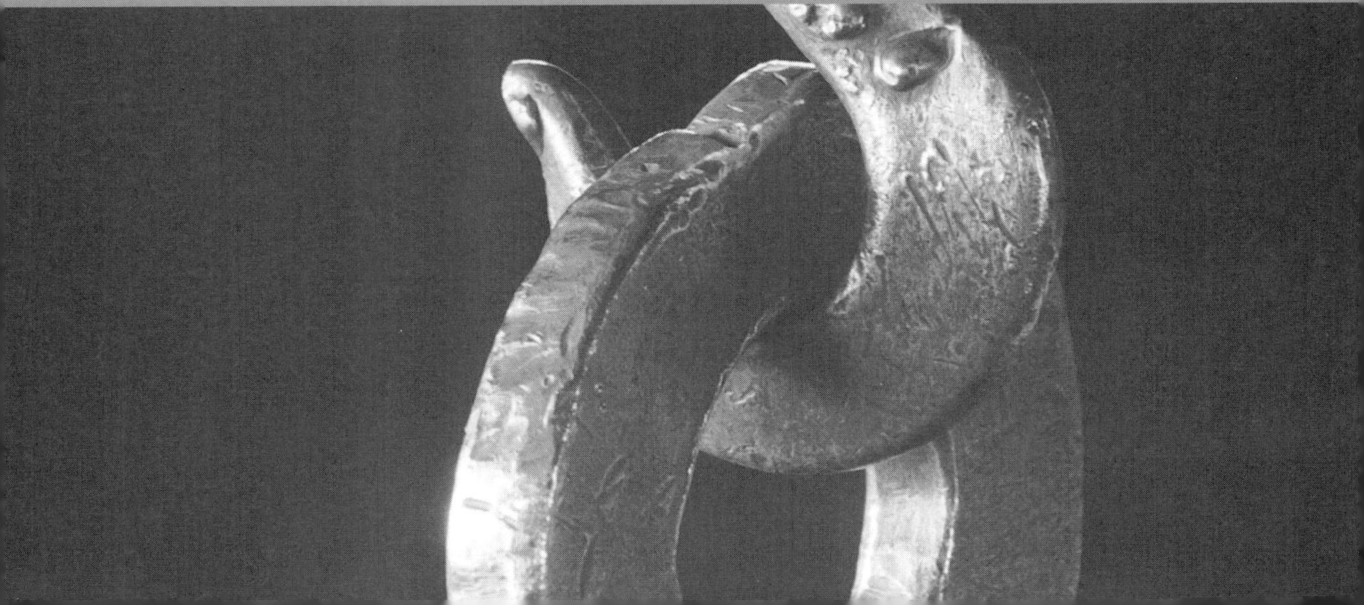

Overview

In this chapter, we look at the properties of the `FTPDirItem` object. This object contains information about a file on the FTP server that was parsed from the FTP server's response to the RFC-959 `List` or `NameList` commands that are issued by the `List` or `NameList` methods. Note that the `ListItem` event only occurs when the FTP property `ListItemNotify` is set to `true`. Otherwise the directory information is returned through the `DocOutput` event. I believe that using the `FTPDirItem` object is somewhat easier than using the `DocOutput` object because the information is returned in a much simpler format. This information is already broken into fields that indicate the date the file was last modified, the name of the file or directory, and its size in kilobytes. In case the control is unable to parse the information correctly from the server, the raw data from is also made available to the program.

By the end of this chapter, you should be able to answer the following questions:

- What information is returned in this object?
- What methods are used to generate this information?

Properties

The `FTPDirItem` object consists of a set a properties that describe a single file on the remote FTP server. It includes a property that can be used to separate files from directories. It also includes properties that contain such information as the size of the file, the name of the file, and the date the file was last modified. The raw data as returned from the server is also available as a property.

Attributes

Format: `FTPDirItemObject.Attributes`

`Attributes` is a read-only property that returns an integer indicating whether the object is a file or a directory.

Table 8-1 *Attributes* Values

Attributes Value	Description
1	This object is a directory.
2	This object is a file.

Date

Format: `FTPDirItemObject.Date`

The `Date` property returns a string that holds the date the file or directory was last modified.

Details

Format: `FTPDirItemObject.Details`

The `Details` property returns a string that contains the raw information returned from the FTP server about this directory entry. This is the information that the FTP client control parses to determine the values of the other properties in this object. This information is typically not needed because the important information is returned using other properties.

Filename

Format: `FTPDirItemObject.Filename`

The `Filename` property returns a string containing the name of the file or directory. You can use the `Attributes` property to determine whether the entry is a file or a directory.

Size

Format: `FTPDirItemObject.Size`

The `Size` property returns a long that holds the size of the file or directory in kilobytes.

Example

The following code fragments show how to display directory information from an FTP server using the `FTPDirItem` object. These fragments assume that an FTP control called `FTP1`, two ListBoxs called `lstRemoteDirList` and `lstRemoteFileList`, and a command button called `cmdListRemoteDir` have been defined on the main form. Also, all the code necessary to log onto the server has been provided in other events. (Chapter 10 contains a complete example of an FTP program.)

In Listing 8-1, you see the code necessary to request the directory information from the FTP server. This code is included in the `Click` event of the `cmdListRemoteDir` command button. Basically, the code instructs the `FTP1` control to direct any output in response to an RFC-959 `List` or `NameList` command through the `ListItem` event. Then the `List` method is used to send the RFC-959 `List` command to the server.

Listing 8-1 ***cmdListRemoteDir*_Click Event**

```
Private Sub cmdListRemoteDir_Click()

FTP.ListItemNotify = True
FTP.List

End Sub
```

The `List` method asks the server for a list of files and directories, which are returned through the `ListItem` event (see Listing 8-2). For each object returned from the server, first check to see if the information refers to a file or a directory. If the object contains information about a directory, the name is added to the `lstRemoteDirList` ListBox. If the object contains information about a file, the information is formatted and added to the `lstRemoteFileList` ListBox.

Listing 8-2 *FTP_ListItem* Event

```
Private Sub FTP_ListItem(ByVal Item As FTPDirItem)

dim strTemp as string

if Item.Attributes = 1 then
  lstRemoteDirectoryList.Additem Item.Filename

else
  lstRemoteFileList.Additem Item.Filename
   & " " & Item.Date & " " & format(Item.Size, "999,999")

end if

End Sub
```

Summary

In this chapter we discussed the `FTPDirItem` object. This object contains information about a file on the remote FTP server, which is retrieved from the FTP server's directory by either the `List` or `NameList` methods. While this information can be retrieved from the server using the `DocOutput` object, using the `FTPDirItem` lets the Visual Basic programmer write less code to perform the same work.

In case you want to check your answers to the questions in the Overview section, here are the answers:

- *What information is returned in this object?*

  `Attributes` is the object a file or a directory.

  `Date` is the last time the file was modified.

  `Filename` is the name of the file or directory.

`Size` is the size of the file or directory in kilobytes.

`Details` is the raw information that the above attributes were extracted from.

- *What methods are used to generate this information?*

  The `List` and `NameList` FTP methods generate this information.

Chapter 9

icError Object and the icErrors Collection

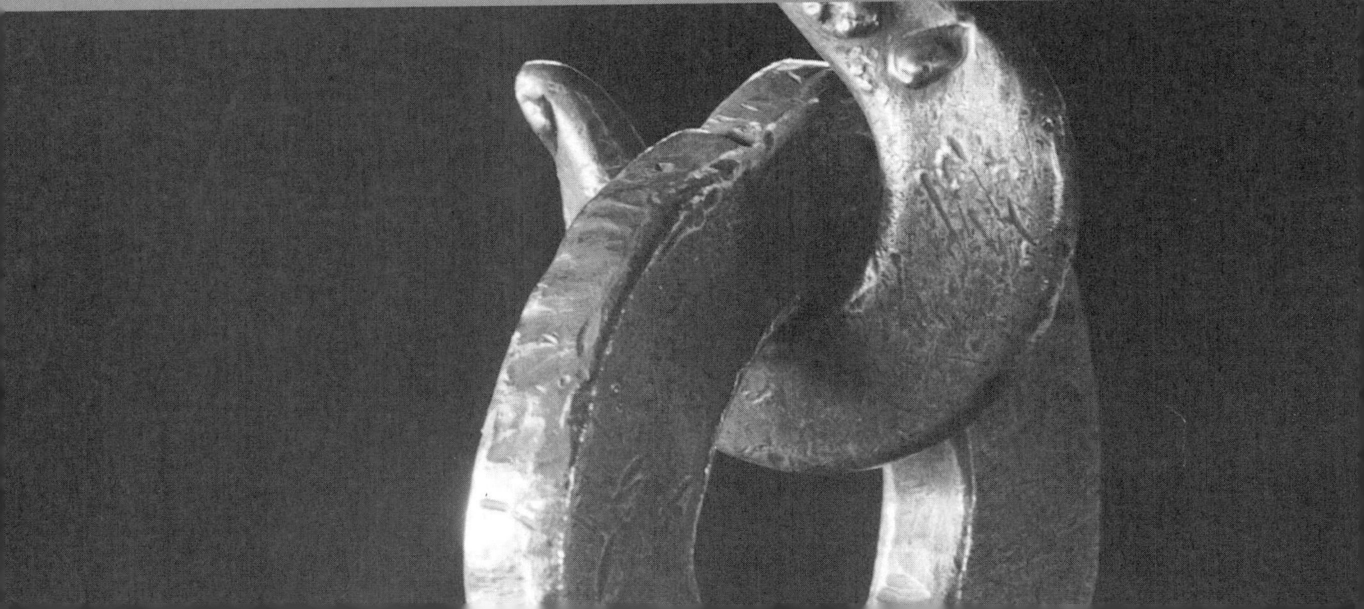

Overview

In this chapter we discuss the properties of the `icError` object and the `icErrors` collection. This object contains information about errors that occur during the operation of the client control. The `icError` object is accessed through the `Error` property on the FTP control. This object provides easy access to the errors that can occur while interacting with the FTP server.

The `icError` object is also part of the `icErrors` collection. In this case, multiple `icError` objects are contained in one object.

The `icError` object and the `icErrors` collection are used by the rest of the ActiveX client controls (HTTP, NNTP, POP, and SMPT). This information is typically used with the `DocInput` and `DocOutput` objects, which we discuss in more detail in the Part Three.

By the end of this chapter, you should be able to answer the following questions:

- What information is returned in the `icErrors` collection?
- What information is returned in the `icError` object?

Properties—icErrors

The `icErrors` object is a collection of `icError` objects. This object follows the Microsoft practice in which multiple occurrences of a simple object are grouped together as a single higher level object. Then the information from the lower level objects can be easily accessed though the higher level object. Additional information that is common to the set of lower level objects can be stored once at the higher level rather than in each of the individual lower level objects. In this case, the `icErrors` object contains a set of `icError` objects, plus other properties such as the source of the errors and the number of `icError` objects.

icErrors.Count

Format: `FTPObject.Errors.Count`

`HTTPObject.Errors.Count`

`NNTPObject.Errors.Count`

`POPObject.Errors.Count`

`SMTPObject.Errors.Count`

The `icErrors.Count` property is a read-only property that returns the number of errors in the icErrors collection.

icErrors.Item

Format: `FTPObject.Errors.Item(x)`

`HTTPObject.Errors.Item(x)`

`NNTPObject.Errors.Item(x)`

`POPObject.Errors.Item(x)`

`SMTPObject.Errors.Item(x)`

The `icErrors.Item` property, when used with a valid subscript (x), returns an `icError` object. Valid subscripts range from `1` to `icErrors.Count`.

icError.Source

Format: `FTPObject.Errors.Source`

`HTTPObject.Errors.Source`

`NNTPObject.Errors.Source`

`POPObject.Errors.Source`

`SMTPObject.Errors.Source`

The `icErrors.Source` property returns a variant that contains the name of the object that caused the most recent error.

Methods—icErrors

The icErrors object contains only one method, Clear, which is used to clear all the values of the icErrors object.

icErrors.Clear

Format: FTPObject.Errors.Clear

HTTPObject.Errors.Clear

NNTPObject.Errors.Clear

POPObject.Errors.Clear

SMTPObject.Errors.Clear

The icErrors.Clear method is used to remove all errors from this collection.

Properties—icError

Now that we have seen the icErrors object and understand how to access the individual icError objects, we can look at the properties associated with the icError object.

icError.Code

Format: FTPObject.Errors.Item(x).Code

HTTPObject.Errors.Item(x).Code

NNTPObject.Errors.Item(x).Code

POPObject.Errors.Item(x).Code

SMTPObject.Errors.Item(x).Code

The icError.Code property is a read-only property that returns a long value for the given error type. This requires a valid subscript for x that is between 1 and FTPObject.Errors.Count.

Table 9-1 Code Values

Code Value	Description
1	This object is a directory.
2	This object is a file.

icError.Description

Format: `FTPObject.Errors.Item(x).Description`

`HTTPObject.Errors.Item(x).Description`

`NNTPObject.Errors.Item(x).Description`

`POPObject.Errors.Item(x).Description`

`SMTPObject.Errors.Item(x).Description`

The `icError.Description` property returns a string that holds the text message corresponding to the error code. This requires a valid subscript for x that is between `1` and `FTPObject.Errors.Count`.

icError.Type

Format: `FTPObject.Errors.Item(x).Type`

`HTTPObject.Errors.Item(x).Type`

`NNTPObject.Errors.Item(x).Type`

`POPObject.Errors.Item(x).Type`

`SMTPObject.Errors.Item(x).type`

The `Type` property returns a string that contains a standard label indicating the type of error. This includes such values as "protocol" and "transport". This requires a valid subscript for x that is between `1` and `FTPObject.Errors.Count`.

Example

The following code fragment (see Listing 9-1) assumes that a control `FTP1` is defined and that the information is to be displayed in a Msgbox. When one or more errors occur during an FTP transfer, they are collected and stored in the `FTP1.Errors` property, which is defined to be an `icErrors` object.

When the `FTP1_Error` event is triggered in response to an error, the code associated with the event loops through the `icErrors` collection and displays each error using MsgBox. Because the first item in the collection has a value of 1, I can use a `For` loop that begins with one and goes until I reach the number of items in the collection (`FTP1.Errors.Count`).

I then use a `With` statement so that I do not have to type the entire object reference to access one of its properties. I only supply the leading period and object defined in the `With` statement, which is assumed to be in front of the property. Finally, I use a MsgBox statement to display each of the key properties to the user.

While this example shows how to access the error information, you still need to write the rest of the FTP program to access the server and perform some functions that generate the error. We see a much more complete example in Chapter 10 when we build the FTPRunner program.

Listing 9-1 ***FTP1_Error*** **Event**

```
Private Sub FTP1_Error(Number as Integer, Description as String, Scode as long, Source
as String, HelpFile as String, HelpContext as Long, CancelDisplay as Boolean)

Dim i as integer

For I = 1 to FTP1.Errors.Count
  With FTP1.Errors.Item(I)
   Msgbox "FTP Error: " & .type & " " & format(.code) & _
    ": " & .Description
  End With
Next i

End Sub
```

Summary

In this chapter we discuss the `icError` object. This object contains information about errors encountered while using an ActiveX control.

In case you want to check your answers to the questions in the Overview section, here are the answers:

- *What information is returned in the `icErrors` collection?*

  `Count` is the number of errors in the `icErrors` Collection.

  `Item(x)` is a reference to a single `icError` object, where the subscript x is in the range of `1` and `Count`.

  `Source` is the name of the object that caused the most recent error.

- *What information is returned in the `icError` object?*

  `Code` is the error code returned.

  `Description` is the text message associated with the error code.

  `Type` is the area within the control that generated the error.

Chapter 10

FTPRunner

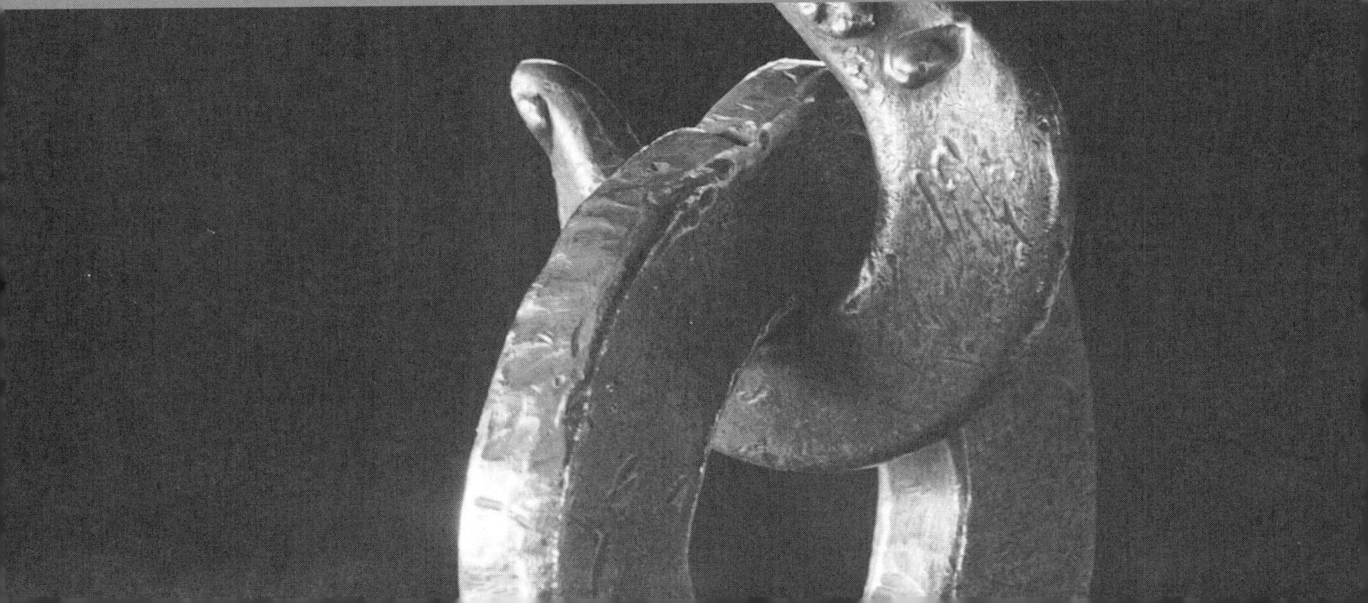

Overview

In this chapter, we build a program called FTPRunner using the FTP ActiveX client control. This is a general-purpose FTP program, but without all the bells and whistles that are typical of commerical FTP programs. The main purpose of FTPRunner is to provide sample code that you can incorporate into your own applications.

I'm not going to go through every line of code in the program. That's why there is a CD-ROM included with the book. I want to focus on the more important aspects of using the FTP control (connecting, listing directories, and transferring files). My goal is to provide sufficient information so that you can write your own program or incorporate the FTP client control into your own programs.

By the end of this chapter, you should be able to answer the following questions:

- What are some problems one might encounter when connecting to a remote computer?
- Why is the `Busy` property important?
- How does the Abort process work?

How to Use FTPRunner

The user interacts with FTPRunner with menu commands or toolbar buttons. With only two exceptions (the Exit and About commands), every command available as a menu item is also available as a toolbar button. When the program is first started, this main form is displayed (see figure 10-1). Notice that only the Connect, New Host, and Del Files buttons are active. The rest of the buttons require that the program be connected to a remote FTP server.

Clicking the Connect button causes the program to connect to the remote system shown in the Remote Host field. If this field is blank, the user is prompted by the Connect form as shown in figure 10-2. The user fills in the Remote Host field, the User Id field, the Password field, and the Remote Port field. Clicking OK results in the program trying to connect to the remote system; clicking Cancel abandons the changes and returns back to the main form.

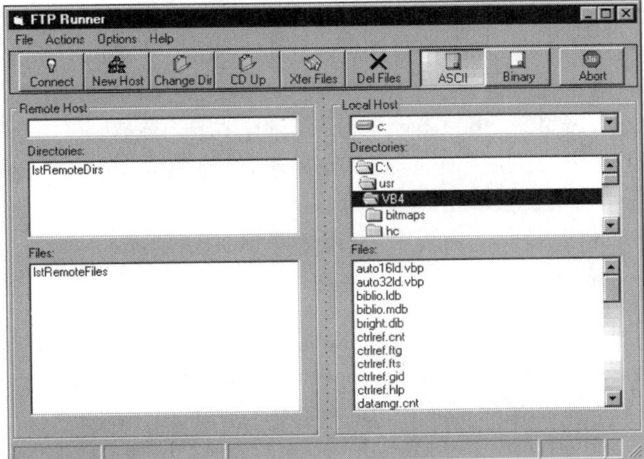

FIGURE 10-1

The FTPRunner form.

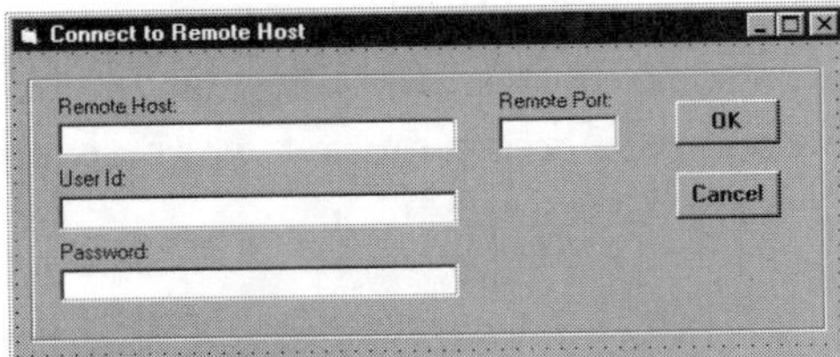

FIGURE 10-2

The FTPRunner Connect form.

When the connection is established, the lightbulb icon on the Connect button is turned on, and so are the rest of the buttons on the toolbar (except for the Abort button, which is enabled only when a transfer is taking place). The directory information on the remote system is retrieved automatically and displayed in the Remote Directories and Remote Files boxes.

The Change Dir and CD Up buttons can be used to switch remote directories on the remote system. The Change Dir button prompts for the name of the new directory, while the CD Up button simply changes the directory to the parent directory. Also, the user can click the name of any of the directories listed in the Remote Directories box. Any of these changes cause the list of files in the Remote Files box to be updated.

Like the Remote Directories box, the Local Directories box works the same way. Selecting a new directory causes the list of files in the Local files box to be updated. In addition to the Directories and Files boxes, the top box in the Local Hosts part of the form includes a Drive box that can be used to select the different disk drives available on the local PC.

Transferring files is done by clicking on the files to be transferred in both the Remote and Local Files boxes and either clicking the the Xfer Files button, or right-clicking the Local or Remote Files box and dragging it to the other box. While transferring files, the Abort button is enabled, which enables the user to stop the transfer process. Clicking the Abort button causes a message to be displayed saying that the Abort command has been sent to the remote server. It is followed by another message when the server acknowledges the abort request. Selecting ASCII or Binary transfers is as easy as clicking the ASCII or Binary button.

The Del Files button is always enabled because files can always be deleted from the local machine. However, if a connection to a remote FTP server is active, files can be deleted on the server also. Deleting files works similar to the way the Xfer Files process works. Simply select the files to be deleted and click the Del Files button. Of course, you need permission to delete files on the FTP server.

All the commands that we have discussed are also available as menu commands. There are two additional menu commands that do not exist as buttons. These are the Exit command, which is used to leave the program; and the About command, which displays an About form that includes the name of the program and its version.

The Program Structure

From the preceding description, you can tell this is a relatively simple program. It has only three forms and one module. The forms are: FTPRunner, About, and Connect. The module is Global.

The Global module includes a few definitions that are common to all of the routines and two subroutines: Initialize and Main. Listing 10-1 shows the global definitions. Only three global variables are defined: `FTPAborted`, `FTPConnected`, and `FTPStartTime`. `FTPAborted` is a flag used when someone wants to abort connection to an FTP server. `FTPStartTime` is the starting date and time when the connection to the server was made. Also notice that I include an `Option Explicit` statement. This forces all variables to be declared before they are used, and helps to keep Visual Basic from assisting you by creating variables that you do not want.

Listing 10-1 Global Variables

```
' Form/Module:   Global
' Author:        Wayne S. Freeze
' Version        1.0
' Date Written:  18 June 1996
' Date Revised:  18 June 1996
' Description:
'    This module initialized the global variables
'    and starts the main FTP form.

Option Explicit

' True when the program is trying to abort
' a transfer
Global FTPAborted As Integer

' True when the program is talking to a remote
' system, false otherwise
Global FTPConnected As Integer

' Used to track when the FTP connection was
' started
Global FTPStartTime As Date
```

The main subroutine is shown in Listing 10-2. From past experience, I prefer to launch my Visual Basic programs from a `Main` Subroutine rather than just starting by loading the main form. This gives me a chance to ensure that the global variables are properly initialized. And if any clean-up work is necessary, it can be done when the program returns.

Listing 10-2 The Main Subroutine

```
Sub main()

'  The is the main starting point for the program
'  Initialize the global variables and show the
'  main form.  When the main form unloads itself
'  the program will end.
Initialize

frmFTPRunner.Show 1

End

End Sub
```

After the main suboutine initializes the global variables, the FTPRunner form is displayed. When this form is closed, control returns back to the main subroutine where the program ends.

When the main form appears, a little more initialization occurs. (The code can be found in Listing 10-3.) First, the timer interval is set to 1 second (actually a thousand milliseconds). This is useful because on the FTPRunner form, the status bar at the bottom displays a timer showing the time that the user has been connected to the server. Then the routine initalizes the rest of the fields in the status bar and disables the toolbar buttons that cannot be used until after a connection to the FTP server is established.

Listing 10-3 The FTPRunner *Form_Load* Subroutine

```
Private Sub Form_Load()

'  When we load this form, initialize controls
Timer1.Interval = 1000

StatusBar.Panels(1).Text = "not connected"
```

```
StatusBar.Panels(2).Text = "xxx"
StatusBar.Panels(4).Text = "00:00:00"
StatusBar.Panels(5).Text = " "

Toolbar.Buttons("Change Dir").Enabled = False
Toolbar.Buttons("CD Up").Enabled = False
Toolbar.Buttons("Xfer Files").Enabled = False
Toolbar.Buttons("ASCII").Enabled = False
Toolbar.Buttons("Binary").Enabled = False
Toolbar.Buttons("Abort").Enabled = False

End Sub
```

I discuss the code controlling actions in the toolbar here (shown in Listing 10-4) because it is more interesting, and because you can look at the rest of the code on the CD-ROM to see how I handle the menu events. For the most part, the user interface controls merely call other subroutines that do the real work. We explore these in a little more depth later in this chapter.

The Connect button works like many power switches—push it to turn it on, and push it again to turn it off. In this case turning it on (`FTPConnected = False`) causes the program to run the `DoConnect` routine, while turning it off (`FTPDisconnected = True`) runs the `DoDisconnect` routine.

To switch to a different FTP server, the New Host button is used. Clicking this button disconnects you if you are connected to an FTP server. Then the name of the remote host is erased. This forces the `DoConnect` routine to display the FTPConnect form prompting you for new connection information.

Changing directories is done through two different buttons. The Change Dir button prompts the user for a new directory and passes this value to the `DoChangeDir` routine. The CD Up button simply issues a `DoChangeDir` with the dot dot ("..") value that means parent directory.

The next button is the Del Files button, which is used to delete files that are on the remote and local machines. Because the program may not have a connection to a remote FTP server, there is a check to ensure the connection is active before trying to delete any remote files.

The ASCII and Binary buttons control the value used for `Type` in the data transfer. Clicking ASCII changes the `FTP.Type` property to `ftpAscii`. Clicking the Binary button changes the `FTP.Type` property to `ftpImage`. Because both buttons are members of the same button group, only one button is clicked at a time.

The last button on the toolbar is the Abort button. This button is active only during FTP transfers. Clicking it sends an ABORT message to the FTP server. Because we have to wait for the acknowledgment from the server, which could take several seconds, I notify the user that the abort request was sent and then disable the Abort button.

Listing 10-4 The *Toolbar_ButtonClick* Subroutine

```
Private Sub Toolbar_ButtonClick(ByVal Button As Button)

'  Handle the Toolbar Buttons
Select Case Button.Key

Case "Connect"
   If FTPConnected Then
      DoDisconnect

   Else
      DoConnect
   End If

Case "New Host"
   If FTPConnected Then
      DoDisconnect
   End If
   txtRemoteHost.Text = ""
   DoConnect

Case "Change Dir"
   DoChangeDir InputBox("Enter new directory path:")
```

```
Case "CD Up"
   DoChangeDir ".."

Case "Xfer Files"
   DoPutLocal
   DoGetRemote

Case "Del Files"
   DoDelLocal
   If FTPConnected Then
      DoDelRemote
   End If

Case "ASCII"
   FTP.Type ftpAscii

Case "Binary"
   FTP.Type ftpImage

Case "Abort"
   FTPAborted = True
   MsgBox "Abort request sent to the server, please wait."
   FTP.Abort
   Toolbar.Buttons("Abort").Enabled = False

End Select

End Sub
```

Connecting to the Server

The `DoConnect` subroutine (see Listing 10-5) is called whenever we want to establish a connection to a remote FTP server. The first step in this process is to get the host name, userid, and password information if we do not already have it. We do this by checking to see if there is a value for the host name in the Remote Host field on the form. Rather than checking to see if the field is the null string (`""`), I prefer to check for length equal to zero. This is faster than doing a string comparison because the length of a string is stored as part of the string.

If the connect information is needed, the ConnectFTP form is displayed. As you saw in figure 10-2, this form is very simple, it displays only the RemoteHost, the Userid, the Password, and the RemotePort fields with OK and Cancel buttons. The code merely collects the current connection information from the FTP client control, places it into the form, and then allows the user to change it. If the user clicks OK, the information on the form is stored back in the FTP client control and in the remote host field on the FTPRunner form. If the Remote Host field is still a null string after the ConnectFTP form was displayed, the `DoConnect` subroutine assumes that the user selected Cancel and stops the connect process.

After the connection information has been set in the FTP client control, the `DoConnect` routine sets `FTPStartTime` to the current time and starts the timer. Then the `FTP.Connect` method is used to start the FTP connection process. In theory, when the `Connect` method finishes, the `FTP_Connect` event should be called, but in practice, I've found this approach unreliable. What I've done in this routine is put logic in to watch various FTP `status` properties to determine when the actual connection is made.

There is something I should take a moment to point out. It may be obvious to many people, but it is very important. Because of the way Windows works, it is necessary to return control of the CPU back to Windows periodically. For the most part this is not necessary when you spend a lot of time waiting for input from the user. However, if you have a long task (in this case long means anything over a half a second or so) that doesn't involve user input, you need to do something explicit in the code. The way this is done is by putting calls to `DoEvents` in the code.

`DoEvents` returns control back to Windows. Windows, in turn, checks to see if any other processes need CPU resources. After Windows determines that no other programs need the CPU, it returns control back to your program immediately after the `DoEvents` routine. In the case of the FTP client control, we are merely doing nothing while waiting for the connection process to complete. Why not let something else take advantage of the time we are wasting?

When the connection process finally finishes, I go through the `FTP.Authentication` method. As with the `FTP.Connect` method, I prefer to wait until the process completes, rather than relying on the `Authentication` event to be properly triggered.

When the Authentication process is finished, I trigger the `FTP.PrintDir` method to get the current working directory. This also triggers a request to get a copy of the files in the current directory. We go through this process a little later in this chapter. Finally, I update the FTPConnected flag and enable all the buttons that only work while the connection is up.

Listing 10-5 The *DoConnect* Subroutine

```
Private Sub DoConnect()

'  Connect to the remote FTP server.

'  Do we have a host, if not then get one.
If Len(txtRemoteHost.Text) = 0 Then
   frmConnectFTP.Show 1

   '  Cancel the connect if the user didn't specify
   '  a host name.
   If Len(FTP.RemoteHost) = 0 Then
      Exit Sub
   Else
      txtRemoteHost.Text = FTP.RemoteHost
   End If
End If

FTPStartTime = Now
Timer1.Enabled = True

'  Start the connection process.
FTP.Connect
```

```
'  Wait for the connection process to complete
Do While (FTP.State = prcConnecting) _
   Or (FTP.State = prcResolvingHost) _
   Or (FTP.State = prcHostResolved)
   DoEvents
Loop

'  Check to see if the connection process worked
If FTP.State <> prcConnected Then
   Exit Sub
End If

'  Wait some more before we try to logon
Do While (FTP.State = prcConnected) _
     And (FTP.ProtocolState = ftpBase)
   DoEvents
Loop

'  Send the userid and password
FTP.Authenticate

'  Wait for the authenticate process to complete
Do While (FTP.State = prcConnected) _
     And (FTP.ProtocolState = 1)
   DoEvents
Loop

Do While (FTP.Busy)
   DoEvents
Loop

'  Now that we're logged on, get the current
'  directory which will also get a listing of
'  the remote directory.
```

```
FTP.PrintDir

'  With the directory process started, set the
'  connected flag and enable the toolbar buttons
FTPConnected = True
Toolbar.Buttons("Connect").Image = 2
Toolbar.Buttons("Change Dir").Enabled = True
Toolbar.Buttons("CD Up").Enabled = True
Toolbar.Buttons("Xfer Files").Enabled = True
Toolbar.Buttons("ASCII").Enabled = True
Toolbar.Buttons("Binary").Enabled = True

End Sub
```

Disconnecting from the Server

After all the complexity involved in connecting to the FTP server, it is nice to have a relatively simple process to disconnect. In Listing 10-6, I issue the `FTP.Quit` method to disconnect from the FTP server and then clean up a few things like resetting the FTPConnected flag to `false`, disabling the toolbar buttons that rely on the connection being active, and clearing the list boxes used to store the directory information from the remote system.

Listing 10-6 The *DoDisconnect* Subroutine

```
Private Sub DoDisconnect()

'  Close the connection, reset the flags and
'  buttons and clear the directory and file
'  information
FTP.Quit

FTPConnected = False
```

```
Timer1.Enabled = False
Toolbar.Buttons("Connect").Image = 1
Toolbar.Buttons("Change Dir").Enabled = False
Toolbar.Buttons("CD Up").Enabled = False
Toolbar.Buttons("Xfer Files").Enabled = False
Toolbar.Buttons("ASCII").Enabled = False
Toolbar.Buttons("Binary").Enabled = False

lstRemoteDirs.Clear
lstRemoteFiles.Clear

End Sub
```

Listing a Directory

Earlier we discussed how you can trigger a process to get files in the remote directory by using the `FTP.PrintDir` method. The `PrintDir` method merely returns the current working directory. When the response is received by the FTP client control, the `FTP_PrintDir` event occurs. In the `FTP_PrintDir` event (Listing 10-7), the first thing I do is show the current directory as the first line in the RemoteDirs list box. Then I set the ListItemNotify flag `true`, and trigger the `FTP.List` method. This returns each line of the directory through the `FTP_ListItem` event.

In the `FTP_ListItem` event, I put the file into either the RemoteDirs list box or the RemoteFiles list box depending on the value of the `Item.Attributes` value. This routine can be enhanced to show some other information about the files such as the file size and the last accessed date. (Does this sound like a future exercise perhaps?)

Listing 10-7 The *FTP_PrintDir* Event

```
Private Sub FTP_PrintDir()

'  This Event is triggered when the result of a
'  PWD command is received.  When this happens
```

```
'  the directories and files lists are cleared
'  and a List command is sent to the FTP server
'  which will in turn trigger the FTP_ListItem Event
lstRemoteDirs.Clear
lstRemoteFiles.Clear

lstRemoteDirs.AddItem FTP.RemoteDir

FTP.ListItemNotify = True
FTP.List FTP.RemoteDir

End Sub
```

Listing 10-8 The *FTP_ListItem* Event

```
Private Sub FTP_ListItem(ByVal Item As FTPDirItem)

'  This is triggered each time a LIST or NLST command
'  is sent to the FTP server.  Each line of the directory
'  is parsed by the ActiveX control and returned as
'  an FTPDirItem object.

'  The simple logic here simply checks to see if the
'  object is a directory or a file and add it to the
'  end of the appropriate list.
If Item.Attributes = 1 Then
   lstRemoteDirs.AddItem FTP.RemoteDir & "/" & Item.filename

Else
   lstRemoteFiles.AddItem Item.filename
End If

End Sub
```

Changing Directory

Changing a directory is even easier than listing a directory. Essentially all you need to do is issue the `FTP.ChangeDir` method with a new directory, and that is nearly all the code in Listing 10-9 does. Because changing the directory invalidates the files listed in the RemoteDirs and RemoteFiles text boxes, we play the waiting game and issue the `FTP.PrintDir` method to update both text boxes.

Listing 10-9 The *DoChangeDir* Subroutine

```
Private Sub DoChangeDir(strDir As String)

'  Change remote directory and get new file listing
'  from the FTP server.
FTP.ChangeDir strDir

Do While FTP.Busy
   DoEvents
Loop

FTP.PrintDir

End Sub
```

Sending a File

If you thought changing directories was easy, sending a file is even easier, as Lising 10-10 illustrates. This suboutine takes two parameters: one with the local file name, and one with the remote file name. It then issues the `FTP.PutFile` method to begin the file transfer. The only tricky part here is to recognize that transferring a file takes time, so I've included a wait until the FTP client control has finished processing. This prevents two FTP transfers from running at the same time. (Remember that only one transfer between the client DTP and the server DTP can take place at a time.)

Listing 10-10 The *DoPutALocalFile* Subroutine

```
Private Sub DoPutALocalFile(strLocal As String, strRemote As String)

' Start the transfer and wait for it to finish.
FTP.PutFile strRemote, strLocal

Do While FTP.Busy
   DoEvents
Loop

End Sub
```

Receiving a File

Similar to the `DoPutALocalFile` suboutine is the `DoGetARemoteFile` subroutine (see Listing 10-11). It functions the same way as the `DoPutALocalFile` subroutine, but because the transfer is from the remote FTP server to the local machine, the `FTP.GetFile` method is used.

Listing 10-11 The *DoGetAFile* Subroutine

```
Private Sub DoGetARemoteFile(strLocal, strRemote)

' Start the transfer and wait for it to finish.
FTP.GetFile strRemote, strLocal

Do While FTP.Busy
   DoEvents
Loop

End Sub
```

Transferring Multiple Files

With subroutines available to transfer a single file, the next step is to transfer multiple files. The Xfer Files button transfers all the selected files on the local machine to the remote machine, or all the files from the remote machine to the local machine. Listing 10-12 illustrates the code used to transfer files from the local machine to the remote machine.

We start by enabling the Abort button. While issuing an an RFC-959 ABORT command to stop a single file is easy, we need to worry about stopping not only the current file, but all other files that have yet to be transferred.

First, we scan the Local Files box looking for selected files. When we find one, we put a message in the status bar at the bottom of the form saying that we are transferring the file. Because we already have a routine that puts a file onto the remote system (`DoPutALocalFile`), all we need to do at this point is to call it with the name of the file to be transferred. Because I'm trying to keep things simple, I assume that the name of the file on the server is the same as the local file name.

When we return from `DoPutALocalFile`, we deselect the file we have just transferred. Then we refresh the remote directory by using the `FTP.PrintDir` method we previously discussed. After updating the status bar with the transfer information, we check the FTPAbort flag to see if the file transfer was aborted. If it was aborted, we leave this routine and return back to the main menu. Otherwise, we start the process all over again with the next file in the list.

After all the selected files have been transferred, the Abort button is disabled and we leave the routine. There is a similar routine available for retrieving files from the remote machine called `DoGetLocal`. It works basically the same way as `DoPutLocal`, so I'm not going to discuss it here. You can take a look at it on the CD-ROM.

Listing 10-12 The *DoPutLocal* Subroutine

```
Private Sub DoPutLocal()

'  This process scans all of the list of selected
'  local files and transfers them to the remote
'  system.
```

```
Dim i As Integer

'Enable the abort button
Toolbar.Buttons("Abort").Enabled = True
FTPAborted = False

For i = 0 To filLocalFiles.ListCount - 1
   If filLocalFiles.Selected(i) Then

     StatusBar.Panels(3).Text = _
         "Transferring file " & filLocalFiles.List(i)

      DoPutALocalFile filLocalFiles.List(i), _
         filLocalFiles.List(i)

      '  After transfer, unselect the file and
      '  refresh the remote directory by retrieving
      '  the remote directory triggering a cascade
      '  to list the files
      filLocalFiles.Selected(i) = False
      FTP.PrintDir

      '  Update the status bar
      StatusBar.Panels(3).Text = FTP.ReplyString
      FTP_ProtocolStateChanged FTP.ProtocolState

      '  If the transfer was aborted, return back to the user
      If FTPAborted Then
         Exit Sub
      End If

   End If
Next i
```

```
'  Disable the abort button
Toolbar.Buttons("Abort").Enabled = False

End Sub
```

Summary

We discussed how to implement the FTP client control in a simple FTP client program. This program incorporates the most important functions of the control, which should provide sufficient information about how the control works to include it in other Visual Basic programs.

This brings to a close our discussion of the FTP ActiveX client control. In the next part, we resume our tour of the ActiveX controls with the NNTP client control and how to build a program to access Usenet news. However, before we start that, here are the answers to the questions I asked at the start of this chapter.

- *What are some problems one might encounter when connecting to a remote computer?*

  The ActiveX control `Connected` and `Authenticated` events do not always occur when they should, forcing the user to watch various FTP properties to know when to start the next part of the connection process.

- *Why is the `Busy` property important?*

  The `Busy` property lets the program know when the FTP client control is performing a command. In most cases, you do not want to start another command until the first command finishes. A good example of this would be transferring multiple files. You must wait until the previous transfer to complete before starting the next transfer. One exception to this would be the Abort process.

- *How does the Abort process work?*

  The Abort process starts by notifying the server that the current data transfer in progress should be stopped and then waiting for an acknowledgment from the server.

PART III

Reading News with NNTP

What Is the NNTP Client Control

The NNTP client control provides an easy way to access Usenet news articles from a Network News Transport Protocol server. Usenet news is the most popular form for exchanging information over the Internet. Essentially, articles are sent to a news server, which then forwards them to other news servers around the world. Users may then access the articles on their local news server and respond with a message of their own.

In some ways, this is similar to some discussion group functions provided by Bulletin Board Systems (BBS), except that the information is exchanged with everyone on the Internet rather than those individuals who may subscribe to the BBS.

The other way to exchange the type of information contained in a typical Usenet article is to send electronic mail to everyone that should receive the information. With an NNTP server, only one copy of the information is stored locally then transmitted to other sites. This reduces the network bandwidth needed to send the material, and also reduces the storage necessary to hold this information.

Where Would I Use the NNTP Client Control

Obviously the world does not need yet another Usenet newsreader, however, with the advent of the intranet, news servers are being implemented with restrictions on who may access them. Thus local newsgroups can be created, and privileged users may take advantage of Internet technology to access them.

With many custom Visual Basic applications being developed, it is feasible to include a small newsreader that is integrated with the application. This can be used to hide the underlying technology from the user, yet permit them to receive important information without resorting to a custom application.

For example, you can include a function in an application that checks for news each time the application is started. This provides an easy method to communicate to the user that the system may be down for maintenance over the weekend, or announce updates or new features in the application. This is especially useful when the users of the application are spread over a large geographic area.

Another example is when you need to promote group discussion on a limited topic, but do not want the users to have full access to a Usenet newsreader. You can develop other examples, but they tend to follow the same pattern. You have a need to distribute information to your user community (and perhaps to accept questions and comments from the users), but do not want them to use a general purpose Usenet newsreader.

It can be argued that a custom database file with a few Visual Basic forms can provide the same basic function. I agree, however, the NNTP server is independent of the platform that the client may be using. Thus while some users may be better off using the custom application, others could access the same NNTP server with a standard newsreader.

Summary

The NNTP client control offers a lot of capabilities that are easy to include in Visual Basic programs. The best situation to use it is when you want to hide the full capabilities of a normal Usenet newsreader from the end user. In the following chapters, we explore how the NNTP protocol actually works, discuss how the ActiveX NNTP control can be used to access an NNTP news server, and we also start building an integrated Internet tool that starts with the FTP and NNTP ActiveX controls and is expanded as we learn more about the other ActiveX controls.

Chapter 11—NNTP Protocols and Functions

This chapter discusses in detail how NNTP works from a functional level and the protocols that are used to communicate between the client and the server. This serves as background material for understanding the NNTP client control and the NewsRunner sample program.

- Overview
- The NNTP Model
- News Article Format
- NNTP Protocol Commands
- NNTP Reply Codes and Messages

- Accessing the Server
- Reading News
- Posting
- Other Facilities
- Extended NNTP Protocol Commands
- Extended NNTP Reply Codes and Messages
- Example
- Summary

Chapter 12—The NNTP Client Control

This chapter discusses all the programming aspects (properties, events, and methods) provided by the NNTP client control. Aspects necessary for fundamental usage are emphasized, but the advanced aspects are briefly discussed.

- Overview
- Properties
- Methods
- Events
- Summary

Chapter 13—The DocHeader, DocHeaders, DocInput, and DocOutput Objects

This chapter discusses all the programming facilities provided by the `DocInput`, `DocOutput`, and `DocHeader` objects. Aspects necessary for fundamental usage are emphasized, but the advanced aspects are briefly touched upon.

- Overview
- Properties—DocHeaders Collection

- Methods—DocHeaders
- Properties—DocHeader
- Properties—DocInput
- Methods—DocInput
- Properties—DocOutput
- Methods—DocOutput
- Summary

Chapter 14—NewsRunner

This chapter presents a program called NewsRunner, which allows the user to read Usenet news using the NNTP control.

- Overview
- How to Use NewsRunner
- The Program Structure
- Connecting to the Server
- Retrieving Information from the News Server
- Retrieving Data from the Server with the DocOutput Event
- Posting and Replying to Articles
- Summary

Chapter 15—NetRunner—Part One

This chapter shows the user how to combine the NewsRunner program with the FTPRunner program into a single Internet access tool. While these programs do not integrate well, NetRunner—Part One serves as a basis for adding future programs like MailRunner and WebRunner.

- Overview
- How to Use NetRunner

- The Program Structure
- Changing the Timer
- Forms Placement
- Forms Sizing
- Summary

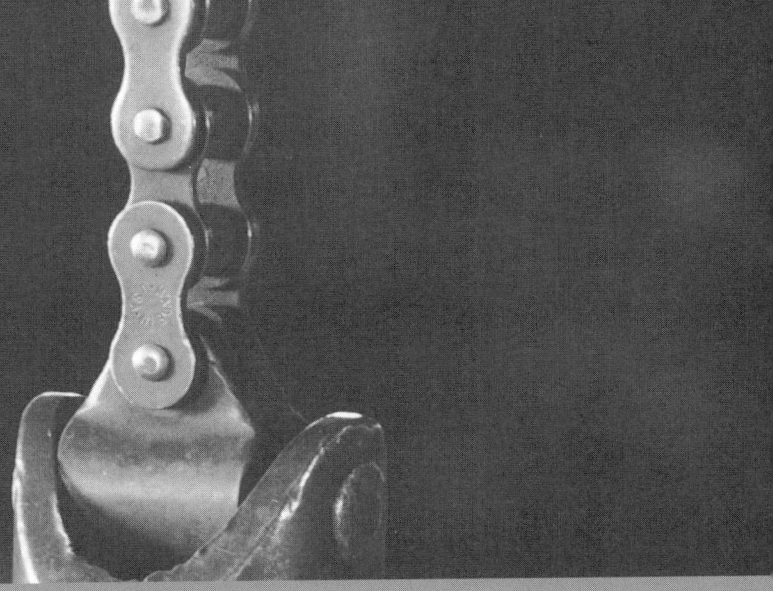

Chapter 11

NNTP Protocols and Functions

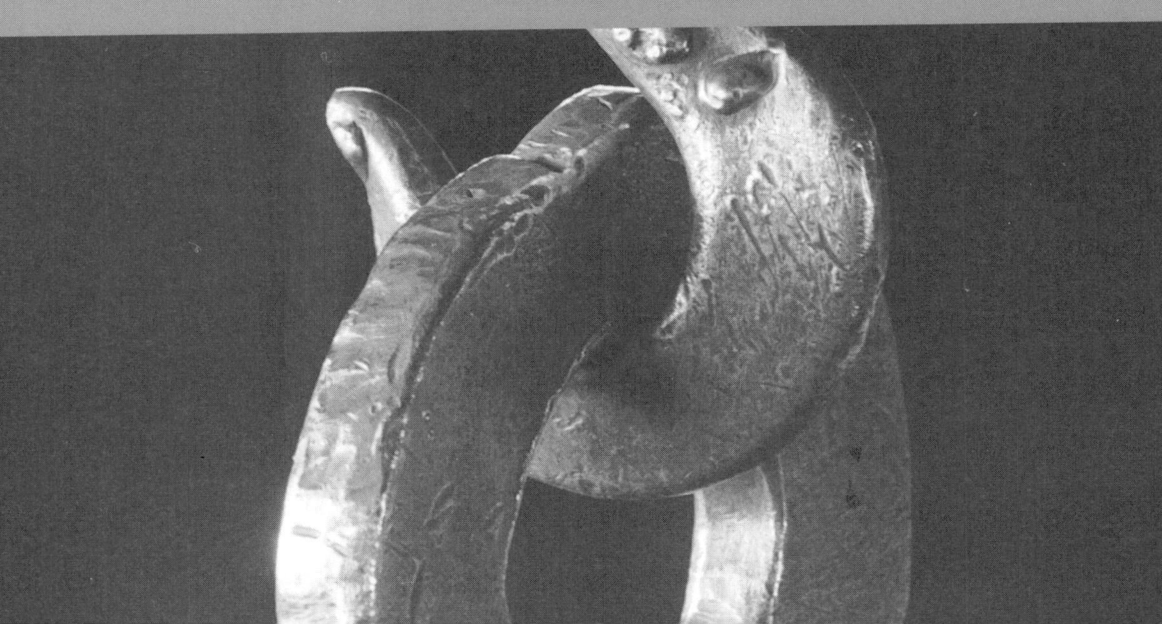

Overview

In this chapter, we discuss how NNTP works from a functional level. *NNTP* (which stands for *Network News Transport Protocol*) specifies the protocols that are used to communicate between a client and a Usenet news server. The protocols for NNTP are described in RFC-977 (which is available on the CD-ROM, along with all the other RFCs referenced in this book), while the format of the news articles is specified in RFC-1036. The NNTP ActiveX control takes advantage of a number of extensions to the commands described in RFC-977.

By the end of this chapter, you should be able to answer the following questions:

- How do you access the server?
- How do you retrieve lists of newsgroups?
- How do you retrieve a list of articles in a newsgroup?
- How do you retrieve a specific article from a newsgroup?
- What extensions are used by the NNTP client control?

The NNTP Model

Usenet news was developed to permit users to communicate items of interest to multiple people. Prior to Usenet, the only method available was for people to send e-mail to everyone who was interested in a particular topic. This was viewed as extremely wasteful because each person received his or her own copy of the e-mail. This method not only wasted disk space on their local machine, but network bandwidth as well. Consider this: Today's typical Internet user has a Pentium PC, a gigabyte hard disk, and 28.8 kilobaud modem; a typical user from 15 years ago used a VT-52 terminal to access a single UNIX host with many other people. The UNIX system probably only had 200MB of disk space, and users had to connect using 1,200 baud modems. Also, most of the computer-to-computer connections back then used only 9,600 baud lines, while today we consider a 1.5 megabit T-1 connection slow. So an alternate method evolved where the e-mail notes became news articles, and common servers were used to hold the information rather than individual e-mail messages. This became known as Usenet.

Under Usenet, a user interacts with a news server to view existing news articles and post new articles. The server makes the new article available to everyone on that specific server and propagates this new information to other news servers. This is much more efficient because only one copy of the article is stored on the local server. Also, only one copy of the message needs to be passed to the nearby servers. The nearby servers, in turn, pass the message to other nearby servers, thus letting the message reach the entire network community (see figure 11-1). Notice that it is possible for the same articles to be received from more than one news server. A unique messageid is included with each article that permits clients and servers to recognize when a message has been received more than once. This prevents users from seeing the same article twice (and also saves storage and transmission time).

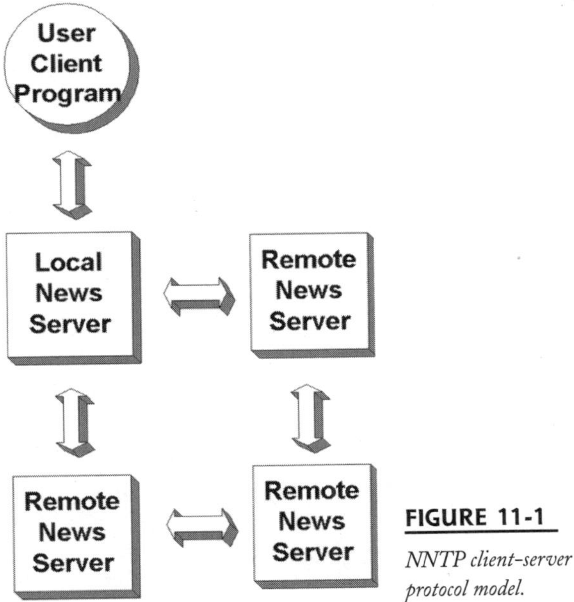

FIGURE 11-1

NNTP client-server protocol model.

The NNTP protocol is used to access Usenet news articles on an NNTP server. Like most Internet protocols, NNTP defines the communication process between a local client and a remote server. NNTP also defines the communication process between NNTP servers to exchange new news articles. Other techniques have been used in the past, but today nearly all news servers are based on NNTP.

News Article Format

RFC-1036 describes the format for a Usenet message. One of the key elements of a Usenet message is that it is formatted according to the same rules as Internet mail messages (RFC-822) with some restrictions and limitations. This gives the format some compatibility with existing Internet tools and makes it easier to extend with new features.

Essentially, news articles are composed of two parts: a header and a body. While the body is free text and has no real structure, the header is a different story. Here is an example of a sample news article:

```
Path: hecate.umd.edu!jillion
From: WFreeze@umdacc.umd.edu
Newsgroups: um.test
Subject: Test news post
Date: 26 Jun 1996 15:32:36 GMT
Organization: University of Maryland, College Park
Lines: 2
Distribution: um
Message-ID: <4qrl6k$fu4@hecate.umd.edu>
NNTP-Posting-Host: annex13-27.dial.umd.edu
X-Newsreader: News Xpress Version 1.0 Beta #4

Here is a test news post.
    ......Wayne
.
```

Notice at the start of the article is a series of lines, each with a keyword, followed by a colon (:), followed some text. This is the article header. After the header is a blank line and the body of the article. The blank line serves to separate the body from the header; it is required by the standard.

The header keywords fall into two categories: required and optional. The required keywords are: From, Date, Newsgroups, Subject, Message-Id, and Path. Followup-To, Expires, Reply-To, Sender, References, Control, Distribution, Keywords, Summary,

Approved, Lines, Xref, and Organization are optional keywords. In the above sample, notice that all the required keywords are present (though not in the order listed), and Lines and Distribution are optional keywords present. Also note that two additional header keywords are present: NNTP-Posting-Host and X-Newsreader. These are additional keywords not included in the standard, but they follow the standard header format.

From

This is a valid Internet mail-style address of the user who posted the message and must be in one of the following three formats:

```
wfreeze@umdacc.umd.edu

wfreeze@umdacc.umd.edu (Wayne S. Freeze)

Wayne S. Freeze <wfreeze@umdacc.umd.edu>
```

Date

The *date* keyword precedes the date the message was originally posted to the newsgroup. In the above example, the date is formatted as: Day, Month, Year, Hour, :, Minute, :, second, GMT. Because news articles are transmitted around the world, it is important to specify the time either in terms of GMT (Greenwich Mean Time), or to include the time zone or offset from GMT to uniquely identify when the message was sent.

Newsgroups

This is a list of newsgroups to which the article was posted. If the article was posted to more than one newsgroup, each group listed is separated by a comma.

Subject

This is simply the subject line of the article. The contents are left up to the original poster, but hopefully it represents something descriptive about the article.

Message-Id

This keyword precedes a unique identifier for the article. Because this value is always unique for a particular news article, it can be used to determine if an article was received from multiple places. A simple way to create a message-id is to take the current date, time, and host name and append them together into a single string. (If you are working on a multi-user computer, you may have to add something else to ensure that it is unique.) There is a set of rules contained in RFC-822 (which can be found on the CD-ROM) that describe some better methods to generate this value.

Path

The *Path* keyword shows the path the article took to reach the server. As an article is transferred from one machine to another, the machines are appended to the front of the path. Practically speaking, this information is only useful to NNTP servers to track message flow between each other.

Optional Headers

The *Reply-To* keyword provides a way to specify an alternate e-mail address to which replies should be directed. If present, this e-mail address should be used rather than the From e-mail address. The *Sender* keyword is similar to the *Reply-To* keyword and is used primarily when articles are posted by someone using someone else's account. *Followup-To* forces follow-up postings to a different newsgroup. This might be used to redirect replies from comp.sys.lang.visual.basic.announce to comp.sys.lang.basic.misc to minimize the traffic in the .announce group.

Expires is used to suggest when an article should be deleted from a server. Generally, it is better to let the servers delete news articles according to their own policies. However, it may be beneficial for some articles such as FAQs, which should probably be kept around until the next time they are re-posted. *Control* indicates an article that is passing information relevant to the server and is not designed to be read by users.

Distribution is an important keyword. Because newsgroups span the world, sometimes it is desirable to limit their geographic distribution. In the above example, I limited distribution of the test group to the news servers at the University of Maryland. After all, would someone in Japan really want to see this test post?

Organization helps to identify where the message was originally posted. It is helpful to include the *Keywords* keyword with values that help to identify the content of the article. *Summary* is similar to keywords, but contains a quick description of the article rather than a few choice words. *Approved* is required for posting into a moderated newsgroup. *Lines* contains the number of lines in the body of an article. Note that the blank line that separates the header from the body is not counted. *Xref* includes information about other newsgroups to which this article was posted. Its information is only meaningful on the local system, and is used to help client programs skip over articles that have been posted in more than one newsgroup.

NNTP Protocol Commands

NNTP protocol commands are very similar to the FTP commands we saw in Chapter 6. They are basically character strings that are followed by a carriage return and line feed. Responses from the server are also text-based and relatively easy to understand, although they are generally not passed onto the user directly. Unlike the FTP protocol, there is not a separate data port for bulk transfers. All data exchanges between the client and server occur over the standard NNTP port.

Table 11-1 lists the NNTP protocol commands and their syntax, and Table 11-2 shows the syntax of the parameters.

Table 11-1 NNTP Protocol Commands

Command	Syntax
Article	`ARTICLE [ <message-id> ] ¦ [ <article-number> ]`
Body	`BODY [ <message-id> ] ¦ [ <article-number> ]`
Group	`GROUP <group-name>`
Head	`HEAD [ <message-id> ] ¦ [ <article-number> ]`
Help	`HELP`

continues

Table 11-1 Continued

Command	Syntax
IHave	IHAVE<message-id>
Last	LAST
List	LIST
Newgroups	NEWGROUPS <date> <time> [GMT] [<distribution>]
Newnews	NEWNEWS <group-name> <date> <time> [GMT] [<distribution>]
Next	NEXT
Post	POST
Quit	QUIT
Slave	SLAVE
Stat	STAT [<message-id>] ¦ [<article-number>]

Table 11-2 NNTP Command Parameter Syntax

Parameter	Syntax
<article-number>	::= valid article number
<date>	::= six digits in the form YYMMDD
<distribution>	::= list of distribution groups
<group-name>	::= valid Usenet group name
<message-id>	::= valid Usenet message-id
<time>	::= six digits in the form HHMMSS

NNTP Reply Codes and Messages

Messages returned by the server consist of three parts: a reply code, a reply string (which make up a single line of response), and an optional part consisting of a block information returned by the server. This may be a list of newsgroups or a single article. This is significantly different from the FTP process where blocks of information are usually returned through a separate process.

Like the FTP reply code, NNTP uses a highly structured three-digit number. The first digit indicates whether or not the command was successful.

1 An informational message. For example, help information follows a reply code of 100.
2 The command executed properly.
3 The command is okay as far as it can be processed, but additional information is needed before the command can be completed.
4 The command is correct, but for some reason could not be executed. This could mean that the server is out of disk space or a transmission error occurred.
5 Some kind of permanent error, like a syntax error or a serious program error.

The second digit of the reply code further refines the type of information returned.

0 Refers to connection, setup, and miscellaneous messages.
1 Related to newsgroup selection.
2 Related to article selection.
3 The reply code contains information related to distribution functions.
4 Posting reply code.
8 or 9 Indicates nonstandard extensions to NNTP and debugging information respectively.

The text part of the messages listed in Table 11-3 may vary from those listed. In many cases they contain more information than what is shown. For example, the message for reply code 200 may contain the name of the host machine.

Table 11-3 NNTP Reply Codes and Reply Text

Reply Code	Reply Text
100	`help text follows.`
199	`debug output.`
200	`server ready - posting allowed.`
201	`server ready - no posting allowed.`
202	`slave status noted.`
205	`closing connection - goodbye!`
211	`n f l s group selected.`
215	`list of newsgroups follows.`
220	`n <a> article retrieved - head and body follow.`
221	`n <a> article retrieved - head follows`
222	`n <a> article retrieved - body follows.`

continues

Table 11-3 Continued

Reply Code	Reply Text
223	`n <a> article retrieved - request text separately`
230	`list of new articles by message-id follows`
231	`list of new newsgroups follows`
235	`article transferred ok`
240	`article posted ok`
335	`send article to be transferred. End with <cr-lf>.<crlf>`
340	`send article to be posted. End with <cr-lf>.<cr-lf>`
400	`service discontinued.`
411	`no such news group.`
412	`no newsgroup has been selected.`
420	`no current article has been selected.`
421	`no next article in this group.`
422	`no previous article in this group.`
423	`no such article number in this group.`
430	`no such article found.`
435	`article not wanted - do no sent it.`
436	`transfer failed - try again later.`
437	`article rejected - do not try again.`
440	`posting not allowed.`
441	`posting failed.`
500	`command not recognized.`
501	`command syntax error.`
502	`access restriction or permission denied`
503	`program fault - command not performed.`

Accessing the Server

A client process initiates a connection request to the NNTP server on port 119, and the server either accepts or rejects the request. Assuming that the connection request is successful, the server waits for commands to be issued from the client. Like many Internet protocols, NNTP issues commands and responses much like a user does on a Telnet session. In fact, it is possible to Telnet to an NNTP news server, execute the commands, and see the responses that the client program normally sees. (See the example later in this chapter for more information on how to do this.)

Unlike FTP servers, NNTP servers do not worry about user IDs and passwords. Generally, the server checks your IP address against an internal list of IP addresses that are permitted to access the server. Assuming that you have access to the server, the server responds with either a 200 or 201 message, indicating that you can go ahead and issue the NNTP protocol commands.

There are two commands that are used to manage newsgroups. The `List` command is used to retrieve the list of all newsgroups available on the server. The `Newgroups` command lists all newsgroups that have been created since a specified date and time. The `List` command is typically used the first time someone uses a news server to retrieve all the newsgroups on the server. Then each time after that, the `newsgroups` commands are used to retrieve all newsgroups that have been created since the last time the user connected to the server. This approach is important because some NNTP servers have more than 10,000 different newsgroups. It could take 10 to 15 minutes to download this information each time you connect to the server. Typically, the newsreader program keeps a list of available newsgroups locally and then only adds the newly created newsgroups each time you connect to the server.

Quit

This command is used to disconnect from the NNTP server. If the server accepts this command, it returns a reply code of 205.

List

This command is used to retrieve all the newsgroups on the server. It returns a reply code of 215, followed by the listing of all newsgroups. The listing takes the form of:

```
<group> <last> <first> <p>
```

where `<group>` is the name of the newsgroup; `<last>` is the number of the last known article; `<first>` is the first available article; and `<p>` is "y" if posting is permitted to the newsgroup and "n" if it is not. (Posting may be restricted because the newsgroup is moderated or because the system administrator prefers not to allow people to post articles through their news server.)

Newgroups

The `Newgroups` command takes the form of "NEWGROUPS" followed by a space, a date, time, and distribution information. A reply code of 231 is generated, followed by a listing of all newsgroups created after the specified date and time and belonging to the specified distribution groups. This listing uses the same format as the listing discussed in the `List` command.

Reading News

After you have a valid list of newsgroups, the user can select a newsgroup and begin to read articles. To aid the NNTP client developer, the news server maintains an internal current article pointer. This pointer can be set directly by using the `Article`, `Body`, `Head`, and `Stat` commands when they specify an article number or retrieve information about the current article if no parameters are specified. The `Next` and `Last` commands can be used to move the pointer to the following and previous articles.

Group

This command establishes the group that is used for any subsequent `Article`, `Body`, `Head`, and `Stat` commands. A reply code of 211 means that the group was found, and a reply code of 411 means that no such group exists on the server.

Article, Body, Head, and Stat

The `Article`, `Body`, `Head`, and `Stat` commands all work basically the same way. The only difference is the information returned. The `Article` command returns the entire article; the `Body` command returns only the body of the article; the `Head` command returns only the header information from the article; and the `Stat` command returns nothing (this is usually used to set the internal current article pointer). If successful, the `Article` command returns a reply code of 220, the `Body` command returns a reply code of 222, the `Head` command returns a reply code of 221, and the `Stat` command returns a reply code of 223. Unsuccessful reply codes include 412, 420, 423, and 430.

There are three different ways to use each of the four commands. The first way is to enter the command by itself. The server then returns the article, body, head, or stat information for the current article. The second is to specify the article number that you want to retrieve. The server returns the information requested and moves the internal current article pointer to this article. The third is to specify the messageid of the article you want to retrieve. The server then returns the information, but does not change the internal current article pointer.

Next and Last

These serve to move the internal current article pointer to either the article following the current article (`Next`) or the previous article (`Last`).

Posting

Now that we have talked about how to retrieve articles from the server, we are going to talk about how to create an article for the server. Only one command is used to do this, the `Post` command. Note that even though the group may have been marked as posting is permitted (see the `List` command above), there may be a restriction on the server that may prevent people from posting articles.

Post

If the command is accepted, a return code of 340 is returned to which the client should respond with the message (formatted according to RFC-1036) followed by a <cr> <lf> . <cr> <lf> stream of characters. A reply code of 440 is returned in response to a Post command if posting is not allowed. After the article is sent, a reply code of 240 is returned if the process is successful. A reply code of 441 is returned otherwise.

Other Facilities

There are several other commands worth mentioning. The Help command provides information about the commands supported by the NNTP server. The Slave, IHave, and NewNews commands are used primarily by servers exchanging new news articles.

Help

If the command is successful, a reply code of 100 is returned. The help information follows this response as a block of text followed by a single line with only a period in it, or if you want to think about it as a stream of characters it would look like <cr> <lf> "." <cr> <lf>.

Slave

A proper response to this command is a reply code of 202. The Slave command is used to indicate that the connection is coming from another NNTP server. In many cases, the Slave command is used to prioritize requests from this computer at a lower priority than a normal interactive user. However, no specific action must be taken by the server other than returning the proper response code.

IHave

This information can be used by a server to accept or reject the specified article. If the server responds with a reply code of 335, it expects the article to be transmitted. A 435 reply code means that the article is not wanted. After the article has been sent, a 235 response is sent indicating that the article was received okay. Reply codes of 436 and 437 refer to transmission errors and whether or not to try again later.

Newnews

This command is used by servers to retrieve a list of all news articles that have been posted or received to the specified newsgroups since the specified date and time. The only reply code used is 230. Following the reply code is a list of all the message-ids that meet the date, time, and distribution information criteria, followed by a line that consists of only a single period. Note that it is possible there may be no new news items, so no entries may be in the list of message-ids.

Extended NNTP Protocol Commands

Over the years since RFC-977 was issued, there have been a number of extensions to the commands available. Most of these were done by the implementors attempting to improve the functions of their NNTP servers, or to address problems and limitations in the original specifications. While many of these commands may be available on NNTP servers, you should not assume that they will always be there. In many cases it is a good idea to check if the command is available and take advantage of it, but also include code in your program to handle the situation where you do not have these extensions available. Of course, if you are working with only one server, this advice may not be necessary.

Table 11-4 lists the extended NNTP protocol commands and their syntax, and Table 11-5 shows the syntax of the parameters.

Table 11-4 Extended NNTP Protocol Commands

Command	Syntax
Authinfo User	`AUTHINFO USER <username>`
Authinfo Pass	`AUTHINFO PASS <password>`
Listgroup	`LISTGROUP [<group-name>]`
List Overview.FMT	`LIST OVERVIEW.FMT`
XHDR	`XHDR <header> [<range> ¦ <message-id>]`
XMOTD	`XMOTD <date> <time> [GMT]`
XOVER	`XOVER [<range>]`

Table 11-5 Extended NNTP Command Parameter Syntax

<table>
<tr><th>Parameter</th><th>Syntax</th></tr>
<tr><td><article-number></td><td>::= valid article number</td></tr>
<tr><td><date></td><td>::= six digits in the form YYMMDD</td></tr>
<tr><td><group-name></td><td>::= valid Usenet group name</td></tr>
<tr><td><header></td><td>::= valid newsgroup header</td></tr>
<tr><td><message-id></td><td>::= valid Usenet message-id</td></tr>
<tr><td><password></td><td>::=a valid password for the userid</td></tr>
<tr><td><range></td><td>::= <article-number> | <article-number> - | <article-number> - <article-number></td></tr>
<tr><td><time></td><td>::= six digits in the form HHMMSS</td></tr>
<tr><td><username></td><td>::=a valid userid for the server</td></tr>
</table>

Extended NNTP Reply Codes and Messages

As with the standard reply codes and messages, the extended NNTP reply codes and messages follow the same formatting rules. Existing reply codes and messages are often used to prevent confusion.

Table 11-6 Extended NNTP Reply Codes and Reply Text

Reply Code	Reply Text
211	`list of article numbers follow.`
215	`information follows.`
221	`header follows.`
224	`overview information follows.`
281	`authentication accepted.`
381	`more authentication information required.`
412	`not currently in newsgroup.`
420	`no current article selected.`
430	`no such article.`
480	`authentication required.`
482	`authentication rejected.`
502	`no permission.`
503	`program error, function not performed.`

Authinfo

The `Authinfo` is used to provide logon information to a server. Authentication information consists of a user ID, followed by an optional password. In response to a reply code of 480, a client program responds with the `AUTHINFO USER` command to pass a valid userid to the server. If the server requires a password, a reply code of 381 is returned. A successful login returns a reply code of 281. If unsuccessful, the server sends reply codes of 482 or 502, depending on the error.

List Overview.FMT

The `List Overview.FMT` command is used to send a list of headers in the order that they are sent by the XOVER command. Note that the header information follows the standard described in RFC-1036. If the header title is included with the header information returned by the XOVER command, ":full" is appended to the end of the header. If successful, the server returns a reply code of 215, followed by the list of headers one header per line, followed by a line with only a period. If unsuccessful, the command returns a reply code of 503.

Listgroup

The `Listgroup` command returns a list of all the article numbers for the specified newsgroup. If the newsgroup is not specified, the current newsgroup is used. If this command is successful, a reply code of 211 is returned with a list of article numbers followed by a line with only a period. Unsuccessful reply codes are 412 and 502.

XHDR

The `XHDR` command is used to retrieve a list of headers from one or more articles in a newsgroup. A single header is specified and only the header information from the specified article range is returned. If nothing is specified for the range, the current article is assumed. Otherwise the header information for the article or articles is returned. If successful, a reply code of 221 is returned followed by the line of header information, followed by a line with a single period. If not successful, a reply code of 412, 420, 430 or 502 is returned.

XMOTD

The `XMOTD` command is used to retrieve the administration file from the server. This is sometimes called the Message Of The Day file. If successful, a reply code of 215 is returned followed by the administration file, followed by a single period. Otherwise a reply code of 503 is returned.

XOVER

The `XOVER` command works with the `List Overview.FMT` command to retrieve overview information for the specified articles. The `List Overview.FMT` command provides list of headers in the order they will be presented when the `XOVER` command is used. If this command is successful, a reply code of 224 is returned, followed by one line for each article retrieved. The format for the line is the article number, followed by each of the headers separated by a tab character. If a header is missing for a particular article, a null field is sent (i.e., two tab characters will be next to each other). Unsuccessful reply codes are 412, 420, and 502.

Example

In the following example, I used Windows 95 `telnet` command to connect to a news server. If you want to try this, Telnet to your local news server using port 119 instead of port 23. You need to set local echo on and be a good (or very good) typist, because the server does not allow you to use backspace or delete to correct any typing errors.

Commands that I typed are prefixed by `->`, and responses from the server begin with the three digit reply code that we previously discussed.

```
200 hecate.umd.edu InterNetNews NNRP server INN 1.4unoff4 05-Mar-96 ready (posting ok).
>help
100 Legal commands
  authinfo user Name¦pass Password¦generic <prog> <args>
  article [MessageID¦Number]
  body [MessageID¦Number]
  date
  group newsgroup
  head [MessageID¦Number]
  help
  ihave
  last
  list [active¦newsgroups¦distributions¦schema]
  listgroup newsgroup
  mode reader
  newgroups yymmdd hhmmss ["GMT"] [<distributions>]
  newnews newsgroups yymmdd hhmmss ["GMT"] [<distributions>]
  next
  post
  slave
  stat [MessageID¦Number]
  xgtitle [group_pattern]
  xhdr header [range¦MessageID]
  xover [range]
  xpat header range¦MessageID pat [morepat...]
  xpath MessageID
```

```
Report problems to <news@csc.umd.edu>
.
->newgroups 960625 000000
231 New newsgroups follow.
alt.tv.robotech 29 1 y
alt.sports.college.acc 4 1 y
alt.books.kurt-vonnegut 2 1 y
rec.music.artists.reb-st-james 0 1 y
alt.usenet.kooks 70 1 y
alt.humor.best-of-usenet.d 10 1 y
alt.usenet.offline-reader.forte-agent 128 1 y
comp.os.os2.networking.server 0 1 y
.
->group um.test
211 1 3384 3384 um.test
->head 3384
221 3384 <4qrl6k$fu4@hecate.umd.edu> head
Path: hecate.umd.edu!jillion
From: WFreeze@umdacc.umd.edu
Newsgroups: um.test
Subject: Test news post
Date: 26 Jun 1996 15:32:36 GMT
Organization: University of Maryland, College Park
Lines: 2
Distribution: um
Message-ID: <4qrl6k$fu4@hecate.umd.edu>
NNTP-Posting-Host: annex13-27.dial.umd.edu
X-Newsreader: News Xpress Version 1.0 Beta #4
.
->body 3384
222 3384 <4qrl6k$fu4@hecate.umd.edu> body
Here is a test news post.
    ......Wayne
.
```

```
->article 3384
220 3384 <4qrl6k$fu4@hecate.umd.edu> article
Path: hecate.umd.edu!jillion
From: WFreeze@umdacc.umd.edu
Newsgroups: um.test
Subject: Test news post
Date: 26 Jun 1996 15:32:36 GMT
Organization: University of Maryland, College Park
Lines: 2
Distribution: um
Message-ID: <4qrl6k$fu4@hecate.umd.edu>
NNTP-Posting-Host: annex13-27.dial.umd.edu
X-Newsreader: News Xpress Version 1.0 Beta #4

Here is a test news post.
    ......Wayne
.
->quit
205
```

The first message that we receive after establishing the connection has a reply code of 200. This message provides information about the host system and the NNTP server software. Note that none of this is really important. Only the reply code is significant because it means that the server will accept any messages we choose to post.

The first command I entered is the `Help` command, which generates a reply code of 100 and a listing of the available commands. Notice that this particular server supports a number of commands that are extensions to the commands from RFC-977. But it does not list the `XMOTD` and the `List Overview.FMT` commands used by the NNTP ActiveX control. You should also note that the list is ended by a single period (".") on a line by itself.

The next command I entered is the `Group` command. I had previously posted a test message in the newsgroup um.test for this example. (Most Internet providers have either their own test group or another place to test posting messages. You may want to remember this when you begin testing your NNTP program later on.) The command returned a 211 message with three numbers and the name of the newsgroup. The first number is the number of articles in the newsgroup, in this case only my test article is present so its value is one. The next two numbers are the starting number and stopping numbers. Because there is only one article in this newsgroup, the first and last numbers are identical, 3384 and 3384.

The `Head` command followed by the article number 3384 was entered next. This returns a reply code of 221 with the article number (3384), the messageid (<4qrl6k$fu4@hecate.umd.edu>), and the word head. Notice that the messageid is the unique identifier that is associated with this article. It remains unchanged no matter where the news article is retrieved from. Looking at the information returned from the header information, you can see the subject (Test news post), who posted it (Wfreeze@umdacc.umd.edu), and the date and time it was posted (26 June 1996 15:32:26 GMT).

After the `Head` command, I entered the `Body` command with the same article number. This time I received a reply code of 222 with the same messageid as the head command returned and three lines of text, the two lines of the article body and the standard termination line.

Finally, I used the `Article` command to retrieve the entire article. Notice that this time I received everything that both the `Head` and `Body` commands returned.

To end this example, I entered the `Quit` command. The server responded with a reply code of 205, followed immediately by terminating the session.

Summary

In this chapter, we talked about the NNTP protocol used to retrieve and post news articles with a Usenet NNTP server. This protocol is described in detail in RFC-977. While we did not discuss how an article is formatted, this information is described in RFC-1036. We discussed how to retrieve the list of all the available newsgroups from the server, and how to retrieve any updates to the list rather than retrieving the whole list each time. Then we covered how to select a newsgroup and retrieve articles from the group. Finally, we discussed how to post new articles to the server.

In the next chapter, we begin to explore the ActiveX controls for NNTP by looking at the NNTP client control.

In case you want to check your answers to the questions in the Overview section, here are the answers:

- *How do you access the server?*

  You access the server by simply establishing a session with the server. No user IDs or passwords are required.

- *How do you retrieve lists of newsgroups?*

  The `List` command retrieves a list of all newsgroups available on the server, and the `Newgroups` command retrieves all newsgroups that have been created after a specified date and time.

- *How do you retrieve a list of articles in a newsgroup?*

  By using the `Group` command with the name of a valid newsgroup that returns the first and last numbers of the articles in the newsgroup. Then the `Head` command can be used to retrieve information from each of the headers in the newsgroup.

- *How do you retrieve a specific article from a newsgroup?*

  The `Article`, `Head`, and `Body` commands followed by a valid article number return the entire article, the header information, or the body of the article respectively.

- *What NNTP extensions are used by the NNTP client control?*

  The `Authinfo`, `List Overview.FMT`, `Listgroup`, `XHDR`, `XMOTD`, and `XOVER` NNTP extensions are used by the NNTP client control to provide increased function when used with servers that support these commands.

Chapter 12

The NNTP Client Control

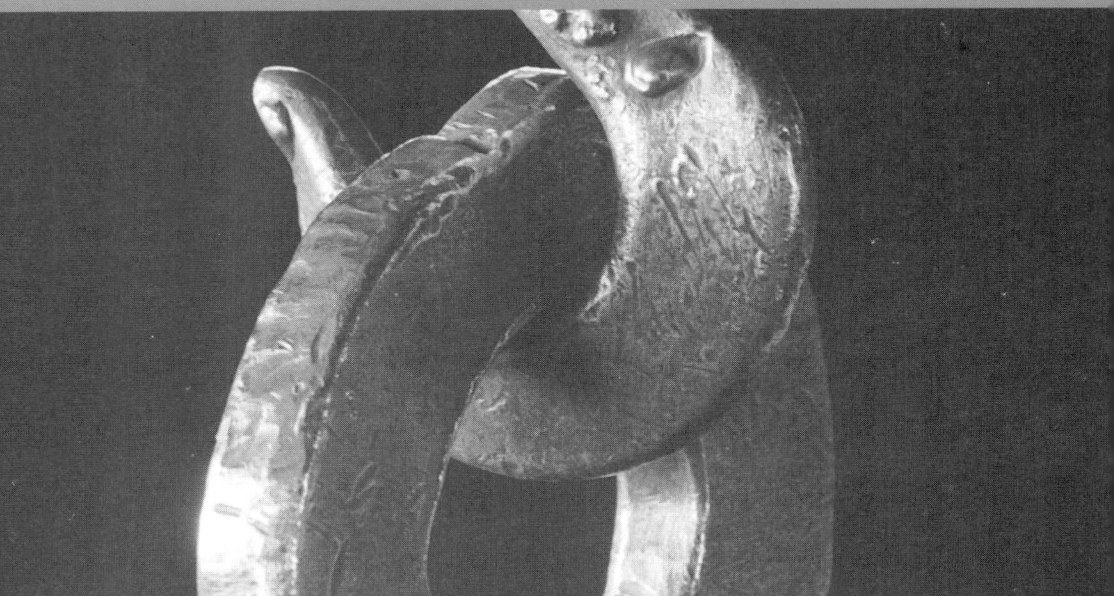

Overview

In this chapter, we discuss the properties, events, and methods of the NNTP client control. This control handles the protocol interaction with a remote NNTP server and provides a high-level method of interacting with the server.

Yes, this is another one of those reference chapters that I know you are not going to bother reading. However, you may want to skim through and just look at some of the highlights. They will most likely come in handy later.

By the end of this chapter, you should be able to answer the following questions:

- What other objects are used by this control?
- What methods are used to retrieve information about newsgroups?
- What methods are used to manage a connection?

Properties

The NNTP control has a number of properties that provide default values for various methods, describe the facilities available on the remote server, and provide status information about the control's state.

ArticleNumbersSupported

Format: `NNTPObject.ArticleNumbersSupported`

The `ArticleNumbersSupported` property returns a boolean that indicates whether the server supports the `ListGroups` command so that articles may be retrieved by using the `GetArticleNumbers` method.

Table 12-1 ***ArticleNumbersSupported*** **Values**

ArticleNumbersSupported **Value**	**Description**
`True`	The `GetArticleNumbers` method may be used to retrieve articles from the server.

ArticleNumbersSupported Value	Description
False	The GetArticleNumbers method does not work with this server.

Busy

Format: NNTPObject.Busy

The Busy property returns true if the NNTP client control is executing a command. Most commands cannot be started until the current command is finished.

Table 12-2 *Busy* Values

Busy Value	Description
True	The NNTP client control is executing a command.
False	The NNTP client control is not executing a command.

DocInput

Format: NNTPObject.DocInput

The DocInput property returns a reference to the DocInput object associated with the control. It is used primarily to access the various properties of the DocInput object.

DocOutput

Format: NNTPObject.DocOutput

The DocOutput property returns a reference to the DocOutput object associated with the control. It is used primarily to access the various properties of the DocOutput object.

EnableTimer

Format: `NNTPObject.EnableTimer(event) [= boolean]`

The `EnableTimer` property sets or returns a flag that controls one of several different timers.

Table 12-3 *EnableTimer* Events

EnableTimer Event Name	*EnableTimer* Event Value	Description
`prcConnectTimeout`	1	If a connection is not made within the time-out period, the `TimeOut` event is triggered.
`prcReceiveTimeout`	2	If no data arrives for a receive process within the timeout period, the `TimeOut` event is triggered.
`prcUserTimeout`	65	User defined `TimeOut` event.

Table 12-4 *Timeout* Values

Timeout Value	Description
`True`	The timer for this event is enabled.
`False`	The timer for this event is not enabled.

Errors

Format: `NNTPObject.Errors`

The `Errors` property returns an `icErrors` collection that contains information about the last error that occurred. It is used primarily to access the properties of the `icErrors` object. (For more information about the `icErrors` and `icError` objects, see Chapter 9.)

LastUpdate

Format: `NNTPObject.LastUpdate [= date]`

The `LastUpdate` property returns or sets a date value that is used when processing the `GetAdministrationFile` and the `ListNewGroups` methods. The `GetAdministrationFile` is retrieved if it has been updated since the specified date value. The `ListNewGroups` command retrieves all new newsgroups that have been added or received by the server since the specified value in `LastUpdate` property.

NotificationMode

Format: `NNTPObject.NotifictionMode [= integer]`

The `NotificationMode` property returns or sets an integer that indicates when notification should be provided for incoming data. This is most useful when working with the `DocInput` and `DocOutput` objects.

Table 12-5 *NotificationMode* Values

NotificationMode Value	Description
0	**Complete:** Notification is given when the response is complete.
1	**Continuous:** Notification is given as new data is received.

OverviewSupported

Format: `NNTPObject.OverviewSupported`

The `OverviewSupported` property is used to determine if the NNTP server supports the `XOVER` and `LIST OVERVIEW.FMT` commands. If they are supported, the `GetOverviewFormat` and `GetOverView` methods can be used to retrieve overview information.

Table 12-6 *OverviewSupported* Values

OverviewSupported Value	Description
True	The GetOverview and GetOverviewFormat methods can be used to retrieve data.
False	The GetOverview and GetOverviewFormat methods cannot be used to retrieve data.

PostingAllowed

Format: NNPObject.PostingAllowed

The PostingAllowed property returns a boolean that indicates whether the server permits posting. Note that this information is based on the initial reply code of 200 or 201. Posting to individual newsgroups may or may not be permitted. You need to check the individual newsgroup to determine if you can post to it.

Table 12-7 *PostingAllowed* Values

PostingAllowed Value	Description
True	The NNTP server permits articles to be posted.
False	The NNTP server does not permit articles to be posted.

ProtocolState

Format: NNTPObject.ProtocolState

The ProtocolState property is used to determine which state the protocol is in.

Table 12-8 *ProtocolState* Values

ProtocolState Value Name	*ProtocolState* Value	Description
ftpBase	0	**Base state:** Before a connection is established with the server.

ProtocolState Value Name	*ProtocolState* Value	Description
ftpAuthorization	1	**Authorization state:** After connection is established and before the user has been granted access to the server.
ftpTransaction	2	**Transaction state:** After the user has been granted access to the server. The client can now interact with the server.

RemoteHost

Format: `NNTPObject.RemoteHost [= string]`

The `RemoteHost` property is a string that contains the host name or IP address of the remote host. It is used with the `Connect` method to establish a connection to the remote computer.

RemotePort

Format: `NNTPObject.RemotePort [= long]`

The `RemotePort` property is a long that contains the port number that the NNTP server is listening to. Usually this value is 119.

ReplyCode

Format: `NNTPObject.ReplyCode`

The `ReplyCode` property is a long that contains the reply code of the most recent message generated by the NNTP server. See Table 11-3 for a list of valid reply codes and sample messages.

ReplyString

Format: `NNTPObject.RemoteString`

The `ReplyString` property is a string that contains the text of the last message received from the NNTP server. See Table 11-3 for a list of valid reply codes and sample messages.

State

Format: `NNTPObject.State`

The `State` property returns an integer and is used to determine which state the connection is in.

Table 12-9 *State* Values

State Value Name	*State* Value	Description
`prcConnecting`	1	**Connecting state:** A connection has been requested and is waiting for an acknowledgment.
`prcResolvingHost`	2	**Resolving Host state:** Waiting for a host name to be translated into its IP address. (Not entered if an IP address was supplied as the `RemoteHost` property.)
`prcHostResolved`	3	**Host Resolved state:** After the host name has successfully translated into an IP address. (Not entered if an IP address was supplied as the `RemoteHost` property.)
`prcConnected`	4	**Connected state:** A connection has been successfully established.
`prcDisconnecting`	5	**Disconnecting state:** A request to disconnect has been requested.
`prcDisconnected`	6	**Disconnected state:** Before a connection is requested and after a connection has been closed.

TimeOut

Format: `NNTPObject.TimeOut(event) [= long]`

The `TimeOut` property sets or returns a flag that controls how much time must pass before a `TimeOut` event.

Table 12-10 *TimeOut* Events

TimeOut Event Name	*TimeOut* Event Value	Description
prcConnectTimeout	1	If a connection is not made within the timeout period, the `TimeOut` event is triggered.
prcReceiveTimeout	2	If no data arrives for a receive process within the timeout period, the `TimeOut` event is triggered.
prcUserTimeout	65	User defined `TimeOut` event.

URL

Format: `NNTPObject.URL [= string]`

The `URL` property is a string that holds the name of the current document being transferred. The URL may be set before using the `SendDoc` or `GetDoc` methods. This property is used primarily to support the `DocInput` and `DocOutput` objects.

Methods

The NNTP ActiveX client control provides many methods to work with a news server. Note that some of the commands depend on extensions to the basic NNTP protocol. Because not all news servers have these extensions, you should not rely on these methods unless you verify that the server has these extensions available.

Cancel

Format: `NNTPObject.Cancel`

The `Cancel` method is used to cancel a pending request. After this method finishes, the `cancel` event is triggered.

Connect

Format: `NNTPObject.Connect [remotehost] [,remoteport]`

The `Connect` method is used to establish a connection to a remote NNTP server. Both parameters are optional, but if they are not specified, the values from the `RemoteHost` and the `RemotePort` properties are used. After this method is finished, the `Connect` event is triggered. If an error occurs during the process, the `Error` event is invoked.

Table 12-11 *Connect* Method Arguments

Argument Name	Argument Type	Description
`remotehost`	variant	Either a remote host name or an IP address.
`remoteport`	variant	Numeric port value.

GetAdministrationFile

Format: `NNTPObject.GetAdministrationFile [lastupdate]`

The `GetAdministrationFile` method uses the `XMOD` command to retrieve the administrator's information file from the server if it is newer than the value of `lastupdate`. If `lastupdate` is not supplied, the value of the `LastUpdate` property is used. Note that not all NNTP servers support the `XMOD` command because it is not part of the RFC-1063 standard.

Table 12-12 *GetAdminisrationFile* Method Arguments

Argument Name	Argument Type	Description
`lastupdate`	date	Retrieves information if newer than this date.

GetArticleByArticleNumber

Format: `NNTPObject.GetArticleByArticleNumber [articlenumber]`

The `GetArticleByArticleNumber` method is used to retrieve an article from the NNTP server. The `articlenumber` parameter can be either an integer or a string. This method essentially executes the RFC-1063 `Article` command with an `articlenumber` as the parameter. If `articlenumber` is not specified, the current article is used.

Table 12-13 ***GetArticleByNumber* Method Arguments**

Argument Name	Argument Type	Description
`articlenumber`	variant	Article number of the article to be retrieved.

GetArticleByMessageId

Format: `NNTPObject.GetArticleByMessageId [Messageid]`

The `GetArticleByMessageId` method is used to retrieve an article from the NNTP server. This method essentially executes the RFC-1063 `Article` command with a `messageid` as the parameter. If `Messageid` is not specified, the current article is used.

Table 12-14 ***GetArticleByMessageId* Method Arguments**

Argument Name	Argument Type	Description
`Messageid`	string	Messageid of the article to be retrieved.

GetArticleHeaders

Format: `NNTPObject.GetArticleHeaders header [, [firstarticle] [, lastarticle]]`

The `GetArticleHeaders` method is used to retrieve all the article headers from a newsgroup. `Header` refers to a valid header line from RFC-1036. `Firstarticle` and `lastarticle` are both optional and specify the starting and ending article numbers from which the header information should be obtained. If `firstarticle` is omitted, it defaults to the first article available. If `lastarticle` is omitted or set to zero, the range ends with the last article available on the server. Note that this method uses the `XHDR` command, so all NNTP servers may not be able to use this method.

Table 12-15 *GetArticleHeaders* Method Arguments

Argument Name	Argument Type	Description
`header`	string	Header field to retrieve.
`firstarticle`	variant	First article number to retrieve.
`lastarticle`	variant	Last article number to retrieve.

GetArticleNumbers

Format: `NNTPObject.GetArticleNumbers [newsgroup]`

The `GetArticleNumbers` method retrieves a list of article numbers for the specified newsgroup. If `newsgroup` is omitted, it defaults to the current newsgroup. This method executes the RFC-977 `Listgroup` command. All output is directed to the `DocOutput` event.

Table 12-16 *GetArticleNumbers* Method Arguments

Argument Name	Argument Type	Description
`group`	string	Name of a newsgroup.

GetBodyByArticleNumber

Format: `NNTPObject.GetBodyByArticleNumber [articlenumber]`

The `GetBodyByArticleNumber` method retrieves the body of an article from the NNTP server. The `articlenumber` parameter can be either an integer or a string. This method essentially executes the RFC-1063 `Body` command with an `articlenumber` as the parameter. If `articlenumber` is not specified, the current article is used.

Table 12-17 ***GetBodyByNumber*** **Method Arguments**

Argument Name	Argument Type	Description
`articlenumber`	variant	Article number of the body to be retrieved.

GetBodyByMessageId

Format: `NNTPObject.GetBodyByMessageId [Messageid]`

The `GetBodyByMessageId` method is used to retrieve the body of an article from the NNTP server. This method essentially executes the RFC-1063 `Body` command with a `messageid` as the parameter. If `Messageid` is not specified, the current article is used.

Table 12-18 ***GetBodyByMessageId*** **Method Arguments**

Argument Name	Argument Type	Description
`Messageid`	string	Messageid of the body to be retrieved.

GetDoc

Format: `NNTPObject.GetDoc [url] [,[headers] [,outputfile]]`

The `GetDoc` method works with the `DocOutput` object to transfer a file from the remote NNTP server to the local machine. All three arguments are optional and if not specified, the appropriate values from the `DocOutput` object are used.

The `URL`, if specified, should be of the form: `News://remotehost/messageid`

where

`News:` is optional when used with the NNTP client control.

`remotehost` is optional and assumed to be the current machine.

`Messageid` is required and is the name of the message to be retrieved from the remote NNTP server.

Table 12-19 ***GetDoc*** **Method Arguments**

Argument Name	Argument Type	Description
`url`	string	Name of the file on the remote system to be retrieved in URL format.
`Headers`	DocHeaders	A list of header keyword value pairs from the received article.
`outputfile`	string	Name of the output file on the local machine.

GetHeaderByArticleNumber

Format: `NNTPObject.GetHeaderByArticleNumber [articlenumber]`

The `GetHeaderByArticleNumber` method is used to retrieve the header of an article from the NNTP server. The `articlenumber` parameter can be either an integer or a string. This method essentially executes the RFC-1063 `Header` command with an `articlenumber` as the parameter. If `articlenumber` is not specified, the current article is used.

Table 12-20 ***GetHeaderByNumber*** **Method Arguments**

Argument Name	Argument Type	Description
`articlenumber`	variant	Article number of the header to be retrieved.

GetHeaderByMessageId

Format: `NNTPObject.GetHeaderByMessageId [Messageid]`

The `GetHeaderByMessageId` method is used to retrieve the header of an article from the NNTP server. This method essentially executes the RFC-1063 `Header` command with a `messageid` as the parameter. If `Messageid` is not specified, the current article is used.

Table 12-21 ***GetHeaderByMessageId*** **Method Arguments**

Argument Name	Argument Type	Description
`Messageid`	string	messageid of the header to be retrieved.

GetOverview

Format: `NNTPObject.GetOverview [firstarticle] [,lastarticle]`

The `GetOverview` method uses an extension to many NNTP servers called the `XOVER` command to retrieve overview information from the server. The output from this method is returned through the `DocOutput` event. Check the `OverviewSupported` property after a connection is made to a server to determine if this method can be used. If `firstarticle` is omitted, it defaults to the first article available. If `lastarticle` is omitted or set to zero, the range ends with the last article available on the server.

Table 12-22 *GetOverview* Method Arguments

Argument Name	Argument Type	Description
`firstarticle`	variant	First article number to be retrieved.
`lastarticle`	variant	Last article number to be retrieved.

GetOverviewFormat

Format: `NNTPObject.GetOverviewFormat`

The `GetOverviewFormat` method queries the NNTP server to determine the list of headers returned as an overview. This information is needed when using the `GetOverview` method to retrieve information from the server. While many NNTP servers support this function (`LIST OVERVIEW.FMT` command), you should check the `OverviewSupported` property after a connection is made to a server to determine if this method can be used. The output from this method is returned through the `DocOutput` event.

GetStatByArticleNumber

Format: `NNTPObject.GetStatByArticleNumber [articlenumber]`

The `GetHeaderByArticleNumber` method is used to set the current article pointer to this article. Any output generated by this method is directed to the `DocOutput` event. The `articlenumber` parameter can be either an integer or a string. This method essentially executes the RFC-1063 `Stat` command with an `articlenumber` as the parameter. If `articlenumber` is not specified, the current article is used.

Table 12-23 *GetStatByArticleNumber* Method Arguments

Argument Name	Argument Type	Description
articlenumber	variant	Article number of the header to be retrieved.

ListGroupDescriptions

Format: `NNTPObject.ListGroupDescriptions`

The `ListGroupDescriptions` method requests the server to return descriptions of the newsgroups. This method executes the `List Newsgroups` command. Because not all news servers support this command, you need to check the status of the reply code to ensure proper execution. Any data generated by this method is returned through the `DocOutput` event.

ListGroup

Format: `NNTPObject.ListGroup`

The `ListGroup` method requests a complete list of all the newsgroups on the server, including the first article number, the last article number, and a y/n flag that indicates whether you can post to a particular newsgroup. This command is the RFC-1073 `List` command and should be available on all news servers. All output generated by this command is returned through the `DocOutput` event.

ListNewGroups

Format: `NNTPObject.ListNewGroups [lastupdate]`

The `ListNewGroups` method uses the RFC-1063 `Newgroups` command to retrieve a list of all newsgroups that have been created since the specified date. If the `lastupdate` parameter is not specified, the value of the `LastUpdate` property is used. Typically, the first time a connection is made to the server the `ListGroups` method is used to retrieve all the groups on the server. Then the `ListNewGroups` method is used each time after that when the client connects to the server to get all the updates since the last time connected.

Table 12-24 *ListNewGroups* Method Arguments

Argument Name	Argument Type	Description
`lastupdate`	date	Retrieves information if newer than this date.

Quit

Format: `NNTPObject.Quit`

The `Quit` method is used to disconnect from the NNTP server.

SelectGroup

Format: `NNTPObject.SelectGroup newsgroup`

The `SelectGroup` method sets the name of the current newsgroup inside the news server to the specified newsgroup. This method executes the RFC-977 `Group` command. If successful, the `SelectGroup` event occurs.

Table 12-25 *SelectGroup* Method Arguments

Argument Name	Argument Type	Description
`group`	string	Name of a newsgroup.

SendDoc

Format: `NNPObject.SendDoc [url] [,[headers] [,[inputdata] [,[inputfile] [,outputfile]]]]`

The `SendDoc` method works with the `DocInput` object to transfer a file to the remote NNTP server from the local machine. All five arguments are optional and if not specified, the appropriate values from the `DocInput` object are used.

The `URL`, if specified, should be of the form: `News://remotehost/filename` where

`News` is optional when used with the NNTP client control

`remotehost` is optional and assumed to be the current machine

`filename` is required and is the fully qualified name of the file on the local machine.

Table 12-27 *SendDoc* Method Arguments

Argument Name	Argument Type	Description
`url`	string	Name of the file on the remote system to be retrieved in URL format.
`headers`	DocHeaders	The list of header keywords and values that are attached to the article.
`inputdata`	variant	Optional data buffer containing the document to be sent.
`Inputfile`	variant	Optional file containing the document to be sent.
`outputfile`	string	Name of the output file on the local machine to which the reply document is written.

SelectLastArticle

Format: `NNTPObject.SelectLastArticle`

The `SelectLastArticle` method is used to move the server's internal article pointer to the article that immediately precedes the current article.

SelectNextArticle

Format: `NNTPObject.SelectNextArticle`

The `SelectNextArticle` method is used to move the server's internal article pointer to the article that immediately follows the current article.

Events

The NNTP events are called in response to various conditions that happen during the execution of a program using the NNTP ActiveX control.

AuthenticateRequest

Format: `NNTPObject_AuthenticateRequest(userid as string, password as string)`

The `AuthenticateRequest` event occurs after the news server requests userid and password information.

Table 12-28 *AuthenticateRequest* Event Parameters

Parameter Name	Argument Type	Description
`userid`	string	The userid to be returned to the server.
`Password`	string	The password to be returned to the server.

AuthenticateResponse

Format: `NNTPObject_AuthenticateResponse(authenticated as boolean)`

The `AuthenticateResponse` event occurs after the news server has processed the information sent via the `AuthenticateRequest` event.

Table 12-29 *AuthenticateResponse* Event Parameters

Parameter Name	Argument Type	Description
`authenticated`	boolean	Status of the authentication process.

Table 12-30 *authenticated* Values

authenticated Value	Description
`True`	The user has been granted access to the system.
`False`	The user has not been granted access to the system.

Banner

Format: `NNTPObject_Banner(ByVal banner as string)`

The `Banner` event occurs after the client program has successfully signed onto the news server.

Table 12-31 *AuthenticateResponse* Event Parameters

Parameter Name	Argument Type	Description
`banner`	string	Banner string returned by the news server.

Busy

Format: `NNTPObject_Busy(ByVal isBusy As Boolean)`

The `Busy` event occurs when the `NNTPObject.Busy` property changes state. This event occurs when a command begins execution, or when a command finishes execution.

Table 12-32 ***Busy*** **Event Parameters**

Parameter Name	Argument Type	Description
`isBusy`	boolean	Indicates when a command is being executed.

Table 12-33 ***isBusy*** **Values**

isBusy Value	Description
`True`	A command is being executed.
`False`	A command is not being executed.

Cancel

Format: `NNTPObject_Cancel`

The `Cancel` event occurs after the `Cancel` method is invoked.

DocInput

Format: `NNTPObject_DocInput(ByVal docinput as DocInput)`

The `DocInput` event occurs when data has been transferred to this control.

Table 12-34 ***DocInput*** **Event Parameters**

Parameter Name	Argument Type	Description
`docinput`	DocInput	Object that describes the current input data for this transfer.

DocOutput

Format: `NNTPObject_DocOutput(ByVal docinput as DocInput)`

The `DocOutput` event occurs when data has been transferred from this control.

Table 12-35 *DocOutput* Event Parameters

Parameter Name	Argument Type	Description
`docoutput`	DocOutput	Object that describes the current output data for this transfer.

LastArticle

Format: `NNTPObject_LastArticle(ByVal articlenumber as long, Messageid as string)`

The `LastArticle` event occurs when the NNTP client control is set to the previous article in the newsgroup. This event is usually triggered by the `NNTPObject.SelectLastArticle` method.

Table 12-36 *LastArticle* Event Parameters

Parameter Name	Argument Type	Description
`articlenumber`	long	The article number of the last article.
`Messageid`	string	The messageid of the last article.

NextArticle

Format: `NNTPObject_NextArticle(ByVal articlenumber as long, Messageid as string)`

The `NextArticle` event occurs when the NNTP client control is set to the next article in the newsgroup. This event is usually triggered by the `NNTPObject.SelectNextArticle` method.

Table 12-37 ***NextArticle*** **Event Parameters**

Parameter Name	Argument Type	Description
`articlenumber`	long	The article number of the next article.
`Messageid`	string	The messageid of the next article.

ProtocolStateChanged

Format: `NNTPObject_ProtocolStateChanged(ByVal protocolstate as integer)`

The `ProtocolStateChanged` event occurs whenever the protocol state is changed.

Table 12-38 ***ProtocolStateChanged*** **Event Parameters**

Parameter Name	Argument Type	Description
`protocolstate`	integer	The value of the protocol state.

Table 12-39 ***protocolstate*** **Values**

protocolState **Value Name**	***protocolState*** **Value**	Description
`ftpBase`	0	**Base state:** Before a connection is established with the server.
`ftpAuthorization`	1	**Authorization state:** After connection is established and before the user has been granted access to the server.
`ftpTransaction`	2	**Transaction state:** After the user has been granted access to the server. The client can now interact with the server.

SelectGroup

Format: `NNTPObject_SelectGroup(ByVal newsgroup as string, ByVal firstarticle as long, ByVal lastarticle as long, ByVal messagecount as long)`

The SelectGroup event occurs in response to the SelectGroup method.

Table 12-40 *SelectGroup* Event Parameters

Parameter Name	Argument Type	Description
newsgroup	string	The name of the newsgroup.
firstarticle	long	The starting article number in the newsgroup.
lastarticle	long	The ending article number in the newsgroup.
messagecount	long	Total messages in the newsgroup.

StatArticle

Format: `NNTPObject_StatArticle(ByVal articlenumber as long, ByVal Messageid as string)`

The StatArticle event occurs after the StatArticle method is used. This event returns information about the current article.

Table 12-41 *StatArticle* Event Parameters

Parameter Name	Argument Type	Description
articlenumber	long	The article number of the current article.
Messageid	string	The messageid for the current article.

StateChanged

Format: `NNTPObject_StateChanged(ByVal state as integer)`

The StateChanged event occurs whenever the transport state is changed.

Table 12-42 *StateChanged* Event Parameters

Parameter Name	Argument Type	Description
state	integer	The value of the transport state.

Table 12-43 *state* Values

state Value Name	*state* Value	Description
prcConnecting	1	**Connecting state:** A connection has been requested and is waiting for an acknowledgment.
prcResolvingHost	2	**Resolving Host state:** Waiting for a host name to be translated into its IP address. (Not entered if an IP address was supplied as the RemoteHost property.)
prcHostResolved	3	**Host Resolved state:** After the host name has successfully translated into an IP address. (Not entered if an IP address was supplied as the RemoteHost property.)
prcConnected	4	**Connected state:** A connection has been successfully established.
prcDisconnecting	5	**Disconnecting state:** A request to disconnect has been requested.
prcDisconnected	6	**Disconnected state:** Before a connection is requested and after a connection has been closed.

TimeOut

Format: `NNTPObject_TimeOut(ByVal event as integer, continue as boolean)`

The `TimeOut` event occurs when the specified event does not occur within the interval defined in the `TimeOut` property for that event.

Table 12-44 *TimeOut* Event Parameters

Parameter Name	Argument Type	Description
event	integer	Event to which the timer interval applies.
continue	boolean	Determines if the timer will remain active.

Table 12-45 *event* Values

event Name	*event* Value	Description
prcConnectTimeout	1	If a connection is not made within the timeout period, the Timeout event is triggered.
prcReceiveTimeout	2	If no data arrives for a receive process within the timeout period, the Timeout event is triggered.
prcUserTimeout	65	User defined Timeout event.

Table 12-46 *continue* Values

continue Value	Description
True	The timer continues to run.
False	The timer stops.

Summary

In this chapter we discussed the NNTP client control. This control provides the basic functions needed to access Usenet news servers. Unlike the FTP ActiveX control, the DocInput and DocOutput objects must be used to handle communications with the NNTP server. The DocHeaders collection and the DocHeader object are also used by the NNTP control and the DocInput and DocOutput objects to simplify the process of building a program. These objects are discussed in the next chapter.

In case you want to check your answers to the questions in the Overview section, here are my answers:

- *What other objects are used by this control?*

  DocInput is used for information coming to this control.

  DocOutput is used for information leaving this control.

  icErrors is used to hold error information.

- *What methods are used to retrieve information about newsgroups?*

  GetArticleByArticleNumber and GetArticleByMessageId retrieve the header and the body of an article.

`GetBodyByArticleNumber` and `GetArticleByMessageId` retrieve the body of an article.

`GetHeaderByArticleNumber` and `GetArticleByMessageId` retrieve the header of an article.

The following methods retrieve information about newsgroups:

`ListGroups` retrieves all the newsgroups available on the server.

`ListNewGroups` retrieves the newsgroups created after a specified date.

- *What methods are used to manage a connection?*

`Connect` is used to connect to the remote server.

`AuthenticateRequest` executes when the server requests authentication information.

`AuthenticateResponse` returns the results of the authentication information sent to the server.

`Quit` is used to disconnect from the remote server.

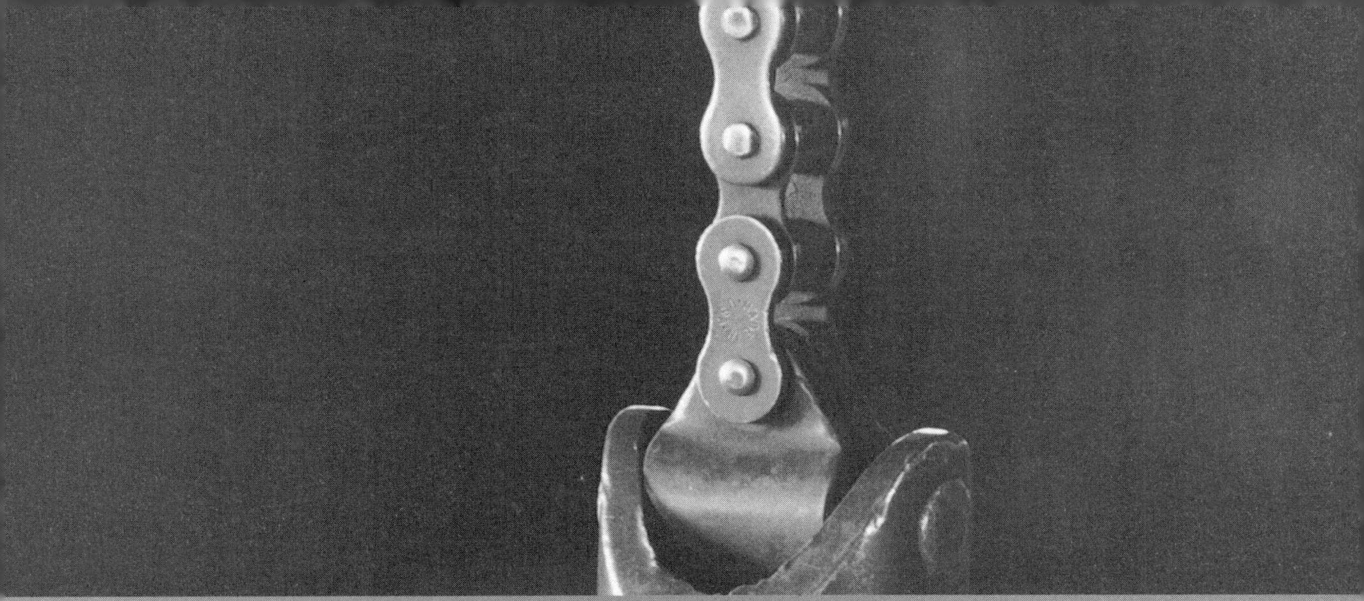

Chapter 13

The DocHeader, DocHeaders, DocInput, and DocOutput Objects

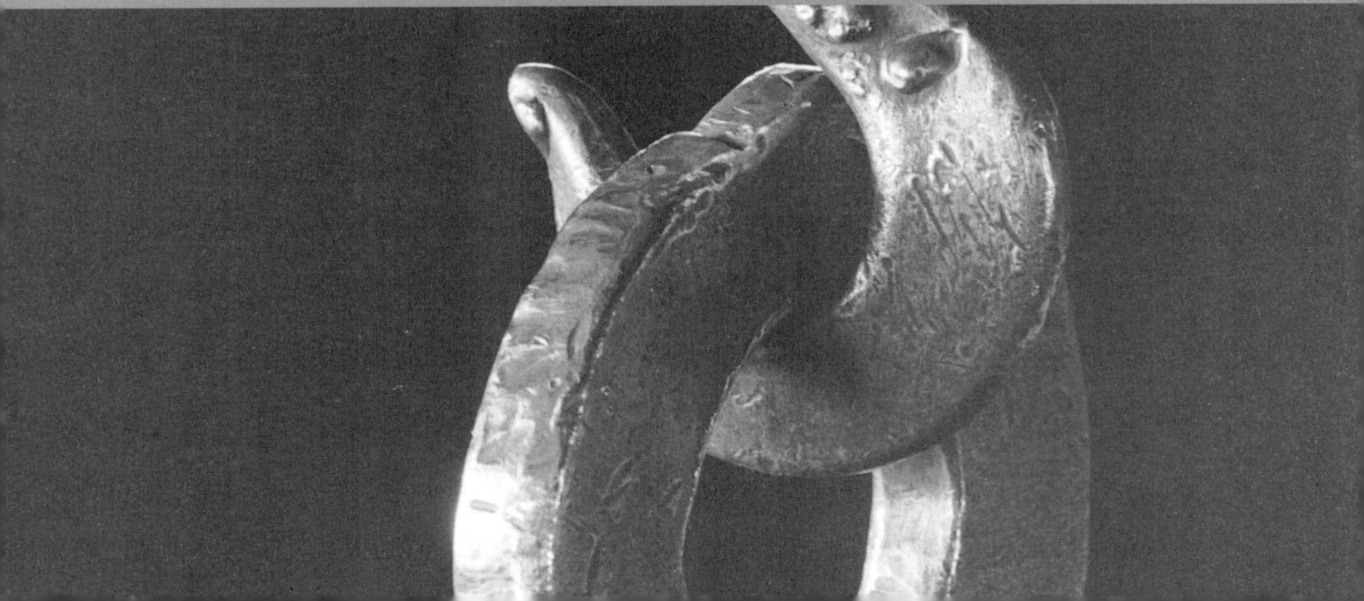

Overview

In this chapter, we discuss the properties and methods of the DocHeader, DocInput, and DocOutput objects, as well as the DocHeaders collection. These objects are available for all the client controls. We did not talk about these objects in the FTP ActiveX control section because that control has the option to use the DocObjects or the ListItem event. The NNTP control must use the DocObjects to handle transfers between the client and the server because it does not have any support objects similar to the FTP control's ListItem event.

The DocInput and DocOutput objects handle data as a stream of characters. It is up to the programmer to properly recognize the data contained in the stream of characters and to extract the formatted information.

By now you may be thinking, "This is yet another boring reference chapter," however, this chapter covers one of the most confusing parts of the Internet ActiveX controls. Take a few minutes to flip through the material, and then come back later when you realize you need more information about these objects.

By the end of this chapter, you should be able to answer the following questions:

- What is the difference between DocHeaders and DocHeader?
- What techniques are available for receiving data from a remote server?
- What is data linking?

Properties—DocHeaders Collection

The DocHeaders collection is a set of DocHeader objects. This object is used to store header information for a news article or mail message, and information is formatted according to RFC-1036. The header information is automatically parsed from the information returned from the server. For information that is sent to the server, header information is constructed separately from the data. The headers information and data are combined when sent to the remote server. Two properties are available: Count (the number of DocHeader objects in the collection) and Text (a list of the header values available).

Count

Format: `DocHeadersObject.Count`

The `Count` property returns the number of `DocHeader` objects in the `DocHeaders` collection.

Text

Format: `DocHeadersObject.Text [ = string ]`

The `Text` property contains the list of headers available in MIME (Multipurpose Internet Mail Extensions) or RFC-1036 news article header format.

Methods—DocHeaders Collection

`DocHeaders` provide four methods to manage the set of headers in the collection. They are `Add` to create a new `DocHeader` object, `Clear` to delete all of the `DocHeader` objects in the collection, `Item` to reference a single `DocHeader` object, and `Remove` to delete a single `DocHeader` object.

Add

Format: `DocHeadersObject.Add name, value`

The `Add` method inserts a new `DocHeader` object into the `DocHeaders` collection. `Name` is used to hold the header keyword, and `value` is used to hold the text associated with the keyword. Together these items represent a single line in a news article or mail message.

Table 13-1 ***Add*** **Method Arguments**

Argument Name	Argument Type	Description
`name`	variant	The name of a header keyword.
`value`	variant	The value for the specified header keyword.

Clear

Format: `DocHeadersObject.Clear`

The `Clear` method is used to remove all the objects in the `DocHeaders` collection.

Item

Format: `DocHeadersObject.Item(index)`

The `Item` method returns the `DocHeader` object specified by `index`.

Table 13-2 *Item* Method Arguments

Argument Name	Argument Type	Description
index	variant	Identifies the `DocHeader` object.

Remove

Format: `DocHeadersObject.Remove index`

The `Remove` method deletes the `DocHeader` object specified by `index` from the `DocHeaders` collection.

Table 13-3 *Remove* Method Arguments

Argument Name	Argument Type	Description
index	variant	Identifies the `DocHeader` object.

Properties—DocHeader Object

The `DocHeader` object is very simple, consisting of only two properties: `Name` and `Value`. Basically this is a single line in a news article or mail message. It can contain information like Subject and text that would be included in the subject line or From and the userid that is associated with the article or message.

Name

Format: `DocHeaderObject.Name [= string]`

The `Name` property sets or returns a string that contains a valid MIME header (without the colon). This property is usually set by using the `DocHeaders.Add` method.

Value

Format: `DocHeaderObject.Value [= string]`

The `Value` property sets or returns a string that contains the value associated with the `DocHeaderObject.Name` property.

Properties—DocInput Object

The `DocInput` object is used to generate data that is sent to a server using the ActiveX controls. Because most documents are relatively complex, consisting of MIME header information as well as a body of text, it is useful to have a tool like the `DocInput` object to pull it all together.

BytesTotal

Format: `DocInputObject.BytesTotal`

The `BytesTotal` property returns the number of bytes to be transferred. This property returns zero if the value is not known.

BytesTransferred

Format: `DocInputObject.BytesTransferred`

The `BytesTransferred` property returns the number of bytes transferred. When the transfer begins, the `BytesTransferred` property is set to zero. Then before the `DocInput` occurs each time, the `BytesTransferred` property is updated. Combined with the information in the `BytesTotal` property, displaying a progress bar becomes very easy. Note that this information is only valid during a transfer and should not be used after the transfer is finished.

DocLink

Format: `DocInputObject.DocLink [= string]`

The `DocLink` property returns or sets a string value that is used with data linking. When the `DocInputObject.DocLink` property is set to the `DocOutputObject.DocLink` property, data that is passed to the `DocOutput` object is passed to the `DocInput` object. Note that the `DocInputObject.FileName` property must be set to an empty string, or the `FileName` property overrides the DocLink Property. If no values are specified for the `DocLink` and `FileName` parameters, the data is expected to be created by the `DocInput` event.

One case where this may be useful is when you want to mail a news article. As the article is retrieved from an NNTP client control, the NNTP's `DocOutput` object passes the stream of characters to the SMTP's `DocInput` object. Then the SMTP's `DocInput` object passes the data onto the SMTP server.

FileName

Format: `DocInputObject.FileName [= string]`

The `FileName` property returns or sets a string value that contains the name of a file to be read and sent as input. Setting the `FileName` property to a non-empty value causes the `DocLink` property to be set to an empty string. If both the `FileName` and `DocLink` properties have no values, the `DocInput` event generates the data to be sent to the server.

Headers

Format: `DocInputObject.Headers`

The `Headers` property returns a reference to a `DocHeaders` collection.

PushStreamMode

Format: `DocInputObject.PushStreamMode [= boolean]`

The `PushStreamMode` property sets or returns a boolean value that indicates the state of the PushStream mode. Setting the `FileName` or `DocLink` properties automatically sets the `PushStreamMode`.

Table 13-4 *PushStreamMode* Values

PushStreamMode Value	Description
`true`	The control is in Push mode.
`false`	The control is in Pull mode.

State

Format: `DocInputObject.State`

The `State` property returns an integer and is used to determine which state the object is in. This is important when processing data through the `DocInput` event to determine what actions are necessary to process the data.

Table 13-5 *State* Values

State Value Name	*State* Value	Description
`icDocNone`	0	No transfer is in progress.
`icDocBegin`	1	The transfer being initiated.
`icDocHeaders`	2	Document headers are being transferred.

continues

Table 13-5 Continued

State Value Name	*State* Value	Description
icDocData	3	Document data is being transferred.
icDocError	4	An error occurred during the transfer.
icDocEnd	5	The transfer is finished.

Suspended

Format: `DocInputObject.Suspended`

The `Suspended` property returns a boolean flag that indicates whether the transfer process is suspended or not. The transfer is suspended by using the `Suspend` method.

Table 13-6 *Suspended* Values

TimeOut Event Name	Description
true	The transfer process is suspended.
false	The transfer process is not suspended.

Methods—DocInput Object

The `DocInput` object has methods available to manage the data stream. `GetData` retrieves data from the server. `Setdata` sends data to the server. `Suspend` pauses or resumes the data flow. `PushStream` provides an alternate way to transfer data in the data stream.

GetData

Format: `DocInputObject.GetData data [,type]`

The `GetData` method retrieves the data that caused the `DocInput` event to be called. If there is not sufficient data to fill the data type, the variable is set to `Empty`.

Table 13-7 *GetData* Method Arguments

Argument Name	Argument Type	Description
`data`	variant	The current block of data.
`type`	long	Optional type of the variable that receives the data.

Table 13-8 *type* Values

type Value Name	State Value	Description
`vbByte`	17	Byte data type.
`vbInteger`	2	Integer (2 bytes) data type.
`vbLong`	3	Long (4 bytes) integer data type.
`vbSingle`	4	Single (4 bytes) floating point data type.
`vbDouble`	5	Double (8 bytes) floating point data type.
`vbCurrency`	6	Currency data type.
`vbDate`	7	Date data type.
`vbBoolean`	11	Boolean data type.
`vbError`	10	Undefined data type.
`vbString`	8	String data type.
`vbByte+vbArray`	8209	Byte array data type.

PushStream

Format: `DocInputObject.PushStream`

The `PushStream` method provides an alternate method of sending data to a remote system. When the `PushStreamMode` is set to `true`, you can use the `PushStream` method to call the `DocInput` event of an ActiveX control to process data that is ready to be sent.

Normally (when the `PushStreamMode` property is set to `false`) when the server is ready for data, the `DocInput` event is invoked. Also remember this method is not available when either the `FileName` property or the `DocLink` property is set.

SetData

Format: `DocInputObject.SetData data`

The `SetData` method is used to send data to the remote server using the `DocInput` event.

Table 13-9 *SetData* Method Arguments

Argument Name	Argument Type	Description
`data`	variant	The current block of data to be transmitted.

Suspend

Format: `DocInputObject.Suspend suspend`

The `Suspend` method is used to temporarily stop the data transfer process. For each call to `Suspend` with suspend set to `true`, there must be another call to `Suspend` with suspend set to `false`. Otherwise, the data transfer process will never complete.

Table 13-10 *Suspend* Method Arguments

Argument Name	Argument Type	Description
`suspend`	boolean	Stops or starts the transfer process.

Table 13-11 *suspend* Values

suspend Value	Description
`true`	Suspends the transfer process.
`false`	Resumes the transfer process.

Properties—DocOutput Object

The `DocOutput` object is used to receive data from a remote server. It assists with the unpackaging process to extract header information from the data.

BytesTotal

Format: `DocOutputObject.BytesTotal`

The `BytesTotal` property returns the number of bytes to be transferred, or a zero if the value is not known.

BytesTransferred

Format: `DocOutputObject.BytesTransferred`

The `BytesTransferred` property returns the number of bytes transferred. When the transfer begins, the `BytesTransferred` property is set to zero. Then, before each `DocOutput` event occurs, the `BytesTransferred` property is updated. Combined with the information in the `BytesTotal` property, this makes it easy to display a progress bar. Note that this information is only valid during a transfer and should not be used after the transfer is finished.

DocLink

Format: `DocOutputObject.DocLink`

The `DocLink` property returns a string value that is used with data linking. When the `DocInputObject.DocLink` property is set to the `DocOutputObject.DocLink` property, data that is passed to the `DocOutput` object is passed to the `DocInput` object. Note that unlike the `DocInput` object, output can be directed via data linking, files, and data streaming.

FileName

Format: `DocOutputObject.FileName [= string]`

The `FileName` property returns or sets a string value that contains the name of a file to be written with the data that has been received from the remote server.

Headers

Format: `DocOutputObject.Headers`

The `Headers` property returns a reference to a `DocHeaders` collection.

PushStreamMode

Format: `DocOutputObject.PushStreamMode`

The `PushStreamMode` property returns a boolean value that indicates the state of the PushStream mode. Unlike the `DocInput` object, this property is read only.

Table 13-12 *PushStreamMode* Values

PushStreamMode Value	Description
`true`	The control is in Push mode.
`false`	The control is in Pull mode.

State

Format: `DocOuputObject.State`

The `State` property returns an integer and is used to determine which state the object is in. This is important when processing data through the `DocOutput` event to determine what actions are necessary to process the data.

Table 13-13 ***State*** **Values**

State Value Name	*State* Value	Description
icDocNone	0	No transfer is in progress.
icDocBegin	1	The transfer is being initiated.
icDocHeaders	2	Document headers are being transferred.
icDocData	3	Document data is being transferred.
icDocError	4	An error occured during the transfer.
icDocEnd	5	The transfer is finished.

Suspended

Format: `DocOutputObject.Suspended`

The `Suspended` property returns a boolean flag that indicates whether the transfer process is suspended or not. The transfer is suspended by using the `Suspend` method.

Table 13-14 ***Suspended*** **Values**

Suspended Event Name	Description
true	The transfer process is suspended.
false	The transfer process is not suspended.

Methods—DocOutput Object

The `DocOutput` object has methods that almost totally mirror the `DocInput` object's methods except for the direction the data is sent.

GetData

Format: `DocOutputObject.GetData data [,type]`

The `GetData` method is used to retrieve the data that causes the `DocInput` event to be called. If there is not sufficient data to fill the data type, the variable is set to `Empty`.

Table 13-15 *GetData* Method Arguments

Argument Name	Argument Type	Description
`data`	variant	The current block of data.
`type`	long	Optional type of the variable that receives the data.

Table 13-16 *type* Values

type Value Name	State Value	Description
`vbByte`	17	Byte data type.
`VbInteger`	2	Integer (2 bytes) data type.
`vbLong`	3	Long (4 bytes) integer data type.
`vbSingle`	4	Single (4 bytes) floating point data type.
`vbDouble`	5	Double (8 bytes) floating point data type.
`vbCurrency`	6	Currency data type.
`vbDate`	7	Date data type.
`vbBoolean`	11	Boolean data type.
`vbError`	10	Undefined data type.
`vbString`	8	String data type.
`vbByte+vbArray`	8209	Byte array data type.

SetData

Format: `DocOutputObject.SetData data`

The `SetData` method is used to send data to the remote server using the `DocOutput` event.

Table 13-17 *SetData* Method Arguments

Argument Name	Argument Type	Description
`data`	variant	The current block of data to be transmitted.

Suspend

Format: `DocOutputObject.Suspend suspend`

The `Suspend` method is used to stop the data transfer process temporarily. For each call to `Suspend` with `suspend` set to `true`, there must be another call to `Suspend` with `suspend` set to `false`, otherwise the data transfer process will never complete.

Table 13-18 *Suspend* Method Arguments

Argument Name	Argument Type	Description
`suspend`	boolean	Stops or starts the transfer process.

Table 13-19 *suspend* Values

suspend Value	Description
`true`	Suspends the transfer process.
`false`	Resumes the transfer process.

Summary

In this chapter we discussed the `DocHeader` collection and the `DocHeader`, `DocInput`, and `DocOutput` objects.

In case you want to check your answers to the questions in the Overview section, here are the answers:

- *What is the difference between* `DocHeaders` *and* `DocHeaders`*?*

  The `DocHeader` object consists of a single header keyword and a value, while the `DocHeaders` object consists of a set of `DocHeader` objects.

- *What techniques are available for receiving data from a remote server?*

  Data can be stored a file, received inside the `DocOutput` object, and then processed as part of the program, or it can be sent to `DocInput` object using data linking.

- *What is data linking?*

  Data linking occurs when the output of a `DocOutput` object is connected into the input of a `DocInput` object. An example where this would be useful is when you want to mail a news article.

Chapter 14

NewsRunner

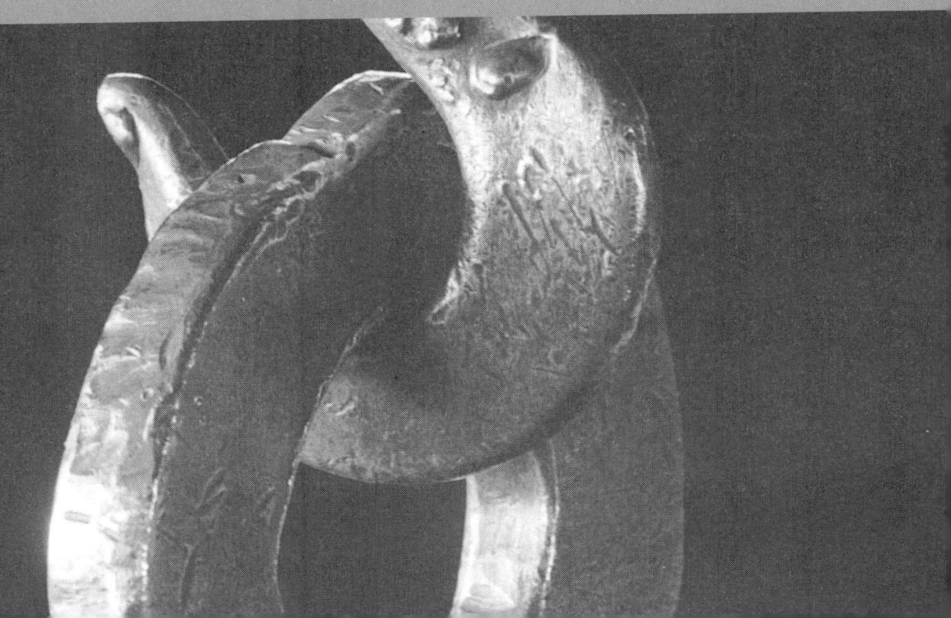

Overview

In this chapter, we build a program called NewsRunner using the News ActiveX client control. Like the FTPRunner program we built in Chapter 10, this program is not a replacement for a commercial newsreader program. It does, however, provide all the basic functions that are necessary in a newsreader.

The complete source code is provided on the CD-ROM, so I'm only going to present the more interesting parts of the code, including such topics as how to connect to the news server, how to retrieve newsgroup information, how to retrieve article header information, and how to retrieve the articles themselves.

By the end of this chapter, you should be able to answer the following questions:

- What are some problems one might encounter when connecting to a remote computer?
- What is a spin loop?

How to Use NewsRunner

Unlike the FTP program, which consisted of only one primary form, the NewsRunner program has three main forms. These forms mirror the hierarchy of the Usenet news structure. The first form is the NewsRunner form where all newsgroups are displayed. The second form is the ArticleList form where the list of articles in a particular newsgroup are displayed. The third form is used to display and post news articles. Like the FTPRunner program, the user can execute functions by selecting either menu commands or clicking toolbar buttons (with the exceptions of the Exit and About functions).

In the NewsRunner form shown in figure 14-1, the Connect button (and the Actions | Connect menu item) cause the program to connect to the remote system. If a remote system has not been specified, the Connect to Remote Host form is displayed so the user can fill in the name of the remote NNTP system along with the port number to use (see figure 14-2). Clicking OK on this form continues with the connection process. When a connection has successfully been made, the light bulb changes from white to yellow. Clicking this button again closes the connection and causes the light bulb's color to return to white.

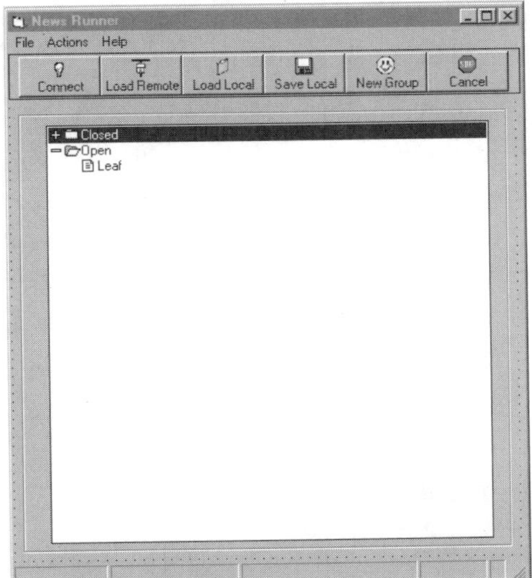

FIGURE 14-1

The NewsRunner form.

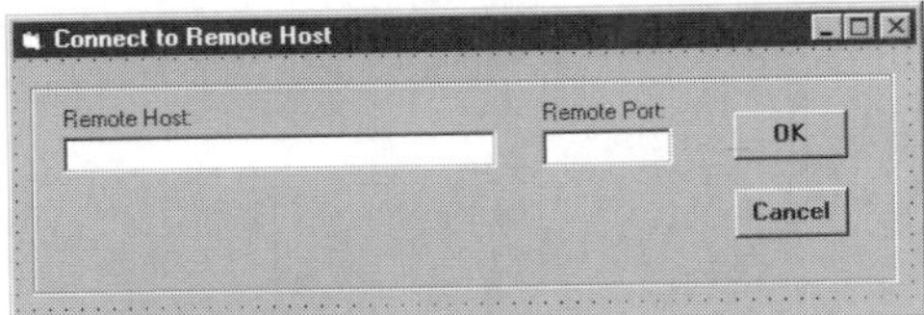

FIGURE 14-2

The Connect to Remote Host form.

When the connection is established, the rest of the NewsRunner functions become available. Load Remote retrieves a current copy of the newsgroups from the server and displays them in the outline box below the buttons. The Load Local command loads a file of newsgroups from the PC's hard disk. The Save Local saves the information in the outline box to a disk file. The New Group button prompts you for the name of a newsgroup and then displays the ArticleList form with all the articles in that newsgroup. The Cancel button is used to cancel the current action from the NNTP client control. Use this button with care because it often leaves the control in a state where no other functions can be executed.

The outline box that contains the list of newsgroups works just like you would expect. To see the comp.lang.basic.visual.misc newsgroup, you first open the comp folder, then the lang folder, the basic folder, and finally the visual folder. Inside the visual folder, you see 3rdparty, announce, database, and misc. Double-clicking misc displays the ArticleList form with all the articles in the comp.lang.basic.visual.misc newsgroup.

The ArticleList form shown in figure 14-3 contains only three buttons: Refresh, New Group, and Return. The Refresh button goes to the server and loads all the news articles for the current newsgroup. The New Group button works exactly the same as the New Group button on the NewsRunner form: it prompts the user for the name of a newsgroup, and then loads the article information into the ArticleList form. The Return button simply closes the ArticleList form and returns to the NewsRunner form. Double-clicking an article listed in the main part of the ArticleList form loads the article into the Article form.

FIGURE 14-3

The ArticleList form.

The buttons on the Article form provide easy access to various NewsRunner functions (see figure 14-4). Previous and Next provide a way to look at the last or next article in the newsgroup in article number order. Post and Reply prepare the form to send an article to the news server, and the Send button actually completes the Post or Reply process. The Return button simply returns to the ArticleList form.

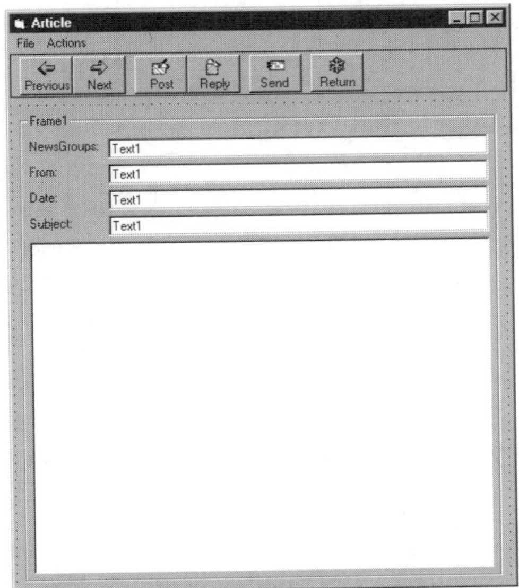

FIGURE 14-4

The Article form.

The Program Structure

This program contains three main forms, two secondary forms, and one module. The main forms are NewsRunner, ArticleList, and Article; the secondary forms are NewsConnect and AboutNews; the module is NewsGlobal.

The NewsGlobal module includes a few definitions that are common to all the routines and two subroutines: Initialize and Main. In Listing 14-1, I show the global definitions. Note that after the module definition, I include the highly recommended `Option Explicit` statement. I know I talked about it in Chapter 10, but if you want to build complex and reliable Visual Basic programs, you really should use this statement. I've used more programming languages than I can count, and in every language that automatically declares variables, I get into trouble. By now you have seen that I use the variable `i` as a general purpose loop counter or index pointer throughout my programs. (Yes, I really did write FORTRAN programs a long time ago!)

Now consider what happens if I did not declare `i` in a subroutine and just started using it. Best case, Visual Basic will declare a floating point variable for `i` that takes more CPU time to do the arithmetic and has to be converted to an integer (or long) when using it as an array index. Your program will run a little slower, but for the most part no one will probably notice. Big deal. But if you happen to misspell it (trust me, you can; I've done it myself), Visual Basic will automatically declare it and assign it a value of zero. This can cause serious problems when you try to execute the program. If the block of code is relatively complex, you may not be able to find the problem for a day or two, which is too much time to spend on such a simple error. Take my advice and just use it. You'll thank me one day down the road when you see a highly caffeinated fellow programmer pulling his hair out over an error that you recognize immediately!

You see that there are only five variables that are declared global: `NewsConnected`, `NewsStartTime`, `NewsType`, `CurrentArticle`, and `CurrentGroup`. Of these five, you saw similar variables in FTP for `NewsConnected` and `NewsStartTime`. `NewsConnected` is `true` when a connection has successfully been made to a remote NNTP server. `NewsStartTime` is a date/time variable that is set to the time when the connection to the server was made.

One new variable is `NewsType`. This variable holds a value that is used by the `DocOutput` routine to determine the type of data transmission. Remember when I talked about `DocOutput` in Chapter 13? I said it was a useful object to have because it simplifies the handling of header information. What I did not go into detail about was the fact that `DocOutput` does not really know anything about the type of data you are receiving. In the case of NewsRunner, we will be receiving three basic types of data from the server: a list of newsgroup names, header information that is to be displayed in the ArticleList form, and header and body information that is to be displayed in the Article form. `NewsType` is used to differentiate between these three types of data transfers. We see more about this later when we talk about the `News_DocOutput` routine.

The other new variables are `CurrentArticle` and `CurrentGroup`. These are used to pass the current article number and the current newsgroup to other routines that may want to read these values. For example, the Article form takes advantage of this information and displays the article number as the frame header that surrounds the article itself.

Listing 14-1 Global Variables

```
' Form/Module:   NewsGlobal
' Author:        Wayne S. Freeze
' Version        1.0
```

```
'  Date Written:  26 June 1996
'  Date Revised:  26 June 1996
'  Description:
'     This module initializes the global variables
'     and starts the main News form.

Option Explicit

'  True when the program is talking to a remote
'  system, false otherwise
Global NewsConnected As Integer

'  Used to track when the FTP connection was
'  started
Global NewsStartTime As Date

'  Define the type of data being retrieved
'  from the NNTP server
'  0 = undefined
'  1 = Newsgroup List
'  2 = Article List
'  3 = Article
Global NewsType As Integer

'  The article number
Global CurrentArticle As Long

'  The current news group
Global CurrentGroup As String
```

The main subroutine is shown in Listing 14-2. It is nearly identical to the main program we discussed in Chapter 10 for the FTP program. The only difference is the name of the form that is displayed. Why mess with something that works?

Listing 14-2 The *Main* Subroutine

```
Sub main()

'  The is the main starting point for the program
'  Initialize the global variables and show the
'  main form.  When the main form unloads itself
'  the program will end.

Initialize

NewsRunner.Show 0

End Sub
```

Unlike the FTPRunner program, which has only one main form, the NewsRunner program has three. I could have chosen to use the Multiple Document Interface and place all three forms in one big form, or I could do something fancy with the tab control, but I personally like the way Visual Basic pops unconnected forms all over the place. That way I can place the forms where I feel most comfortable with them and go directly to the form I want from the taskbar. (Besides, it takes less work to do it this way than any of the other approaches.)

This approach, however, has one small drawback, which is the placement of the NNTP control and all of the functions that access the control. For the sake of simplicity (and future expandibility), I put all of the important code into this NewsRunner form and provide standard routines that other forms can call to use NNTP functions. Also, the NNTP supports a number of extensions that I have chosen not to use. I figure that once you see the basic functions implemented, implementing the extensions is merely a matter of checking the appropriate property to see if the extension is available and using an extension rather than the standard method. In either case, the results should be similar to what I've included in the program.

Starting with the `Form_Load` routine shown in Listing 14-3, you can see that I followed the same basic procedure I used in the FTPRunner program. I set the timer at one second intervals (or a thousand milliseconds) and start it when I connect to the server. Then

I initialize the statusbar and disable the toolbar buttons, which are not available until I connect to the server.

Listing 14-3 The NewsRunner *Form_Load* Subroutine

```
Private Sub Form_Load()

'  When we load this form, initialize controls
Timer1.Interval = 1000

StatusBar.Panels(1).Text = "Not Connected"
StatusBar.Panels(2).Text = "xxx"
StatusBar.Panels(4).Text = "00:00:00"
StatusBar.Panels(5).Text = " "

Toolbar.Buttons("Load Remote").Enabled = False
Toolbar.Buttons("New Group").Enabled = False
Toolbar.Buttons("Cancel").Enabled = False

End Sub
```

The toolbar buttons and menu commands essentially work the same way, so I'm going to talk about how the toolbar buttons work. The complete code is on the CD-ROM, so if you are curious about how the menu commands work, start Visual Basic and load the NewsRunner program. The toolbar code can be found in Listing 14-4.

The Connect button works like many power switches—push it to turn it on, and push it again to turn it off. In this case, turning it on (`NewsConnected = False`) causes the program to run the `DoConnect` routine, while turning it off (`NewsDisconnected = True`) runs the `DoDisconnect` routine.

The Load Remote button is one part of the code I'm not really happy with. (It took a week of writing and rewriting to get it this good. I'll discuss the problems in more detail later when I talk about retrieving information from the news server.) Essentially, I broke this function into three different phases: Retrieve all the newsgroups from the server, sort them, and then load them into the outline control on the NewsRunner form. The first task was relatively easy. The second was a little more difficult. There is no function in Visual Basic to sort a string array, so I wrote the newsgroups into a disk file and called the DOS sort to sort the file. This was very quick, but I had no way to determine when the sort was finished, so I placed `MsgBox` statements before and after the sort so that the user could watch the sort execute and continue when the sort was finished. After the sort finishes, I load the file into the Outline1 control so that the user may choose the newsgroup that he or she wants to view. I talk about this a lot more when I discuss the `DoLoadGroups` and the `AddNewsGroup` functions later in the chapter.

The Load Local button is very straightforward. Because I already had a routine to load a disk file into the Outline1 control, I chose to use that function to load the disk file. The Save Local button simply copies the contents of the outline control to a disk file.

The New Group button is a way to bypass the outline control and simply type in the name of the newsgroup that you want to view. This is handy to use when testing various parts of the ArticleList and Article forms, though a user will find it a little difficult to use because he must enter the exact name of the newsgroup. While alt.test may be easy to type, try typing comp.lang.visual.basic.misc correctly.

The Cancel button was added late in the development of the program when I encountered some problems with the `GetHeaderByArticleNumber` method. Pushing this button causes the `NNTP.Cancel` method to run, which stops whatever the NNTP control is doing. However, this causes other problems because the NNTP control apparently does not recover cleanly from this situation and you eventually have to close the connection and restart the program.

Listing 14-4 The *`Toolbar_ButtonClick`* Subroutine

```
Private Sub Toolbar_ButtonClick(ByVal Button As Button)

Dim s As Long

'  Handle the Toolbar Buttons
Select Case Button.Key

Case "Connect"
```

```
    If NewsConnected Then
        DoDisconnect

    Else
        DoConnect
    End If

Case "Load Remote"
    DoGetAllGroups
    MsgBox "Newsgroups loaded"

    s = Shell("\SORTNEWS.BAT")

    MsgBox "Newsgroups sorted"

    DoLoadGroups

Case "Load Local"
    DoLoadGroups

Case "Save Local"
    DoSaveGroups

Case "New Group"
    GetNewsGroup InputBox("Enter the name of a newsgroup")
    ArticleList.Show 0

Case "Cancel"
    News.Cancel

End Select

End Sub
```

Connecting to the Server

The `DoConnect` subroutine (see Listing 14-5) establishes a connection to a remote NNTP server. For the most part, this routine is very similar to the logic used for FTPRunner. The first part of the code asks the user for the name and port number of an NNTP server by displaying the ConnectNews form. With this information, it then displays the server name in the frame that surrounds the outline control.

At this point, a value for the start time is saved into `NewsStartTime` and the timer is started. Then the `NNTP.Connect` method is executed. This starts a number of things happening. First, the host name needs to be translated into a numeric IP address (assuming that a host name was entered as the server name—this step would be skipped if the IP address was entered). We can watch the control go through this part of the connect process by examining the protocol's state value (`News.State`) and checking to see what state the protocol is in. Specifically, we check for `prcConnecting`, `prcResolvingHost`, and `prcHostResolved` in a loop that executes `DoEvents` between each test. (Remember, we have to give control back to Windows periodically so that the control has CPU resources to do its thing.) If we see anything except `prcConnected` after this phase, we know that there is a problem making the connection and may as well give up and try another server.

The next phase involves some more waiting until the `ProtocolState` is ready for processing and the server has a reply code of either 200 (posting permitted) or 201 (posting is not permitted). Any other reply code means that there is a problem with the connection and we cannot proceed. This could range from something like the server is offline to the server not accepting connections from your IP address.

After the connection is established, the toolbar buttons that were disabled until a connection is made are now enabled. The `NewsConnected` flag also needs to be set and the light bulb in the Connect button needs to be turned on.

Listing 14-5 The *DoConnect* Subroutine

```
Private Sub DoConnect()

'   Connect to the remote News server.

If Len(Frame1.Caption) = 0 Then
```

```
   ConnectNews.Show 1
   If Len(News.RemoteHost) = 0 Then
      Exit Sub
   Else
       Frame1.Caption = News.RemoteHost
   End If
End If

NewsStartTime = Now
Timer1.Enabled = True

News.Connect
Do While (News.State = prcConnecting) _
   Or (News.State = prcResolvingHost) _
   Or (News.State = prcHostResolved)
   DoEvents
Loop

If News.State <> prcConnected Then
   MsgBox "Error in DoConnect(Connect). Unable to connect to news server."
   Exit Sub
End If

Do While (News.State = prcConnected) _
   And (News.ProtocolState = 1)
   DoEvents
Loop

Do While News.Busy
   DoEvents
Loop

If (News.ReplyCode <> 200) And (News.ReplyCode <> 201) Then
```

continues

Listing 14-5 Continued

```
   MsgBox "Error in DoConnect(Connect). Reply text is: " & News.ReplyString
End If

NewsConnected = True
Toolbar.Buttons("Connect").Image = 2
Toolbar.Buttons("Load Remote").Enabled = True
StatusBar.Panels(1).Text = "Connected"

End Sub
```

Disconnecting from the Server

Listing 14-6 shows how easy it is to disconnect from the server. Essentially you just use the `News.Quit` method to send an RFC-977 `Quit` command to the server and wait for the server to return a reply code of 205, meaning that you have successfully disconnected. Then the program cleans up the flags and buttons and panels and timers so that it can reconnect again later.

Listing 14-6 The *DoDisconnect* Subroutine

```
Private Sub DoDisconnect()

'  Close the connection, reset the flags and
'  buttons and clear the directory and file
'  information

News.Quit
Do While News.Busy
   DoEvents
Loop
```

```
If (News.ReplyCode <> 205) Then
   MsgBox "Error in DoDisConnect(Quit). Reply text is: " & News.ReplyString
End If

NewsConnected = False
Timer1.Enabled = False
Toolbar.Buttons("Connect").Image = 1
Toolbar.Buttons("Load Remote").Enabled = False
StatusBar.Panels(1).Text = "Not Connected"

End Sub
```

Retrieving Information from the News Server

Until now, everything we did was nearly identical to what we did with the FTPRunner program. That is because all the controls basically work the same way for establishing connections. From now on, however, we see a lot of different functions that are all very specific to reading Usenet news. Retrieving the newsgroups from the server is a three-step process, as we saw in the toolbar code: get the groups from the server, sort them, and finally load them into the outline control.

Why are these three steps necessary? Three reasons: First, the list of newsgroups is not in alphabetical order when it is sent from the server. Even if a particular server sends them in sorted order, it is not a good idea to assume that all servers will do so. Second, I found that both the Outline and TreeView controls are relatively slow to load large numbers of unsorted records. Loading the records in sorted order makes the time to load all the newsgroups barely tolerable, though not what I really consider acceptable. Third, Visual Basic does not have any sorting functions. I tried a quick bubble sort and could not get the speed I felt I needed to achieve a tolerable level of performance.

The real solution is to do something other than what I did. This is what Microsoft chose to do in its examples because it used either an unsorted TextBox or a database. Of the two solutions, the database is probably better, but it requires distributing all the database controls and DLLs with the newsreader package, which makes the package relatively large. The TextBox approach has a problem with the 64KB limit of the size of the TextBox. Because I was testing against two NNTP servers with about 3,500 and 9,500 newsgroups, the simple Microsoft program would not run.

An alternate approach is to write a C language subroutine that can be called by Visual Basic to do the sort. This is relatively easy to write, but it still leaves the problem of the long time it takes the Outline and TreeView controls to load the information. Probably the best alternative is one in which the data is loaded into the control only for those newsgroups that need to be displayed. Thus the lengthy load time can be replaced with shorter load times. But you still may have long load times when you have to load a lot of newsgroups.

Another option is to not bother sorting the newsgroups and let the user specify a keyword and then search the list for a set of acceptable matches. Entries selected by the user can then be added to a short list of favorite groups. There are a number of other alternatives that could be used. This discussion could go on for pages, but I'm going to stop here. As quote from a number of other books I've read over the years, "The solution to this problem is left as an exercise for the reader."

DoGetAllGroups

The `DoGetAllGroups` subroutine is used to start a transfer of all the newsgroups on the server to the NewsRunner program (see Listing 14-7). Executing the `News.ListGroups` method results in the NNTP control issuing a RFC-977 `LIST` command to the server. The server then responds with a list of newsgroups that the NNTP control returns to the NewsRunner program using the `DocOutput` event. Because the `DocOutput` event does not know where the output is generated, I need to set `NewsType` to identify that the type of output is a list of newsgroups. I'll defer the rest of the discussion about how the `DocOutput` routine processes the returned data until we cover the other routines that returns data from the server through the `DocOutput` event.

Listing 14-7 The *DoGetAllGroups* Subroutine

```
Private Sub DoGetAllGroups()

'  Get a copy of all newsgroups into a disk file for
```

```
'  later processing

NewsType = 1

News.ListGroups

Do While News.Busy
   DoEvents
Loop

If News.ReplyCode <> 215 Then
   MsgBox "Error in DoGetAllGroups(ListGroups). Reply text is: " & News.ReplyString
End If

NewsType = 0

End Sub
```

GetNewsGroup

Moving from the previous problem to the next one, I'm going to talk about the `GetNewsGroup` function (see Listing 14-8). This function is used to select a newsgroup and display its contents in the ArticleList form. For this type of data, I set `NewsType` to two and begin the real work. The same function handles both loading a new newsgroup and refreshing the current group. The refresh process can be done by specifying this function with the current newsgroup, or by calling it with a null string as the group name. In the latter case, it assumes that you want to reload the current group.

The next step is to load the current newsgroup name into the frame that surrounds the list of articles in the form, and then save the specified newsgroup name into the global variable `CurrentGroup`. By issuing the `News.SelectGroup` method, the NNTP client control sends an RFC-977 `Group` command to the NNTP server. This makes the specified newsgroup the current group and makes the first available article in that group the current article on the server.

Because there is nothing the program can do but wait until the server responds to the Group command, I put the program into a *spin loop* (yes, I know that this is a mainframe term, but it fits) to wait for the News.Busy flag to become false. If I do not receive the proper reply code (211), I display an error message and then exit the function.

Continuing on with the program, I now request header information for each of the articles in the newsgroup. Assuming that the NNTP control worked properly, I issue a News.GetHeaderByArticleNumber (which issues an RFC-977 Head command) without any parameters to retrieve information on the current article.

After much pain and suffering, however, I discovered that this method does not properly return data in DocOutput. I attempted a fix (which we see later), but that did not work either, so I was forced to retrieve the entire article (using the RFC-977 Article command) even though I only wanted the header information. This causes significant performance problems, especially if the articles you retrieve are longer than one or two lines.

The best way to solve this problem is to retrieve the information using the GetOverView and GetOverViewFormat methods (assuming that they are available on your news server). This should perform much better than the method I used, and may even perform better than the GetHeaderByArticle method. In fact, this routine would be a good place to check the OverviewSupported property and use the GetOverView method if it is available. (You may want to consider trying this for yourself.)

When you really look at the rest of the function, you end up with a loop that waits for a reply code of 421 and then executes two NNTP methods: the GetArticleByArticleNumber method and the SetNextArticle method. The rest of the loop involves spin loops to check for the ActiveX control's busy state after each NNTP method used, followed by a check of the reply code to determine if an error really occurred. Note that a reply code of 220 is generated in response to a successful Article command, and a reply code of 221 is generated in response to a successful Head command. The 421 reply code is returned by the SetNextArticle method (which issues the RFC-977 Next command) and means that there are no more articles in the newsgroup.

Listing 14-8 The *GetNewsGroup* Function

```
Function GetNewsGroup(g As String) As Integer

'  Specify NewsType to retrive a list of articles in the
```

```
'  DocOutput routine, for the specified newsgroup.
'  DocOutput will put the information directly onto the
'  ArticleList form.

NewsType = 2

If Len(g) = 0 Then
   g = CurrentGroup
End If

ArticleList.Frame1.Caption = g
CurrentGroup = g

News.SelectGroup g
Do While News.Busy
   DoEvents
Loop

If News.ReplyCode <> 211 Then
   MsgBox "Error in GetNewsGroup(SelectGroup). Reply text is: " & News.ReplyString
   GetNewsGroup = News.ReplyCode
   NewsType = 0
   Exit Function
End If

Do While News.ReplyCode <> 421
   News.GetArticleByArticleNumber
'    News.GetHeaderByArticleNumber
   Do While News.Busy
      DoEvents
   Loop

   If News.ReplyCode <> 220 Then
```

continues

Listing 14-8 Continued

```
'    If News.ReplyCode <> 221 Then
        MsgBox "Error in GetNewsGroup(GetHeaderByArticleNumber). Reply text is: " _
           & News.ReplyString
        GetNewsGroup = News.ReplyCode
        NewsType = 0
        Exit Function
     End If

     News.SetNextArticle
     Do While News.Busy
        DoEvents
     Loop

     If (News.ReplyCode <> 223) And (News.ReplyCode <> 421) Then
        MsgBox "Error in GetNewsGroup(SetNextArticle). Reply text is: " _
           & News.ReplyString
        GetNewsGroup = News.ReplyCode
        NewsType = 0
        Exit Function
     End If

Loop

NewsType = 0

GetNewsGroup = News.ReplyCode

End Function
```

GetCurrentArticle

The last of the three routines that generates `DocOutput` information is the `GetCurrentArticle` function (see Listing 14-9). As its name implies, the `GetCurrentArticle` function uses the `GetArticleByArticleNumber` method to retrieve the current article. Because the output from the server is different from the other routines we have discussed, I assign `NewsType` a value of three so that the `DocOutput` event can properly handle the data.

Listing 14-9 The *GetCurrentArticle* Function

```
Function GetCurrentArticle() As Integer

'  Specify NewsType to retrive an article in the
'  DocOutput routine, then retrieve the current
'  article. DocOutput will set the header
'  information and display the body of the article.

NewsType = 3
News.GetArticleByArticleNumber
Do While News.Busy
   DoEvents
Loop

If News.ReplyCode <> 220 Then
   MsgBox "Error in GetCurrentArticle(GetArticleByArticleNumber). Reply text is: " _
      & News.ReplyString
End If
NewsType = 0

Article.Frame1.Caption = "Article: " & Format(CurrentArticle)

GetCurrentArticle = News.ReplyCode

End Sub
```

Retrieving Data from the Server with the DocOutput Event

The final block of code I'm going to talk about in this section is the DocOutput event (found in Listing 14-10). All three of the previous routines requested information from the server, which is returned through the DocOutput event. While this routine is rather long, it is very structured. A DocOutput event has only five states: icDocBegin, icDocEnd, icDocHeaders, icDocData, and icDocErrors. Because we are retrieving data from three different routines, we have a total of 15 possible combinations (i.e., a set of icDocBegin logic for NewsType = 1, a set of icDocBegin logic for NewsType = 2, through icDocError logic for NewsType = 3). In practice, we do not need all of the possible combinations. To simplify the explanations, I'm going to discuss the states for each value of NewsType.

Basically this subroutine is written as one large select statement with the various DocOutput.States values, with smaller select statements inside each DocOutput.State value that select the proper value of NewsType.

Retrieving Newsgroups

With a NewsType = 1, we know that the server is returning a list of newsgroups. In this case, our job is relatively simple: to write the data to a disk file. As you would expect, we put in the icDocBegin state statements to open a disk file. However, because we are retrieving a raw stream of files (with other information) from the server, we do not know exactly where the buffer is going to be split, so we define a Static variable, y, that holds the leftover data from the previous transmission. Because y must have a valid value later in the icDocData logic, we set y to the null string.

In the icDocData state we use the GetData method to retrieve the data that triggered the DocOutput event. This data is appended to the value of y that we held from the previous time this routine was called. Then we simply search through this buffer looking for carriage return line feed pairs, which indicates the end of a line of data. As you remember from Chapter 11, the format for a list of newsgroups is the name of the newsgroup followed by a space, followed by the starting article number, another space, the ending article number, yet another space, and a Y/N flag that indicates if the newsgroups permit posting. Because all I want it to capture is the newsgroup name, I simply look for the first space after the carriage return line feed pair.

The `InStr` function is really good at searching for these values, so I use the variable `i` as the starting index into `x`, and I use `j` as the position of the next carriage return line feed pair. Then all I have to do is write the disk file, a substring of `x` starting at location `i` until I find the first space. I step my way through the loop until I cannot find a carriage return line feed pair. At that point, the loop ends and saves the remainder of `x` into `y` for processing the next time around.

At the end of all the data, the `icDocEnd` state occurs, and we then need to close the file we opened when the transmission began. Note that I do not worry about the `icDocError` or the `icDocHeader` states for this value of `NewsType` because there is no header information associated with the list of newsgroups, and I have a general purpose error routine.

Retrieving Article Headers

Article headers are retrieved when a `NewsType` of two is set. Because the data retrieved from the server is going to the `ArticleList.ListView1` control on the form, the only thing necessary to do in `icDocBegin` is to clear the `ListView` control of its previous contents. There are no actions required for `icDocEnd` or `icDocData` because there is no need to clean up after all the data is processed, and there is no data that will be retrieved from the server. The only data to be transferred should be header information because we are using the `GetHeaderByArticleNumber` method.

Well, we would be using the `GetHeaderByArticleNumber` if it worked, but because it does not, I wrote logic similar to the logic used when retrieving newsgroups to parse out the input data and to find and extract the header information. This logic is included in the `icDocData` section for `NewsType = 2`, but I have commented it out. For some reason unknown to me, the NNTP control becomes busy on selected news articles. Other newsreaders were able to correctly process the information, but NewsRunner works properly when I use the `GetArticleByArticleNumber` method rather than the `GetHeaderByArticleNumber` method.

Anyway, it really does not matter how the header information is transmitted from the server because the code in `icDocHeaders` is independent of the method used to get the data. I create a new entry in the `ArticleList.ListView1.ListItems` collection by using the `.Add` property and saving the pointer into the object pointer l. I then step through the `DocHeaders` collection and select the headers that I am interested in displaying to the user. In this case, I'm looking for the subject, from, date, and lines header keywords, and I save them in the object I just created. (If you are curious about what life would be like without the DocHeaders collection, take a look at the code that I wrote to handle this manually. I prefer DocHeaders much more.)

Earlier I referred to the generic icDocError routine I wrote. Essentially any error generates an error message using a MsgBox routine. However, because a reply code of 421 is a useful reply code (meaning that we have processed all of the articles), I take the time to suppress this error message in the icDocError state.

Retrieving an Article

Of the three values of NewsType we have discussed so far, the third is the most interesting. Retrieving an article involves both the icDocHeader and icDocData states. This situation shows the advantages of handling the data stream from the server in this fashion.

As with the previous examples, the icDocBegin logic consists mainly of erasing the previous contents of the form. The icDocError logic is the same generic routine we used before, and no code is necessary for the icDocEnd state.

The icDocHeaders state consists of very similar logic that we used to parse the header information for the ArticleList form. In this case, however, we direct the data to be displayed on the Article form. The icDocData state simply appends the data to the end of the Article.ArticleBox object. Because this is a RichTextBox object, we do not have to worry about exceeding the 64KB limit of a regular TextBox. In fact, this is the only reason I'm using this object.

Now that I have described it, it seems relatively simple and that is the important point. The DocOutput object handles the hard work. It separates the headers from the rest of the document and permits us to write some easy to maintain code to process the data. (Now if only the GetHeaderByArticleNumber method had worked properly. Sigh.)

Listing 14-10 The *DocOutput* Event

```
Private Sub News_DocOutput(ByVal DocOutput As DocOutput)

'  Check the DocOutput.State value to determine
'  the state of the transmission process (Begin, End,
```

```
' Headers, Data, or Errors). Within each state,
' choose the appropriate action based on the
' value of NewsType (1=newsgroup list, 2=article list,
' 3=article header and body).

Dim hdr As DocHeader
Dim i As Long
Dim j As Long
Dim l As ListItem
Dim x As Variant
Static y As Variant

Select Case DocOutput.State

Case icDocBegin
   Select Case NewsType
   Case 1
      y = ""
      Open App.Path & "\news.raw" For Output As #1
   Case 2
      ArticleList.ListView1.ListItems.Clear
   Case 3
      Article.articlebox.Text = ""
   End Select

Case icDocEnd
   Select Case NewsType
   Case 1
      Close #1

   End Select

Case icDocHeaders
```

continues

Listing 14-10 Continued

```
  Select Case NewsType
  Case 2
     Set l = ArticleList.ListView1.ListItems.Add(, , Format(CurrentArticle))
     For Each hdr In DocOutput.Headers
        Select Case LCase(hdr.Name)
        Case "subject"
           l.SubItems(1) = hdr.Value
        Case "from"
           l.SubItems(2) = hdr.Value
        Case "date"
           l.SubItems(3) = hdr.Value
        Case "lines"
           l.SubItems(4) = hdr.Value
        End Select
     Next hdr
  Case 3
     For Each hdr In DocOutput.Headers
        Select Case LCase(hdr.Name)
        Case "newsgroups"
           Article.Newsgroup.Text = hdr.Value
        Case "subject"
           Article.subject.Text = hdr.Value
        Case "from"
           Article.From = hdr.Value
        Case "date"
           Article.DateTime = hdr.Value
        End Select
     Next hdr
  End Select

Case icDocData
  Select Case NewsType
  Case 1
```

```
    DocOutput.GetData x
    x = y & x
    i = 1
    j = InStr(x, vbCrLf) - 1
    Do While (i < Len(x)) And (j > 0)
       Print #1, Mid(x, i, InStr(i, x, " ") - i)
       i = j + 3
       j = InStr(i, x, vbCrLf) - 1
    Loop
    y = Right(x, Len(x) - i + 1)
    DoEvents

 Case 2
' This situation should not occur, since the GetHeadersByArticleNumber should
' not return data, only header information. This appears to be a bug.

'     DocOutput.GetData x
'     If CurrentArticle = 9203 Then MsgBox "bad record"
'     Set l = ArticleList.ListView1.ListItems.Add(, , Format(CurrentArticle))
'     i = 1
'     j = InStr(x, vbCrLf) - 1
'     If j < 0 Then j = Len(x)
'     Do While i < Len(x)
'        If LCase(Mid(x, i, 7)) = "subject" Then
'           l.SubItems(1) = Trim(Mid(x, i + 8, j - i - 7))
'        ElseIf LCase(Mid(x, i, 4)) = "from" Then
'           l.SubItems(2) = Trim(Mid(x, i + 5, j - i - 4))
'        ElseIf LCase(Mid(x, i, 4)) = "date" Then
'           l.SubItems(3) = Trim(Mid(x, i + 5, j - i - 4))
'        ElseIf LCase(Mid(x, i, 5)) = "lines" Then
'           l.SubItems(4) = Trim(Mid(x, i + 6, j - i - 5))
'        Else
'           MsgBox Format(CurrentArticle) & " " & Mid(x, i, j - i - 1)
```

continues

Listing 14-10 Continued

```
'           End If
'           i = j + 3
'           j = InStr(i, x, vbCrLf) - 1
'           If j < 0 Then j = Len(x)
'       Loop

    Case 3
       DocOutput.GetData x
       Article.articlebox.Text = Article.articlebox.Text & x
    End Select

Case icDocError
    Select Case NewsType
    Case 2
       If News.ReplyCode <> 421 Then
          MsgBox "Docoutput error: " & Format(News.ReplyCode)
       End If
    Case Else
       MsgBox "DocOutput Error: " & Format(News.ReplyCode)
    End Select

End Select

End Sub
```

Posting and Replying to Articles

If you thought what we have done so far was hard, then take a look at something relatively easy. Assume that we have used the NewsRunner program to read some articles from a newsgroup and we want to share our ideas with the rest of the world. NewsRunner has three subroutines that handle all the necessary work: `DoPost`, `DoReply` (both of which are found in the Article form), and `SendArticle` (which is in the

NewsRunner form). Basically the `DoPost` and `DoReply` routines prepare the article to be sent to the server, and the `SendArticle` routine actually sends the article.

Posting an Article

When the user clicks the Post button on the Article form, I call the `DoPost` subroutine (see Listing 14-11). In this routine, I prepare the article for sending by clearing all the old information from the form. Posting an article sends a brand new article to the server, so any information already in the form needs to be erased so the user can enter new information. The only piece of information that the server requires that I generate at this time is the current date and time.

Listing 14-11 The *DoPost* Subroutine

```
Private Sub DoPost()

'  Prepare the form to post a new article, by
'  filling in the header information.

Frame1.Caption = "Post"

From.Text = ""
DateTime.Text = Format(Date, "ddd, dd mmm yyyy ") & Format(Time, "hh:mm:ss ") & "GMT"
Newsgroup.Text = ""
subject.Text = ""

End Sub
```

Replying to the Article

Replying to an article is very similar to posting so the `DoReply` subroutine (see Listing 14-12) is similar to the `DoPost` subroutine. The main differences are a "re:" is placed in front of the subject line (if it is not already there), the name of the person that sent the article is listed, and a ">" is placed in front of each line of the rest of the existing text. This marks the existing text as being quoted from the original author. Then the user is free to type additional text or delete the original text before sending the article to the server.

Listing 14-12 The *DoReply* Subroutine

```
Private Sub DoReply()

'  Prepare the form to reply to the current
'  article by preparing the header fields
'  and inserting a "> " in front of all of
'  the lines of existing text.

Dim i As Integer

Frame1.Caption = "Reply"

DateTime.Text = Format(Date, "ddd, dd mmm yyyy ") & Format(Time, "hh:mm:ss ") & "GMT"
If Left(LCase(Trim(subject.Text)), 3) <> "re:" Then
   subject.Text = "re: " & subject.Text
End If

articlebox.Text = "In the previous article " & From.Text & " wrote  " _
   & vbCrLf & articlebox.Text
articlebox.Text = "> " & articlebox.Text
i = InStr(articlebox.Text, vbCrLf)
Do While i <> 0
   i = InStr(i + 2, articlebox.Text, vbCrLf)
   articlebox.Text = Left(articlebox.Text, i + 1) & "> " & Right(articlebox.Text,
(Len(articlebox.Text) - i - 1))
Loop

From.Text = ""

End Sub
```

Sending the Article

After the article has been prepared for sending by using either the `DoPost` or `DoReply` routines, the user clicks the Send button, which calls the `SendArticle` function (see Listing 14-13). This function takes the information in the Article form and prepares the article for posting using the `DocInput` object.

First, I create a `DocHeaders` collection (which for some reason is called `DocHeadersCls`) and add the header information from the Article form (subject, from, date, and newsgroup), plus a Message-Id header and a Path header, both of which are required. In a more complex newsreader, you would allow the user to specify additional headers, but these six headers are the minimum necessary for a post to succeed.

Then I use the `News.SendDoc` method to send the data to the server using the `DocInput` object. Note that I did not have to write any code other than this for the `DocInput` object to work properly. All the defaults were sufficient for handling this posting.

Finally, I use the spin loop to wait for the NNTP ActiveX control to finish, and then check the reply code. A 240 reply code means the article was posted successfully.

Listing 14-13 The *SendArticle* Subroutine

```
Function SendArticle() As Integer

'  After the article has been prepared for sending,
'  build the DocHeaders collection, and sent the
'  article to the server.



Dim hdr As New DocHeadersCls

hdr.Clear
hdr.Add "From", Article.From.Text
hdr.Add "Date", Article.DateTime.Text
hdr.Add "Newsgroups", Article.Newsgroup.Text
```

continues

Listing 14-13 Continued

```
hdr.Add "Subject", Article.subject.Text
hdr.Add "Message-ID", "<" & Trim(Format(Date, "mmddyyy")) & _
   Trim(Format(Time, "hhmmss")) & Article.From.Text & ">"
hdr.Add "Path", News.RemoteHost

News.SendDoc , hdr, Article.articlebox.Text

Do While News.Busy
   DoEvents
Loop

If News.ReplyCode = 440 Then
   MsgBox "Posting is not allowed on this server."
ElseIf News.ReplyCode <> 240 Then
   MsgBox "Error encountered in SendArticle(SendDoc). Reply text is: " &
News.ReplyString
End If

SendArticle = News.ReplyCode

End Function
```

Summary

We discussed how to implement the NNTP ActiveX client control in a simple program. This program incorporates the most important functions of the control, which should provide sufficient information about how the control works to include it in other Visual Basic programs. We also discussed the problems that exist in the controls and how to create work-arounds for most of the problems.

In the next chapter, we are going to take the FTPRunner program we developed in the previous part and combine it with this program to create the NetRunner program. Then, as we add new programs using the ActiveX controls, we add them to NetRunner until we have a very interesting Internet utility.

In case you want to check your answers to the questions at the front of the chapter, here are the answers:

- *What are some problems one might encounter when connecting to a remote computer?*

  Unlike the FTP control where a userid and password were required, this program reacts only to a successful or unsuccessful connection to the server.

- *What is a spin loop?*

  A spin loop is the term I use to indicate a small loop that constantly checks an ActiveX control's `Busy` property and executes `DoEvents` while the property is true. This permits other work in Windows to proceed while the program waits for the operation to be completed.

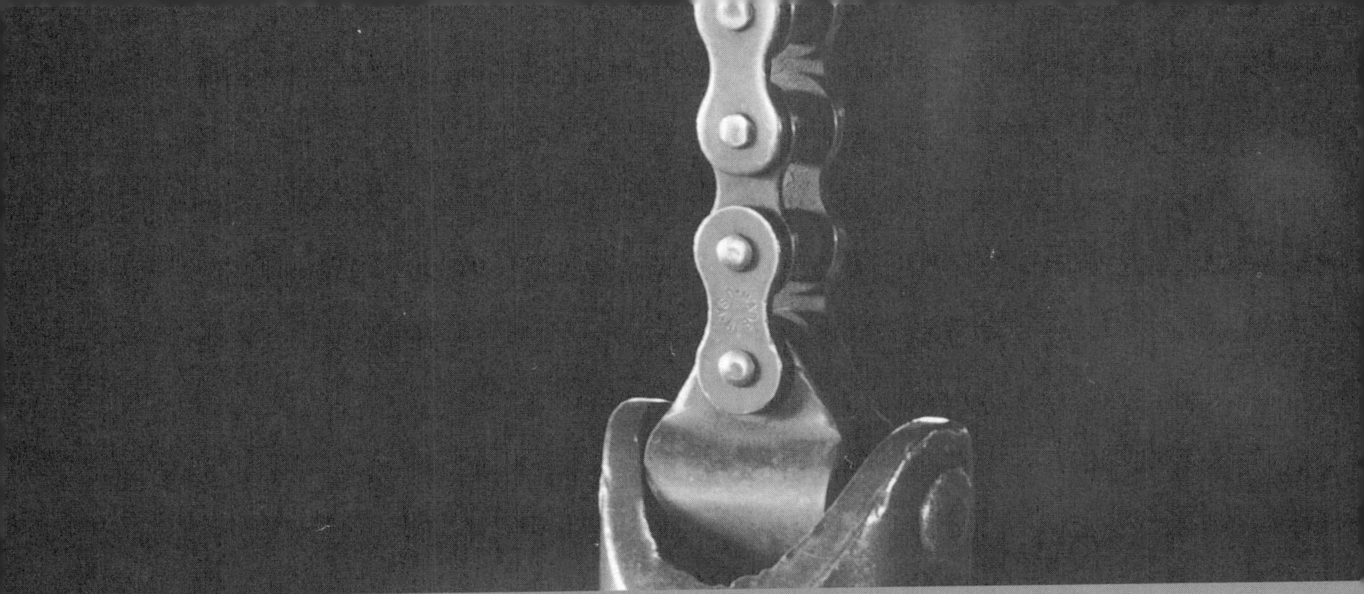

Chapter 15

NetRunner—Part One

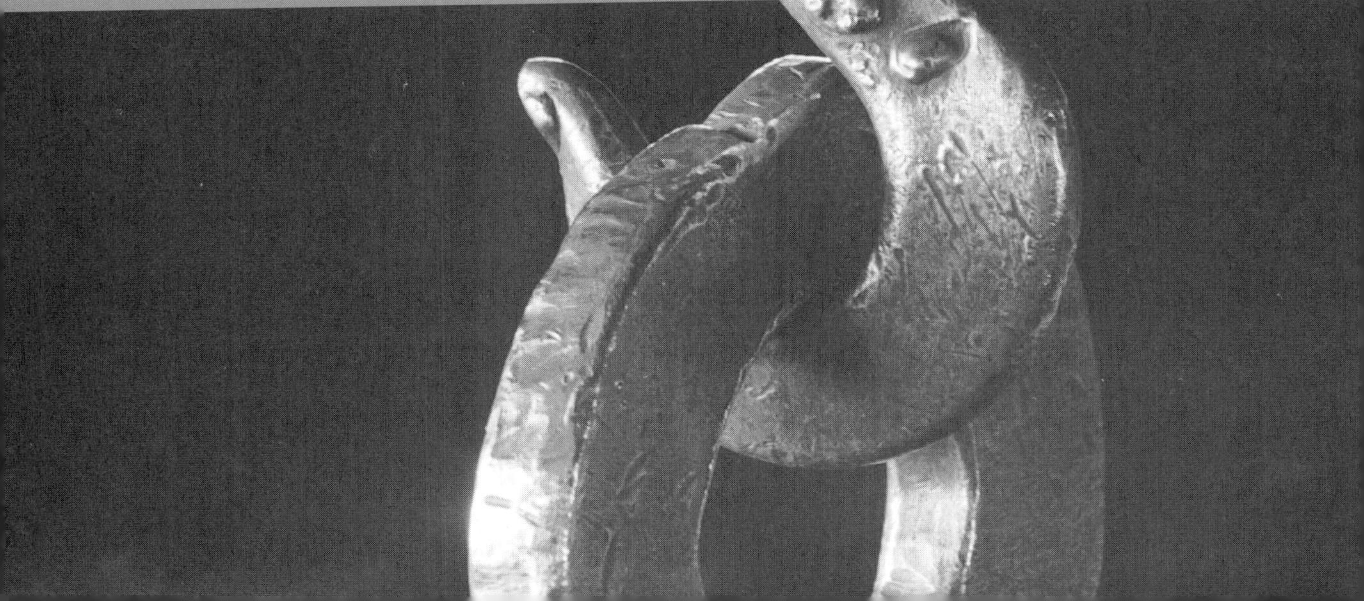

Overview

In this chapter, we are going to start building a program called NetRunner. NetRunner is designed to be a multipurpose Internet tool that integrates all the ActiveX controls into a single program. To create this program, we combine and enhance the stand-alone programs we built already: FTPRunner and NewsRunner. While the look and feel of the individual programs remains basically the same, we try to include additional refinements and new capabilities each time we add one of the programs.

We start building NetRunner by creating a new master control form that can start either FTPRunner or NewsRunner. As I have done in previous chapters, I'm only going to highlight the more interesting blocks of code because the complete source code is on the CD-ROM. However, unlike the previous chapters, I spend a little time talking about parts of the program that do not directly relate to the ActiveX controls.

By the end of this chapter, you should be able to answer the following question:

- What is the system registry?

How to Use NetRunner

We start creating the NetRunner program by building a new form that the user sees when the program starts (see figure 15-1). This form consists of some menu controls, a Tab control, and a status bar. Each tab on the Tab control contains the parameters and a button to launch the specified application. There are tabs for NetRunner, WebRunner, MailRunner, NewsRunner, and FTPRunner. Because the NetRunner-specific features do not exist and we have yet to write MailRunner and WebRunner, those tabs are blank. That is not the case, however, for FTPRunner and NewsRunner.

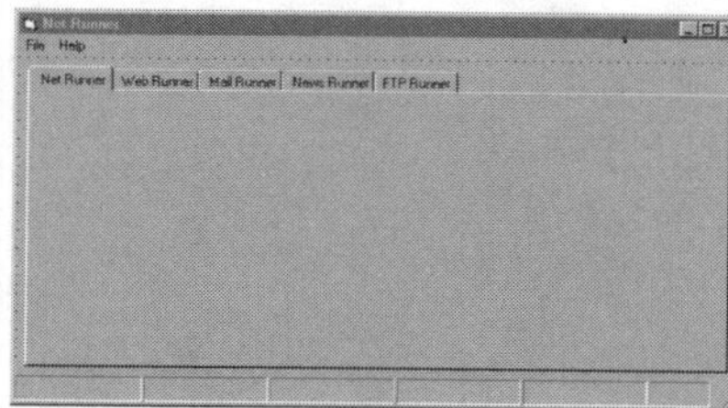

FIGURE 15-1

The NetRunner form.

Clicking the FTPRunner tab shows the form illustrated in figure 15-2. You will notice that I have put all the parameters that were on the FTPConnect form on this form as well. This enables me to eliminate the FTPConnect form and now these parameters are in an easy-to-access place. After the parameters are filled in, you can launch the FTPRunner program by clicking the FTPRunner button. Then the FTPRunner form is loaded and the `DoConnect` routine automatically starts.

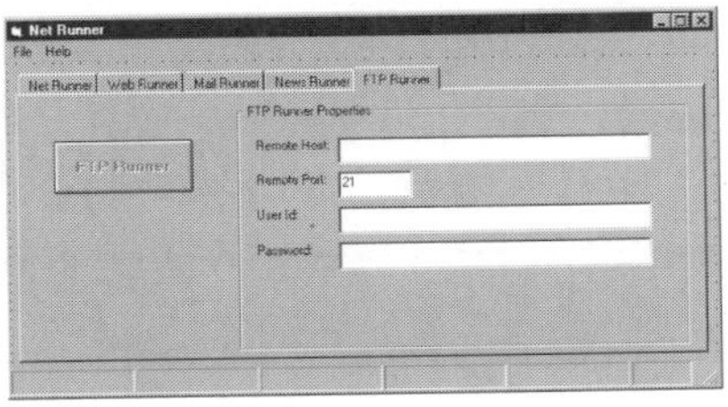

FIGURE 15-2

The NetRunner form, FTPRunner tab.

Like the FTPRunner tab, the NewsRunner tab contains the information necessary to connect to a news server (see figure 15-3). Clicking the NewsRunner button launches the NewsRunner form and establishes a connection to the specified news server.

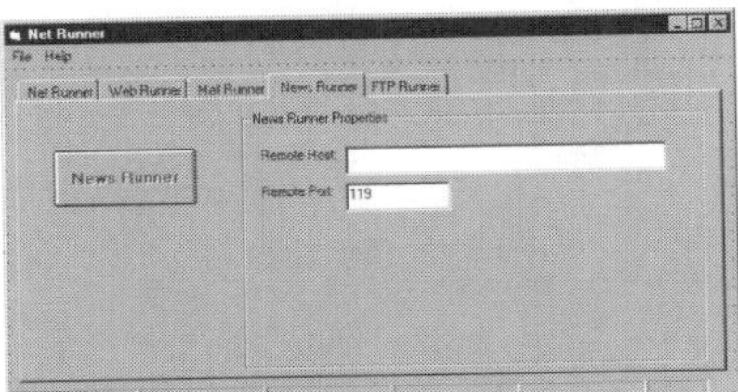

FIGURE 15-3

The NetRunner form, NewsRunner tab.

The Program Structure

This program consists of the main NewsRunner form (refer to figure 15-1), the FTPRunner and NewsRunner forms, plus the NewsRunner's ArticleList and Article forms. In addition, About forms are included for NetRunner, FTPRunner, and NewsRunner. There is also one module, called NetGlobal. This is very similar to the global modules used for the stand-alone NewsRunner and FTPRunner programs. As you can see in Listing 15-1, these two modules were merged together to create the NetGlobal module. Note that all FTP-related global variables are prefixed by FTP, and all News-related global variables are prefixed with News. We continue with this pattern as we add other variables to the NetGlobal.

The main subroutine used to start NetRunner is identical to the main subroutine in NewsRunner, and the `Initialize` subroutine merely consists of the two previous subroutines merged together. Rather than listing them here, please refer to the CD-ROM or look in Chapter 10 in Listing 10-2, or Chapter 14 in Listing 14-2, for more information.

Listing 15-1 Global Variables

```
' Form/Module:   NetGlobal
' Author:        Wayne S. Freeze
' Version        2.0
' Date Written:  22 July 1996
' Date Revised:  22 July 1996
' Description:
'    This module initialized the global variables
'    and starts the Net Runner form.

Option Explicit

' Define the FTP Runner Global Variables
' =============================================

' True when the program is trying to abort
' a transfer
Global FTPAborted As Integer

' True when the program is talking to a remote
' system, false otherwise
Global FTPConnected As Integer
```

```
'  Used to track when the FTP connection was
'  started
Global FTPStartTime As Date

'  Define the News Runner Global Variables
'  ==============================================

'  True when the program is talking to a remote
'  system, false otherwise
Global NewsConnected As Integer

'  Used to track when the FTP connection was
'  started
Global NewsStartTime As Date

'  Define the type of data being retrieved
'  from the NNTP server
'  0 = undefined
'  1 = Newsgroup List
'  2 = Article List
'  3 = Article
Global NewsType As Integer

'  The article number
Global NewsCurrentArticle As Long

'  The current news group
Global NewsCurrentGroup As String
```

Changing the Timer

Timers are a relatively scarce resource in Windows. It is very wasteful to have multiple timers, especially when it's relatively easy to combine them into one. Essentially, all I did was strip the `Timer1_Timer` event from the both the NewsRunner and FTPRunner forms and combine them into a new `Timer1_Timer` event in the NetRunner form. Of course, I also had to delete the Timer control from each form and any other Timer-related code in the two forms.

Listing 15-2 The *Timer1_Timer* Subroutine

```
Private Sub Timer1_Timer()

'  There are only a few timers in Windows, so rather than
'  let each ActiveX control use it's own timer, the Net
'  Runner timer will handle all of there events.

Dim h As Long
Dim m As Long
Dim s As Long
Dim X As Long

StatusBar.Panels(6).Text = Format(Now, "Long Time")

If FTPConnected Then
   FTPRunner.StatusBar.Panels(3).Text = FTPRunner.FTP.ReplyString
   X = DateDiff("s", FTPStartTime, Now)
   s = X Mod 60
   m = (X / 60) Mod 60
   h = (X / 3600) Mod 60
   FTPRunner.StatusBar.Panels(4).Text = Format(h, "00") & ":" & Format(m, "00") & ":" &
➥Format(s, "00")

   If FTPRunner.FTP.Busy Then
      FTPRunner.StatusBar.Panels(5).Text = "*"
   Else
      FTPRunner.StatusBar.Panels(5).Text = " "
   End If
```

```
End If

If NewsConnected Then
   NewsRunner.StatusBar.Panels(3).Text = NewsRunner.News.ReplyString

   X = DateDiff("s", NewsStartTime, Now)
   s = X Mod 60
   m = (X / 60) Mod 60
   h = (X / 3600) Mod 60

   NewsRunner.StatusBar.Panels(4).Text = Format(h, "00") & ":" & Format(m, "00") & ":" &
➥Format(s, "00")

   If NewsRunner.News.Busy Then
      NewsRunner.StatusBar.Panels(5).Text = "*"
   Else
      NewsRunner.StatusBar.Panels(5).Text = " "
   End If

End If

End Sub
```

Forms Placement

The following block of code has absolutely nothing to do with the ActiveX controls, but is a dirty trick I learned a while ago. When developing programs like NetRunner where multiple forms are displayed all over the screen, I found it handy to be able to adjust the placement of the forms while the program was running, and be able to restore that placement the next time I ran the program. After much head scratching, I figured out the following simple solution. Each time the form is loaded, it checks the system registry for information about the placement of the form. And each time the form is unloaded, it updates the system registry with the current placement values.

In Listing 15-3, I show the code I used in the NetRunner form to find out the last position it occupied on the screen, and in Listing 15-4, I show how to save the current position. Based on my experience, the user isn't really aware of the time required to do the updates, and the `GetSetting/SaveSetting` routines make it relatively easy to include in your code.

In general, I use the name of my application as the first parameter to the `SaveSetting/GetSetting` routines. For parameters that are local to a particular form, I use the form name as the second level. This leaves the parameter name itself as the third level in the hierarchy.

Listing 15-3 The NetRunner *Form_Load* Subroutine

```
Private Sub Form_Load()

NetRunner.Show 0

NetRunner.Top = GetSetting("NetRunner", "NetRunner", "Top", 660)
NetRunner.Left = GetSetting("NetRunner", "NetRunner", "Left", 660)

Timer1.Interval = 1000

End Sub
```

Listing 15-4 The NetRunner *Form_Unload* Subroutine

```
Private Sub Form_Unload(Cancel As Integer)

Timer1.Enabled = False

SaveSetting "NetRunner", "NetRunner", "Top", NetRunner.Top
SaveSetting "NetRunner", "NetRunner", "Left", NetRunner.Left

End Sub
```

For those who may not be familiar with the system registry, think of it as a super INI file. They both serve the same purpose, that is, to preserve information about the application that is local to the machine on which it is running. Both the system registry and the typical INI file can be viewed as a hierarchical storage bin. In general, the first level of the system registry corresponds to the name of an INI file. The second level corresponds to the major category inside the INI file. The third level corresponds to a line inside the major category. If the data were stored in an INI file, it would look like this:

```
[NetRunner]
Top=660
Left=660
```

Because the system registry cannot be viewed with a text editor like an INI file, you should know about the RegEdit tool. This tool is available in the \Windows directory, but for some reason Microsoft chose not to include it as part of the programs available under the taskbar's Start button. The best way to run it is to go to Start | Run and enter **\Windows\RegEdit**. Then I use the Edit | Find command to search for my application name. Next, I open the NetRunner folder and the NetRunner folder inside that one. Finally, I see the screen shown in figure 15-4, which shows the exact same information as in the INI file shown previously.

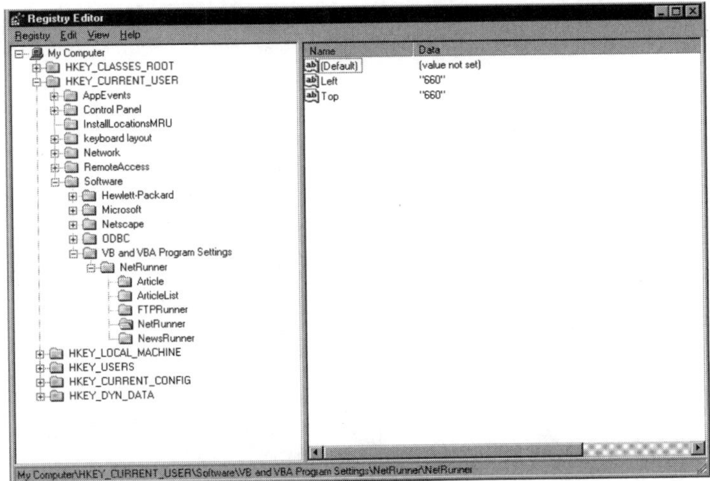

FIGURE 15-4

The system registry view of the NetRunner parameters.

Forms Sizing

Continuing with my diversion from the ActiveX controls, I attack the issue of how to resize a form. (If you are wondering why I'm spending so much time talking about issues other than ActiveX, consider how well an FTP program and a newsreader program can be integrated. As they have almost nothing in common, we have to wait until we have a few more Internet functions available. Just wait until Chapter 23, "The HTTP Client Control," where we really begin to integrate the controls in a useful way.) Resizing a form is useful when you have a form that lends itself to resizing. The NetRunner form we just looked at is not a good candidate for resizing because all the controls on its form are relatively fixed in size. The NewsRunner form in figure 15-5, however, is a perfect candidate because resizing a form can potentially dramatically increase the amount of data able to be viewed in a single window.

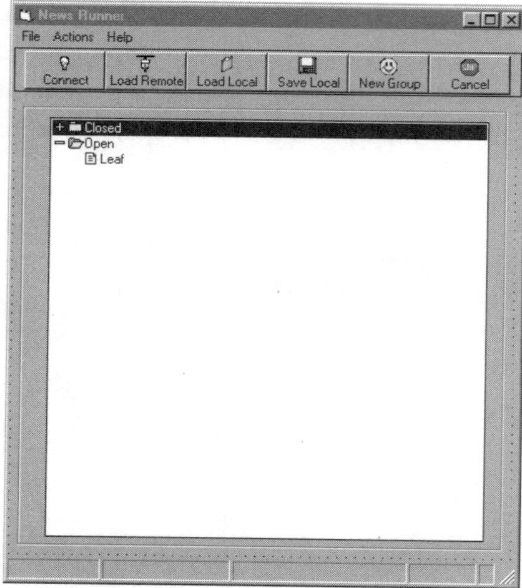

FIGURE 15-5

The NewsRunner form.

To find a good candidate for window resizing, look for controls on a form that have scroll bars or whose field sizes can really vary in size. The NewsRunner form has this because the Outline and Frame controls are easily resized. The status bar is also easily resized. The toolbar control can be resized as well; however, if all the buttons cannot be displayed on a single row, the control automatically puts the buttons in a second row. The way to handle this situation is to prevent the form from being made smaller than a certain minimum size.

In Listing 15-5, you see the `Form_Resize` subroutine for the NewsRunner form. Notice that the first thing I do is ensure that the form is not resized smaller than 2,400 twips in height and 6,700 twips in width. How did I choose these values? The lazy way. I resized the form in Visual Basic to what I felt was a good minimum, and then hard-coded those parameters into this routine. It is a simple solution, and it has the side benefit of preventing users from resizing the form so small that they get confused.

The rest of the subroutine is devoted to resizing the frame (`Frame1`) and outline (`AllGroups`) controls on the screen. Because the Top and Left values for both controls are fixed, all I need to do is adjust the width and height of the controls whenever the form is adjusted. The way I do this is by keeping a constant distance between the edge of the form and the edge of the control. I call this constant a *gap*. Because we have a bottom edge that is controlled by the form's height and a right edge that is controlled by the form's width, I call the frame's constants `fhgap` (for frame, Height gap), and `fwgap` (for frame, Width gap). The corresponding constants for the outline control are `ahgap` and `awgap`.

Listing 15-5 The NewsRunner *Form_Resize* Subroutine

```
Private Sub Form_Resize()

If NewsRunner.Height < 2400 Then
   NewsRunner.Height = 2400
End If

If NewsRunner.Width < 6700 Then
   NewsRunner.Width = 6700
End If

If (fwgap > 0) Then
   Frame1.Width = NewsRunner.Width - fwgap
   Frame1.Height = NewsRunner.Height - fhgap
   AllGroups.Width = NewsRunner.Width - awgap
   AllGroups.Height = NewsRunner.Height - ahgap
End If

End Sub
```

Because the gap values are constants, they must be computed or derived at some point. The best time is to compute them before the form is actually displayed on the screen. To do this, I declare the gap variables as Singles in the Global declarations for the form. Then I compute them based on the current values for the form's and control's sizes.

After I have the gap values, I force the form to be displayed to the user by executing a `Show` method against the NewsRunner form. Then the subsequent lines of code cause the `resize` event to be invoked with new values for the form size.

Listing 15-6 The NewsRunner *Form_Load* Subroutine

```
Private Sub Form_Load()

fwgap = NewsRunner.Width - Frame1.Width
fhgap = NewsRunner.Height - Frame1.Height
awgap = NewsRunner.Width - AllGroups.Width
ahgap = NewsRunner.Height - AllGroups.Height

NewsRunner.Show 0

NewsRunner.Top = GetSetting("NetRunner", "NewsRunner", "Top", 660)
NewsRunner.Left = GetSetting("NetRunner", "NewsRunner", "Left", 660)
NewsRunner.Height = GetSetting("NetRunner", "NewsRunner", "Height", NewsRunner.Height)
NewsRunner.Width = GetSetting("NetRunner", "NewsRunner", "Width", NewsRunner.Width)

'  When we load this form, initialize controls

StatusBar.Panels(1).Text = "Not Connected"
StatusBar.Panels(2).Text = "xxx"
StatusBar.Panels(4).Text = "00:00:00"
StatusBar.Panels(5).Text = " "

Toolbar.Buttons("Load Remote").Enabled = False
Toolbar.Buttons("New Group").Enabled = False
```

```
Toolbar.Buttons("Cancel").Enabled = False

DoConnect

End Sub
```

A more complicated example is found in the FTPRunner form. This form has many elements that need to be managed. While the same basic principles apply here, the actual code requires a little more thought. As with the previous example, I prevent the form from being resized beyond a minimum size, and then I begin the hard stuff.

As you remember from Chapter 10, the FTPRunner form consists of a toolbar, a status bar, and two frames that each occupy about half the remaining space on the form. This makes it necessary to expand both frames at the same time so they remain the same size relative to each other. We do this with the same technique used in the last example. However, this time, we compute the gap value based on the unused space between both frames and the form. We then want to position the each frame with 1/4 the space between the sides of the frame and the side of the form and with 1/2 the space between the frames. Note we also have to reposition the `Left` property for both frames; we cannot assume that they will be in the same relative position.

Likewise, we need to do the same for each control within the frame that will vary in size. This includes the `txtRemoteHost`, `lstRemoteDirs`, and the `LstRemoteFiles` controls in the `fraRemoteHost` frame and the `drvLocalDrives`, `dirLocalDirs`, and `filLocalFiles` controls in the `fraLocalHost` frame. Note that these fields are a little easier to deal with because their `Left` and `Width` properties are relative to the frame, not the form.

Changing the form height, however, is a little (maybe a lot?) more complicated. This is because some controls should not have their height changed (like a Label control), but they need to have their height changed (like a multiple-line TextBox). The first step in handling this situation is to resize the frame like we have done in the other examples. Because the frames are side by side, we do not have to do anything special to ensure that the frames are properly positioned other than reset the `Height` property.

Now comes the tricky part. Because the same basic code applies to both frames, I'm only going to talk about the `fraRemoteHost` frame. Starting at the top of the frame, the `txtRemoteHost` control is left alone along with the `Label` control immediately below it. This means that the `Top` of the `txtRemoteDirs` control also does not change. The first value that needs to be changed is the `Height` of the `txtRemoteDirs` control. For some reason (probably because it looks right), I change the `Height` of this control to one fourth of the `Height` of the frame.

Then I must reposition the label (`Lable3`) control immediately below it. I compute the value for the `Top` of the control by taking the bottom of the `txtRemoteDirs` control (`txtRemoteDirs.Top + txtRemoteDirs.Height`) and leaving a small gap (100 twips). Because I'm not changing its `Height` property, I move onto the final control in the frame, the `lstRemoteFiles` control.

Placing this control is fairly easy. First, I set the `Top` of the `lstRemoteFiles` control to the bottom of the `Label3`. (I do not bother to leave a gap because it looks better that way.) Then, I set the height by computing the space available (`fraRemoteHost.Height - lstRemoteFiles.Top`) and leaving a small gap (100 twips) between the bottom of the control and the bottom of the frame.

To finish the resizing subroutine, all you need to do is to copy the `Top` and `Height` values of the controls that were changed in the `fraRemoteHost` frame to their counterparts in the `fraLocalHost` frame. That is all it takes to resize a complex form like FTPRunner. The key is just to take things one step at a time and whenever possible break the problem into a series of smaller, more easily solved ones. (Boy, this sounds like something one of my professors might have said—but it works!)

Listing 15-7 The FTPRunner *Form_Resize* Subroutine

```
Private Sub Form_Resize()

If FTPRunner.Height < 3000 Then
   FTPRunner.Height = 3000
End If

If FTPRunner.Width < 8700 Then
   FTPRunner.Width = 8700
End If

fraRemoteHost.Width = (FTPRunner.Width - fwgap) / 2
```

```
fraRemoteHost.Left = fwgap / 4

txtRemoteHost.Width = fraRemoteHost.Width - dwgap
txtRemoteHost.Left = dwgap / 2
lstRemoteDirs.Width = fraRemoteHost.Width - dwgap
lstRemoteDirs.Left = dwgap / 2
lstRemoteFiles.Width = fraRemoteHost.Width - dwgap
lstRemoteFiles.Left = dwgap / 2

fraLocalHost.Width = fraRemoteHost.Width
fraLocalHost.Left = fraRemoteHost.Width + fwgap / 2

drvLocalDrives.Width = fraLocalHost.Width - dwgap
drvLocalDrives.Left = dwgap / 2
dirLocalDirs.Width = fraLocalHost.Width - dwgap
dirLocalDirs.Left = dwgap / 2
filLocalFiles.Width = fraLocalHost.Width - dwgap
filLocalFiles.Left = dwgap / 2

fraRemoteHost.Height = FTPRunner.Height - fhgap
lstRemoteDirs.Height = fraRemoteHost.Height / 4
Label3.Top = lstRemoteDirs.Height + lstRemoteDirs.Top + 100
lstRemoteFiles.Top = Label3.Top + Label3.Height
lstRemoteFiles.Height = fraRemoteHost.Height - lstRemoteFiles.Top - 100

fraLocalHost.Height = FTPRunner.Height - fhgap
dirLocalDirs.Height = lstRemoteDirs.Height
Label5.Top = Label3.Top
filLocalFiles.Top = lstRemoteFiles.Top
filLocalFiles.Height = lstRemoteFiles.Height

End Sub
```

Listing 15-8 The FTPRunner *Form_Load* Subroutine

```
Private Sub Form_Load()

'  When we load this form, initialize controls

fwgap = FTPRunner.Width - fraLocalHost.Width - fraRemoteHost.Width
dwgap = fraLocalHost.Width - txtRemoteHost.Width
fhgap = FTPRunner.Height - fraLocalHost.Height
fwgap = fraLocalHost.Height = lstRemoteDirs.Top

FTPRunner.Show 0

FTPRunner.Top = GetSetting("NetRunner", "FTPRunner", "Top", 660)
FTPRunner.Left = GetSetting("NetRunner", "FTPRunner", "Left", 660)
FTPRunner.Height = GetSetting("NetRunner", "FTPRunner", "Height", FTPRunner.Height)
FTPRunner.Width = GetSetting("NetRunner", "FTPRunner", "Width", FTPRunner.Width)

StatusBar.Panels(1).Text = "not connected"
StatusBar.Panels(2).Text = "xxx"
StatusBar.Panels(4).Text = "00:00:00"
StatusBar.Panels(5).Text = " "

Toolbar.Buttons("Change Dir").Enabled = False
Toolbar.Buttons("CD Up").Enabled = False
Toolbar.Buttons("Xfer Files").Enabled = False
Toolbar.Buttons("ASCII").Enabled = False
Toolbar.Buttons("Binary").Enabled = False
Toolbar.Buttons("Abort").Enabled = False

txtRemoteHost.Text = NetRunner.FTPRemoteHost.Text

DoConnect

End Sub
```

Summary

We discussed how to combine the FTPRunner and the NewsRunner programs into a single program. While each of these programs cannot easily take advantage of the other's features, they form the foundation that we expand on and add new features to and provide better integration between the various controls through the rest of the book. We also spent time discussing how to provide some nice frills to the program that permit users to resize and relocate the various forms and save that information in the system registry so those values can be restored the next time the program is run.

In case you want to check your answer to the question at the front of the chapter, here is the answer:

- *What is the system registry?*

  The system registry is a convenient place to store information that is specific to a single machine and that spans multiple sessions of the program. A good example of this type of information is the size and location of the various forms used in the program.

PART IV

Sending and Receiving Mail with SMPT and POP

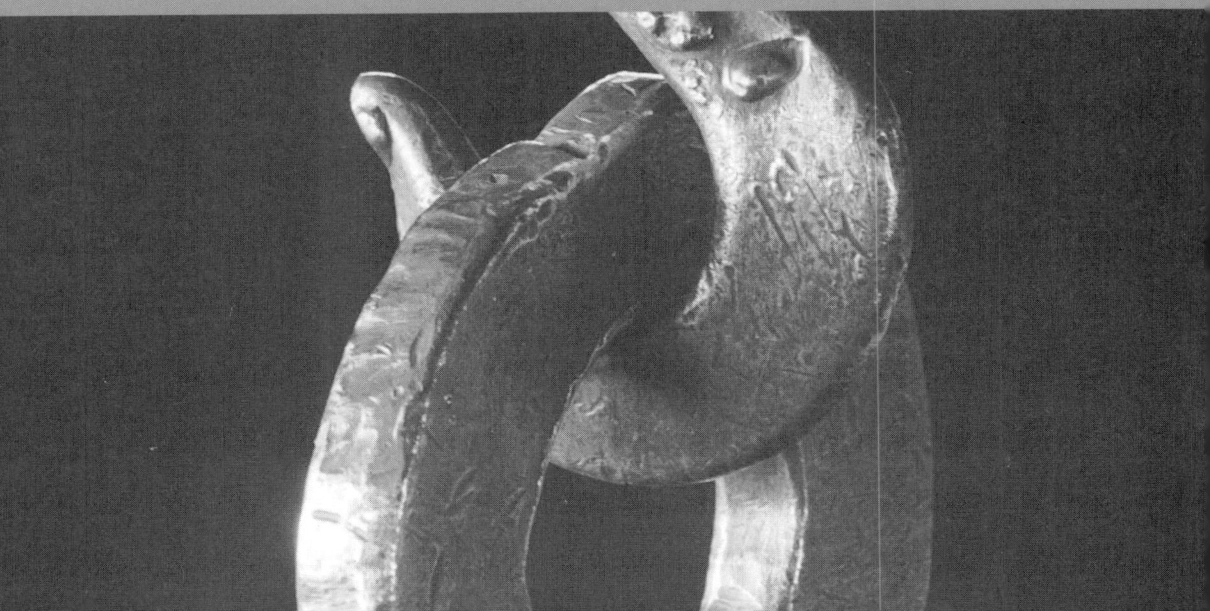

What Are the SMTP and POP Client Controls?

The SMTP and POP client controls provide an easy way to access Internet electronic mail using a Simple Mail Transport Protocol server and a Post Office Protocol server. Electronic mail (or e-mail) has become one of the most fundamental uses of the Internet. Its impact on our culture is astonishing. Many people would rather do without a telephone than without electronic mail (assuming you did not need the telephone to access the Internet). In some parts of the world, electronic mail service is more reliable than the local telephone company. It has been responsible for the @ (at sign) becoming one of today's most popular icons.

In fact, the very term electronic mail brings to mind the concept of writing a letter and dropping it in a mailbox for pickup, knowing that eventually the mail will reach the person to whom it was addressed. Rather than waiting days for the mail to reach someone, e-mail is delivered to the person in a matter of seconds. However, just because the mail is delivered quickly, the recipient must still check his mailbox in order to see if he has any new mail.

In many ways electronic mail is very similar in concept to the Usenet newsgroups we discussed in the part three of this book—both contain text documents that are transported across the Internet into the hands of the reader, and then the reader may reply to the message in the same fashion. Unlike Usenet news, however, e-mail messages are not intended for public distribution. With any e-mail message, there is a specific list of intended recipients that will receive the mail.

Where Would I Use the SMTP and POP Client Controls?

SMTP and POP provide the capability to send and receive electronic mail. With these controls it is possible for an application to generate electronic messages and send them to other individuals.

One practical application of automatically generating a message is in an inventory system when the system determines that the supply of a specific item has reached the reorder point. The application sends an e-mail message to the person responsible for ordering the item.

Send Us YOUR COMMENTS

Dear Reader:

Thank you for buying this book. In order to offer you more quality books on the topics ***you*** would like to see, we need your input. At Prima Publishing, we pride ourselves on timely responsiveness to our readers' needs. If you complete and return this brief questionnaire, ***we will listen!***

Name (First) ______ (M.I.) ______ (Last) ______

Company ______ Type of business ______

Address ______ City ______ State ______ ZIP ______

Phone ______ Fax ______ E-mail address: ______

May we contact you for research purposes? ❑ Yes ❑ No

(If you participate in a research project, we will supply you with the Prima computer book of your choice.)

❶ How would you rate this book, overall?

- ❑ Excellent
- ❑ Very good
- ❑ Good
- ❑ Fair
- ❑ Below average
- ❑ Poor

❷ Why did you buy this book?

- ❑ Price of book
- ❑ Author's reputation
- ❑ Content
- ❑ Prima's reputation
- ❑ CD-ROM/disk included with book
- ❑ Information highlighted on cover
- ❑ Other (please specify): ______

❸ How did you discover this book?

- ❑ Found it on bookstore shelf
- ❑ Saw it in Prima Publishing catalog
- ❑ Recommended by store personnel
- ❑ Recommended by friend or colleague
- ❑ Saw an advertisement in: ______
- ❑ Read book review in: ______
- ❑ Saw it on Web site: ______
- ❑ Other (please specify): ______

❹ Where did you buy this book?

- ❑ Bookstore (name): ______
- ❑ Computer store (name): ______
- ❑ Electronics store (name): ______
- ❑ Wholesale club (name): ______
- ❑ Mail order (name): ______
- ❑ Direct from Prima Publishing
- ❑ Other (please specify): ______

❺ Which computer periodicals do you read regularly? ______

❻ Would you like to see your name in print?

May we use your name and quote you in future Prima Publishing books or promotional materials?

❑ Yes ❑ No

❼ Comments & suggestions: ______

TAPE HERE

❽ I am interested in seeing more computer books on these topics

- ❑ Word processing
- ❑ Databases/spreadsheets
- ❑ Networking
- ❑ Programming
- ❑ Desktop publishing
- ❑ Web site development
- ❑ Internetworking
- ❑ Intranetworking

❾ How do you rate your level of computer skills?

- ❑ Beginner
- ❑ Intermediate
- ❑ Advanced

❿ What is your age?

- ❑ Under 18
- ❑ 18–29
- ❑ 30–39
- ❑ 40–49
- ❑ 50–59
- ❑ 60–over

SAVE A STAMP

Visit our Web site at **http://www.primapublishing.com**

and simply fill out one of our online response forms.

PRIMA PUBLISHING
Computer Products Division
701 Congressional Blvd., Suite 350
Carmel, IN 46032

PLEASE PLACE STAMP HERE

Messages could also be sent to the people that use that specific item to notify them that the item count is low. An e-mail note could also be sent directly to the supplier so that it ships more of the item.

Another interesting application where these controls would be useful is to help an organization reduce paperwork. A Visual Basic application could present the electronic equivalent of a paper form. The application would capture the user's input and save it in a database. It would then forward an electronic note to the person that must approve the request, letting them know that they must use the application to review and approve the request. While this may not be useful in a small organization, it would be extremely useful in a large organization, especially where the people who must approve requests spend a lot of time doing tasks other than waiting for requests to approve.

A really off-the-wall application of the SMTP control would be to include it in your program's error logic. Imagine a situation where you have a widely distributed application that is relatively complex. There are always situations where you find bad data that the program cannot resolve, and the application displays a message saying "Program error. Please report the following information." Rather than display that message and the information that follows, it may be reasonable to package all of that material into an e-mail note and send it to the person that is responsible for fixing this problem. This technique would not work for all errors because many will cause the program to crash, but it will help in those situations where you suspect that the data the program is using may have gotten corrupted or worse yet, have gotten into a part of the code that you do not expect to be executed. (This would be great as the `Case Else` in a `Select Case` statement where you expect all cases to be handled by specific logic.) You could also create a button that will pop up a problem report form where the user can fill in any relevant problem information.

Of course, the best application would be a highly specialized mail program that could send and receive encoded messages. While encrypted messages are a good way to ensure privacy, an encoded message is even better. An encoded message substitutes a word or phrase for another word or phrase. Consider the following message: "Mary had a little goat. Paris bridge is falling down. Old McDonald had a horse." This could be translated into: "The rebel forces are in place and will begin their attack on the palace at midnight. They request that the additional funds for replacement arms should be transferred to them via their account in Bermuda. They acknowledge the presidential order to assassinate the…" (The rest of this paragraph has been determined to be in violation of national security and has been removed from this book!)

Summary

In the following chapters, we discuss how the SMTP and POP protocols work together with their servers to exchange electronic mail; how the ActiveX controls use the SMTP and POP protocols to send and receive electronic mail; and how to build an electronic mail program. We also discuss how to add these functions to the NetRunner program and how that can be integrated with the existing functions.

Chapter 16—SMTP Protocols and Functions

This chapter discusses in detail how SMTP works from a functional level and the protocols that are used to communicate between the client and the server. This serves as background material for understanding the SMTP client control and the MailRunner sample program.

- Overview
- The SMTP Model
- Electronic Mail Format
- SMTP Protocol Commands
- SMTP Reply Codes and Messages
- Accessing the Server
- Sending a Note
- Other Facilities
- Example
- Summary

Chapter 17—The NNTP Client Control

This chapter discusses all the programming aspects (properties, events, and methods) provided by the SMTP client control. Aspects necessary for fundamental usage are emphasized, but the advanced aspects are briefly discussed.

- Overview

- Properties
- Methods
- Events
- Summary

Chapter 18—POP Protocols and Functions

This chapter discusses in detail how POP works from a functional level and the protocols that are used to communicate between the client and the server. This serves as background material for understanding the POP client control and the MailRunner sample program.

- Overview
- The POP3 Model
- POP Protocol Commands
- POP Reply Codes and Messages
- Accessing the Server
- Transaction Commands
- Other Facilities
- Example
- Summary

Chapter 19—The POP Client Control

This chapter discusses all the programming aspects (properties, events, and methods) provided by the POP client control. Aspects necessary for fundamental usage are emphasized, but the advanced aspects are briefly discussed.

- Overview
- Properties
- Methods
- Events
- Summary

Chapter 20—MailRunner

This chapter introduces a program called MailRunner that allows the user to send and receive electronic mail over the Internet using the SMTP and POP controls.

- Overview
- How to Use MailRunner
- The Program Structure
- Connecting to the Server
- Interacting with the POP Server
- DeleteNote
- Interacting with the SMTP Server
- Summary

Chapter 21—NetRunner—Part Two

This chapter shows the user how to add the MailRunner program to the NetRunner program we built in Chapter 15. We continue the process of integration of the functions by adding a facility to mail news articles and offer some other improvements to NetRunner—Part One and MailRunner.

- Overview
- How to Use NetRunner—Part Two
- Merging MailRunner into NetRunner
- Sending Articles from NewsRunner
- Sort ListViews in ArticleList and MailRunner
- The Assign Function
- Delete Registry Information
- Summary

Chapter 16

SMPT Protocols and Functions

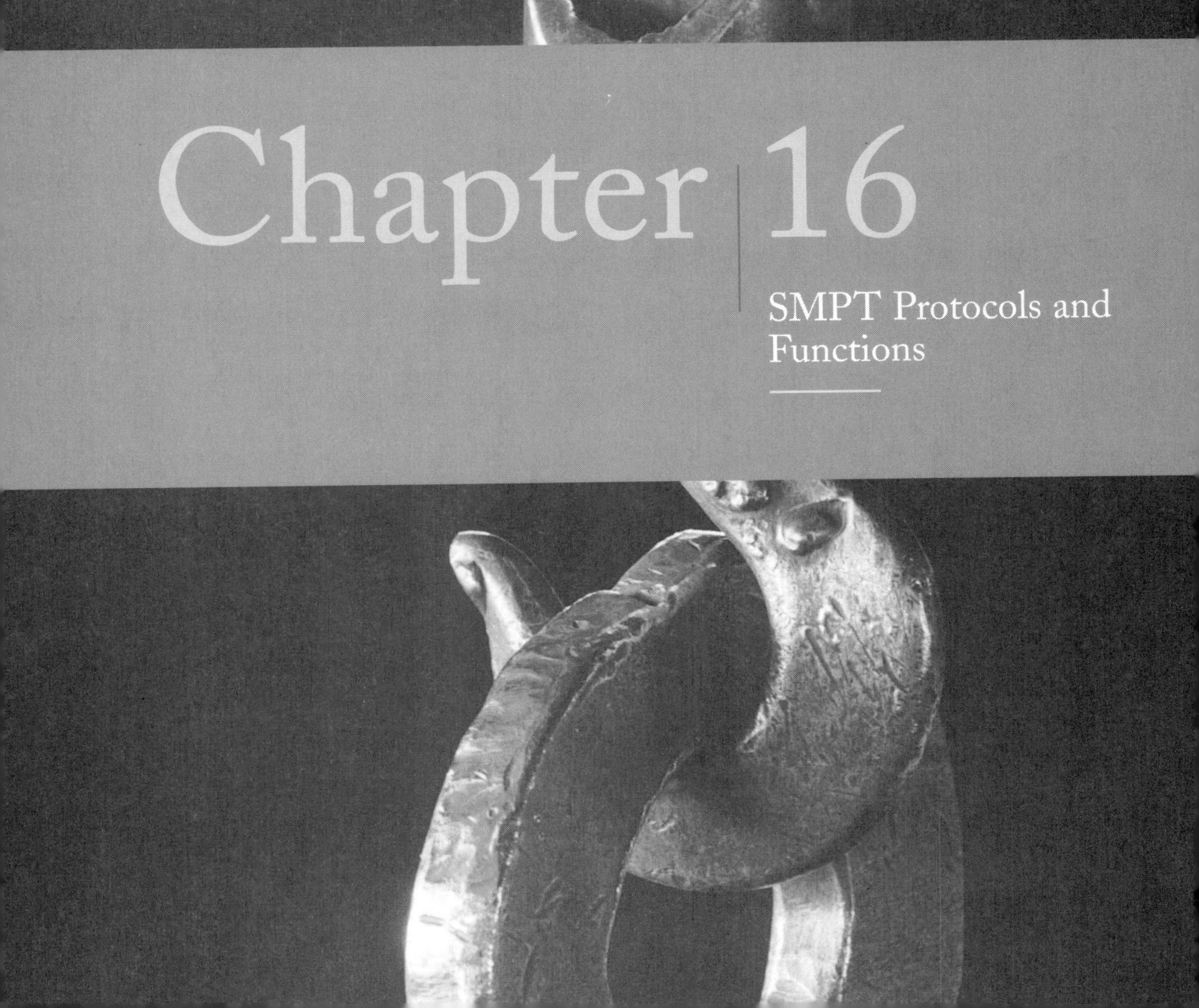

Overview

In this chapter, we talk about how the SMTP protocols work between the client and the server. For more details about this protocol, see RFC-821. This protocol specifies how to send mail and how to receive mail. As you will see in a few moments, it is not practical for the average PC to receive mail, so we are going to try to limit ourselves to discussions about how to send mail.

By the end of this chapter, you should be able to answer the following questions:

- How do you access the server?
- What header keywords should be included in the note?
- How do you send a message?

The SMTP Model

The *Simple Mail Transport Protocol (SMTP)* is a protocol that was developed to send and receive electronic mail over computer networks. It also provides other features besides straight transport of electronic messages, such as relaying messages between different networks, and forwarding messages to a user on a different machine.

Mail is sent from one SMTP server to another much in the same way that news is sent from one news server to another. Unlike moving news from one server to another, the user directly initiates the transfer process when sending mail. Received mail from another SMTP server, however, is generally processed and stored directly in the host system's file system. From there, a program can scan the location in the file system where mail files are stored and display the received mail to the user.

When the user's program is ready to send a piece of mail, it connects to an SMTP server using port 25. In figure 16-1, this server is referred to as the "sending SMTP server." The user sends SMTP commands to the sending server with information about who should receive the mail message along with the message itself. The SMTP server stores this information locally in the host's file system, and then attempts to transmit it to the specified recipients. If it cannot transmit it to all recipients, it saves it and tries to retransmit it later. Eventually, if it is not successful, the message is returned to the sender.

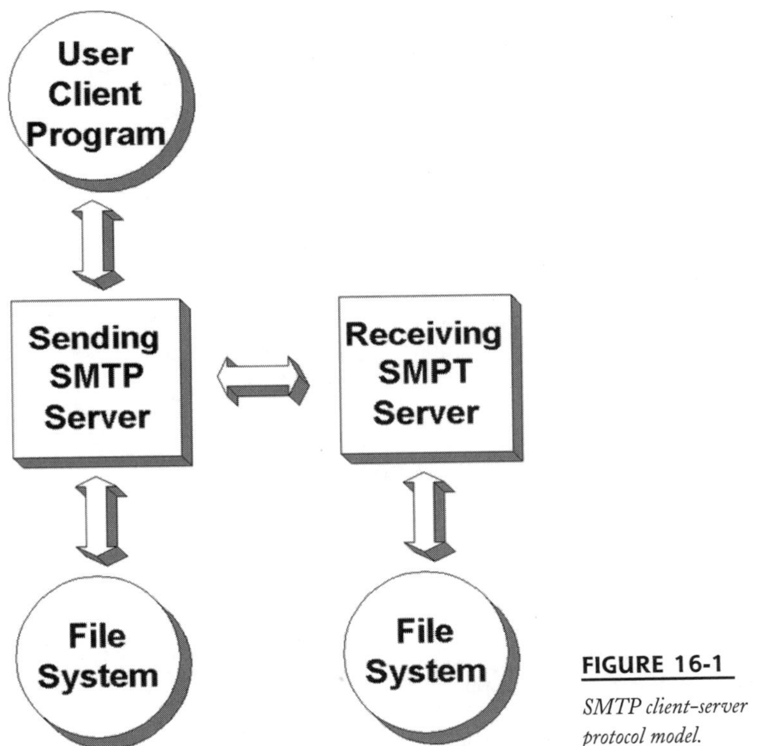

FIGURE 16-1

SMTP client-server protocol model.

Like most servers, SMTP expects to have a full-time connection to the network. This is not possible with a Windows 95 PC over a dial-up connection. Because a connection is not always there, messages cannot be received on the local machine. For that reason, using SMTP is not a total solution to processing mail on the Internet. An easy solution is to have a server that can scan the file system on demand for mail files and download them to the Windows 95 PC. Such a server exists and is called a *Post Office Protocol* (*POP*) server. We explore this function more in Chapter 18, "POP Protocols and Functions."

Electronic Mail Format

RFC-822 describes the format for an e-mail message. As we saw in Chapter 11, a news article is formatted according to the same rules used to format electronic mail. The same overall structure for the document exists; that is, a header followed by a blank line and finally the body of the message. The headers are formatted according to rules outlined in the RFC-822 document and the body is essentially unstructured text. Here is an example of a sample electronic mail message:

```
Date:     4 Jul 1996 15:06:00 -0400
From:     Wayne S. Freeze <WFreeze@umdacc.umd.edu>
To:       WFreeze@umdacc.umd.edu
Subject: Test note

Testing the SMTP mail server.

                  ...............Wayne
.
```

In this example, we have three lines of header information, which is the practical minimum for sending a note. The *Date:* header lets the reader know when the note was sent. The *From:* header identifies the sender's e-mail address. The *To:* header identifies the e-mail address of the person who will receive the mail. The *Subject:* header contains information that helps the recipient understand the content of the note.

Each header is formatted in the same way as the headers in the news article. Each line begins with a keyword that is followed by a colon (":") and then some text.

Date

The date keyword indicates the date the e-mail note was composed and sent. In the preceding example, the date is formatted as: Day, Month, Year, Hour, :, Minute, :, second, and offset from Greenwich Mean Time (GMT). Just in case you are not familiar with GMT, this is the time that is defined to be time on the planet. All local times are defined in terms of the number of hours before or after GMT. Because Eastern Daylight Savings Time is four hours behind GMT, the local time that this note was written is a little after 1:00pm.

From

This is a valid Internet mail-style address of the user who wrote the note and must be in one of the following three formats:

```
WFreeze@umdacc.umd.edu
WFreeze@umdacc.umd.edu (Wayne S. Freeze)
Wayne S. Freeze <WFreeze@umdacc.umd.edu>
```

Notice that I used multiple formats for the e-mail address in this example. You are always free to choose which format you want to use.

To

The To header is a list of one or more e-mail addresses that are formatted in the same fashion as the From header.

Subject

This is simply the subject line of the note. Its contents are left up to the original poster, but hopefully it contains something meaningful about the note. While the RFC-822 standard classifies this as an optional component of a note, I strongly suggest you consider it a required component because every mail program I've ever used includes the subject line when displaying a list of e-mail messages. Including a subject header makes it easier for the user to determine the contents and urgency of your e-mail message.

Optional Headers

While we covered the four most important header keywords for an e-mail note, there are a few others that are worth mentioning. The *CC:* keyword is used to send the message to a secondary user. The *BCC:* keyword also sends the message to a secondary user, however, no users listed in the To: and CC: headers see the BCC header. (By the way, "CC" stands for Carbon Copy and "BCC" stands for Blind Carbon Copy. These terms date back to the days before copiers when the only way for someone to create another copy of a letter was to use carbon paper.)

Other interesting header keywords include Message-Id (which we saw in Chapter 11), which has the same meaning here; References, which is used to refer to one or more previous e-mail notes; and Keywords, which is a list of one or more words that describe the note. Also, it is possible to create other header keywords that include useful information, like X-NNTP-NewsReader, which indicates the name of the newsreader that posted the article.

SMTP Protocol Commands

The SMTP commands we are going to discuss relate only to the sending of mail using the SMTP command. While there are other commands available, they are not used by the ActiveX control, so I'm not going to discuss them in this chapter. You can read about them in RFC-821.

Table 16-1 lists the SMTP protocol commands and their syntax, while Table 16-2 shows the syntax of the parameters.

Table 16-1 SMTP Protocol Commands

Command	Syntax
Data	`DATA`
Hello	`HELO [<domain>]`
Help	`HELP [<help-string>]`
Mail	`MAIL FROM: <reverse-path>`
Quit	`QUIT`
Recipient	`RCPT TO: <forward-path>`

Table 16-2 SMTP Command Parameter Syntax

Parameter	Syntax
`<domain>`	::=
`<forward-path>`	::= email address of recipient
`<help-string>`	::= SMTP command
`<reverse-oath>`	::= email address of the sender

SMTP Reply Codes and Messages

The SMTP protocol is very similar to the NNTP protocol in the way that reply codes and messages are handled. These reply codes consist of three parts: a three-digit reply code, a reply string, and an optional block information returned by the server. Like the FTP and NNTP protocols, the reply code and reply message are returned in a single line. Like the NNTP server, the optional block of text is included in the data stream on the same port.

SMTP uses a highly structured three-digit number for the reply code. The first digit indicates whether or not the command was successful.

1 Indicates a positive preliminary reply, where the command is partially complete and the server is waiting for confirmation of the information in this reply. (Believe it or not, this value is defined as part of the standard even though no SMTP commands generate this message.)

2 The command executed properly.

3 The command is okay as far as it can be processed, but additional information is needed before the command can be completed.

4 The command is correct, but for some reason could not be executed.

5 Some kind of permanent error, such as a syntax error or a serious program error.

The second digit of the reply code further refines the type of information returned.

0 Refers to syntax errors or unimplemented commands.

1 Indicates informational messages.

2 Contains information about connections.

3, 4 Are unspecified and available for future use.

5 The reply refers to mail system status.

The last digit does not have a defined set of categories, but is available to refine the meaning of the various reply codes. The text part of the messages is not fixed and probably contains more specific information than listed in Table 16-3. However, if the message occupies more than one line, the reply code followed immediately by a dash ("-") starts each line but the last. In the last line, the reply code is followed by a space and then the text. If there is only one line to the message, there is a space between the reply code and the message's text.

Table 16-3 SMTP Reply Codes and Reply Text

Reply Code	Reply Text
211	System status, or system help reply.
214	Help message.
220	<domain> Service ready.
221	<domain> service closing transmission channel.
250	Requested mail action okay, completed.
251	User not local; will forward to <forward-path>.
354	Start mail input; end with <crlf> . <crlf>
421	<domain> service not available.
450	Requested mail action not taken: mailbox unavailable (E.g., mailbox busy).
451	Requested action aborted: local error in processing.
452	Requested action not taken: insufficient system storage.
500	Syntax error, command unrecognized.
501	Syntax error in parameters or arguments.
502	Command not implemented.
503	Bad sequence of commands.
504	Command parameter not implemented.
550	Requested action not taken: mailbox unavailable (E.g., mailbox not found, no access).
551	User not local; please try <forward-path>.
552	Requested mail action aborted: exceeded storage allocation.
553	Requested action not taken: mailbox name not allowed (E.g., Mailbox syntax incorrect).
554	Transaction failed.

Accessing the Server

Sending a note is a fairly straightforward process. The client program initiates a connection to an SMTP server on port 25. If the server accepts the request, it responds with a reply code of 220. A reply code of 221 indicates that the server is running, but not accepting service requests.

Unlike the servers we have already discussed, the SMTP server is not that concerned about security. After the connection is made, the client program issues a `Hello` command to identify itself to the system. Closing the connection is done by using the `Quit` command. The `Help` command is available to determine what commands are available for use. To send a message, the `Mail` command is used, followed by one or more `Recipient` commands. Finally, the `Data` command is used to submit the actual document to be mailed.

Hello

The `Hello` command is used to identify the local machine to the server. It has an optional parameter that is the name of your local machine. The reason this parameter is optional is that the server knows your IP address and has the capability to use standard Internet utilities to translate the IP address into a host name.

As you can see, this isn't really a good security check, but because SMTP attaches your real address to your mail (take a look at your mail header sometime), this is not as big a problem as it might seem. If the `Hello` command is successful, a reply code of 250 is returned. Otherwise, one of the following reply codes identifies the error: 500, 501, 504, and 421.

Quit

The `Quit` command is used to disconnect from the SMTP server. If the server accepts this command, it returns a reply code of 221.

Help

The `Help` command provides information about the commands available on the server. A reply code of 211 or 214 is generated along with a text message that is designed to be read by a human. The `Help` command also takes one parameter, which is usually the name of one of the available commands. This returns more detailed information about the selected command.

Sending a Note

After connecting to the server, three commands are needed to send a message: the `Mail` command, the `Recipient` command, and the `Data` command.

Mail

The `Mail` command begins the process of sending a piece of electronic mail by identifying the sender. In this case, the sender is your e-mail address. If the command is successful, a reply code of 250 is returned. Unsuccessful reply codes are 552, 451, and 452. The usual 500 series error codes also apply.

Recipient

The `Recipient` command follows the `Mail` command when sending a piece of e-mail. This command supplies the e-mail address of a single person you want to receive your message. If the note is sent to multiple addresses, each address must be supplied as a separate `Recipient` command. If successful, the server returns a reply code of 250 or 251. Otherwise, the reply code could be any one of the following: 450, 451, 452, 550, 551, 552, or 553.

Data

The `Data` command is used to transfer the actual e-mail note after all the recipients have been specified. This note must be properly formatted including all the headers in the proper place, a blank line before the body, and the free-form text of the body. Then the `Data` command simply passes the note from the sending SMTP server to the receiving SMTP server. The header information is used eventually by the mail client, but SMTP does not use this information because all the recipients have been specified explicitly by using the `Recipient` command.

After the `Data` command has been submitted, the server responds with a reply code of 354 (send the message). The client then responds with the electronic mail note as described above, followed by a line with only a single period. If the command is successful, a reply code of 250 is returned by the server. Otherwise, codes of 451, 452, 500, 501, 504, or 552 could be returned depending on the error.

Other Facilities

While I said I was going to focus on the parts of the SMTP command that are used by the SMTP ActiveX control, I would be remiss in not telling you that the actual SMTP design is a lot more complex and flexible. SMTP is designed to work between two host machines. It provides additional commands to perform tasks such as forwarding mail through multiple servers and across multiple networks until the mail reaches its ultimate destination and displaying messages on the user's terminal. (Of course, you need a session on the host machine that has the SMTP server for this function to work.) SMTP also has commands that can verify e-mail addresses and treat an e-mail address as a distribution list and expand it into a list of individual e-mail addresses.

Most of these other facilities are important only when implemented in a more complex environment. Mail forwarding was more important few years ago when multiple networks were very common. Likewise, because multiuser host systems were also more popular years ago, sending messages to a user's terminal was also a more useful feature.

Example

In the following example, I use the Windows 95 `Telnet` command to connect to a machine with an SMTP server. If you want to try this, Telnet to your local SMTP server using port 25 instead of port 23. You need to set local echo on and be a good (or very good) typist, because the server does not allow you to use backspace or delete to correct any typing errors.

Commands that I type are prefixed by -‡, and responses from the server begin with the three-digit reply code that we previously discussed.

```
220 dbserva.acc.umd.edu Sendmail AIX 3.2/UCB 5.64/4.03 ready at Thu, 4 Jul 1996 15:04:54
-0400
-‡helo
```

```
250 dbserva.acc.umd.edu Hello  (annex12-60.dial.umd.edu)
help
214-Commands:
214-     HELO     MAIL     RCPT     DATA     RSET
214-     NOOP     QUIT     HELP     VRFY     EXPN
214-For more information use HELP followed by the topic.
214-For local information contact postmaster at this site.
214 End of HELP information.
-‡help data
214-Usage: DATA
214-     The following text is collected as the message.
214-     End with a line containing only the . character.
214 End of HELP information.
-‡mail from:WFreeze@umdacc.umd.edu
250 WFreeze@umdacc.umd.edu... Sender is valid.
-‡rcpt to:WFreeze@umdacc.umd.edu
250 WFreeze@umdacc.umd.edu... Recipient is valid.
-‡data
354 Enter mail. End with the . character on a line by itself.
-‡Date:     4 Jul 1996 15:06:00 -0400
-‡From:     Wayne S. Freeze <WFreeze@umdacc.umd.edu>
-‡To:       WFreeze@umdacc.umd.edu
-‡Subject: Test note
-‡
-‡Testing the SMTP mail server.
-‡
-‡                 ...............Wayne
-‡.
250 Ok
-‡quit
221 dbserva.acc.umd.edu: closing the connection.
```

Connecting to the server generates a return code of 220 with a reply message that includes the name of the host system. At this point, the server is ready to accept commands. The first command I enter is the Hello command (`HELO`). Notice that I didn't bother to tell the server my domain name. The server responded with a reply code of 250 and a message that repeated its own domain name and also responded with my domain name in parentheses.

After I established the connection, I tried the `Help` command to get a list of commands available on the server. The server returned a reply code of 214 and the help text. Notice that each line begins with 214 and all lines except last have a dash ("-") after the reply code. In this example, I executed a second `Help` command that specified the `Data` command as a parameter and received some basic help information about the `Data` command.

At this point, I begin a sequence of commands that result in a piece of mail being sent. First, I enter the `Mail` command and specify my e-mail address as the parameter to the FROM: clause. The server then responds with a reply code of 250 with an acknowledgment that the sender e-mail address was acceptable.

Then I submitted a Recipient command (`RCPT`) with another e-mail address. Note that this e-mail address is the same as the other e-mail address. (Yes, it is legal to send mail to yourself.) As before, the server responded with a reply code of 250 like the mail command, but this time the server's text message differed in that the mail recipient was valid. While I specified only one recipient, you could specify as many as you desire (or the server will accept).

Next, I submitted a mail message. Note that this mail message includes mail headers for From, To, and Subject, and then a blank line and the body of the text. The header information for From and To headers are required even though SMTP commands contain the same information. I terminated the message with a period on a line by itself. Upon receiving the period, the server responded with a reply code of 250, saying that the message was accepted.

Finally, I enter the SMTP `Quit` command to close the connection. The server responded with a reply code of 221 and then closed the connection.

Summary

In this chapter, we talked about the SMTP features that are used by the SMTP ActiveX control. For a complete description of the protocol, see RFC-821. We discussed how to connect to a server, and how to submit the commands necessary to send an e-mail message.

In the next chapter, we continue our discussion of SMTP by looking at how the SMTP client control works.

In case you want to check your answers to the questions in the Overview section, here are the answers:

- *How do you access the server?*

  You access the server by simply establishing a session with the server and then executing the `Hello` command.

- *What header keywords should be included in the note?*

  The Date header keyword indicates the day and time the note was created. The To header keyword has the list of users that will receive the note. The From header keyword lets the recipient know who sent the note. The Subject header keyword provides a simple summary of the contents of the note.

- *How do you send a message?*

  You send a message by using the `Mail` command to identify yourself as the sender, and then executing one or more `Recipient` commands for each person that will receive the e-mail note, and finally the `Data` command is executed to send the actual note to the server.

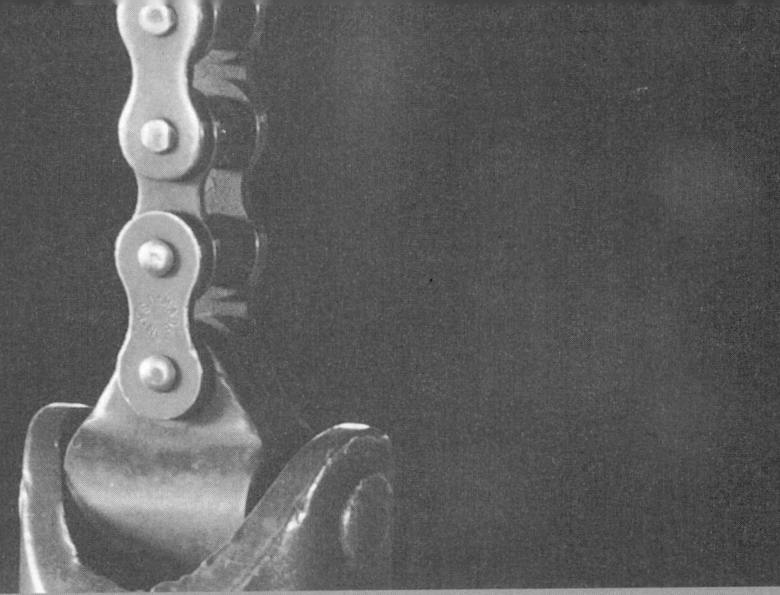

Chapter 17

The SMTP Client Control

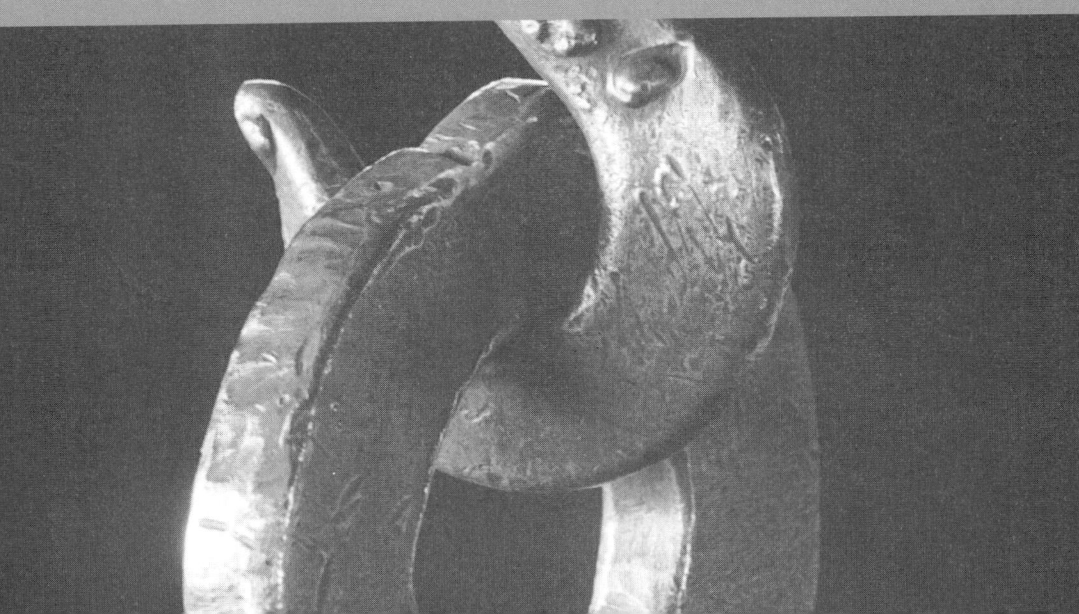

Overview

In this chapter, we discuss the properties, events, and methods of the SMTP client control. This control handles the protocol interaction with a remote SMTP server and provides a high-level method of interacting with the server.

By the end of this chapter, you should be able to answer the following questions:

- What other objects are used by this control?
- What methods are used to send an e-mail message?
- What methods are used to manage a connection?

Properties

The SMTP control has a number of properties that provide default values for various methods, describe the facilities available on the remote server, and provide status information about the control's state.

Busy

Format: `SMTPObject.Busy`

The `Busy` property returns `true` if the SMTP client control is executing a command. Most commands cannot be started until the current command is finished.

Table 17-1 *Busy* Values

Busy Value	Description
`True`	The SMTP client control is executing a command.
`False`	The SMTP client control is not executing a command.

DocInput

Format: `SMTPObject.DocInput`

The `DocInput` property returns a reference to the `DocInput` object associated with the control. It is used primarily to access the various properties of the `DocInput` object. Note that unlike the NNTP and FTP controls, this control does not have a `DocOutput` object because it never receives data from a server.

EnableTimer

Format: `SMTPObject.EnableTimer(event) [= boolean]`

The `EnableTimer` property sets or returns a flag that controls one of several different timers.

Table 17-2 *`EnableTimer`* Events

`EnableTimer` Event Name	*`EnableTimer`* Event Value	Description
`prcConnectTimeout`	1	If a connection is not made within the time out period, the `TimeOut` event is triggered.
`prcReceiveTimeout`	2	If no data arrives for a receive process within the timeout period, the `TimeOut` event is triggered.
`prcUserTimeout`	65	User defined `TimeOut` event.

Table 17-3 *`Timeout`* Values

`Timeout` Value	Description
`True`	The timer for this event is enabled.
`False`	The timer for this event is not enabled.

Errors

Format: `SMTPObject.Errors`

The `Errors` property returns an `icErrors` collection that contains information about the last error that occurred. It is used primarily to access the properties of the `icErrors` object. (For more information about the `icErrors` and `icError` objects, see Chapter 9.)

NotificationMode

Format: `SMTPObject.NotifictionMode [= integer]`

The `NotificationMode` property returns or sets an integer that indicates when notification should be provided for incoming data. This property is used when working with the `DocInput` object.

Table 17-4 *NotificationMode* Values

NotificationMode Value	Description
0	**Complete:** Notification is given when the response is complete.
1	**Continuous:** Notification is given as new data is received.

ProtocolState

Format: `SMTPObject.ProtocolState`

The `ProtocolState` property is used to determine which state the protocol is in.

Table 17-5 *ProtocolState* Values

ProtocolState Value Name	*ProtocolState* Value	Description
`ftpBase`	0	**Base state:** Before a connection is established with the server.

ProtocolState Value Name	*ProtocolState* Value	Description
`ftpAuthorization`	1	**Authorization state:** After connection is established and before the user has been granted access to the server.
`ftpTransaction`	2	**Transaction state:** After the user has been granted access to the server. The client can now interact with the server.

RemoteHost

Format: `SMTPObject.RemoteHost [= string]`

The `RemoteHost` property is a string that contains the host name or IP address of the remote host. It is used with the `Connect` method to establish a connection to the remote computer.

RemotePort

Format: `SMTPObject.RemotePort [= long]`

The `RemotePort` property is a long that contains the port number that the SMTP server is listening to. Usually this value is 25.

ReplyCode

Format: `SMTPObject.ReplyCode`

The `ReplyCode` property is a long that contains the reply code of the most recent message generated by the SMTP server. See Table 16-3 for a list of valid reply codes and sample messages.

ReplyString

Format: `SMTPObject.RemoteString`

The `ReplyString` property is a string that contains the text of the message last received from the SMTP server. See Table 16-3 for a list of valid reply codes and sample messages.

State

Format: `SMTPObject.State`

The `State` property returns an integer and is used to determine which state the connection is in.

Table 17-6 *State* Values

State Value Name	*State* Value	Description
`prcConnecting`	1	**Connecting state:** A connection has been requested and is waiting for an acknowledgment.
`prcResolvingHost`	2	**Resolving Host state:** Waiting for a host name to be translated into its IP address. (Not entered if an IP address was supplied as the `RemoteHost` property).
`prcHostResolved`	3	**Host Resolved state:** After the host name has successfully translated into an IP address. (Not entered if an IP address was supplied as the `RemoteHost` property.)
`prcConnected`	4	**Connected state:** A connection has been successfully established.
`prcDisconnecting`	5	**Disconnecting state:** A request to disconnect has been requested.
`prcDisconnected`	6	**Disconnected state:** Before a connection is requested and after a connection has been closed.

TimeOut

Format: `SMTPObject.TimeOut(event) [= long]`

The `TimeOut` property sets or returns a flag that controls how much time must pass before a `TimeOut` event.

Table 17-7 *TimeOut* Events

TimeOut Event Name	*TimeOut* Event Value	Description
`prcConnectTimeout`	1	If a connection is not made within the timeout period, the `TimeOut` event is triggered.
`prcReceiveTimeout`	2	If no data arrives for a receive process within the timeout period, the `TimeOut` event is triggered.
`prcUserTimeout`	65	User defined `TimeOut` event.

URL

Format: `SMTPObject.URL [= string]`

The `URL` property is a string that holds the name of the current document being transferred. The `URL` may be set to a URL that you want to retrieve before using the `SendDoc` method. If the `URL` is not set before the `SendDoc` method is used, this information must be included as a parameter to the `SendDoc` method. This property is used primarily to support the `DocInput` object.

Methods

The SMTP ActiveX client control provides many methods to work with a news server. Note that some of the commands depend on extensions to the basic SMTP protocol. Because not all news servers have these extensions, you should not rely on these methods unless you have verified that the server has these extensions available.

Cancel

Format: `SMTPObject.Cancel`

The `Cancel` method is used to cancel a pending request. After this method is finished, the `Cancel` event is triggered.

SendDoc

Format: `SMTPObject.SendDoc [url] [,[headers] [,[inputdata] [,[inputfile] [,output-file]]]]`

The `SendDoc` method works with the `DocInput` object to transfer a file to the remote SMTP server from the local machine. All five arguments are optional and if they are not specified, the appropriate values from the `DocInput` object are used.

The URL, if specified, should be of the form: `Mailto://remotehost/filename` where

`News` is optional when used with the SMTP client control.

`remotehost` is optional and assumed to be the current machine.

`filename` is required and is the fully qualified name of the file on the local machine.

Table 17-8 *SendDoc* Method Arguments

Argument Name	Argument Type	Description
`url`	string	Name of the file on the remote system to be retrieved in URL format.
`headers`	DocHeaders	Header information.
`inputdata`	variant	Optional data buffer containing the document to be sent.
`Inputfile`	variant	Optional file containing the document to be sent.
`outputfile`	string	Name of the output file on the local machine to which the reply document is written.

Events

The SMTP events are called in response to various conditions that happen during the execution of a program using the SMTP ActiveX control.

Busy

Format: `SMTPObject_Busy(ByVal isBusy As Boolean)`

The `Busy` event occurs when the `SMTPObject.Busy` property changes state. This event occurs when a command begins execution, or when a command finishes execution.

Table 17-9 *Busy* Event Parameters

Parameter Name	Argument Type	Description
`isBusy`	boolean	Indicates when a command is being executed.

Table 17-10 *isBusy* Values

isBusy Value	Description
`True`	A command is being executed.
`False`	A command is not being executed.

Cancel

Format: `SMTPObject_Cancel`

The `Cancel` event occurs after the `Cancel` method is invoked.

DocInput

Format: `SMTPObject_DocInput(ByVal docinput as DocInput)`

The `DocInput` event occurs when data has been transferred from this object to the remote SMTP server.

Table 17-11 *DocInput* Event Parameters

Parameter Name	Argument Type	Description
`docinput`	DocInput	Object that describes the current input data for this transfer.

ProtocolStateChanged

Format: `SMTPObject_ProtocolStateChanged(ByVal protocolstate as integer)`

The `ProtocolStateChanged` event occurs whenever the protocol state is changed.

Table 17-12 *ProtocolStateChanged* Event Parameters

Parameter Name	Argument Type	Description
`protocolstate`	integer	The value of the protocol state.

Table 17-13 *protocolstate* Values

protocolState Value Name	*protocolState* Value	Description
`ftpBase`	0	**Base state:** Before a connection is established with the server.
`ftpAuthorization`	1	**Authorization state:** After connection is established and before the user has been granted access to the server.
`ftpTransaction`	2	**Transaction state:** After the user has been granted access to the server. The client can now interact with the server.

StateChanged

Format: `SMTPObject_StateChanged(ByVal state as integer)`

The `StateChanged` event occurs whenever the transport state is changed.

Table 17-14 *StateChanged* Event Parameters

Parameter Name	Argument Type	Description
`state`	integer	The value of the transport state.

Table 17-15 *state* Values

state Value Name	*state* Value	Description
`prcConnecting`	1	**Connecting state:** A connection has been requested and is waiting for an acknowledgment.
`prcResolvingHost`	2	**Resolving Host state:** Waiting for a host name to be translated into its IP address. (Not entered if an IP address was supplied as the `RemoteHost` property).
`prcHostResolved`	3	**Host Resolved state:** After the host name has successfully translated into an IP address. (Not entered if an IP address was supplied as the `RemoteHost` property.)
`prcConnected`	4	**Connected state:** A connection has been successfully established.
`prcDisconnecting`	5	**Disconnecting state:** A request to disconnect has been requested.
`prcDisconnected`	6	**Disconnected state:** Before a connection is requested and after a connection is closed.

TimeOut

Format: `SMTPObject_TimeOut(ByVal event as integer, continue as boolean)`

The `TimeOut` event occurs when the specified event does not occur within the interval defined in the `TimeOut` property for that event.

Table 17-16 *TimeOut* Event Parameters

Parameter Name	Argument Type	Description
`event`	integer	Event to which the timer interval applies.
`continue`	boolean	Determines if the timer will remain active.

Table 17-17 *event* values

event Name	*event* Value	Description
`prcConnectTimeout`	1	If a connection is not made within the time out period, the `TimeOut` event is triggered.
`prcReceiveTimeout`	2	If no data arrives for a receive process within the timeout period, the `TimeOut` event is triggered.
`prcUserTimeout`	65	User defined `TimeOut` event.

Table 17-18 *continue* Values

continue Value	Description
`True`	The timer continues to run.
`False`	The timer is stopped.

Summary

In this chapter, we discussed the SMTP client control. This control provides a method that enables you to send an e-mail message to an SMTP server that is in turn delivered to the recipient. Unlike the FTP and NNTP controls, this control only permits a one way transfer to the server. In the next chapter, we look at the POP control that enables the user to receive e-mail.

In case you want to check your answers to the questions in the Overview section, here are the answers:

- *What other objects are used by this control?*

  `DocHeader` is used to hold a single header.

  `DocHeaders` is used to hold all the message's headers.

  `DocInput` is used to information coming to this control.

  `icErrors` is used to hold error information.

- *What method is used to send an e-mail message?*

  The `SendDoc` method is used to send an e-mail note to the server.

- *What methods are used to manage a connection?*

  This is a trick question—no methods are used to connect to the server or quit the connection.

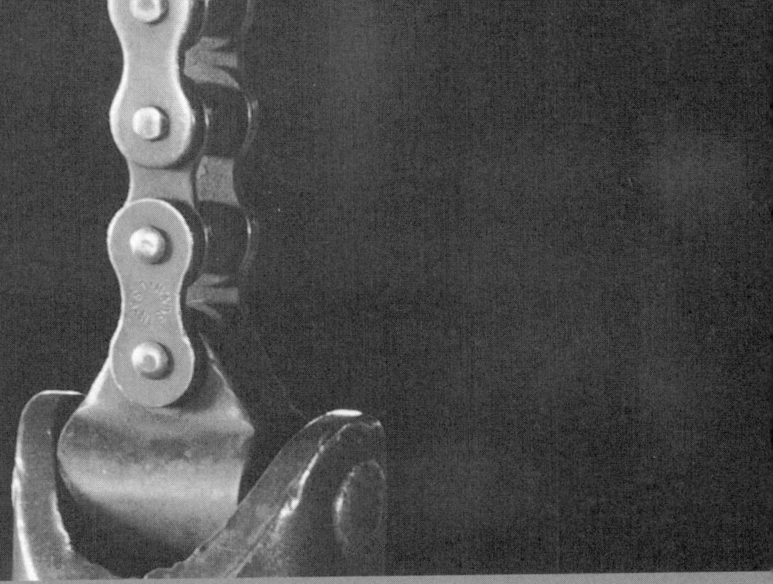

Chapter 18

POP Protocols and Functions

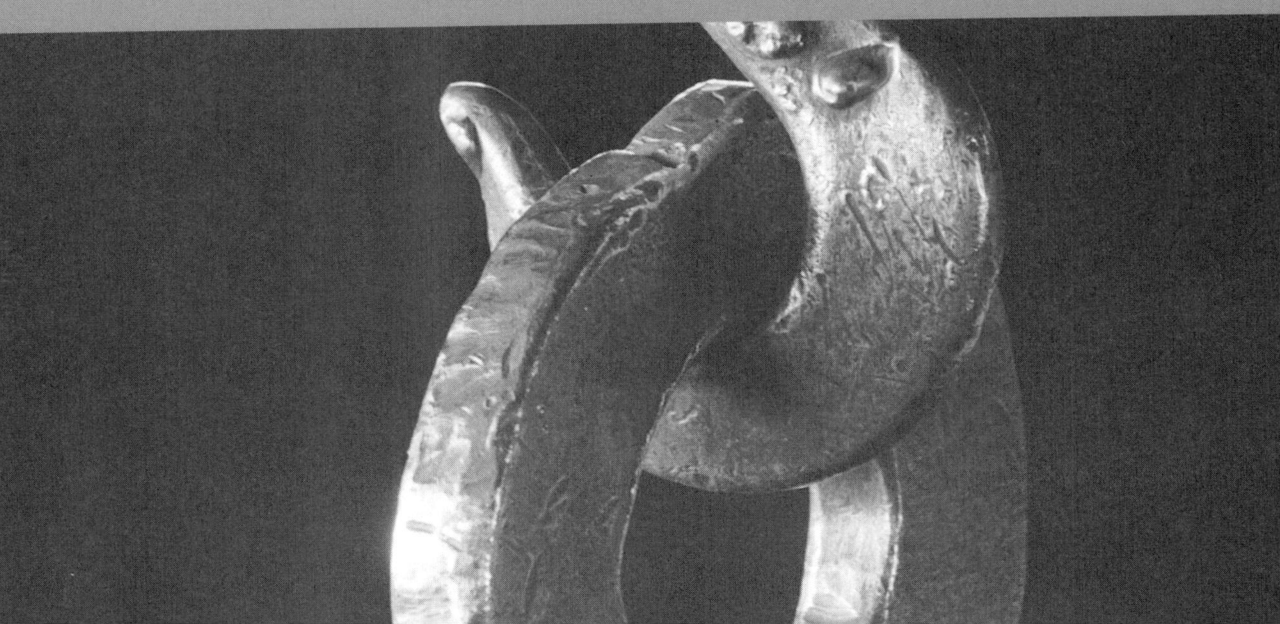

Overview

In this chapter, we talk about how the POP3 protocols work between the client and the server. For more details about this protocol, see RFC-1939. This protocol is used to download mail from a server, but it does not send mail. The POP3 and the SMTP work together to permit a Windows 95 system with the ActiveX controls to send and receive mail.

By the end of this chapter, you should be able to answer the following questions:

- How do you access the server?
- How to you list the messages to be received?
- How do you send a message?

The POP3 Model

In Chapter 16, we talked about how SMTP handles sending and receiving mail. However, in order to receive mail, the SMTP server must be connected to the Internet when another SMTP server attempts to send mail. If it is not, the sending SMTP server must hold the message and try again later. After several unsuccessful attempts, the sending SMTP server usually returns the mail to the sending user as undeliverable. This causes serious problems with computers that are not directly connected to the Internet, such as a Windows 95 PC with a dial-up connection.

Windows 95 does not include an SMTP server, but it can connect to a SMTP server when it is ready to send mail. The same SMTP server can be used to receive mail for the Windows 95 PC, but the mail is saved on the SMTP server's host machine, not the Windows 95 PC. While this solves the issue of how to send mail over the Internet, it still leaves the problem of how to receive mail from the Internet.

The *Post Office Protocol* solves this problem. This protocol works with an SMTP server on a remote host that has a direct connection to the Internet. This remote host is called the *mail server*. The SMTP server on the mail server is used to send and receive mail with the rest of the Internet. Because the server is always connected, it can always receive mail. All the client program needs to do is periodically connect to the mail server using the Post Office Protocol and check for mail.

In figure 18-1 you can see that the mail server actually consists of two servers, an SMTP server and a POP server. The user is assigned an e-mail address on the mail server. Mail is sent and received from the mail server just as if it were the user's machine. The SMTP server receives mail from the Internet and saves it in the local file system, and then the user can access the POP server to receive mail when desired.

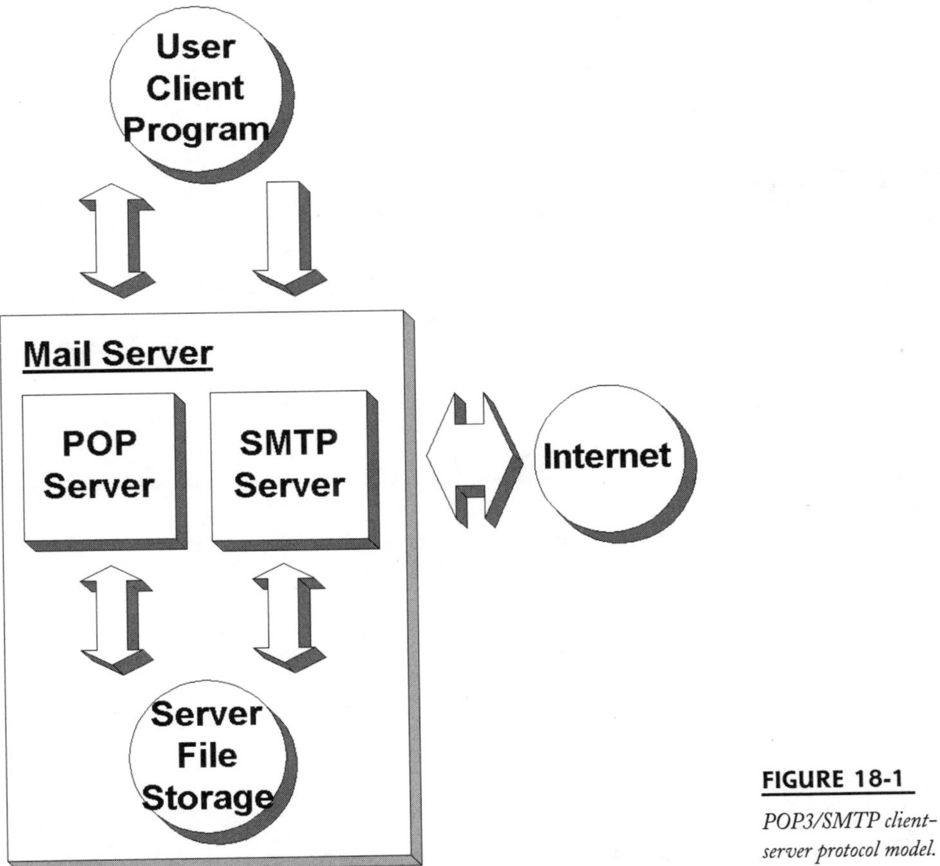

FIGURE 18-1

POP3/SMTP client-server protocol model.

To check to see if there is incoming mail, the client program uses the POP ActiveX control to connect to the POP server on port 110. Using POP commands, the program can check the mail server's file system for mail, retrieve a list of mail messages, and then download each one. After the mail is retrieved, the client has the option to either leave it on the server or delete it.

While it is possible to leave mail on the server, it is not practical to leave it there for a long time—all the mail will be treated as new mail each time the user retrieves mail. There is also no method to transfer mail from the client to the server for storage. There is another protocol that addresses this problem called *IMAP* (*Internet Mail Access Protocol*). IMAP includes functions that enable a user to retrieve new mail from the server and to store documents on the server in a hierarchical format (much like the Windows 95 directory structure). While IMAP is not widely supported today, it is gaining popularity and may eventually replace POP as the protocol of choice. But today POP is the most popular method to access mail on a remote mail server.

POP Protocol Commands

The ActiveX POP client control works very much like the other protocols we have already discussed. It takes the form of a series of commands with parameters.

Table 18-1 lists the POP protocol commands and their syntax; Table 18-2 shows the syntax of the parameters.

Table 18-1 POP Protocol Commands

Command	Syntax
APOP	`APOP <user-name> <digest>`
Delete	`DELE <message-number>`
List	`LIST [ <message-number> ]`
Noop	`NOOP`
Password	`PASS`
Quit	`QUIT`
Retrieve	`RETR <message-number>`
Reset	`RSET`
Top	`TOP <message-number> <number-of-lines>`
UIDL	`UIDL [ <message-number> ]`
User	`USER <user-name>`

Table 18-2 POP Command Parameter Syntax

Parameter	Syntax
`<digest>`	::=
`<message-number>`	::= the message number.
`<number-of-lines>`	::= the number of lines to be sent.
`<password>`	::= the password for the associated username.
`<username>`	::= a userid that is used to access the POP server.

POP Reply Codes and Messages

The POP protocol uses a different reply code from any other server we have seen so far. Instead of returning a three-digit number that has information about the successful or unsuccessful execution of the command, POP simply returns `+OK` or `-ERR`. (I refer to these messages through the rest of this chapter as *okay* or *error*.) A text message generally follows the reply code. This message may provide additional information to the user, however, most client programs do not take advantage of this information because there is not a standard for the messages. (That is not exactly true as we see later on, but for the purpose of this discussion lets go on this assumption.) After the line that contains the reply code and the reply text, additional information may follow as a series of one or more lines of text followed by a single line consisting only of a period. (We've seen this type of data transfer before in other protocols such as NNTP and SMTP.)

Accessing the Server

Using the POP server is similar to using the NNTP server. A connection is established from the client program to the server using port 110. If successful, the server responds with an okay, otherwise the server responds with an error. The client responds to the okay reply with the `User` command and follows that with the `Password` command. Assuming that both commands return okay messages, the user program is free to submit the transaction commands. Then when the user is finished, the `Quit` command is executed to terminate the session.

User

The `User` command is used to identify the person who wants to access the POP server. This is the same as the user's mailbox (i.e., Mailbox@POPServer). Note that the username does not have to be a valid userid that can access the host system using Telnet or FTP. The username can be local to the POP server (and the SMTP server). That decision is up to the implementor.

The `User` command may respond okay even if the username is not defined to the server. This may happen if the server needs both the username and the password to check to see if the user can access the server.

Password

The `Password` command supplies security information associated with the username. If the combination of password and username is valid, the server attempts to place an exclusive lock on the mailbox to prevent multiple sessions from updating the same mailbox. (It would cause problems if one session were about to retrieve a piece of mail just after another session deleted it.) If the username and password are bad, or if the POP server cannot lock the mailbox, the server returns an error reply code.

Quit

The `Quit` command is used to disconnect from the POP server. This command deletes all the messages marked for deletion and then releases the lock on the mailbox. Finally, it responds with a reply code of okay and drops the connection.

Transaction Commands

After a successful connection to the server is made, the user can submit a series of transaction commands. These commands enable the user to retrieve a list of messages, retrieve the messages themselves, and delete those messages that the user (or the client program) wants to delete.

Message numbers are assigned at this time. They always begin with one and are assigned sequentially. Note that each time the server is accessed, the message numbers are assigned all over again. This means that you should not make any assumptions about the message numbers from one session to the next.

Stat

The `Stat` command is usually the first command issued to the POP server. Its purpose is to determine the number of mail messages on the server as well as the total size of the messages. This is one of two cases in this protocol where the reply text (after the `+OK`) has a specific format. Immediately following the `+OK` is a single space followed by the number of mail messages in the mailbox, followed by another single space and the total size of the mailbox in bytes. Note that RFC-1093 refers to the size in octets, which is another name for an 8-bit byte. (This definition is important for systems like the DEC-10, DEC-20, and the Unisys 1100/2200, which do not use 8-bit bytes.)

List

The `List` command is similar to the `Stat` command in that it returns information about the number and size of the messages in the mailbox. While the `Stat` command returns information about the total mailbox, the `List` command returns a list of message numbers and message sizes. The list is terminated by a line with only a single period. Each line in the list consists of a message number, followed by a single space, followed by the message size in bytes.

A message number may be supplied with the `List` command as a parameter. In this case, the reply text is formatted similar to the `Stat` command, complete with information about the specified message. So following the `+OK` is a space, the message number, another space, and the size of the message.

Retrieve

The `Retrieve` command is used to get a copy of the specified mail message. If successful, the server returns a reply code of okay, the mail message, and finally a line with only a single period on it. The server returns an error if the message does not exist or has been deleted.

Top

The `Top` command takes two parameters, a message number and the number of lines of the message to return. The server then returns the specified number of lines from the specified message number. This command works in exactly the same way as the `Retrieve` command, but it limits the number of lines that can be returned. This command is useful to retrieve header information, such as the From, To, Date and Subject header keywords, and then to display the information to the user. If the message does not exist or has been deleted, this command returns an error.

Note that this command is an optional POP3 command and may not be available on all servers.

Delete

The `Delete` command is used to mark a specified mail message on the server as deleted. The server returns an error if the message does not exist or has already been deleted. Note that the message is not physically deleted when the command is executed. The messages are only physically deleted when the `Quit` command is executed.

Reset

The `Reset` command is used to remove the delete mark from any messages that have been marked for deletion.

Other Facilities

We've gone over most of the commands available on a POP server, but there are a couple of other commands that are worth highlighting.

Noop

The `Noop` command is a simple command that causes the server to respond with a reply code of okay. This command is useful to determine if the connection to the server is still working.

UIDL

The `UIDL` command works very similar to the `List` command, but instead of returning the size of the message, it returns a unique identifier for a specific message.

APOP

Most client programs automatically access a POP server periodically to check for new messages. Because both the `User` and `Password` commands send the userid and password over the network in clear text, it is possible for an unauthorized person to capture this information and use it to access the server. The more frequently you access your mail, the more often you establish a session with the server, thus increasing the possibility that someone could capture your username and password.

The `APOP` command addresses this loophole by establishing an alternate way to log onto the server. Basically, each time a connection is established with the server, the server provides a unique identifier for that session. The client can calculate a value for the digest parameter based on this identifier and a known "shared secret." When the `APOP` command is executed, the server can determine if this value is correct. Thus, the password need not be sent over the network each time the client needs to check for new mail. (This may be a little confusing, so if you are really interested in how this works, take some time to read the RFC-1939. It spends a lot of time explaining how this command works, including some nice examples.)

Example

I used Windows 95 Telnet command to connect to a machine with an POP3 server. You can try the same thing by Telnetting to your local POP server using port 110 instead of the standard Telnet port 23. Unless you set local echo on, you will not be able to see anything you type. Commands that I type are prefixed by ->, all other text is generated by the server.

```
+OK dbserva.acc.umd.edu POP3 3.3(20) w/IMAP2 client (Comments to MRC@CAC.Washington.EDU)
➥at Sun, 7 Jul 1996 17:14:46 -0400 (EDT)
->user wfreeze
+OK User name accepted, password please
->pass xxxxxx
+OK Mailbox open, 3 messages
->list
+OK Mailbox scan listing follows
1 769
2 776
3 1797
.
->top 1 15
+OK Top of message follows
Received: from umdacc.umd.edu by dbserva.acc.umd.edu (AIX 3.2/UCB 5.64/4.03) id AA23282;
➥Sun, 7 Jul 1996 16:56:04 -0400
Received: from UMDACC.UMD.EDU by UMDACC.UMD.EDU (IBM VM SMTP V2R2)with BSMTP id 0187;
➥Sun, 07 Jul 96 16:59:55 EDT
Received: from UMDACC (WFREEZE) by UMDACC.UMD.EDU (Mailer R2.08 R208004) with BSMTP
➥id 0496; Sun, 07 Jul 96 16:59:55 EDT
Message-Id:  <19960707.165955.WFREEZE@ACCMAIL.UMD.EDU>
Date: 07 Jul 96 16:59:54 EDT
From: Wayne Freeze      <WFREEZE@ACCMAIL.UMD.EDU>
To: "Wayne S. Freeze" <wfreeze@dbserva.acc.umd.edu>
Subject: Test Note #1
Status:

From:     Wayne S. Freeze, <WFreeze@ACCMAIL.umd.edu, 405-1080>
          Administrative Computer Center, Technical Support
.
```

```
->retr 1
+OK 769 octets
Received: from umdacc.umd.edu by dbserva.acc.umd.edu (AIX 3.2/UCB 5.64/4.03) id AA23282;
➥Sun, 7 Jul 1996 16:56:04 -0400
Received: from UMDACC.UMD.EDU by UMDACC.UMD.EDU (IBM VM SMTP V2R2) with BSMTP id 0187;
➥Sun, 07 Jul 96 16:59:55 EDT
Received: from UMDACC (WFREEZE) by UMDACC.UMD.EDU (Mailer R2.08 R208004) with BSMTP
➥id 0496; Sun, 07 Jul 96 16:59:55 EDT
Message-Id:  <19960707.165955.WFREEZE@ACCMAIL.UMD.EDU>
Date: 07 Jul 96 16:59:54 EDT
From: Wayne Freeze      <WFREEZE@ACCMAIL.UMD.EDU>
To: "Wayne S. Freeze" <wfreeze@dbserva.acc.umd.edu>
Subject: Test Note #1
Status:

From:     Wayne S. Freeze, <WFreeze@UMDACC.umd.edu, 405-1080>
          Administrative Computer Center, Technical Support


This is test note #1

     .....Wayne


.
->list
+OK Mailbox scan listing follows
1 769
2 776
3 1797
.
->dele 2
+OK Message deleted
->list
+OK Mailbox scan listing follows
1 769
```

```
3 1797
.
->rset
+OK Reset state
->list
+OK Mailbox scan listing follows
1 769
2 776
3 1797
.
->quit
+OK Sayonara
```

I started this example by Telnetting to my local system with a POP3 server. The server responds with an okay message, followed by the server's host name, the date and time that the connection was established, and some other information. Because I cannot do much without logging onto the server, the next two commands I enter are the `User` and `Password` commands.

After accepting my userid and password, the server responds with a `+OK` and the number of messages that are in my mailbox. Notice that because this message is not part of the RFC, the information is not really that useful. However, you can issue the `List` command as I did to get a list of the messages available on the server and their sizes. In fact, this is probably what most mail client programs do when they connect to the server.

The next thing a mail client program is likely to do is execute the `Top` command to get header information on each of the messages. In this example, I use the `Top` command to get the header information from the first item in my mailbox. Most client programs take this information and look for header keywords such as Subject, From, and Date, and then display that information to the user.

I execute the `Retrieve` command to get the first note in my mailbox. Because this note is relatively small (only 769 bytes), it may have made more sense to retrieve the entire note and hold it in a buffer rather than retrieve only the top of the note.

The next few commands I include in this example show how the `Delete` and `Reset` commands work. First, I execute the `List` command again; there are three messages in my mailbox. Then, I delete the second message and execute the `List` command again. Note that messages 1 and 3 are still available. If I were to execute the `Quit` command at this point and then reconnect to the server, I would find the same two messages there, but they would be numbered 1 and 2. For this example, I execute the `Reset` command, followed by the `List` command again. I see the same three original messages in their original order.

Finally, I execute the `Quit` command. The server responds with the `+OK` response code and drops the connection. Notice that most mail client programs would probably download all the mail to the local machine and then delete them from the server. This time I had only three messages in the mailbox, but if I never deleted any mail, eventually I would get so many messages that it would be impractical to download the header information each time I wanted to check my mail.

Summary

In this chapter, we talked about the Post Office Protocol that is used to retrieve mail from a mail server. Unlike SMTP, POP works well in an environment were the client is not always connected to the Internet. POP commands are used to log onto a server, list the mail on the server, and retrieve and delete individual mail messages.

In the next chapter, we continue our discussion of POP by looking at how the POP client control works.

In case you want to check your answers to the questions in the Overview section, here are the answers:

- *How do you access the server?*

  You access the server by connecting to the server and executing the `User` and `Password` commands.

- *How do you list the messages to be received?*

  The `List` command is used to determine the available messages on the server. The `Top` command is then used to extract the beginning of each mail file to determine the header information.

- *How do you receive a message?*

  A message is received by using the `Retrieve` command. After the message has been transferred, it can be marked for deletion from the server with the `Delete` command. Executing the `Quit` command completes the deletion process.

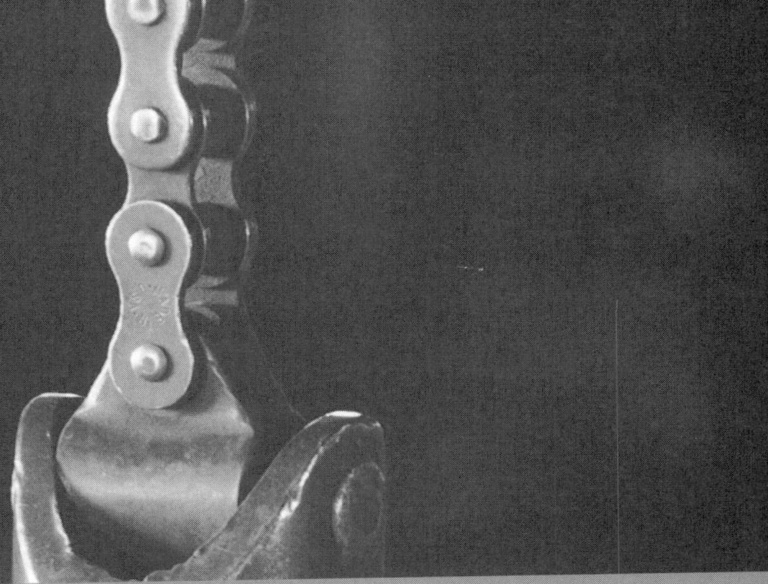

Chapter 19

The POP Client Control

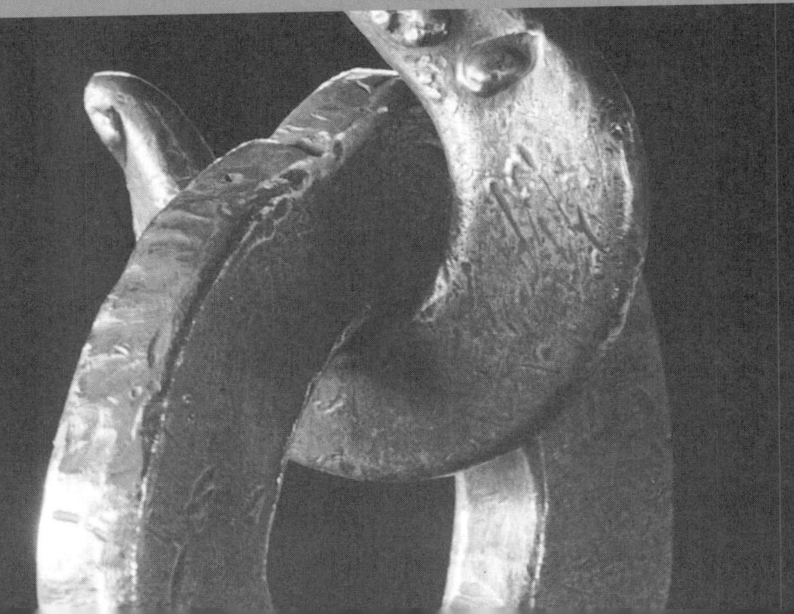

Overview

In this chapter, we discuss the properties, events, and methods of the ActiveX POP client control. This control handles the protocol interaction with a remote POP3 server and provides a high-level method of interacting with the server. While this chapter is organized primarily for quick reference, I urge you to read through it at least once to familiarize yourself with the basic concepts.

By the end of this chapter, you should be able to answer the following questions:

- What other objects are used by this control?
- What methods are used to retrieve information about the messages on the server?
- What methods are used to get messages from the server?
- What methods are used to manage a connection?

Properties

There are a number of properties that support the POP client. Some of the properties help identify methods that may not work on all servers; others communicate additional information about the server. Other properties hold objects for management of the connection and error handling. The `DocOutput` property holds a reference to a document retrieved from the server. Together the POP ActiveX control's properties contain information that is used by the various methods available with the POP control to simplify using the POP server.

Busy

Format: `POPObject.Busy`

The `Busy` property returns `true` if the POP client control is executing a command. Most commands cannot be started until the current command is finished.

Table 19-1 *Busy* Values

Busy Value	Description
`true`	The POP client control is executing a command.
`false`	The POP client control is not executing a command.

DocOutput

Format: `POPObject.DocOutput`

The `DocOutut` property returns a reference to the `DocOutput` object associated with the control. It is used primarily to access the various properties of the `DocOutput` object.

EnableTimer

Format: `POPObject.EnableTimer(event) [= boolean]`

The `EnableTimer` property sets or returns a flag that controls one of several different timers.

Table 19-2 *EnableTimer* Events

EnableTimer Event Name	*EnableTimer* Event Value	Description
`prcConnectTimeout`	1	If a connection is not made within the timeout period, the `TimeOut` event is triggered.
`prcReceiveTimeout`	2	If no data arrives for a receive process within the timeout period, the `TimeOut` event is triggered.
`prcUserTimeout`	65	User defined `TimeOut` event.

Table 19-3 ***Timeout* Values**

Timeout Value	Description
`true`	The timer for this event is enabled.
`false`	The timer for this event is not enabled.

Errors

Format: `POPObject.Errors`

The `Errors` property returns an `icErrors` collection that contains information about the last error that occurred. It is used primarily to access the properties of the `icErrors` object. (For more information about the `icErrors` and `icError` objects, refer to Chapter 9.)

MessageCount

Format: `POPObject.MessageCount`

The `MessageCount` property returns the number of messages on the remote server. The value of this property is undefined until a valid connection has been made.

NotificationMode

Format: `POPObject.NotifictionMode [= integer]`

The `NotificationMode` property returns or sets an integer that indicates when notification should be provided for incoming data. This is most useful when working with the `DocOutput` object.

Table 19-4 ***NotificationMode* Values**

NoticificationMode Value	Description
0	**Complete:** Notification is given when the response is complete.
1	**Continuous:** Notification is given as new data is received.

Password

Format: `POPObject.Password [= string]`

The `Password` property returns or sets the password value used by the `Authenticate` method to access the POP3 server.

ProtocolState

Format: `POPObject.ProtocolState`

The `ProtocolState` property is used to determine which state the protocol is in.

Table 19-5 *ProtocolState* Values

ProtocolState Value Name	*ProtocolState* Value	Description
`prcNone`	0	**Base state:** Before a connection is established with the server.
`prcAuthorization`	1	**Authorization state:** After connection is established and before the user has been granted access to the server.
`prcTransaction`	2	**Transaction state:** After the user has been granted access to the server. The client can now interact with the server.
`prcUpdate`	3	**Update state:** After the `Quit` command has been entered in the transaction state, but before the connection has been disconnected.

RemoteHost

Format: `POPObject.RemoteHost [= string]`

The `RemoteHost` property is a string that contains the host name or IP address of the remote host. It is used with the `Connect` method to establish a connection to the remote computer.

RemotePort

Format: `POPObject.RemotePort [= long]`

The `RemotePort` property is a long that contains the port number that the POP server is listening to. Usually this value is 119.

ReplyCode

Format: `POPObject.ReplyCode`

The `ReplyCode` property is a long that contains the reply code of the most recent message generated by the POP server.

ReplyString

Format: `POPObject.RemoteString`

The `ReplyString` property is a string that contains the text of the message last received from the POP server.

State

Format: `POPObject.State`

The `State` property returns an integer and is used to determine which state the connection is in.

Table 19-6 *State* Values

State Value Name	*State* Value	Description
`prcConnecting`	1	**Connecting state:** A connection has been requested and is waiting for an acknowledgment.
`prcResolvingHost`	2	**Resolving Host state:** Waiting for a host name to be translated into its IP address. (Not entered if an IP address was supplied as the `RemoteHost` property.)
`prcHostResolved`	3	**Host Resolved state:** After the host name has successfully translated into an IP address. (Not entered if an IP address was supplied as the `RemoteHost` property.)
`prcConnected`	4	**Connected state:** A connection has been successfully established.
`prcDisconnecting`	5	**Disconnecting state:** A request to disconnect has been requested.
`prcDisconnected`	6	**Disconnected state:** Before a connection is requested and after a connection is closed.

TimeOut

Format: `POPObject.TimeOut(event) [= long]`

The `TimeOut` property sets or returns a flag that controls how much time must pass before a `TimeOut` event is triggered.

Table 19-7 *TimeOut* Events

TimeOut Event Name	*TimeOut* Event Value	Description
prcConnectTimeout	1	If a connection is not made within the timeout period, the TimeOut event is triggered.
prcReceiveTimeout	2	If no data arrives for a receive process within the timeout period, the TimeOut event is triggered.
prcUserTimeout	65	User defined TimeOut event.

TopLines

Format: `POPObject.TopLines [= integer]`

The `TopLines` property sets or returns the number of lines to be retrieved when the `TopMessage` method is used.

TopSupported

Format: `POPObject.TopSupported`

The `TopSupported` property returns `true` if the POP server supports the `TOP` command. Because not all servers support the `TOP` command, you should check this property before attempting to use the `TopMessage` method.

Table 19-8 *TopSupported* Values

TopSupported Value	Description
true	The POP server supports the TOP command.
false	The POP server does not support the TOP command.

URL

Format: `POPObject.URL [= string]`

The `URL` property is a string that holds the name of the current document being transferred. The URL may be set before the `SendDoc` or `GetDoc` methods are used. If the `URL` property is not specified before the `SendDoc` or `GetDoc` methods are used, the URL must be specified as a parameter when the method is invoked. This property is used primarily to support the `DocOutput` object.

UserId

Format: `POPObject.UserId [= string]`

The `UserId` property sets or returns a string that holds the name of the user on the remote POP3 server. This is used in combination with the `Password` property to gain access to the POP server when using the `Authenticate` method.

Methods

The POP ActiveX client control provides many methods to work with a POP3 mail server.

Authenticate

Format: `POPObject.Authenticate [userid] [,password]`

The `Authenticate` method is invoked after a connection has been established, but before any other methods have been used. Both the `userid` and `password` parameters are optional, and if they are not supplied, they default to the values in the `UserId` property and the `Password` property. After the `Authenticate` method is finished, the `Authenticate` event occurs. If an error occurs during the execution of this method, the `Error` event is invoked.

Table 19-9 *Authenticate* Method Arguments

Argument Name	Argument Type	Description
`userid`	string	The userid (or mailbox name) needed to access the server.
`password`	string	The password needed to access the server.

Cancel

Format: `POPObject.Cancel`

The `Cancel` method is used to cancel a pending request. After this method is finished, the `Cancel` event is triggered.

Connect

Format: `POPObject.Connect [remotehost] [,remoteport]`

The `Connect` method is used to establish a connection to a remote POP server. Both parameters are optional, but if they are not specified, the values from the `RemoteHost` and the `RemotePort` properties are used. After this method is finished, the `Connect` event is triggered. If an error occurs during the process, the `Error` event is invoked.

Table 19-10 *Connect* Method Arguments

Argument Name	Argument Type	Description
`remotehost`	variant	Either a remote host name or an IP address.
`remoteport`	variant	Numeric port value.

Delete

Format: `POPObject.Delete message`

The `Delete` method uses the `Delete` command to delete the e-mail note specified by a message from the POP server. If the e-mail note is successfully marked for deletion, the `Delete` event occurs. Otherwise, the `Error` event occurs. Note that the messages are not actually deleted until the `Quit` method is executed.

Table 19-11 *`Delete`* Method Arguments

Argument Name	Argument Type	Description
`message`	integer	The message number associated with the e-mail note on the server.

GetDoc

Format: `POPObject.GetDoc [url] [,[headers] [,outputfile]]`

The `GetDoc` method works with the `DocOutput` object to transfer a file from the remote POP server to the local machine. All three arguments are optional and if not specified, the appropriate values from the `DocOutput` object are used.

Table 19-12 *`GetDoc`* Method Arguments

Argument Name	Argument Type	Description
`url`	string	Name of the file on the remote system to be retrieved in URL format.
`headers`	DocHeaders	A `DocHeaders` object that will contain the headers from the document.
`outputfile`	string	Name of the output file on the local machine.

Last

Format: `POPObject.Last`

The `Last` method returns the last message number to the `Last` event. If the `Last` method cannot determine the last message number, the `Error` event occurs.

MessageSize

Format: `POPObject.MessageSize message`

The `MessageSize` method is used to determine the size of the specified message. If this method is successful, the `MessageSize` event occurs and displays the size of the message. Otherwise, the `Error` event occurs.

Table 19-13 *MessageSize* Method Arguments

Argument Name	Argument Type	Description
`message`	integer	Message number of the e-mail note.

NOOP

Format: `POPObject.NOOP`

The `NOOP` method checks to see if the server is still connected. If successful, the server returns an `+OK` and the `NOOP` event is triggered. Otherwise, the `Error` event occurs.

Quit

Format: `POPObject.Quit`

The `Quit` method is used to disconnect from the POP server. If successful, the `Quit` event occurs. If it isn't successful, the `Error` event occurs.

Reset

Format: `POPObject.Reset`

The `Reset` method unmarks the messages marked for deletion on the remote POP server. Remember that the messages are not actually removed from the system until the `Quit` method is used, which means that the `Reset` method is always able to recover e-mail notes deleted during the current session. If successful, the `Reset` event occurs. Otherwise, the `Error` event is triggered.

RetrieveMessage

Format: `POPObject.RetrieveMessage message [,docoutput]`

The `RetrieveMessage` method sends the `Retrieve` command to the POP server. The output from this command is returned to the `DocOutput` object specified by `docoutput` or the `POPObject.DocOutput`, if the `docoutput` parameter is omitted. If this method is not successful, the `Error` event is triggered.

Table 19-14 *RetrieveMessage* Method Arguments

Argument Name	Argument Type	Description
`message`	integer	The message number to be retrieved.
`docoutput`	DocOutput object	The `DocOutput` object where the output from this method is directed.

TopMessage

Format: `POPObject.TopMessage message [,docoutput]`

The `TopMessage` method works almost like the `ReceiveMessage` method, except that only the first *n* lines of the article are returned, where *n* is the value found in the `POPObject.TopLines` property. The output from this command is returned to the `DocOutput` object specified by `docoutput` (or the `POPObject.DocOutput` if the `docoutput` parameter is omitted). If this method is not successful, the `Error` event is triggered. Note that not all servers support the `TOP` command, so be sure to check that the `TopSupported` property is `true` before using this method. This method is most useful when trying to extract header information to be displayed about the messages to the user.

Table 19-15 ***TopMessage*** **Method Arguments**

Argument Name	Argument Type	Description
`message`	integer	The message number to be retrieved.
`docoutput`	DocOutput object	The `DocOutput` object where the output from this method is directed.

Events

The POP events are called in response to various conditions that happen during the execution of a program using the POP ActiveX control.

Authenticate

Format: `POPObject_Authenticate`

The `Authenticate` event occurs after the POP server has processed the information sent via the `Authenticate` method.

Busy

Format: `POPObject_Busy(ByVal isBusy As Boolean)`

The `Busy` event occurs when the `POPObject.Busy` property changes state. This event occurs when a command begins execution, or when a command finishes execution.

Table 19-16 ***Busy*** **Event Parameters**

Parameter Name	Argument Type	Description
`isBusy`	boolean	Indicates when a command is being executed.

Table 19-17 *isBusy* Values

isBusy Value	Description
`true`	A command is being executed.
`false`	A command is not being executed.

Cancel

Format: `POPObject_Cancel`

The `Cancel` event occurs after the `Cancel` method is invoked.

Delete

Format: `POPObject_Delete`

The `Delete` event occurs when the `Delete` method is successfully completed.

DocOutput

Format: `POPObject_DocOutput(ByVal docinput as DocInput)`

The `DocOutput` event occurs when data has been transferred from this control.

Table 19-18 *DocOutput* Event Parameters

Parameter Name	Argument Type	Description
`docoutput`	DocOutput	Object that describes the current output data for this transfer.

Error

Format: `POPObject_Error(errcode As Integer, description As String, scode As Long, source As String, helpfile As String, helpcontext As Long, canceldisplay As Boolean)`

The `Error` event occurs whenever the server responds with an error return code.

Table 19-19 *Error* Event Parameters

Parameter Name	Argument Type	Description
`errcode`	integer	The error code.
`description`	string	The text description of the error code.
`scode`	long	The scode of the error.
`source`	string	The name of the source of the error. This is usually the name of the control that caused the error.
`helpfile`	string	Contains the name of the help file with more information about the error.
`helpcontext`	long	Contains the help context reference for the error.
`canceldisplay`	boolean	Displays the standard error message box.

Table 19-20 *canceldisplay* Values

canceldisplay Value	Description
`true`	Display the standard error message box.
`false`	Do not display the standard error message box.

Last

Format: `POPObject_LastArticle(ByVal lastmessage as long)`

The `Last` event occurs when the `Last` method completes successfully. The `lastmessage` parameter indicates the highest message number on the server.

Table 19-21 ***Last* Event Parameters**

Parameter Name	Argument Type	Description
lastmessage	long	The message number of the last e-mail note on the server.

ProtocolStateChanged

Format: `POPObject_ProtocolStateChanged(ByVal protocolstate as integer)`

The `ProtocolStateChanged` event occurs whenever the protocol state is changed.

Table 19-22 ***ProtocolStateChanged* Event Parameters**

Parameter Name	Argument Type	Description
protocolstate	integer	The value of the protocl state.

Table 19-23 ***protocolstate* Values**

protocolState Value Name	*protocolState* Value	Description
ftpBase	0	**Base state:** Before a connection is established with the server.
ftpAuthorization	1	**Authorization state:** After connection is established and before the user has been granted access to the server.
ftpTransaction	2	**Transaction state:** After the user has been granted access to the server. The client can now interact with the server.

Quit

Format: `POPObject_Quit`

The `Quit` event occurs in response to the `Quit` method.

Reset

Format: `POPObject_Reset`

The `Reset` event occurs if the `Reset` method is successful.

StateChanged

Format: `POPObject_StateChanged(ByVal state as integer)`

The `StateChanged` event occurs whenever the transport state is changed.

Table 19-24 *StateChanged* Event Parameters

Parameter Name	Argument Type	Description
state	integer	The value of the transport state.

Table 19-25 *state* Values

state Value Name	*state* Value	Description
prcConnecting	1	**Connecting state:** A connection has been requested and is waiting for an acknowledgment.
prcResolvingHost	2	**Resolving Host state:** Waiting for a host name to be translated into its IP address. (Not entered if an IP address is supplied as the `RemoteHost` property.)
prcHostResolved	3	**Host Resolved state:** After the host name has successfully translated into an IP address. (Not entered if an IP address is supplied as the `RemoteHost` property.)

state Value Name	*state* Value	Description
prcConnected	4	**Connected state:** A connection has been success fully established.
prcDisconnecting	5	**Disconnecting state:** A request to disconnect has been requested.
prcDisconnected	6	**Disconnected state:** Before a connection is requested and after a connection is closed.

TimeOut

Format: `POPObject_TimeOut(ByVal event as integer, continue as boolean)`

The `TimeOut` event occurs when the specified event does not occur within the interval defined in the `TimeOut` property for that event.

Table 19-26 ***TimeOut* Event Parameters**

Parameter Name	Argument Type	Description
event	integer	Event to which the timer interval applies.
continue	boolean	Determines if the timer will remain active.

Table 19-27 ***event* Values**

event Name	*event* Value	Description
prcConnectTimeout	1	If a connection is not made within the timeout period, the `TimeOut` event is triggered.
prcReceiveTimeout	2	If no data arrives for a receive process within the timeout period, the `TimeOut` event is triggered.
prcUserTimeout	65	User defined `TimeOut` event.

Table 19-28 *continue* Values

continue Value	Description
`true`	The timer continues to run.
`false`	The timer is stopped.

Summary

In this chapter we discussed the POP client control. This control provides functions needed to identify and retrieve mail from a remote mail server.

In case you want to check your answers to the questions in the Overview section, here are the answers:

- *What other objects are used by this control?*

  `DocHeader` returns a single header line.

  `DocHeaders` is a collection of `DocHeader` objects.

  `DocOutput` is used for information leaving this control.

  `icErrors` holds error information.

- *What methods are used to retrieve information about the messages on the server?*

  The `Last` method is used to determine the number of messages on the server.

  The `MessageSize` method is used to determine the number of bytes in a message.

  The `TopMessage` method is used to retrieve some of the leading lines of a message. (This is useful for retrieving header information.)

- *What methods are used to get messages from the server?*

  The `RetrieveMessage` method is used to get a message from the server.

  The `Delete` method is used to remove a message from the server. This is typically used after retrieving a message to prevent a large number of messages from building up on the server.

- *What methods are used to manage a connection?*

  `Connect` is used to connect to the remote to the remote server.

  `Authenticate` is used to send userid and password information to the server.

  `Quit` is used to disconnect from the remote server.

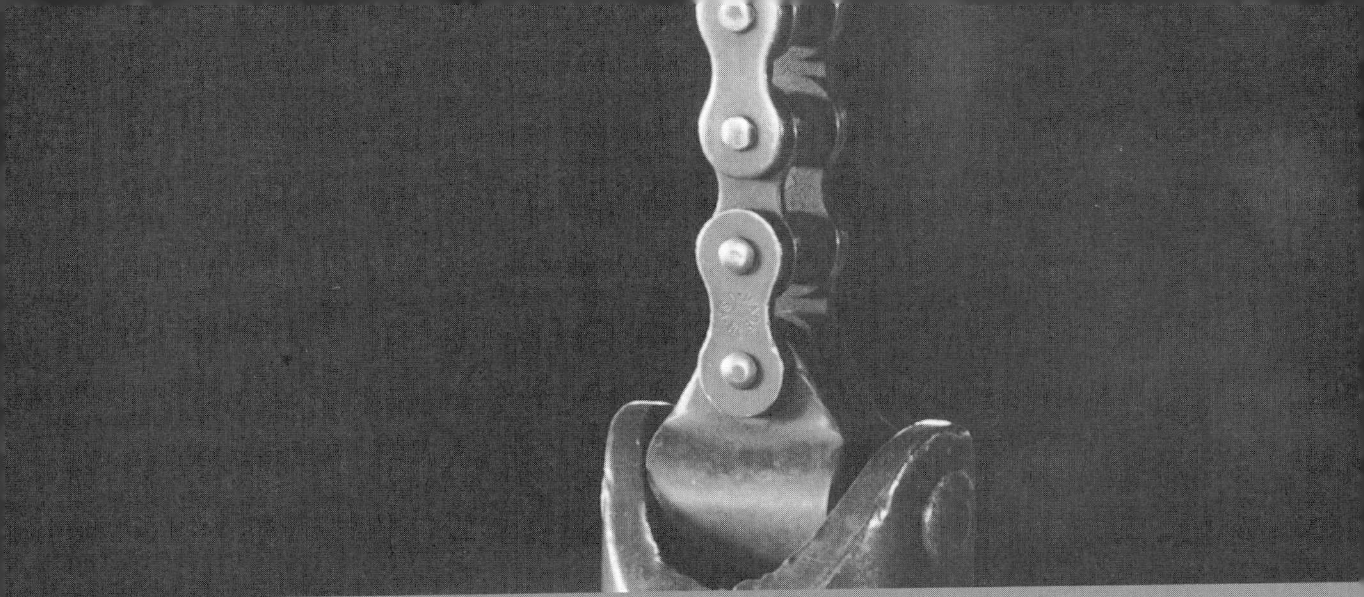

Chapter 20

MailRunner

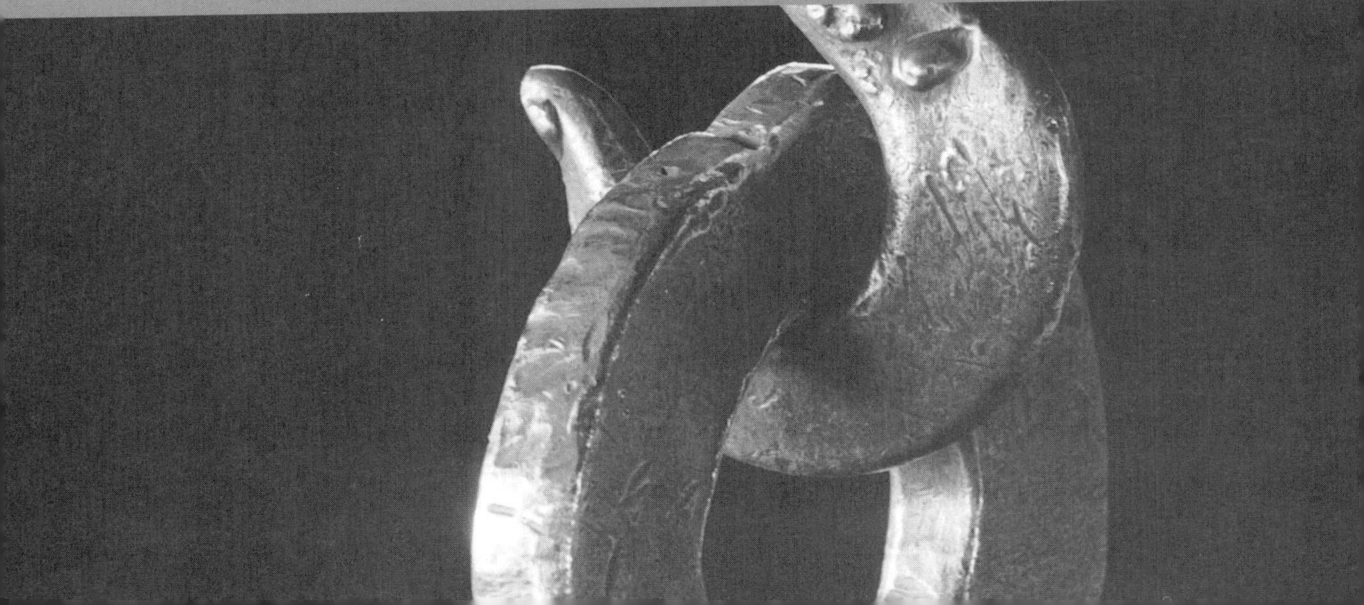

Overview

In this chapter, we build a program called MailRunner that enables you to send and receive mail. This program is based on the POP and SMTP ActiveX controls. Like the rest of the Runner family, this program shows how to build a working Visual Basic program that demonstrates the controls. Also like the rest of the Runner family, it needs a lot of enhancements to make it a viable commercial product.

The complete source code is provided on the CD-ROM, so I'm only going to present the more interesting parts of the code here, including such topics as how to connect to the POP server, how to retrieve a list of notes from the POP server, how to retrieve a single note, and how to send mail using the SMTP server.

By the end of this chapter, you should be able to answer the following question:

- What is the difference between the ActiveX SMTP control and the ActiveX POP control?

How to Use MailRunner

In many respects, the MailRunner program works like the NewsRunner program, but instead of dealing with multiple newsgroups as sources of information, this program deals with only one POP mail server. For this reason, the main form looks like NewsRunner's ArticleList form with a different set of push buttons. While connected to the POP server, this form displays all the mail items on the server that can be retrieved. Then you can double-click a mail item and the Note form is displayed along with the contents of the selected mail item.

Besides the two main forms (the MailRunner form and the Note form), this program also includes two additional forms: the Mail Connect form and the About Mail form. Both of these forms are similar to their counterparts in the NewsRunner program.

The MailRunner form contains three buttons: a Check Mail button, a Send Note button, and a Delete button (see figure 20-1). Clicking the Check Mail button starts the connection process to the remote POP server. If a system has not already been defined, the Mail Connect form is displayed. This form contains information about how to access the POP and SMTP servers. Also, your e-mail address is derived from the POP userid and the

POP server name. (i.e., POPUserId@POPMail.whatever). When the connection is made, the list of e-mail notes on the server is listed on the screen, one per line, and the now familiar light bulb starts to shine.

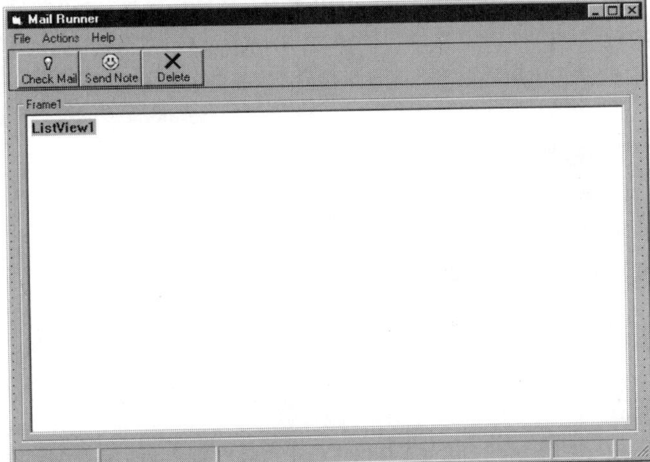

FIGURE 20-1

The MailRunner form.

The connection can also be started by using the Actions | Connect menu command. Disconnecting is also easy because you can simply click the Check Mail button again, which clears the display and turns off the light bulb, or by using the Actions | Disconnect menu command.

Of the other two buttons and commands, the Send Mail function is always available. This is possible because the process to send mail is totally separate from the receiving mail process. (This is because we are using the POP server to receive mail and the SMTP server to send mail.)

The Delete button works only when you are connected to the POP server. It is used to delete the selected message on the screen. After the mail message is deleted, the details of the message are erased and replaced with a message that says the mail has been deleted.

The MailConnect form has more information on it than any of the previous connect forms in the Runner program family because for the first time, we use two different servers in the same program (see figure 20-2). Remember in Chapters 16 and 18 we talked about how the mail is sent to other systems by using the SMTP server and is received by using the POP server? Well, because these services may be provided by two different machines (i.e., pop.JustPC.com and smtp.JustPC.com), we cannot assume that they are on the same machine (though it is very common to find your mail server is something like mail.JustPC.com). Also, it is necessary to specify a userid and password for the POP server because this machine is where you actually receive your mail. Sending mail using an SMTP server needs less security because it is only forwarding something to someone else rather than saving it for someone special to retrieve it.

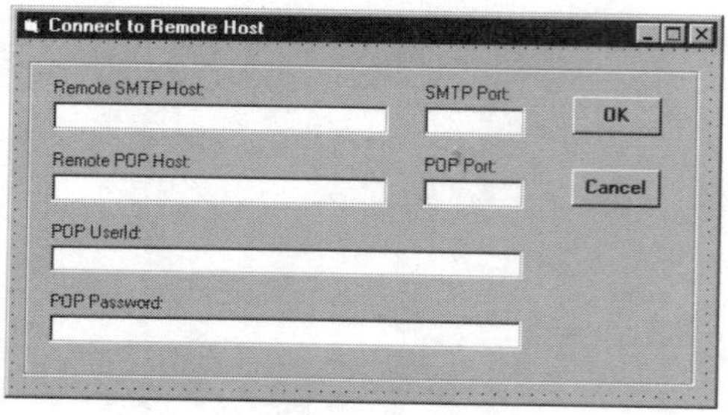

FIGURE 20-2

The MailConnect form.

The Note form is used to display a note retrieved from the server, or to create a new note to send to someone on the Internet (see figure 20-3). Fields are included on the form for values such as the date the note was sent, the subject, who the note was sent to, and who was cc'ed on the note. The person who sent the note is listed in the frame header. I also left room on the form for the note itself. Buttons are available that allow scrolling through the list of notes on the server, preparing to send notes by creating a new note, or replying to the note displayed on the form (sending the note when it is ready and returning to the previous form).

The Previous and Next buttons are disabled when the MailRunner program is sending a message but is not actively connected to the POP server. (It does require that the computer it is running and be connected to the Internet so that it may access the SMTP server.) Menu commands are also available in addition to the buttons.

The Program Structure

This program contains two main forms and two secondary forms, plus one module. The main forms are MailRunner and Note. The secondary forms are MailConnect and AboutMail. The module is MailGlobal. By this time you should be relatively familiar with this structure. The MailGlobal is nearly identical to all the other global modules we have seen.

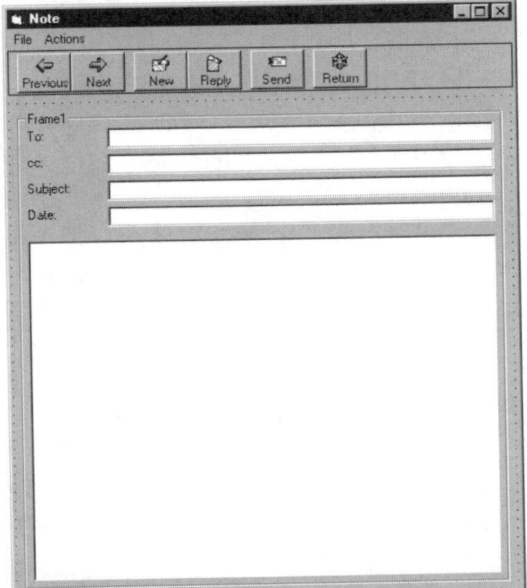

FIGURE 20-3

The Note form.

In Listing 20-1, you find the list of global variables used in this program. There are only four global variables: `MailConnected`, `MailStartTime`, `MailType`, and `MailCurrentNote`. In Chapter 14 you saw that these correspond to the global variables I used in the NewsRunner program. (Well, the NewsRunner program also included a global variable that held the name of the current newsgroup, but because we do not have the concept of a mail group [well maybe if we had multiple mail folders or mail servers] I did not carry it over to this program.)

Just as an aside, it is more than just a coincidence that a lot of these programs look similar. I almost never write a program from scratch. I always borrow code from the last program I wrote to start the new program. It is always faster to cut and paste than it is to write new code. (If you write programs for a living, you know what I am talking about. The last COBOL program I wrote from scratch was in 1980. The last one I wrote, starting from an already existing COBOL program, was about 2 months ago.) This is especially true if you are working on similar programs. Not only do you have a working program at the very beginning of the project, you avoid all the typical problems that come with working with a brand new program.

In fact, this is one of the more important points in this book. I know that very few of you really need to build yet another newsreader or Web browser, but many of you may benefit by adding function to send an e-mail message to a supplier when your inventory application determines that you need more of a particular stock number. Or, perhaps one of the applications running at a remote site needs to upload or download a data file from your central site. While adding Internet capabilities to your applications may add value, you do not have time to learn everything you need to know to make it work. By including some of the code I have written here, you can add these functions quickly and painlessly to your applications without spending all the time I did learning the right combination of things that work. Take advantage of my hard work and impress your customers. Just drop me an e-mail note letting me know what type of application you have and how you used these samples. (Of course, telling your friends to buy this book is an even better way to thank me for my efforts!)

`MailConnected` is `true` when the connection to the POP server is active. We do not need to keep track of the SMTP connection because it is opened and closed each time we send a piece of mail. `MailStartTime` contains the date and time we connected to the POP server. This information is used to determine the total time we are connected to the POP server, which is displayed on the status bar of the MailRunner form. `MailType` is used to determine if the output from the POP server is a list of mail headers to be displayed on the MailRunner form, or a note that is to be displayed on the Note form. `MailCurrentNote` is used to keep track of the current note on the server.

Listing 20-1 MailRunner Global Variables

```
' Form/Module:   MailGlobal
' Author:        Wayne S. Freeze
' Version        1.0
' Date Written:  22 July 1996
' Date Revised:  22 July 1996
' Description:
'   This module initializes the global variables
'   and starts the main Mail form.

Option Explicit
```

```
'  True when the program is talking to a remote
'  system, false otherwise
Global MailConnected As Integer

'  Used to track when the FTP connection was
'  started
Global MailStartTime As Date

'  Define the type of data being retrieved
'  from the NNTP server
'  0 = undefined
'  1 = headers only
'  2 = complete note
Global MailType As Integer

'  Define the current mail message
Global MailCurrentNote As Integer
```

Connecting to the Server

The main subroutine works the same as you have already seen in Chapter 10 (in Listing 10-2) and Chapter 14 (in Listing 14-2), so I do not talk about it here. Nor do I talk about the `Form_Load` logic, because I already discussed that one to death, too. However, I do go through the various command buttons and what they do. Remember that menu commands also work the same way.

The Check Mail button is the same as the Connect button on the previous forms. It calls the `DoConnectPOP` routine when `MailConnected` is `false`, and the `DoDisconnectPOP` routine when `MailConnected` is `true`. This routine is very similar to the previous `DoConnect` routines, especially the FTP one because the POP server requires a userid and password before finishing the connection (see Listing 20-2).

A few minor differences are worth noting: First, I display the name of the server to the user as part of the Frame caption. Second, after the connection is established I know how many mail messages are available on the server for retrieval, so I pass this information on to the user as part of the status bar display. Third, I begin retrieving information from the server to be displayed as part of the MailRunner form by calling the `GetAllMail` function.

One other difference to note is that the POP protocol does not use a reply code in the same fashion that all the other protocols we have discussed so far do. POP protocol simply indicates whether the last command was successful or not. Thus in the ActiveX implementation, a reply code of zero means that the program worked properly, and a non-zero value indicates a problem. For more information about the error, you have to examine the reply string.

While we are talking about how to connect to the server, I need to talk about disconnecting for a moment. This program uses the same basic code that I used in all the previous examples. The only real differences are that I check for a non-zero reply code rather than a specific value, and I clear the MailRunner New Mail display after the connection is closed.

Listing 20-2 The MailRunner *DoConnectPOP* Subroutine

```
Private Sub DoConnectPOP()

'  Connect to the remote POP server.

If Len(POP.RemoteHost) = 0 Then
   ConnectMail.Show 1
   If Len(POP.RemoteHost) = 0 Then
      Exit Sub
   End If
End If

MailStartTime = Now
Timer1.Enabled = True
Frame1.Caption = "Mail from: " & POP.RemoteHost

POP.Connect
Do While (POP.State = prcConnecting) _
   Or (POP.State = prcResolvingHost) _
   Or (POP.State = prcHostResolved)
```

```
    DoEvents
Loop

If POP.State <> prcConnected Then
    MsgBox "Error in DoConnect(Connect). Unable to connect to mail server." & " " &
➥Format(POP.ReplyCode)
    Exit Sub
End If

Do While (POP.State = prcConnected) _
    And (POP.ProtocolState = 1)
    DoEvents
Loop

Do While POP.Busy
    DoEvents
Loop

POP.Authenticate
Do While POP.Busy
    DoEvents
Loop

If (POP.ReplyCode <> 0) Then
    MsgBox "Error in DoConnect(Authenticate). Reply text is: " & POP.ReplyString & " " &
➥Format(POP.ReplyCode)
End If

MailConnected = True
Toolbar.Buttons("Check Mail").Image = 2
Toolbar.Buttons("Delete").Enabled = True
StatusBar.Panels(1).Text = "Connected"
StatusBar.Panels(2).Text = Format(POP.MessageCount) & " message(s) waiting"
```

continues

Listing 20-2 Continued

```
GetAllNotes

End Sub
```

Interacting with the POP Server

After getting the connection to work properly, we can now have fun with the data transfers. Basically we have three different types of interactions: retrieving a summary of the mail to be downloaded, retrieving a note, and deleting a note. Of the three, only two, the `GetAllNotes` and `GetNote`, use the `DocOutput` object. The `DeleteNote` communicates directly with the server to mark a note as being deleted.

GetAllNotes

The `GetAllNotes` function is used to scan the server to retrieve summary information about the mail that is ready to be downloaded, and to display it on the MailRunner form (see Listing 20-3). Because we know how many notes are available on the server and that they are sequentially numbered starting with one, it is a relatively straightforward process to retrieve the header information for each note. That is what the `GetAllNotes` function does.

Listing 20-3 The MailRunner *GetAllNotes* Function

```
Function GetAllNotes() As Integer

'  Specify MailType to retrive a list of notes in the
'  DocOutput routine. DocOutput will, put the
'  information directly onto the MailRunner form.

MailType = 1
MailCurrentNote = 1
POP.TopLines = 20
```

```
Do While MailCurrentNote <= POP.MessageCount
   POP.TopMessage MailCurrentNote
   Do While POP.Busy
      DoEvents
   Loop

   If POP.ReplyCode <> 0 Then
      MsgBox "Error in GetAllNotes(TopMessage). Reply text is: " & POP.ReplyString
      MailType = 0
      Exit Function
   End If
   MailCurrentNote = MailCurrentNote + 1

Loop

MailType = 0
GetAllNotes = POP.ReplyCode

End Function
```

We set `POP.TopLines` to `20`, which means that when we retrieve header information from a note, the critical information is from the first 20 lines of the note. We also set the `MailType` to `1`. The `POP.TopMessage` method is used to send a request to the server to send the top number of lines back to this program and the `DocOutput` object. Because the real work is done in the `DocOutput` subroutine, we continue this discussion shortly, but first I want to talk about the other `DocOutput`-related subroutine.

GetNote

The other `DocOutput`-driven routine is `GetNote` (see Listing 20-4). This function retrieves a specific note and displays it on the Note form. `GetNote` uses the `POP.RetrieveMessage` method to send the RFC-1725 `Retrieve` command to the server. By setting `MailType` to two, the `DocOutput` object is able to recognize that this data is to be displayed on the Note form.

Listing 20-4 The MailRunner *GetNote* Function

```
Function GetNote(n As Integer) As Integer

'  Specify MailType to retrive a note in the
'  DocOutput routine, then retrieve the specified
'  note. DocOutput will set the header information
'  and display the body of the note.

MailType = 2
MailCurrentNote = n
POP.RetrieveMessage MailCurrentNote
Do While POP.Busy
   DoEvents
Loop

If POP.ReplyCode <> 0 Then
   MsgBox "Error in GetNote(RetrieveMessage). Reply text is: " & POP.ReplyString
End If
MailType = 0

GetNote = POP.ReplyCode

End Function
```

The DocOutput Event

The previous routines take advantage of one of ActiveX's strengths: the `DocOutput` object (see Listing 20-5). As we saw in Chapter 14, this can be a relatively complex subroutine. With five different `DocOutput.States` and two different `MailTypes`, we can have as many as 10 different combinations, each with its own unique code. However, in this case, some combinations can be ignored or combined. For instance, because the error logic merely serves to display the `POP.ReplyString`, we do not have to differentiate between the two values for `MailType`.

Starting with `MailType` equal to one, we find that only the `icDocHeaders` state is really required. No initialization code in the `icDocBegin` state is required because all the headers are available at the time this block of code is executed. All we have to do is create an entry in the `ListView` control and add each of the desired headers to the fields associated with the entry we just created.

A `MailType` value of two is a little more complicated because we need to erase whatever was in the Note form previously before loading any new values. This is because we cannot guarantee that all the previous values in the form will be overlaid with new values.

Handling the header information is also straightforward. We simply look at the header keyword and put its associated value into the proper field. The code does, however, allow multiple To and CC keywords, in which case a comma and new the data is appended to the existing value. Also, I chose to display the rest of the header information as part of the body of the note. You may or may not want to do this with your own code—sometimes the extra header information may confuse the casual user. In my case, I found it useful while debugging the program. Perhaps the best solution is to add an option that the user can set that will control whether this information is displayed or not.

Any data that is received for `MailType` equal to 2 is appended to the notebox control on the Note form. Because this is a RichTextBox, we do not have to worry about running out of space to hold the data. A regular TextBox is limited to about 65,000 bytes of information. A RichTextBox is capable of storing an unlimited amount of data (well, it can store as much as it can fit into the available memory).

Listing 20-5 The MailRunner *DocOutput* Event

```
Private Sub POP_DocOutput(ByVal DocOutput As DocOutput)

'  Check the DocOutput.State value to determine
'  the state of the transmission process (Begin, End,
'  Headers, Data, or Errors). Within each state,
'  choose the appropriate action based on the
'  value of MailType (1=mail list, 2=note header and body).
```

continues

Listing 20-5 Continued

```
Dim hdr As DocHeader
Dim l As ListItem
Dim X As Variant

Select Case DocOutput.State

Case icDocBegin
    Select Case MailType
    Case 2
        Note.notebox.Text = ""
        Note.subject.Text = ""
        Note.DateTime.Text = ""
        Note.to.Text = ""
        Note.cc = ""
    End Select

Case icDocEnd

Case icDocHeaders
    Select Case MailType
    Case 1
        Set l = ListView1.ListItems.Add(, , Format(MailCurrentNote))
        For Each hdr In DocOutput.Headers
            Select Case LCase(hdr.Name)
            Case "subject"
                l.SubItems(1) = hdr.Value
            Case "from"
                l.SubItems(2) = hdr.Value
            Case "date"
                l.SubItems(3) = hdr.Value
            End Select
        Next hdr
```

```
  Case 2
     For Each hdr In DocOutput.Headers
        Select Case LCase(hdr.Name)
        Case "to"
           If Len(Note.to.Text) = 0 Then
              Note.to.Text = hdr.Value
           Else
              Note.to.Text = Note.to.Text & "," & hdr.Value
           End If
        Case "subject"
           Note.subject.Text = hdr.Value
        Case "cc"
           if len(Note.cc.Text) = 0 Then
              Note.cc.Text = hdr.Value
           Else
              Note.cc.Text = Note.cc.Text & "," & hdr.value
           End If
        Case "from"
           Note.Frame1.Caption = "From: " & hdr.Value
        Case Else
           Note.notebox.Text = Note.notebox.Text & hdr.Name & ": " & hdr.Value &
➥vbCrLf
        End Select
     Next hdr
  End Select

Case icDocData
    Select Case MailType
    Case 2
       DocOutput.GetData X
       Note.notebox.Text = Note.notebox.Text & X
    End Select
```

continues

Listing 20-5 Continued

```
Case icDocError
   MsgBox "DocOutput Error: " & Format(POP.ReplyCode)

End Select

End Sub
```

DeleteNote

The `DeleteNote` function (see Listing 20-6) is used to delete a note on the POP server. It uses the `POP.Delete` method to send an RFC-1939 `Delete` command to the server to mark the note as deleted. The note is not actually deleted until the `Quit` command is executed. You can provide a way to undelete the notes that were marked for deletion by using the `POP.Reset` method. If the command is successful, update the text associated with the message to indicate that the message was deleted.

Listing 20-6 The MailRunner *DeleteNote* Function

```
Function DeleteNote(n As Integer) As Integer

'  Specify MailType to retrive a note in the
'  DocOutput routine, then retrieve the specified
'  note. DocOutput will set the header information
'  and display the body of the note.

POP.Delete n
Do While POP.Busy
   DoEvents
Loop
```

```
If POP.ReplyCode <> 0 Then
   MsgBox "Error in DeleteNote(DeleteMessage). Reply text is: " & POP.ReplyString
Else
   ListView1.ListItems(n).SubItems(1) = "**********message deleted*********"
   ListView1.ListItems(n).SubItems(2) = ""
   ListView1.ListItems(n).SubItems(3) = ""
End If

DeleteNote = POP.ReplyCode

End Function
```

Interacting with the SMTP Server

The only real trouble I had with this program was writing the code to send a note using the SMTP ActiveX control. I started the process by writing a relatively complex function that included the connection logic and a bunch of other stuff. Eventually, I realized that I was my own worst enemy. I kept removing code from the function that was not needed until I ended up with the code that is currently in the `SendMail` function.

Sending a note is a three-step process. First, we must prepare the note for sending. In preparing the note for sending, we can clear the note form and let the user enter all the information necessary or we can let the user to reply to an existing note so that when the user presses the New button, the `DoNew` subroutine is called. Clicking the Reply button triggers the `DoReply` routine.

The second step after preparing the note for sending is to let the user edit the note. The final step involves actually sending the note. To do this, the user clicks the Send button, which calls the `SendMail` function.

DoNew

The `DoNew` subroutine (see Listing 20-7) is very simple. It builds a From address using the `POP.UserId` and `POP.RemoteHost` properties, and saves it as the frame caption. Then it computes the current time and date and saves it in the DateTime text box. Finally, the rest of the controls on the Note form are cleared so that the user may enter new information. The global variable `MailCurrentNote` is set to zero so that the rest of the program can determine that the contents of the Note form did not come from the POP server.

Listing 20-7 The MailRunner *DoNew* Subroutine

```
Private Sub DoNew()

'  Prepare the form to enter a new note, by
'  filling in the header information.

Frame1.Caption = "From: " & MailRunner.POP.UserId & "@" & MailRunner.POP.RemoteHost
DateTime.Text = Format(Date, "ddd, dd mmm yyyy ") & Format(Time, "hh:mm:ss ")
subject.Text = ""
Note.to.Text = ""
Note.cc.Text = ""
notebox.Text = ""
MailCurrentNote = 0

End Sub
```

DoReply

The `DoReply` logic (see Listing 20-8) is a little more complicated. First, we determine the person to send the mail to by converting the From information in the frame header. Next, we create the new From information by using the `POP.UserId` and the `POP.RemoteHost` values. Then we put a "re:" in front of the subject, unless there is already one there. Finally, we include the previous article in the NoteBox control with a message that indicates who originated the note.

Listing 20-8 The MailRunner *DoReply* Subroutine

```
Private Sub DoReply()

'  Prepare the form to reply to the current
'  article by preparing the header fields
'  and inserting a "> " in front of all of
'  the lines of existing text.

Dim i As Integer

MailCurrentNote = 0

Note.to.Text = Right(Frame1.Caption, Len(Frame1.Caption) - 6)

Frame1.Caption = "From: " & MailRunner.POP.UserId & "@" & MailRunner.POP.RemoteHost
DateTime.Text = Format(Date, "ddd, dd mmm yyyy ") & Format(Time, "hh:mm:ss ")

If Left(LCase(Trim(subject.Text)), 3) <> "re:" Then
   subject.Text = "re: " & subject.Text
End If

notebox.Text = "In the previous article " & Note.to.Text _
               & " wrote  " & vbCrLf & notebox.Text
i = InStr(notebox.Text, vbCrLf)
Do While i > 0
   notebox.Text = Left(notebox.Text, i + 1) & "> " _
                  & Right(notebox.Text, (Len(notebox.Text) - i - 1))
   i = InStr(i + 2, notebox.Text, vbCrLf)
Loop

End Sub
```

SendMail

The first step in the SendMail function (see Listing 20-9) is to ensure that we have the name of an SMTP server. If we do not, display the ConnectMail form. Next, we build the headers needed to send the note from the To, cc, Subject, and DateTime text boxes. Note that I use the DocHeaders collection from the SMTP.DocInput object rather than creating my own. This avoids the problem I had with NewsRunner where the DocHeaders collection was renamed.

After building the headers, simply use the SMTP.SendDoc method to send the headers and the body of the note to the SMTP server. Then do the usual spin loop and check the SMTP.ReplyCode. A value of 221 means that the server has closed the connection and the process is finished.

Note that there is no other code associated with the SMTP control. There is no need to write a DocInput event, although I believe that you can include one and shift functions like building the headers and sending the NoteBox to it. But because the code here is relatively compact and easy to use, I did not want to make this process overly complicated.

Listing 20-9 The MailRunner *SendMail* Function

```
Function SendNote() As Integer

'  After the note has been prepared for sending,
'  build the DocHeaders collection, and send the
'  note to the server.

Dim hdr As DocHeaders

If Len(SMTP.RemoteHost) = 0 Then
   ConnectMail.Show 1
   If Len(SMTP.RemoteHost) = 0 Then
      Exit Function
   End If
End If
```

```
Set hdr = SMTP.DocInput.Headers
hdr.Clear
hdr.Add "From", Note.Frame1.Caption
hdr.Add "To", note.to.text
hdr.Add "Date", Note.DateTime.Text
hdr.Add "Subject", Note.subject.Text
hdr.Add "CC", Note.cc.Text

SMTP.SendDoc , hdr, Note.notebox.Text
Do While SMTP.Busy
   DoEvents
Loop

If SMTP.ReplyCode <> 221 Then
   MsgBox "Error encountered in SendNote(SendDoc). Reply text is: " & SMTP.ReplyString &
➥" " & Format(SMTP.ReplyCode)
Else
   MsgBox "Mail sent to the SMTP server."
End If

SendNote = SMTP.ReplyCode

End Function
```

Summary

In this chapter we discussed how to create a mail program using the POP and SMTP ActiveX controls. Unlike the previous ActiveX controls, these seem to work better and are a little easier to use. The MailRunner program shows how to use the POP control to establish a connection to a POP server and retrieve a list of notes that the user can select. It also shows how to retrieve a note from the POP server and format it for display to the user. Then we discussed how to prepare a note for sending by clearing the form for a new note or converting an existing note for a reply from the user. Finally, we discussed how to send a note to another user or group of users by using the SMTP control.

In the next chapter, we are going to take the MailRunner program we built in this chapter and add it to the NetRunner program we developed in Chapter 15. We extend it by adding the capability to forward news articles to other users using the SMTP control, along with a few other interesting features.

In case you want to check your answer to the question at the front of the chapter, here is the answer:

- *What is the difference between the ActiveX SMTP control and the ActiveX POP control?*

  The ActiveX SMTP control is used to send a piece of electronic mail to an SMTP server that will eventually deliver it to its destination. The ActiveX POP control is used to access a POP server to check for incoming mail that has been sent by other users.

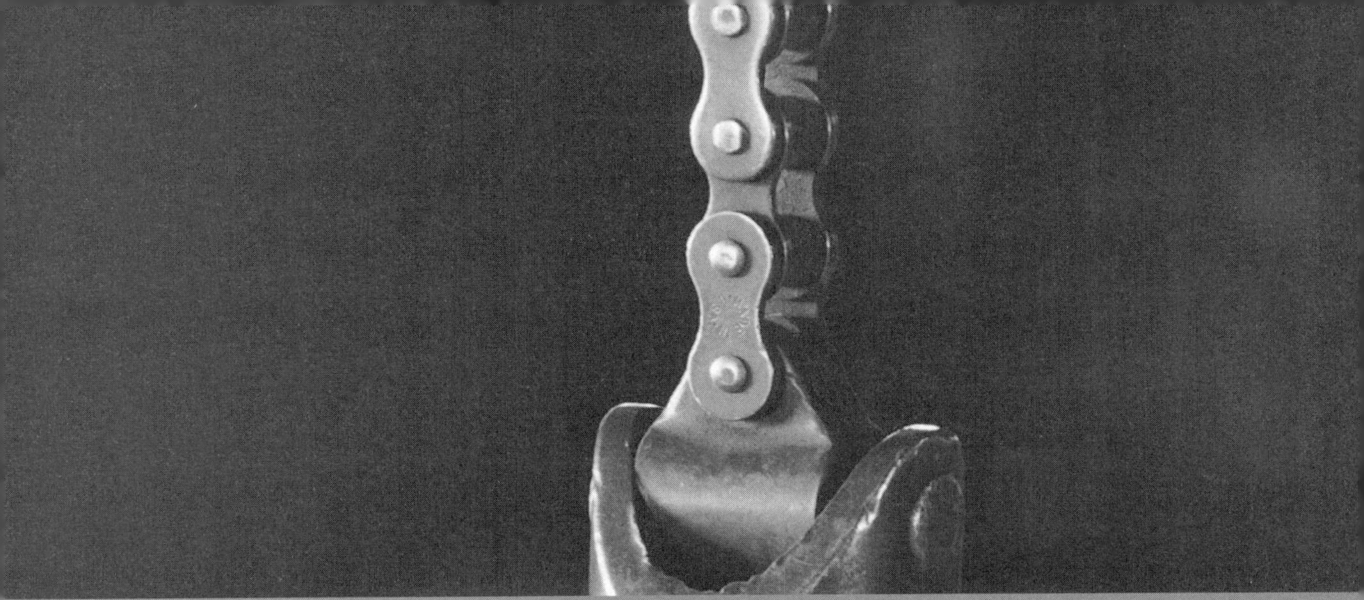

Chapter 21

NetRunner—Part Two

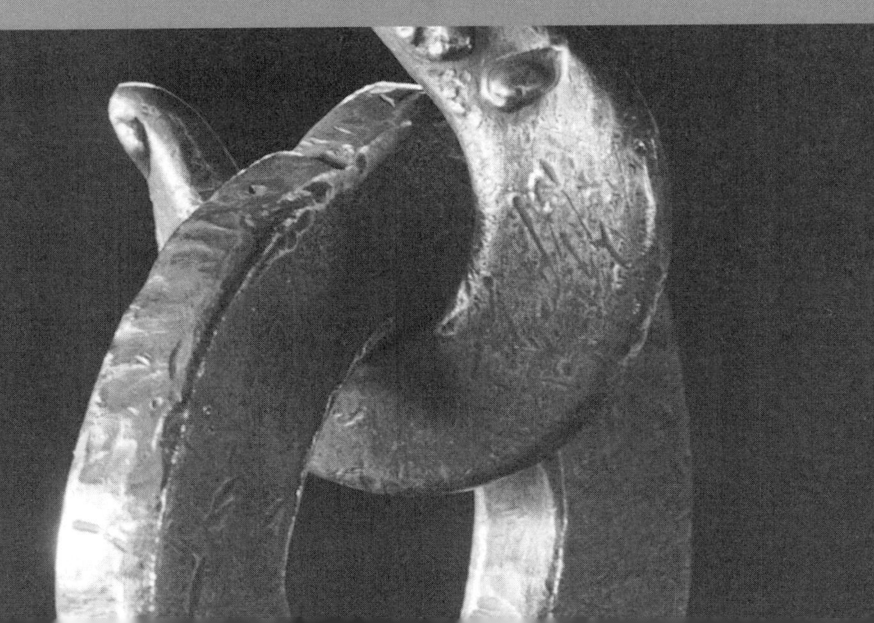

Overview

In Chapter 15 we combined the FTPRunner and NewsRunner programs to form a new program called NetRunner. Eventually, the NetRunner program will include all six of the high-level ActiveX controls. In this chapter, we add support for the mail-related controls: POP and SMTP. To make the program a little more integrated, we are going to add the capability to send a news article as an e-mail message. Also, we are going to spend a few minutes adding a few new enhancements to the NetRunner program.

By the end of this chapter, you should be able to answer the following question:

- Why should the status bar not be updated continuously?

How to Use NetRunner—Part Two

NetRunner—Part Two builds on the work we did in NetRunner—Part One by adding support for MailRunner. The way we do this is by adding information to the MailRunner tab that was found on the MailConnect form (see figure 21-1). This includes the names of the SMTP and POP servers, their port numbers, and the userid and password for the POP server. We also add a button that starts MailRunner function.

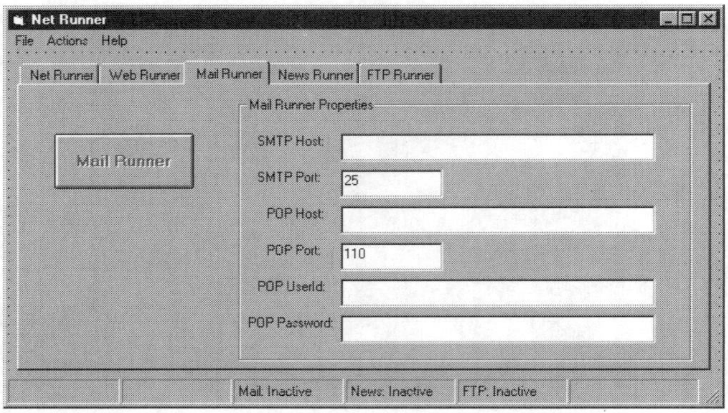

FIGURE 21-1

The NetRunner form, MailRunner tab.

I have also made some changes to the NewsRunner main form by adding another button that enables you to send the current news article to someone as an e-mail message. The article is copied from the Article form to the Note form, and is prepared in the same way as when you reply to an existing note.

Another change I included is a better method of handling newsgroups. Rather than using the DOS sort command to sort and the TreeView control to display the list of newsgroups, I use the ListView control to do both functions. This control is the same control that is used in the ArticleList and has a similar display (see figure 21-2). I also enhanced the ArticleList form with the capability to sort the entries by any of the column headings. Clicking the column heading sorts the list by that value in ascending order. If the list is already sorted, clicking the column header sorts the list in descending order.

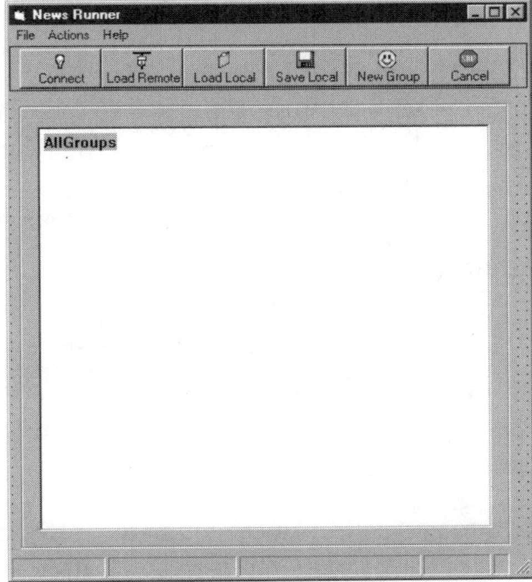

FIGURE 21-2

The NewsRunner form.

I also added the capability to sort the list of notes on the MailRunner form by any of the column headers. Like the ArticleList form, clicking the column header button once sorts the column in ascending order, and clicking it again sorts in descending order.

Finally, I added one last command that allows you to reset the parameters saved in the system registry to their default values. This is useful when you want to return the screen sizes and location to the default values defined in the program. This command is only available from NetRunner's menus because I feel that it would not be frequently used, and adding rarely used buttons to the base applications only confuses the user.

Merging MailRunner into NetRunner

We are going to continue using the same basic program structure that we saw in Chapter 15. The first step is to copy all the old modules (FRM, FRX, and BAS) to the same place in the NetRunner program, and then use the Add File menu item (under File) to add them to the NetRunner project.

Now we can combine the global modules. This is not very hard because MailRunner only has a handful of global variables that need to be declared and initialized. After this is completed, we can discard the old MailGlob.BAS module from the NetRunner program.

In order to eliminate the MailConnect form, we must define all of those fields on the NetRunner form under the MailRunner tab. Then we can delete the MailConnect form. Remember, we need to go through the code and replace the references to MailConnect with references to NetRunner. This can be done in two different ways. The first way is to use the Find and Replace Edit function and simply replace any reference to MailConnect with a reference to NetRunner globally throughout the entire project. The second method is to compile the program with the Full Compile option: you wait until the compiler complains that is cannot find the object, and then you fix it. The first way takes less time because you can change all occurrences at one time. The second way, however, may be somewhat better because you can review the code where the compiler flags the error and perhaps rewrite the code at that point.

As part of the merge process, we also need to update the timer routine to replace the timer routine in the MailRunner program. As you can see in Listing 21-1, there are now three sets of logic that test for each of the major functions in NetRunner. All three sets of logic are nearly identical. The only real difference between them is that they each refer to controls and variables that are specific to that function.

Sending Articles from NewsRunner

Okay, now that we have merged MailRunner with FTPRunner and NewsRunner, what benefits should the user see from this integration (other than the fact that the functions are available in a single program)? Well none, really, unless we start to integrate the functions. We previously decided that FTP and Usenet news did not have much that could be integrated, but is the same situation still true now that Mail is part of the picture? Definitely not.

One of my favorite functions in a news program is the capability to pass on information to people that may not read the newsgroup, or to privately reply to someone that posted a question on the group. Because we just added MailRunner to NetRunner, it is logical to add that function to the Article form. In addition to the changes in the Article form, a few changes are also required in the Note form.

Changes to the Article Form

To send a note, we reuse the existing Note form from MailRunner, add a new button to the toolbar, and create a new routine (see Listing 21-1) that copies the current article to the Note form and prepares it to be mailed. To do this, we need to set header information for To, CC, Subject, and Date. Then we construct a From header using information about the POP server. These statements are very similar to the ones found in the `DoNew` routine in the Note form.

Then we take the current news article and copy it into `Note.Notebox`. Rather than just doing a straight copy, I added a little information that may be useful to the person receiving the note, such as who originally posted the news article and the name of the newsgroup in which the article was found. Then we copy each line of the article and precede each line with a ">", which indicates that the text came from the news article.

Finally, we transfer control to the Note form by using the `Show` method. I also set the global `MailCurrentNote` to -1, which indicates to the Note form that the information in the Notebox did not come from the POP server, but somewhere else.

Listing 21-1 ***DoForward*** **Subroutine**

```
Private Sub DoForward()

'  Forward a note to someone using MailRunner
Dim i As Integer

Note.to.Text = ""
Note.cc.Text = ""
Note.DateTime.Text = Format(Date, "ddd, dd mmm yyyy ") & Format(Time, "hh:mm:ss ")
```

continues

Listing 21-1 Continued

```
Note.subject.Text = Article.subject.Text
Note.Frame1.Caption = "From: " & NetRunner.POPUserId.Text & "@" &
NetRunner.POPRemoteHost.Text
Note.notebox.Text = "In the newsgroups: " & Newsgroup.Text & " " & From.Text & _
                    " wrote " & vbCrLf & Article.articlebox.Text

i = InStr(Note.notebox.Text, vbCrLf)
Do While i <> 0
   i = InStr(i + 2, Note.notebox.Text, vbCrLf)
   Note.notebox.Text = Left(Note.notebox.Text, i + 1) & "> " & _
                       Right(Note.notebox.Text, (Len(Note.notebox.Text) - i - 1))
Loop

MailCurrentNote = -1
Note.Show 0

End Sub
```

Changes to the Note Form

Now that we have inserted code to handle creating a Note form with all the information necessary to forward a news article, there are a couple of changes I decided to make to the Note form. While no changes are really required at this point, using the Note form without loading the MailRunner causes the MailRunner form to be loaded. This happens because the Note form uses the SMTP control from the MailRunner form.

The cure for this problem is to simply move the SMTP control from the MailRunner form to the Note form. The `DoSendNote` routine that is associated with the MailRunner form needs to be revised and moved to the Note form. Also, the events associated with the SMTP control (`DocInput` and `Error`) need to be revised and moved. The revisions to the three routines are very straightforward and are pretty much limited to making sure that the information is referenced in the correct place. Listing 21-2 lists the revised routine that is used to send a note. Because the changes are similar in the other routines, I have simply included them on the CD-ROM rather than deal with them here.

Listing 21-2 ***MenuDefaultParameters*** **Subroutine**

```
Function DoSendNote() As Integer

' After the note has been prepared for sending,
' build the DocHeaders collection, and send the
' note to the server.

Dim hdr As New DocHeadersCls
Dim i As Integer
Dim j As Integer

Toolbar1.Buttons("Send").Enabled = False

If Len(NetRunner.SMTPRemoteHost.Text) = 0 Then
   MsgBox "No remote host system specified."
   NetRunner.Show 0
   Exit Function
End If
SMTP.RemoteHost = NetRunner.SMTPRemoteHost.Text
SMTP.RemotePort = NetRunner.SMTPRemotePort.Text

hdr.Clear
hdr.Add "From", Trim(Right(Frame1.Caption, Len(Frame1.Caption) - 5))
hdr.Add "To", Me.to.Text
hdr.Add "Date", Me.DateTime.Text
hdr.Add "Subject", subject.Text
hdr.Add "CC", cc.Text
```

continues

Listing 21-2 Continued

```
SMTP.SendDoc , hdr, notebox.Text
Do While (SMTP.State = prcConnecting) _
   Or (SMTP.State = prcResolvingHost) _
   Or (SMTP.State = prcHostResolved)
   DoEvents
Loop

If SMTP.State <> prcConnected Then
   MsgBox "Error in DoConnect(Connect). Unable to connect to SMTP server." & " " &
Format(SMTP.ReplyCode)
   Toolbar1.Buttons("Send").Enabled = True
   Exit Function
End If

Do While (SMTP.State = prcConnected) _
   And (SMTP.ProtocolState = 1)
   DoEvents
Loop

Do While SMTP.Busy
   DoEvents
Loop

If SMTP.ReplyCode <> 221 And SMTP.ReplyCode <> 0 Then
   MsgBox "Error encountered in SendNote(SendDoc). Reply text is: " & _
           SMTP.ReplyString & " " & Format(SMTP.ReplyCode)
Else
   MsgBox "Mail sent to the SMTP server."
End If

DoSendNote = SMTP.ReplyCode
```

```
Toolbar1.Buttons("Send").Enabled = True

End Function
```

Sort ListViews in ArticleList and MailRunner

The ListView control offers a number of nice features, some of which we used in both the ArticleList form and the MailRunner form. One feature I find particularly useful is the `ColumnClick` event. This feature applies only to the Report view (`ListView.View = lvwReport`) mode of the control. At the top of the display window, the control automatically lists header information for each of the columns. These columns can be resized by the user by simply putting the cursor on the line between the columns and dragging it to one side or the other, thus increasing the space or decreasing the space used by that column. This allows you to see more information in one column that you might normally see.

Besides changing the size of the columns, the control also recognizes when the user clicks a column header. When this happens, the control triggers the `ColumnClick` event and passes the `ColumnHeader` that the user clicked. Combining this with the control's ability to sort the information displayed on any particular column is a natural idea. The code in Listing 21-5 shows a quick and easy way to implement this function.

First, check to see if the information is already sorted by this column. If it is, then temporarily disable the `Sorted` property and change the sort order, and then re-enable the `Sorted` property. If the data is not already sorted on this column, simply disable the `Sorted` property, change the column, and then re-enable the `Sorted` property. The reason I turn off the `Sorted` property and turn it back on again is to force the control to re-sort the data after I change the sort order.

Now the way I change the `SortOrder` property when the data is already sorted is a little interesting. A value of zero means that the data is to be sorted in ascending order. A value of one means that the data is to be sorted in descending order. This is done by adding one to the current value, and then taking the mod two of the result. (Remember that mod operator returns the remainder after dividing the first value by the second. Thus 0 mod 2

= 0, 1 mod 2 = 1, and 2 mod 2 = 0.) This means that essentially I flip the sort order from ascending to descending to ascending again each time the user clicks the same column, which means that the user has the option to see their mail sorted from oldest to newest, or newest to oldest by merely clicking a column header.

Listing 21-3 ***ListView1_ColumnClick* Event**

```
Private Sub ListView1_ColumnClick(ByVal ColumnHeader As ColumnHeader)

If ListView1.SortKey = ColumnHeader.Index - 1 Then
   ListView1.Sorted = False
   ListView1.SortOrder = (ListView1.SortOrder + 1) Mod 2
   ListView1.Sorted = True

Else
   ListView1.Sorted = False
   ListView1.SortKey = ColumnHeader.Index - 1
   ListView1.Sorted = True
End If

End Sub
```

The Assign Function

While working on this program I noticed a little problem. There was a lot of screen flicker on the status bar when the values were frequently updated, which is caused by a small change to the `DoConnectPOP` routine that displays the state changes during the connection phase. (Check the `Do While` loop in Listing 21-5 immediately after the `POP.Connect` method.) In the past, we would only update the status bar periodically (such as when 100 newsgroups were added or finished). To avoid the screen flicker problem, I created a routine I called Assign (see Listing 21-4) that checks the value in the status bar object and does the assignment only if the values are different. This little bit of code removed the screen flicker. I promptly put a call to this routine anywhere I update the information on the status bar frequently.

Listing 21-4 ***Assign*** **Subroutine**

```
Sub Assign(o As Object, v As String)

If o.Text <> v Then
   o.Text = v
End If

End Sub
```

Listing 21-5 ***MenuDefaultParameters*** **Subroutine**

```
Private Sub DoConnectPOP()

'  Connect to the remote POP server.

If POP.State <> prcDisconnected Then
   Exit Sub
End If

If Len(NetRunner.POPRemoteHost.Text) = 0 Then
   MsgBox "No remote host system specified."
   NetRunner.Show 0
   Exit Sub
End If
POP.RemoteHost = NetRunner.POPRemoteHost.Text
POP.RemotePort = NetRunner.POPRemotePort.Text
POP.UserId = NetRunner.POPUserId.Text
POP.Password = NetRunner.POPPassword.Text

MailStartTime = Now
Frame1.Caption = "Mail from: " & POP.RemoteHost
```

continues

Listing 21-5 Continued

```
POP.Connect
Do While (POP.State = prcConnecting) _
   Or (POP.State = prcResolvingHost) _
   Or (POP.State = prcHostResolved)
   If POP.State = prcConnecting Then
      Assign StatusBar.Panels(1), "Connecting"
   ElseIf POP.State = prcResolvingHost Then
      Assign StatusBar.Panels(1), "Resolving Host"
   ElseIf POP.State = prcHostResolved Then
      Assign StatusBar.Panels(1), "Host Resolved"
   End If
   DoEvents
Loop

If POP.State <> prcConnected Then
   MsgBox "Error in DoConnect(Connect). Unable to connect to mail server."
   Exit Sub
End If

Assign StatusBar.Panels(1), "Loging on"

Do While (POP.State = prcConnected) _
   And (POP.ProtocolState = 1)
   DoEvents
Loop

Do While POP.Busy
   DoEvents
Loop

POP.Authenticate
Do While POP.Busy
   DoEvents
```

```
Loop

If (POP.ReplyCode <> 0) Then
   MsgBox "Error in DoConnect(Authenticate). Reply text is: " & POP.ReplyString & " " &
Format(POP.ReplyCode)
End If

MailConnected = True
Toolbar.Buttons("Check Mail").Image = 2
Toolbar.Buttons("Delete").Enabled = True
StatusBar.Panels(1).Text = "Connected"
StatusBar.Panels(2).Text = Format(POP.MessageCount) & " message(s) waiting"

GetAllNotes

End Sub
```

Delete Registry Info

The last change to NetRunner that I am going to talk about in this chapter lets you reset all the parameters used by NetRunner to their default values. The way this function works is it deletes all the information from the Windows' system registry and resets the values on the appropriate tabs of the NetRunner form. The primary benefit of this function is that it permits you to erase all the form size and placement information and start all over again with the default values from the program.

First, ensure that the user really wants to do this by displaying a message (using the `MsgBox` function) and waiting for the user to respond OK or Cancel. Assuming that the user really wants to do this, use the `DeleteSetting` statement to remove all the NetRunner information from the registry. Because the `DeleteSetting` statement requires both the application and the section values, we cannot delete all of the values in a single statement. Instead, we must explicitly delete each section. (Note that the `DeleteSetting` statement lets you delete a single key within a section. It just doesn't let you delete all sections in a single statement.)

After deleting the information related to the appropriate section, reset the values to their defaults. Because the information related to the form (i.e., position and size) is determined automatically when the form is loaded, you do not have to explicitly reset that information in this routine. All we have to do is put default values in the fields on the NetRunner form. I blanked out every value except for the port numbers, which I set to their well-known port address for the function. (I did this because I never can seem to remember these numbers when I really need them!)

Finally, acknowledge to the user that everything has been updated using another MsgBox. I originally did not bother informing the user when the updates were complete, but after using it a few times I felt that if it was sufficiently important to ask the user if they really want to reset these values, then it is equally important to let them know when the process is finished.

One problem I encountered with this routine was that the `DeleteSetting` statement tended to abort the program if the specified section did not exist. There are two different ways to solve this problem. The first is to check to see if the section exists and then delete it. The other way is just to ignore the error (using the `On Error Resume Next` statement). Because I do not really care if the setting exists before I execute the `DeleteSetting` statement and as long as it does not exist after, can you guess which way I used? (No fair peeking at Listing 21-6 to see the answer!)

Listing 21-6 ***MenuDefaultParameters*** **Subroutine**

```
Private Sub MenuDefaultParameters_Click()

On Error Resume Next

If MsgBox("OK to reset all parameters to their default values?", 1) = 1 Then
   DeleteSetting "NetRunner", "Article"
   DeleteSetting "NetRunner", "ArticleList"
   DeleteSetting "NetRunner", "FTPRunner"
      FTPRemoteHost.Text = ""
      FTPRemotePort.Text = "21"
      FTPUserId.Text = ""
      FTPPassword.Text = ""
```

```
  DeleteSetting "NetRunner", "MailRunner"
     SMTPRemoteHost.Text = ""
     SMTPRemotePort.Text = "25"
     POPRemoteHost.Text = ""
     POPRemotePort.Text = "110"
     POPUserId.Text = ""
     POPPassword.Text = ""
  DeleteSetting "NetRunner", "NetRunner"
  DeleteSetting "NetRunner", "NewsRunner"
     NewsRemoteHost.Text = ""
     NewsRemotePort.Text = "119"
  DeleteSetting "NetRunner", "Note"
  MsgBox "All parameters set to their default values."
End If

End Sub
```

Summary

We continued the process of building NetRunner by incorporating the MailRunner program into the existing NetRunner. With the availability of e-mail support, we added the capability to forward a Usenet news article to an e-mail address. Adding this function required that we restructure MailRunner slightly by moving the SMTP control from the MailRunner form to the Note form.

In case you want to check your answer to the question at the front of the chapter, here is the answer:

- *Why should the status bar not be updated continuously?*

  The status bar is like any display area on the screen. If you send updates to the area continuously, the screen will flicker. It is better to send updates only when the data actually changes or once or twice a second. This helps to prevent screen flicker and also helps the user have enough time to read the information before it changes.

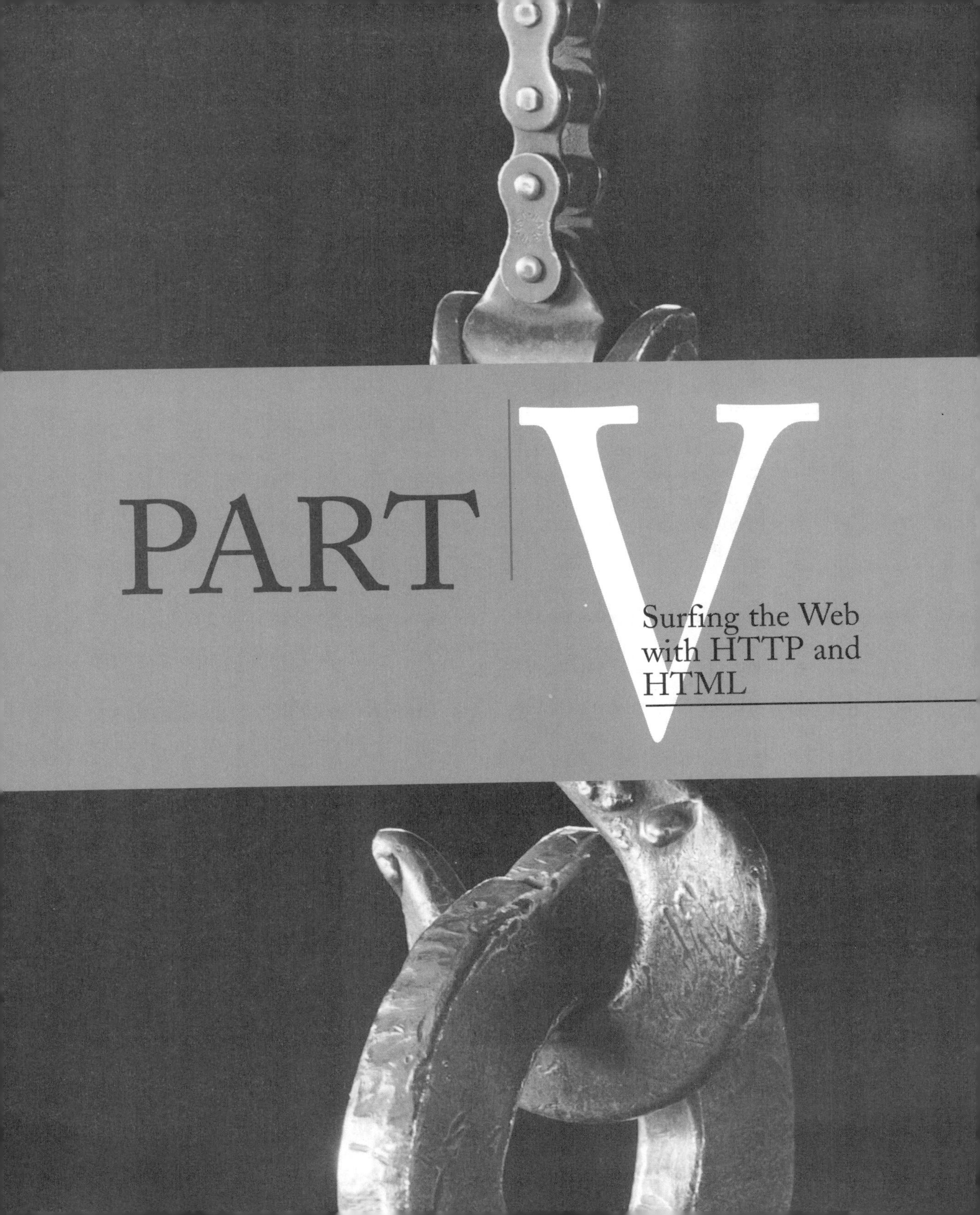

PART V

Surfing the Web with HTTP and HTML

What Are the HTTP and HTML Client Controls?

The HTTP and HTML client controls work together to retrieve documents from the World Wide Web and format them for display to the user. The World Wide Web is the single application responsible for making the Internet a common household word. People who never thought they could use a computer are buying them to access the World Wide Web. The sheer wealth of information on the Web is phenomenal!

Thinking about moving to another state? Use your friendly neighborhood Web browser to check out the houses for sale in that area (http://www.homes.com). Need information about an obscure country for a high school report? Check out the CIA World Fact Book (http://www.odci.gov/cia/publications/pubs.html). Want to find out where and when this week's NASCAR race is telecast? Check out TV Guide at (http://www.iguide.com/tv/).

In fact, there is so much information on the Internet, it is sometimes difficult to find things. Several organizations have addressed this problem by creating Web sites with huge indexes of information on the Internet. You can supply a keyword or two and retrieve a list of Web sites with short descriptions of their contents.

While the HTTP control is similar to the other ActiveX controls we have discussed in that its main function is to transport information from one machine to another, the HTML control is designed primarily to format HTML documents on the computer's screen. Even though the HTML control's function is to format documents, it also has the capability to use the HTTP control to retrieve a document automatically. This makes it much easier to use for the typical application programmer.

One word of caution. This book is not going to discuss the details of how to write HTML documents. I assume that you are somewhat familiar with the material, but if you need additional information there are a number of good books on this subject. For a good tutorial, I suggest reading *Create Your First Web Page in a Weekend* by Steve Callihan, Prima Publishing (ISBN 0-7615-0692-6).

Where Would I Use the HTTP and HTML Client Controls?

If I had to pick just one of the ActiveX controls to use in my programs, my first choice would be the HTML control. While the other controls offer lots of useful functions, the HTML control probably has more practical applications than all of the others combined. (With the possible exception of the SMTP control—I like having the ability to send mail from a program.)

One of the best applications of these controls is to build help files. Building a help file is one of the harder things to do in a Visual Basic application. Unless you are using a special tool, you need to insert a log of cross-linked information. Then you have to compile the help file and hope that you do not get any syntax errors, because if you do, it may take you quite awhile to track down the exact cause of the error. Also, a help file is limited in terms of the graphics it can use. Contrast this with Web documents that are much easier to create and are much more flexible in terms of how information is presented to the user, and it's clear which one is easier to deal with.

In a widely distributed application, using HTML help files means that you do not need to distribute them with the application. You can include information such as Frequently Asked Questions and update them over time without having to distribute the actual files to the user. This also means that the distribution package is much smaller (I have seen cases where the help file actually takes up more space than the application program itself!), which is a big advantage when working with people that have access to the Internet via dial-up modems.

Another use of the HTML control would be to display a welcome message whenever the application starts. This can be used to communicate messages like the database server will be down for service during lunch today, or a new feature is available inside the application—press here for more information.

One more use of HTTP/HTML controls is to allow programs to download new data files as they are made available. Consider the case of a program that keeps a catalog of new versions of small die cast cars such as Hot Wheels and Matchbox cars. This program could check a Web site and download any new information. This information would then be stored locally in a database for quick retrieval and reporting. In fact, the program could also send new information to the server for other users to download. This concept was the reason I began working with the Internet Control Pack in the first place. Back when my die-cast car collection took over the house, I created a program like the one described above called Car Collector to catalogue and inventory the cars. (You can take a look at it by visiting http://www.JustPC.com/cc.html.)

The final application that I am going to discuss here is the use of the HTML and HTTP controls to create self-updating applications. The program would check the Web server periodically and look for a new version. When one is found, the program downloads the updated version and begins the installation process. If the updated version was contained in a self-extracting EXE file, the old application program would start the update EXE file and shut itself down. The update program would wait until the old application had finished, and then start the installation process. As the last step of the installation process, the update program would start the newly updated application.

Summary

The HTTP and HTML client controls offer an easy method to incorporate World Wide Web documents into your Visual Basic programs. You may want to include these functions as an alternative to the traditional help files or simply as a method of providing information to the users of your program. In the following chapters, we explore how the HTTP protocol works and how the HTTP controls can be used to transfer information across the Internet. We also discuss how the HTML control works, but only from a programming level. Then we have a little fun building a Web browser in less than five minutes as well as building a more comprehensive browser called WebRunner. Finally, we incorporate WebRunner into the NetRunner program and add a few interesting touches like recognizing Web page references in e-mail notes and news articles, and then displaying them with the click of a mouse.

Chapter 22—URLs and HTTP Protocols and Functions

This chapter discusses how URLs are formed and how HTTP works from a functional level, and the protocols that are used to communicate between the client and the server. This serves as background material for understanding the HTTP client control and the WebRunner sample program.

- Overview
- URLs
- The HTTP Model
- HTTP Methods
- HTTP Reply Codes and Messages
- Accessing the Server
- Header Keywords
- Posting
- Example
- Summary

Chapter 23—The HTTP Client Control

This chapter discusses all the programming aspects (properties, events, and methods) provided by the HTTP client control. Aspects necessary for fundamental usage are emphasized, but the advanced aspects are briefly discussed.

- Overview
- Properties
- Methods
- Events
- Summary

Chapter 24—The HTMLAttr and HTMLForm Objects

This chapter discusses all the programming facilities provided by the `HTMLAttr` and `HTMLForm` objects. Aspects necessary for fundamental usage are emphasized, but the advanced aspects are briefly touched upon.

- Overview
- Properties—HTMLAttr
- Properties—HTMLAttrs
- Methods—HTMLAttrs
- Properties—HTMLForm
- Methods—HTMLForm
- Properties—HTMLForms
- Methods—HTMLForms
- Example—HTMLAttr and HTMLAttrs
- Example—HTMLForm and HTMLForms
- Summary

Chapter 25—The HTML Client Control

This chapter discusses all the programming aspects (properties, events, and methods) provided by the HTML client control. Aspects necessary for fundamental usage are emphasized, but the advanced aspects are briefly discussed.

- Overview
- Properties
- Methods
- Events
- Summary

Chapter 26—WebRunner

This chapter presents a program called WebRunner, which allows the user to surf various sites on the World Wide Web using the HTML control.

- Overview
- The Five-Minute Web Browser
- How to Use WebRunner
- The Program Structure
- Retrieving a Web Document
- Making History
- Summary

Chapter 27—NetRunner—Part Three

This chapter shows the user how to combine the WebRunner program with the NetRunner program discussed in Chapter 15.

- Overview
- How to Use NetRunner
- The Program Structure
- Changing the Timer
- Forms Placement
- Forms Sizing
- Summary

Chapter 22

HTTP and HTML Protocols and Functions

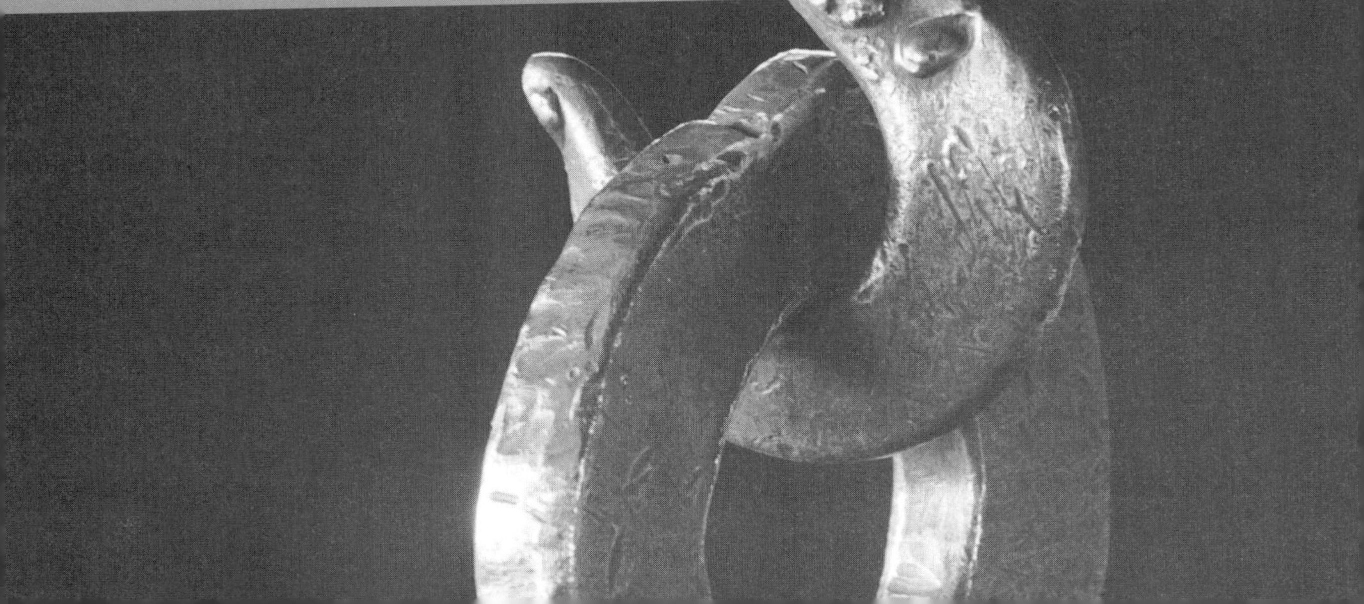

Overview

In this chapter, we talk about *Universal Resource Locators* (URLs) and how they work with the *HyperText Transport Protocol* (HTTP) to transfer documents between a client and a server.

By the end of this chapter, you should be able to answer the following questions:

- How do you access the server?
- How to you retrieve a resource?

URLs

In order to understand how the HyperText Transport Protocol (HTTP) works, we first must start with the fundamental object used with the protocol: the Universal Resource Locator (URL). URLs and their detailed formatting requirements are discussed in RFC-1738. Resources are documents, programs, images, and so on that are available for access on the Internet. URLs are used to uniquely identify these resources.

One way to think about URLs is like an individual's address. The state and city represent the domain and host, while the street name and house address represent the file. Just as all the information needed to find someone's home is available in an address and in a uniform way, all the information needed to find a resource on the Internet is encoded in a URL.

URL Format

The general format for a URL is described in figure 22-1. Each scheme is associated with a particular protocol used on the Internet. Of the protocols listed, the ActiveX controls support FTP (with the FTP control), mailto (with the SMTP control), news and nntp (with the NNTP control), and HTTP with the HTTP control. The host parameter is the remote system's host name or IP address.

Note that both the <user-info> and <port-info> parts of the URL are optional and are usually omitted. In the case of user-info, you can supply either the userid or the userid and password. In cases where this information is not supplied, a reasonable default is generally used. For example, the default userid and password used with the FTP scheme are anonymous and the user's e-mail address, respectively. Port numbers also default to the well-known port address for the specified scheme. (You remember those well-known port addresses from Chapter 2, right?)

The <url-path> is usually the name of the file on the remote system that we want to retrieve. In some cases (such as FTP), the file name is the absolute file name on the remote system. In other cases, such as HTTP and Gopher, the file name is a relative name that is based on definitions inside the server. These definitions may coincide with the physical directory (or more likely provide a shortcut to a directory) and from then on follow the real directory structure.

In some cases, additional information may be included at the end of the <url-path>. This may be something like ";type=typecode" for FTP, which indicates that the file should be transferred as ASCII (a), image (i), or a directory listing (d). An HTTP <url-path> may include a "?" to separate the file name from search information. Other schemes like mail-to and news require radically different formats.

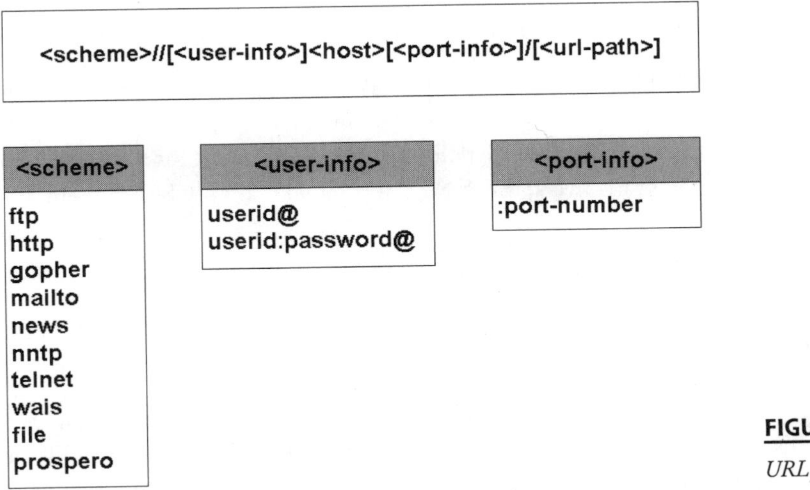

FIGURE 22-1

URL format.

FTP URLs

Incorporating an FTP definition into a URL is a fairly complex task. FTP operates as a state-driven protocol where each command takes advantage of the previous commands, so we must include all of the information that is necessary to access the file into a single

URL. This means that we must include the userid and password, even if it is "anonymous" and an e-mail address. We must also recognize that each request to the FTP server generates all the FTP protocol we have previously discussed for logging onto the server and accessing a file.

In addition to needing the userid and password, a ";type=typecode" parameter may need to be appended to the <url-path> to ensure that the file is transferred with the proper mode. Whenever possible, the client and server try to guess what the proper type is based on the name of the file. Thus, the program should transfer myfile.zip in image mode and myfile.txt in ASCII mode.

News and NNTP URLs

The News scheme is different from the general scheme described in figure 22-1. It takes the form of "News:<newsgroup>" or "News:<message-id>". The former is used to retrieve a list of articles in a particular newsgroup, while the latter is used to retrieve a specific article in a newsgroup.

Unlike the News scheme, the NNTP scheme follows the general format rather closely, differing only in the <url-path>. In this case, the <url-path> takes the form of "/<newsgroup>/<article-number>". Because <article-number> is different for a specific news article on different NNTP servers, the NNTP format should only be used when absolutely necessary.

Mailto URLs

Like the News URL scheme, the mailto URL scheme is totally different than the general format. This format is relatively simple, taking the form of "Mailto:<email-address>". The address must be a properly formatted RFC-822 e-mail address. Definitions for the SMTP server to be used to handle the mail transfer are defined outside the URL.

File URLs

An unusual URL is the File URL. This URL is used to specify the location of a file. Unlike the other URL types, this one does not specify a protocol that should be used to access the file; it uses a format similar to the most of the other URLs, "File://<host>/<path>". Because no protocol is specified, it is really of limited usefulness except in one situation. It is possible to specify "localhost" for <host>. Then <path> is used to search for a file on the local system.

Telnet URLs

Telnet URLs are used to invoke an external Telnet program that allows a user to sign onto a remote system using a dumb terminal. You can also include the <userid>:<password>@ part of the URL to identify the userid and password that is needed to sign onto the remote system.

The HTTP Model

You may have noticed that I did not discuss the HTTP protocol in detail in the previous section. That is because it is impossible to talk about HTTP unless you have a basic understanding of URLs. When HTTP is combined with URLs and the HyperText Markup Language (HTML), you have the basis of the technology used in the World Wide Web.

HTTP was designed to be a light-weight, low-overhead protocol that permits easy access to hypertext documents. It is a stateless protocol because each request is independent of the others. HTTP also builds on existing TCP/IP technologies through the use of the Internet Mail standards and Multipurpose Internet Mail Extensions (MIME) for transferred documents.

Unlike the other protocols we have discussed, the HTTP protocol actually consists of two protocols: HTTP/0.9 and HTTP/1.0. While HTTP/1.0 is really a superset of HTTP/0.9, there are some minor differences that we discuss later. Servers that are designed to meet the HTTP/1.0 protocol are also required to properly respond to HTTP/0.9 protocols.

In figure 22-2, you can see that the protocol model is the classic client-server model. The client program sends a request for information to the server, and the information is retrieved from the server's file system and returned to the client. The client has the option to store this data locally in a cache to improve performance by reducing the number of times the client has to retrieve a document from the server. This is important because most Web browsers are connected to the Internet using relatively slow modems, and many HTML documents frequently use the same graphic images from one page to another. Caching also helps when a browser keeps a history list, which is a list of URLs that the user has visited in the current session. This list is necessary to implement forward and backward functions.

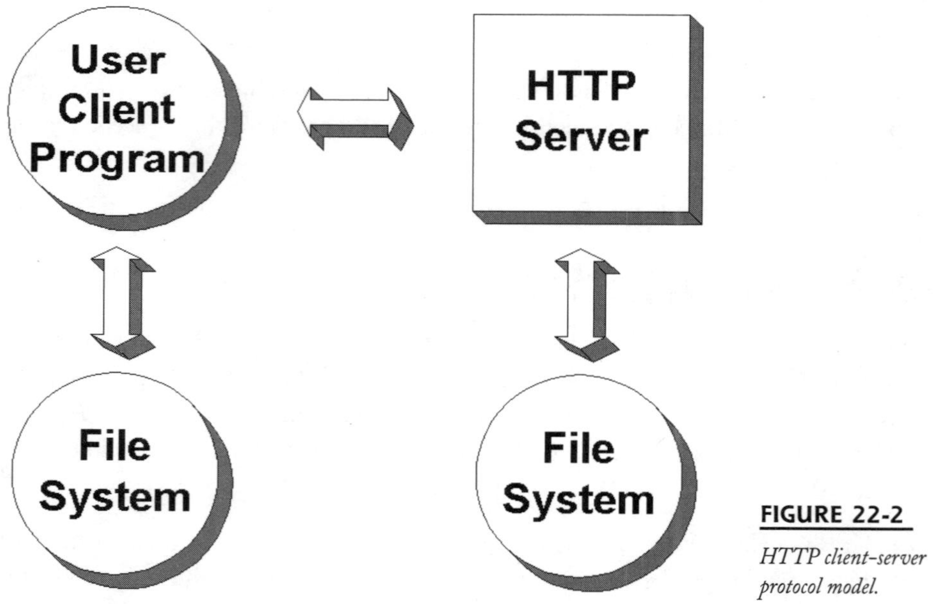

FIGURE 22-2

HTTP client-server protocol model.

HTTP Methods

HTTP/0.9 includes only the `Get` method to access data on the server while HTTP/1.0 adds two more methods: `Head` and `Post`. There are many extensions to these that may or may not be available depending on the server, including `Put`, `Delete`, `Link`, and `Unlink`.

In HTTP/0.9, the client program sends a single line of text to the server. This line is the `Get` method. It is used to retrieve a single document from the server. The server responds with the requested document or a document that contains an error message that is displayed to the user.

In HTTP/1.0, the client program sends a message to the server consisting of one of the methods listed in Table 22-1 and a series of one or more lines of header information listed in Table 22-2. Note that only the first three methods are officially part of HTTP/1.0. The others are extensions to the protocol and may not always be available on all servers.

The server responds to an HTTP/1.0 request by returning a status line that contains the HTTP version, followed by a space and a three-digit reply code. Immediately following this status line is a series of header lines, followed by a blank line, and then the body of the document. These header keywords are listed in Table 22-3.

Table 22-1 HTTP Client Methods

Method	Syntax
`Get`	GET <URL> [HTTP/1.0]
`Head`	HEAD <URL>
`Post`	POST <URL>
`Put`	PUT <URL>
`Delete`	DELETE <URL>
`Link`	LINK <URL>
`Unlink`	UNLINK <URL>

Table 22-2 HTTP Header Keywords for the Client

Keyword	Description
Authorization	Passes security information to the server.
From	E-mail address of the user.
If-Modified-Since	Returns the document if it is newer than the specified date.
Referer	Identifies where the URL was found.
User-Agent	The name of the client that issues the request.

Table 22-3 HTTP Header Keywords for the Server

Keyword	Description
Allow	Lists HTTP methods than can be applied to a resource.
Content-Encoding	Specifies the compression technique used with the resource.
Content-Length	Specifies the size in bytes of the resource.
Content-Type	Specifies the media type of the resource.
Date	Specifies the date the resource was transmitted to the client.
Expires	Specifies the date the resource is no longer current.
Last-Modified	Specifies the date the resource was last modified.
Location	Specifies the exact URL for this resource.
Server	Identifies the name of the software that runs the server.
WWW-Authenticate	Used to verify that the user is permitted to access the resource.

HTTP Reply Codes and Messages

Like all the other protocols we have discussed (except for POP3), in HTTP the server returns a three-digit reply code (see Table 22-4). The first digit determines the general class of message. A `1` in the first position indicates an informational response. While HTTP/1.0 does not define any informational messages, this classification is reserved for future use. A `2` as the first character indicates that the server was able to process the request. A leading character of `3` means that further action must be taken by the server to fulfill the request. A `4` in the first position indicates some kind of error condition that originated from the client. A `5` as the first character indicates an error condition on the server.

Accompanying each reply code is a short description known as the *Reason Phrase*. This is the message often seen as part of the response from the server. Anyone who has used the Web for more than a few minutes is familiar with the `404 Not Found` response.

Table 22-4 HTTP Reply Codes

Reply Code	Reason Phrase	Definition
200	`OK`	The request was successful.
201	`Created`	The request was successful and a new resource was created.
202	`Accepted`	The request was accepted for processing, but the processing is not yet complete.

Reply Code	Reason Phrase	Definition
204	`No Content`	The server has processed the request but there is no new information to be returned.
300	`Multiple Choices`	The requested resource is available at one or more locations.
301	`Moved Permanently`	The requested resource has been assigned a new URL and any further references should use this new URL.
302	`Moved Temporarily`	The requested resource resides at a different location, but will return to this location in the future.
304	`Not Modified`	The requested resource has not been modified since the date specified in the If-Modified-Since header.
400	`Bad Request`	The server could not properly interpret the request.
401	`Unauthorized`	The request requires user authorization.
403	`Forbidden`	The server has understood the request and has refused to satisfy it.
404	`Not Found`	The server cannot find the information specified in the request.
500	`Internal Server Error`	The server could not satisfy the request due to an internal error condition.
501	`Not Implemented`	The server does not support the requested feature.
502	`Bad Gateway`	The server received an invalid response from a server from which it was trying to retrieve information.
503	`Service Unavailable`	The server cannot process this request at the current time.

Accessing the Server

The HTTP server works a little differently than most other servers. The client first establishes a connection to the server's port 80. Rather than waiting for a reply code from the server, the client immediately sends a request message to the server and waits for a response. After the server has accepted the request message, it attempts to process it and returns a reply message. Then the connection is dropped. This is different because in the other protocols the connection to the server is maintained until the client explicitly drops the connection by executing a command.

Get

The `Get` method is used to retrieve a document from the server. It specifies a value for the name of the file to be retrieved or the entire URL. If the HTTP/1.0 version is not specified, the server assumes that the response should be formatted according to HTTP/0.9 specifications (i.e. just the document, no header keywords).

If the HTTP/1.0 is specified, it is possible to include additional header keywords in the request. One common keyword is the If-Modified-Since header. This changes the `Get` method to a conditional `Get` because the document is only transferred if it has been updated since a specified date and time. This is useful when the client has saved a copy of the document in its local cache and wants to ensure that it has the most recent copy.

Head

The `Head` method is used to retrieve only the header information from the server. The results of this method should be identical to the `Get` method except for the exclusion of the document body. This can also be used to determine if a document has been updated on the server; however, you probably should use the more efficient `Get` method with the If-Modified-Since header because the `Head` method requires two accesses (first the `Head` and then a `Get`) to retrieve the data.

Post

The `Post` method is used to return a document that contains information that should be passed from the client to the server. This is commonly used for Web pages that contain forms that are sent to the server for processing. The specified URL contains a program that receives the input and returns a new document.

Put

The `Put` method is an extension to HTTP available on some servers that allows a resource on the server to be updated or a new resource to be added.

Delete

The `Delete` method is an extension to HTTP available on some servers that enables the resource specified in the URL to be deleted.

Link

The `Link` method is an extension to HTTP available on some servers that establishes a Link relationship between the existing resource and other resources on the server.

Unlink

The `Unlink` method is an extension to HTTP available on some servers that removes the Link relationship between two resources on the server.

Header Keywords

The header keywords are used by the client and the server to pass along additional information and to return additional information about the requested resource.

Allow

The Allow header keyword lists the methods that can be applied to a particular resource.

Authorization

The Authorization header keyword passes security credentials from the client to the server. This is usually in response to a 401 (Unauthorized) reply code from the server. If the server does not accept the security credentials, the server responds with a reply code of 403. If the server accepts the security credentials, it responds with a WWW-Authenticate header.

Content-Encoding

The Content-Encoding header keyword enables the server to tell the client that a resource is compressed and needs to use the specified decompression routine when received by the client. This allows the resource to be compressed without destroying any of the underlying information.

Content-Length

The Content-Length header keyword enables the server to pass to the client the total size of the resource in bytes. This field is required on all HTTP/1.0 responses that return a body.

Content-Type

The Content-Type header keyword is used to communicate media information from the server to the client. This information is used to determine what type of resource is being transferred. For example, an HTML document would have a header like "Content-Type: text/html". A JPEG image would have a header like "Content-Type: image/jpeg"

Date

The Date header keyword is used to communicate the date and time the message was created. This information is useful for caching because you have a known date and time of when the information was created. A `Get` command with the If-Modified-Since header that includes the value specified in the cached resource can be used to ensure that the client always receives the most current version of the resource.

Expires

The Expires header keyword is used to communicate to the client when the data should no longer be considered current. This is used primarily to help caching algorithms determine when they should delete a resource from the cache. If the date is zero or not valid, the resource should not be cached. The one exception to this rule is for clients that have a history facility that permits users to move forward and backward through the history. Unless the user has specifically requested that the resources be checked each time for currency, it is acceptable to display an expired resource.

From

The From header keyword is used to send the e-mail address of the user to the server so the server has an address with which to contact the user if their activities are causing problems on the server. (This might happen if someone has a robot searching the Web for information and it gets into an infinite loop requesting the same document.) This field is optional and should not be included without the user's approval because it may violate the user's right to privacy. Also, the information in this field should not be used for security purposes because there is no guarantee that the user has entered the proper e-mail address.

If-Modified-Since

The If-Modified-Since header keyword allows the client to retrieve a document from the server only if it is newer than the specified date.

Last-Modified

The Last-Modified header keyword identifies the last time the document was modified on the server. Because the technique used to determine this value is left up to the implementor, you should not rely on this value for caching. For the most part implementors have extracted this value from the last modified date of the file from the server.

Location

The Location header keyword allows the server to specify the exact location of the resource. If a response code beginning with 3 is returned, this value indicates the preferred location to retrieve the resource.

Referrer

The Referrer header keyword is used by the client to specify the URL of resource that includes the URL that is being retrieved. This is useful for the server to determine the link that enabled the user to get to a specific document.

Server

The Server header keyword is used to send the name of the server product and significant subproducts to the client. Version information may be included.

User-Agent

The User-Agent header keyword is used to send the name of the client program to the server. This information may assist the management of the server to track protocol violations, and may be used by the server to work around limitations in the client program.

WWW-Authenticate

The WWW-Authenticate header keyword is used by the server to present a challenge to the client program. The client program responds to this challenge with the Authorization keyword.

Example

I used a Windows 95 Telnet command to connect to a machine with an HTTP server. You can try the same thing by Telnetting to your local HTTP server using port 80 instead of the standard Telnet port 23. Unless you set local echo on, you will not be able to see anything you type. In the following code, commands that I typed are prefixed by ->, all other text is generated by the server. One note of caution: You will want to turn local echo on in Windows 95 Telnet because when the connection closes at the end of the server's transmission, you cannot access the information on the screen.

```
->GET /
<html>
<head>
<title>Just Plane Crazy</title>
<meta name="GENERATOR" content="Mozilla/2.01Gold (Win32)">
</head>
<body text="#FFFFFF" bgcolor="#C0C0C0" link="#80FFFF" vlink="#551A8B"
alink="#FF0000" background="bricks.gif">
<center><p><img src="jpclogo.gif" border=0></p></center>
<table border=0 cellpadding=0 cellspacing=0>
<tr>
<td width=40% align=left valign=bottom>
<h1 align=center>Just Plane Crazy</h1>
</td>
<td width=60% align=right valign=bottom>
<p><b>This site looks best when viewed with Netscape Navigator 2.0.</b> </p>
<p><b>Download Netscape Now!</b>
<a href="http://home.netscape.com/comprod/mirror/index.html">
<img src="now8.gif" border=2 height=31 width=88></a></p>
</td>
</tr>
</table>
<center><p><img src="jet.gif" border=0 height=10 width=640></p></center>
<b>Welcome to Just Plane Crazy, makers of <a href="cc.html">Car Collector</a>.
We are a small consulting firm operating in Beltsville, Maryland, just
outside our nation's capital. A wide range of management and technical
services are available including: business plan development, computer
application analysis, design and implementation, desktop and web site
publishing, technical writing, and computer technology evaluation. For
more information about these services or other services, please contact
us at either
<i><a href="MAILTO:WFreeze@JustPC.com">WFreeze@JustPC.com</a></i>
or <i><a href="MAILTO:JFreeze@JustPC.com">JFreeze@JustPC.com</a></i>.
<center><p><img src="jet_2.gif" border=0 height=10 width=640></p></center>
```

```
<b><p><font SIZE=-2>Copyright &copy;1996 Just Plane Crazy </font></p>
<p><font SIZE=-2>This page was last updated on 2 May 96. </font></p></b>
</body>
</html>
```

In the next example, I Telnet to WWW.JustPC.COM using port 80. I immediately type "GET /" because all HTTP do not respond with a reply code after the connection is made. This retrieves the default document from the server. Because I did not specify "HTTP/1.0" at the end of the `Get` method, the server merely returns the specified document and drops the connection.

```
->GET / HTTP/1.0

HTTP/1.0 200 OK
Date: Fri, 09 Aug 1996 20:29:19 GMT
Server: Apache/1.0.5
Content-type: text/html
Content-length: 1684
Last-modified: Fri, 03 May 1996 03:32:31 GMT

<html>
.
.
.
Many lines of HTML code deleted.
.
.
.
</html>
```

Here, I retrieve the same document using the HTTP/1.0 method. Note that this time, the server returns a line with the HTTP version before the document, which in this case is version 1.0. It also includes a reply code of 200, which means that the request was successfully executed. The second line returns the message that the request was processed. The third line returns information about the server. The fourth line returns the Content-type of the document. Notice that it is the standard MIME type for an HTML document. The fifth line reports the size of the document in bytes. The sixth line returns that date that this document was last modified. The seventh and last line is a blank line that is used to separate the document headers from the actual document. (Remember this from our mail and news article examples?) Finally, the document is returned. (Rather than repeat the entire Web page, I deleted everything from the `<head>` tag to the `</head>` tag.)

```
->HEAD / HTTP/1.0

HTTP/1.0 200 OK
Date: Fri, 09 Aug 1996 20:32:52 GMT
Server: Apache/1.0.5
Content-type: text/html
Content-length: 1684
Last-modified: Fri, 03 May 1996 03:32:31 GMT
```

The next example is relatively simple. I use the `Head` method to request only the header information from the document. Note that the data returned from the server is nearly identical to the previous example. This time, however, the document is not returned. This method is useful when you have a local cache to store documents and want to verify if the document is still current.

```
->GET / HTTP/1.0
->If-Modified-Since: Sun, 01 Aug 1996 00:00:00 GMT

HTTP/1.0 304 Not Modified
Date: Fri, 09 Aug 1996 20:35:00 GMT
Server: Apache/1.0.5
```

The final example demonstrates another way to verify if the information in the local cache is still current. This time I attempted to retrieve the document from the server using the `Get` method, but I included a header that specifies that the document should be returned only if it has been updated more recently than the first of August. Because the document was last modified on May third (see the Last-Modified header from the previous example), the server does not return the document, but instead returns a status code of 304, which indicates that the document was not modified since the specified date. (Note that if you are caching the document, the date for the If-Modified-Since field should be extracted from the Date: header keyword because the value used in Last-Modified keyword is not strictly defined by RFC-1945.)

Summary

In this chapter, we talked about the Universal Resource Locator (URL) and the HyperText Transport Protocol. URLs are designed to identify any resource that someone may want to access on the Internet, while the HTTP provides simple methods that can be used to access these resources. These standards, along with the HyperText Markup Language, form the core standards for the World Wide Web.

In the next chapter, we continue our discussion of the HTTP ActiveX control by looking at some of the support objects used by the control.

In case you want to check your answers to the questions in the Overview section, here are the answers:

- *How do you access the server?*

  You access the server by connecting to the server and immediately sending the request for information.
- *How do you receive a resource?*

  The `Get` method is used to retrieve a resource from an HTTP server. If you are using HTTP/0.9, the server responds with a resource, either the one you requested or an error document. If you are using HTTP/1.0, you receive a series of headers with information about the server and the resource you requested, including a reply code, the resource size, and other interesting information, plus the resource itself.

Chapter 23

The HTTP Client Control

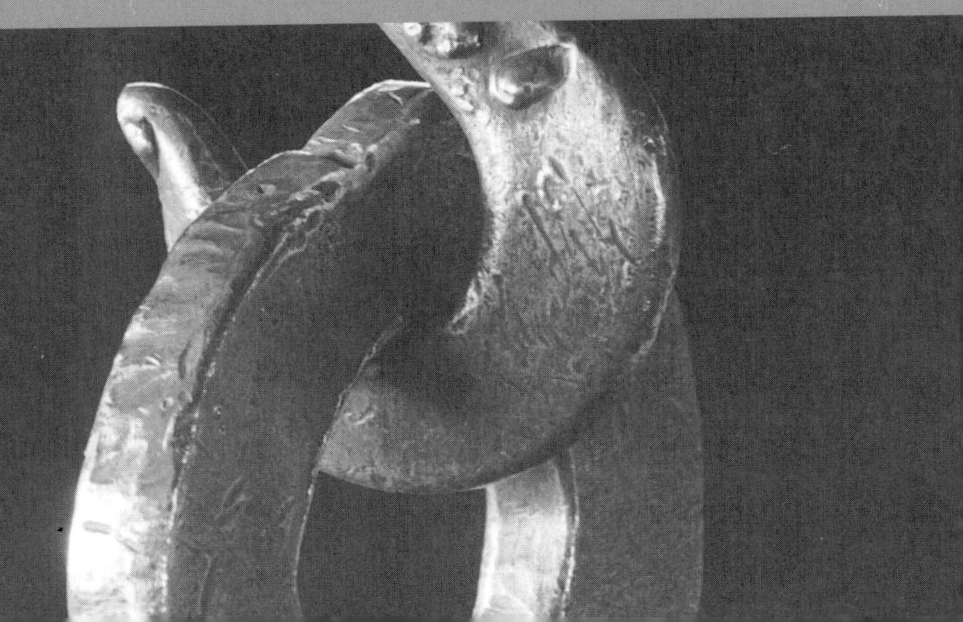

Overview

In this chapter, we discuss the properties, events, and methods of the ActiveX HTTP client control. This control handles the protocol interaction with a remote World Wide Web server and provides a high-level method of interacting with the server. This control only handles the HTTP interaction. Parsing and layout of the HTML document that is most commonly retrieved is handled by the HTML control, which is discussed in the next two chapters.

By the end of this chapter, you should be able to answer the following questions:

- What other objects are used by this control?
- What methods are used to access information on the server?

Properties

Like the other ActiveX controls, there are a number of properties that support the HTTP client control. Many of these we have seen in the previous controls; others are brand new. They work together to provide default values for various methods and to provide information about the state of the control.

Busy

Format: `HTTPObject.Busy`

The `Busy` property returns `true` if the HTTP client control is executing a command. Most methods cannot be used until the current method is finished.

Table 23-1 *Busy* Values

Busy Value	Description
`true`	The HTTP client control is executing a command.
`false`	The HTTP client control is not executing a command.

DocInput

Format: `HTTPObject.DocInput`

The `DocInput` property returns a reference to the `DocInput` object associated with the control. It is used primarily to access the various properties of the `DocInput` object.

DocOutput

Format: `HTTPObject.DocOutput`

The `DocOutput` property returns a reference to the `DocOutput` object associated with the control. It is used primarily to access the various properties of the `DocOutput` object.

Document

Format: `HTTPObject.Document` [= string]

The `Document` property is a string that contains the file part of the URL. The URL can be derived by combining the `RemoteHost` and `Document` properties (for example, `http://HTTPObject.RemoteHost/HTTPObject.Document`).

EnableTimer

Format: `HTTPObject.EnableTimer(event)` [= boolean]

The `EnableTimer` property sets or returns a flag that controls one of several different timers.

Table 23-2 ***EnableTimer* Events**

EnableTimer Event Name	*EnableTimer* Event Value	Description
prcConnectTimeout	1	If a connection is not made within the timeout period, the `TimeOut` event is triggered.
prcReceiveTimeout	2	If no data arrives for a receive process within the timeout period, the `TimeOut` event is triggered.
prcUserTimeout	65	User defined `TimeOut` event.

Table 23-3 *Timeout* Values

Timeout Value	Description
`true`	The timer for this event is enabled.
`false`	The timer for this event is not enabled.

Errors

Format: `HTTPObject.Errors`

The `Errors` property returns an `icErrors` collection that contains information about the last error that occurred. It is used primarily to access the properties of the `icErrors` object. (For more information about the `icErrors` collection and `icError` objects, see Chapter 9.)

Method

Format: `HTTPObject.Method` [=integer]

The `Method` property determines the technique that is used to retrieve a document from the server or send a document to the server. This property should not be confused with the ActiveX methods that are used to initiate an action.

Table 23-4 *Method* Values

Method Value Name	*Method* Value	Description
`prcGet`	0	Retrieves the entire document.
`prcHead`	1	Retrieves only the document headers.
`prcPost`	2	Sends the entire document using the Post technique.
`prcPut`	3	Sends the entire document using the Put technique.

NotificationMode

Format: `HTTPObject.NotifictionMode` [= integer]

The `NotificationMode` property returns or sets an integer that indicates when notification should be provided for incoming data. This is most useful when working the `DocOutput` object.

Table 23-5 ***NotificationMode* Values**

Noticification	Mode Value Description
0	**Complete:** Notification is given when the response is complete.
1	**Continuous:** Notification is given as new data is received.

ProtocolState

Format: `Object.ProtocolState`

The `ProtocolState` property is used to determine which state the protocol is in.

Table 23-6 ***ProtocolState* Values**

ProtocolState Value Name	*ProtocolState* Value	Description
prcNone	0	**Base state:** Before a connection is established with the server.
prcAuthorization	1	**Authorization state:** After connection is established and before the user has been granted access to the server.
prcTransaction	2	**Transaction state:** After the user has been granted access to the server. The client can now interact with the server.
prcUpdate	3	**Update state:** After the `Quit` command has been entered in the transaction state, but before the connection has been disconnected.

RemoteHost

Format: `HTTPObject.RemoteHost` [= string]

The `RemoteHost` property is a string that contains the host name or IP address of the remote host. It is used with the `Connect` method to establish a connection to the remote computer.

RemotePort

Format: `HTTPObject.RemotePort` [= long]

The `RemotePort` property is a long that contains the port number that the HTTP server is listening to. Usually this value is 119.

ReplyCode

Format: `HTTPObject.ReplyCode`

The `ReplyCode` property is a long that contains the reply code of the most recent message generated by the HTTP server.

ReplyString

Format: `HTTPObject.ReplyString`

The `ReplyString` property is a string that contains the text of the message last received from the HTTP server.

State

Format: HTTPObject.State

The `State` property returns an integer and is used to determine which state the connection is in.

Table 23-7 *State* Values

State Value Name	*State* Value	Description
`prcConnecting`	1	**Connecting state:** A connection has been requested and is waiting for an acknowledgment.
`prcResolvingHost`	2	**Resolving Host state:** Waiting for a host name to be translated into its IP address. (Not entered if an IP address was supplied as the `RemoteHost` property.)

`State` Value Name	`State` Value	Description
prcHostResolved	3	**Host Resolved state:** After the host name has successfully translated into an IP address. (Not entered if an IP address was supplied as the `RemoteHost` property.)
prcConnected	4	**Connected state:** A connection has successfully been established.
prcDisconnecting	5	**Disconnecting state:** A request to disconnect has been requested.
prcDisconnected	6	**Disconnected state:** Before a connection is requested and after a connection is closed.

TimeOut

Format: `HTTPObject.TimeOut(event)` [= long]

The `TimeOut` property sets or returns a flag that controls how much time must pass before a `TimeOut` event is triggered.

Table 23-8 *TimeOut* Events

`TimeOut` Event Name	`TimeOut` Event Value	Description
prcConnectTimeout	1	If a connection is not made within the timeout period, the `TimeOut` event is triggered.
prcReceiveTimeout	2	If no data arrives for a receive process within the timeout period, the `TimeOut` event is triggered.
prcUserTimeout	65	User defined `TimeOut` event.

URL

Format: `HTTPObject.URL` [= string]

The `URL` property is a string that holds the name of the current document being transferred. The URL may be set before using the `SendDoc` or `GetDoc` methods to retrieve the

URL. If the URL is not set before using these methods, the URL must be specified as a parameter to the method.

Methods

The HTTP ActiveX client control provides only a few methods to work with a Web server. All deal with the actual transfer of documents from or to the server. In practice, you will probably only use the `RequestDoc` and `Cancel` methods because the other methods are included in them.

Cancel

Format: `HTTPObject.Cancel`

The `Cancel` method is used to cancel a pending request. After this method is finished, the `Cancel` event is triggered.

GetDoc

Format: `HTTPObject.GetDoc [url] [,[headers] [,outputfile]]`

The `GetDoc` method works with the `DocOutput` object to transfer a file from the remote HTTP server to the local machine. All three arguments are optional and if not specified, the appropriate values from the `DocOutput` object are used.

Table 23-9 *GetDoc* Method Arguments

Argument Name	Argument Type	Description
`url`	string	Name of the file on the remote system to be retrieved in URL format.
`Headers`	DocHeaders	A reference to the list of `DocHeaders`.
`outputfile`	string	Name of the output file on the local machine.

PerformRequest

Format: `HTTPObject.PerformRequest [hostname] [,[document] [,[method] [,remoteport]]]`

The `PerformRequest` method performs the same function as the `GetDoc` and `SendDoc` methods, but uses a different set of parameters. All the parameters are optional and the appropriate values from the control's properties are used if they are not specified.

Table 23-10 *PerformRequest* Method Arguments

Argument Name	Argument Type	Description
`hostname`	string	Name of the remote system where the document to be retrieved exists.
`document`	string	Name of the file on the remote system.
`method`	integer	The method used send or retrieve the document.
`remoteport`	long	The port number on the remote host.

Table 23-11 *Method* Values

Method Value Name	*Method* Value	Description
`prcGet`	0	Retrieves the entire document.
`prcHead`	1	Retrieves only the document headers.
`prcPost`	2	Sends the entire document using the Post technique.
`prcPut`	3	Sends the entire document using the Put technique.

SendDoc

Format: `HTTPObject.GetDoc [url] [,[headers] [,[inputdata] [,[inputfile] [,outputfile]]]]`

The `SendDoc` method works with the `DocInput` object to transfer data from the local system to the remote HTTP server. The data is sent to the server using the `DocInput` object, and if the server returns a document, it is returned using the `DocOutput` object. All the arguments are optional, and if they are not specified, the appropriate values from the `DocInput` and the `DocOutput` objects are used.

Table 23-12 *SendDoc* Method Arguments

Argument Name	Argument Type	Description
`url`	string	Name of the file on the remote system to be retrieved in URL format (default value: `DocInput.URL`).
`headers`	DocHeaders	A reference to the list of `DocHeaders` (default value: `DocInput.DocHeaders`).
`inputdata`	variant	A stream of input data (default value: `DocInput.SetData`).
`inputfile`	string	Name of the input file on the local machine (default value: `DocInput.FileName`).
`outputfile`	string	Name of the output file on the local machine (default value `DocOutput.FileName`).

Events

The HTTP events are called in response to various conditions that happen during the execution of a program using the HTTP ActiveX control. They provide information about what is happening inside the control, return information from the server, or request information to be sent to the server.

Busy

Format: `HTTPObject_Busy(ByVal isBusy As Boolean)`

The `Busy` event occurs when the `HTTPObject.Busy` property changes state. This event occurs when a command begins execution, or when a command finishes execution.

Table 23-13 *Busy* Event Parameters

Parameter Name	Argument Type	Description
`isBusy`	boolean	Indicates when a command is being executed.

Table 23-14 *isBusy* Values

isBusy Value	Description
`true`	A command is being executed.
`false`	A command is not being executed.

Cancel

Format: `HTTPObject_Cancel`

The `Cancel` event occurs after the `Cancel` method is invoked.

DocInput

Format: `HTTPObject_DocInput(ByVal docinput as DocInput)`

The `DocInput` event occurs when data has been transferred from this control to the remote host.

Table 23-15 *DocInput* Event Parameters

Parameter Name	Argument Type	Description
`docinput`	DocInput	Object that describes the current input data for this transfer.

DocOutput

Format: `HTTPObject_DocOutput(ByVal docoutput as DocOutput)`

The `DocOutput` event occurs when data has been transferred to this control from the remote host.

Table 23-16 *DocOutput* Event Parameters

Parameter Name	Argument Type	Description
`docoutput`	DocOutput	Object that describes the current output data for this transfer.

Error

Format: `HTTPObject_Error(errcode As Integer, description As String, scode As Long, source As String, helpfile As String, helpcontext As Long, canceldisplay As Boolean)`

The `Error` event occurs whenever the server responds with an error return code.

Table 23-17 *Error* Event Parameters

Parameter Name	Argument Type	Description
`errcode`	integer	The error code.
`description`	string	The text description of the error code.
`scode`	long	The scode of the error.
`source`	string	The name of the source of the error. This is usually the name of the control that caused the error.
`helpfile`	string	Contains the name of the help file with more information about the error.
`helpcontext`	long	Contains the help context reference for the error.
`canceldisplay`	boolean	Displays the standard error message box.

Table 23-18 *canceldisplay* Values

canceldisplay Value	Description
`true`	Display the standard error message box.
`false`	Do not display the standard error message box.

ProtocolStateChanged

Format: `HTTPObject_ProtocolStateChanged(ByVal protocolstate as integer)`

The `ProtocolStateChanged` event occurs whenever the protocol state is changed.

Table 23-19 *ProtocolStateChanged* Event Parameters

Parameter Name	Argument Type	Description
`protocolstate`	integer	The value of the protocol state.

Table 23-20 *protocolstate* Values

protocolstate Value Name	*protocolstate* Value	Description
`prcBase`	0	**Base state:** Before a connection is established with the server.
`prcTransaction`	1	**Transaction state:** After the connection is established and the server is ready to handle requests.

StateChanged

Format: `HTTPObject_StateChanged(ByVal state as integer)`

The `StateChanged` event occurs whenever the transport state is changed.

Table 23-21 *StateChanged* Event Parameters

Parameter Name	Argument Type	Description
`state`	integer	The value of the transport state.

Table 23-22 *state* Values

state Value Name	*state* Value	Description
`prcConnecting`	1	**Connecting state:** A connection has been requested and is waiting for an acknowledgment.
`prcResolvingHost`	2	**Resolving Host state:** Waiting for a host name to be translated into its IP address. (Not entered if an IP address was supplied as the `RemoteHost` property.)
`prcHostResolved`	3	**Host Resolved state:** After the host name has successfully translated into an IP address. (Not entered if an IP address was supplied as the `RemoteHost` property.)
`prcConnected`	4	**Connected state:** A connection has successfully been established.
`prcDisconnecting`	5	**Disconnecting state:** A request to disconnect has been requested.
`prcDisconnected`	6	**Disconnected state:** Before a connection is requested and after a connection is closed.

TimeOut

Format: `HTTPObject_TimeOut(ByVal event as integer, continue as boolean)`

The `TimeOut` event occurs when the specified event does not occur within the interval defined in the `TimeOut` property for that event.

Table 23-23 *TimeOut* Event Parameters

Parameter Name	Argument Type	Description
`event`	integer	Event to which the timer interval applies.
`continue`	boolean	Determines if the timer will remain active.

Table 23-24 ***event* Values**

event Name	*event Value*	Description
prcConnectTimeout	1	If a connection is not made within the timeout period, the TimeOut event is triggered.
prcReceiveTimeout	2	If no data arrives for a receive process within the timeout period, the TimeOut event is triggered.
prcUserTimeout	65	User defined TimeOut event.

Table 23-25 ***continue* Values**

continue Value	Description
true	The timer continues to run.
false	The timer is stopped.

Summary

In this chapter we discussed the HTTP client control. This control provides the methods necessary to interact with a World Wide Web server.

In the next chapter, we begin our discussion of the HTML control with some of the basic objects, and in Chapter 25 we discuss the control itself.

In case you want to check your answers to the questions in the Overview section, here are the answers:

- *What other objects are used by this control?*

  DocHeader returns a single header line.

  DocHeaders is a collection of DocHeader objects.

  DocOutput is used for information leaving this control.

  icErrors is used to hold error information.

- *What methods are used to access information on the server?*

  GetDoc is used to retrieve information from the server.

  SendDoc is used send information to the server for processing; the server responds with another document.

`PerformRequest` is used to send and receive data from the server. It is basically the same as the `GetDoc` and `SendDoc` methods, but it takes a different set of parameters and may be preferred to the `GetDoc` and `SendDoc` methods in some situations.

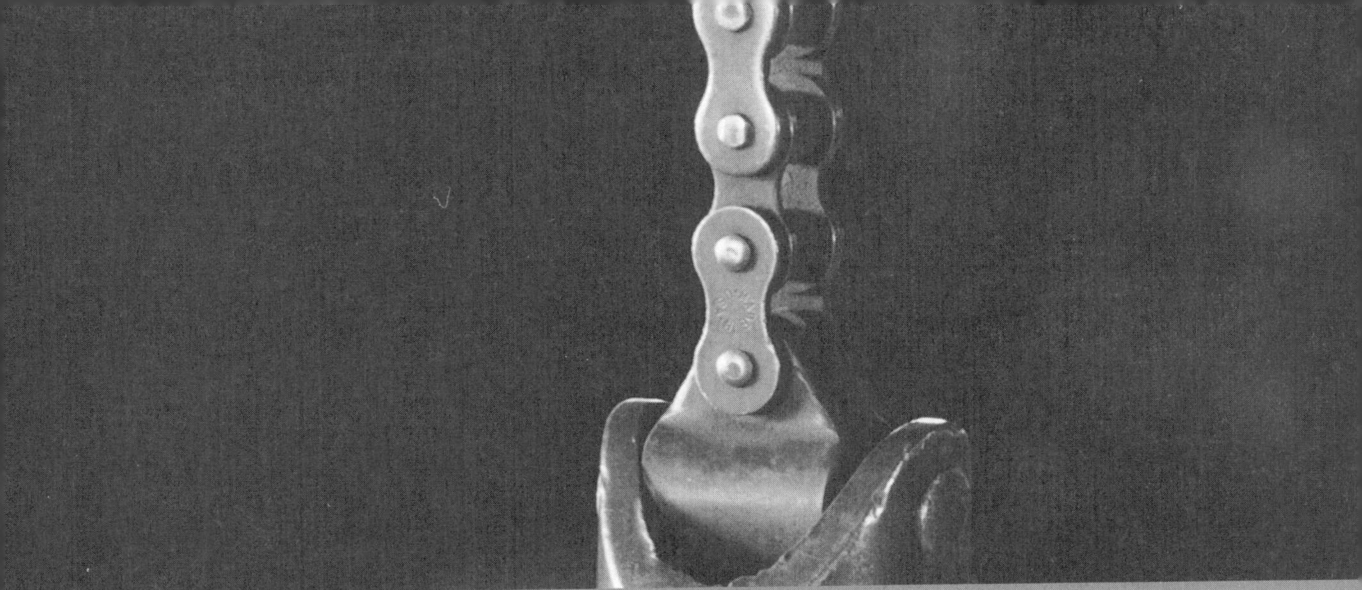

Chapter 24

The HTMLAttr and HTMLForm Objects

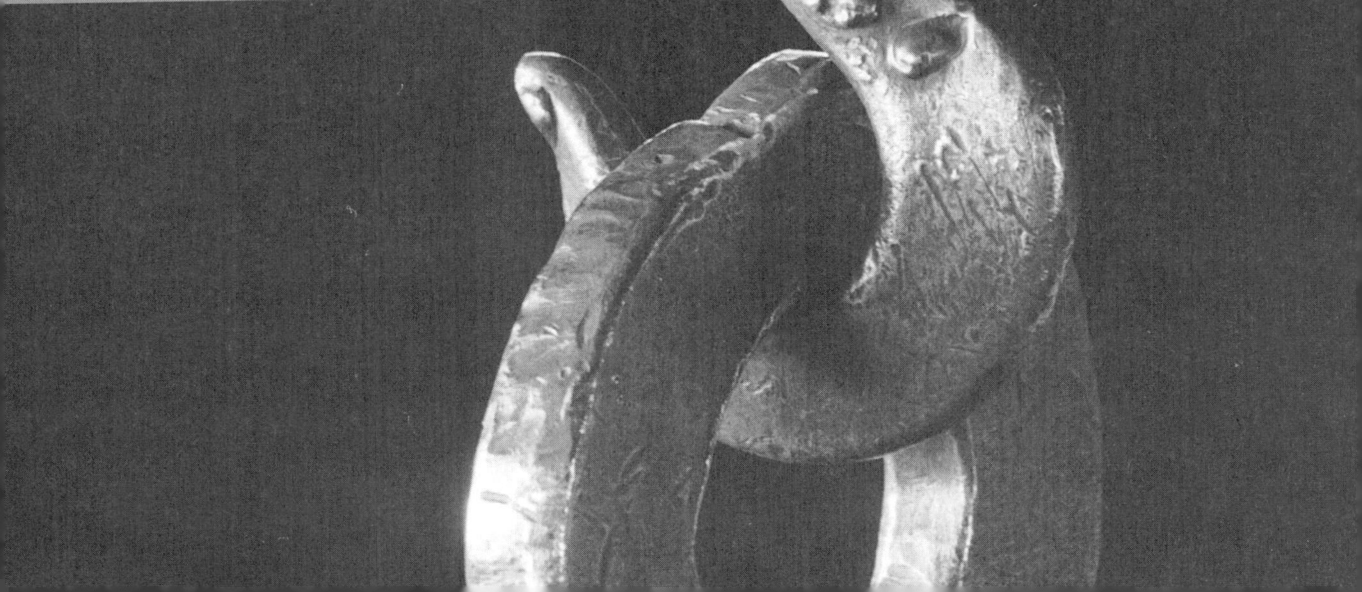

Overview

In the last chapter we discussed properties, methods, and events of the HTTP ActiveX control. In the next chapter, we talk about the HTML ActiveX control that formats the information retrieved from an HTTP server. But before we can talk about the HTML control, we need to discuss two objects and their collections that make the HTML control easier to use.

By the end of this chapter, you should be able to answer the following question:

- What is an HTML element?
- What is an HTML attribute?

Properties—HTMLAttr

The `HTMLAttr` object is used to contain information about a particular part of an HTML element. For example, in the anchor element `<a href="http://www.mysite.com/index.html">`, an attribute name would be the `href` and the attribute value would be `"http://www.mysite.com/index.html"`.

Name

Format: `HTMLAttrObject.Name`

The `Name` property returns a string value that contains the attribute name.

Value

Format: `HTMLAttrObject.Value`

The `Value` property returns the value associated with the attribute name.

Properties—HTMLAttrs

The `HTMLAttrs` object is a collection of `HTMLAttr` objects. It uses the standard collection format, so you can use the `For Each` object in collection statement to process each member of the collection.

Count

Format: `HTMLAttrsObject.Count`

The `Count` property returns the number of items in the `HTMLAttrs` collection.

Methods—HTMLAttrs

The `HTMLAttrs` object is a collection of `HTMLAttr` objects and the following method is used to retrieve a single member of the collection.

Item

Format: `HTMLAttrsObject.Item ( index )`

The `Item` method is used to retrieve an `HTMLAttr` from the collection. The value for the index must be in the range of `0` to `HTMLAttrs.Count -1`.

Table 24-1 *Item* Method Arguments

Argument Name	Argument Type	Description
`index`	long	Reference to a specific `HTLMAttr` object.

Properties—HTMLForm

The `HTMLForm` object is used to store information about the fields in an HTML document that need to be returned using the `Put` or `Post` methods.

Method

Format: `HTMLFormObject.Method` [=integer]

The `Method` property determines the technique that is used to retrieve a document from the server or send a document to the server.

Table 24-2 *Method* Values

Method Value Name	*Method* Value	Description
`prcGet`	0	Retrieves the entire document.
`prcHead`	1	Retrieves only the document headers.
`prcPost`	2	Sends the entire document using the Post technique.
`prcPut`	3	Sends the entire document using the Put technique.

URL

Format: `HTMLFormObject.URL`

The `URL` property returns a string that contains the action URL for the form.

URLEncodedBody

Format: `HTMLFormObject.URLEncodedBody`

The `URL` property returns a string that contains the `URLEncodedBody` text with values for all the form fields used for submission.

Methods—HTMLForm

The `HTMLForm` object contains only one method, the `RequestSubmit`. This method is used to send the `HTMLForm` to an HTTP server for processing. Because you are passing information back to the server for processing, the `HTMLForm.URLEncodedBody` should not be empty.

RequestSubmit

Format: `HTMLFormObject.RequestSubmit`

The `RequestSubmit` method is used to send the form to the server. After the `RequestSubmit` method is invoked, the `DoRequestSubmit` is triggered to determine the target document to be used for submission.

HTMLForms—Properties

The property associated with the `HTMLForms` object is the standard property for any collection.

Count

Format: `HTMLFormsObject.Count`

The `Count` property returns the number of items in the `HTMLForms` collection.

HTMLForms—Methods

The method associated with the `HTMLForms` object is the standard method for any collection. It also permits the use of the Visual Basic `For Each` object construct to iterate through all the members of the collection.

Item

Format: `HTMLFormsObject.Item ( index )`

The `Item` method is used to retrieve an `HTMLForm` from the collection. The value for the index must be in the range of `0` to `HTMLForms.Count -1`.

Table 24-3 *Item* Method Arguments

Argument Name	Argument Type	Description
index	long	Reference to a specific HTLMForm object.

Example—HTMLAttrs and HTMLAttr

If you have gotten this far in the chapter, you are probably as confused as I was when I first encountered these objects. Sometimes a simple example helps to clarify a confusing situation. The block of code below uses the HTMLAttrs and HTMLAttr objects to extract the URL associated with an anchor tag <a> and the text between the anchor tag and an end anchor tag </a>. To keep things simple, I wrote the information to the debug window. In a real program, this information may be saved in memory for later use.

The best way to extract this information is to use the HTML.DoNewElement event. In order to enable this event, you must first set the HTML.ElemNotification property to true. The code in the event is called each time the HTML control detects a new HTML element.

Each time this event is called, the HTML control provides a number of pieces of information. We talk about the parameters in more detail in the next chapter, but I'll briefly go through them here. The ElemType returns the type of tag in the document. The EndTag is set to true when the end tag is found. The Attrs is a collection of attributes from the tag. Text contains text that is not part of the tag. (Either the Text parameter contains a value or the ElemType contains a value, but both can never contain a value at the same time.) The EnableDefault is used to determine whether or not the control should process the information passed to this routine (True) or not process it (False).

The code shown in Listing 24-1 looks for an ElemType of a (for anchor). If it finds one, it scans through the HTMLAttrs collection and prints out the all the tag values associated with the element. If we want only the URL reference, we look for an at.Name of href. Also, because we found an anchor, we also set the global variable FoundA to true.

Next we check for straight text, also checking to see if the length of ElemType is zero. If it is and we have previously found an anchor, we display the text.

Finally, if we look for the EndTag marker and if we have previously found an anchor, we display a marker indicating that we have found everything between the anchor and end anchor tags.

Listing 24-1 *HTMLAttr* Sample Code

```
Private Sub HTML1_DoNewElement(ByVal ElemType As String, ByVal EndTag As Boolean, _
        ByVal Attrs As HTMLAttrs, ByVal Text As String, EnableDefault As Boolean)

Dim at As HTMLAttr

If ElemType = "a" Then
   For Each at In Attrs
      Debug.Print at.Value
   Next
   FoundA = True
End If

If Len(ElemType) = 0 And FoundA Then
   Debug.Print Text; " ";
End If

If EndTag And FoundA Then
   Debug.Print
   Debug.Print "=========="
   FoundA = False
End If

End Sub
```

Example—HTMLForms and HTMLForm

While parsing the document, the HTML control saves the information associated with the forms processing into the property `HTMLObject.Forms`. The code to extract the information from the object is shown in Listing 24-2. I use the `For Each` construct to extract the information from the collection.

Listing 24-2 *HTMLForm* Sample Code

```
Private Sub PrintFormsInfo()

Dim f As HTMLForm

For Each f In HTML1.Forms
   debug.print f.Method
   debug.print f.URL
   debug.print f.URLEncodedBody
   debug.print "===================================="
Next

End Sub
```

Summary

In this chapter we discussed the support objects for the HTML ActiveX control. These objects include two objects, `HTMLAttr` and `HTMLForm`, and their collections, `HTMLAttrs` and `HTMLForms`. The `HTMLAttr` object is used to hold information about a single element of the HTML document. The `HTMLForm` object is used to hold information about the fields on the screen that the user fills out and submits to the server.

In case you want to check your answer to the question in the Overview section, here is the answer:

- *What is an HTML element?*

  An HTML element is a part of an HTML document that is enclosed in < >. For example, `<a href="HTTP://www.mysite.com/index.html">`.

- *What is an HTML attribute?*

  An HTML attribute is a part of an HTML element that consists of a name and a value. Using the example from above, the attribute name would be `href` and the value would be `"HTTP://www.mysite.com/index.html"`.

Chapter 25

The HTML Client Control

Overview

In Chapter 23 we discussed properties, methods, and events of the HTML ActiveX control. However, a Web browser needs to do more than just transfer documents. It must also be able to display the documents it receives. Web documents are almost always formatted using the *HyperText Markup Language* (*HTML*). HTML is a rich language in which complex documents can be written. One aspect that is important to note is that the HTML control automatically invokes the HTTP control to access documents. This simplifies considerably the process of building a Web browser. (In fact, in the next chapter we build a functional Web browser in less than five minutes!)

By the end of this chapter, you should be able to answer the following question:

- What other objects are used by this control?

Properties

Like the other ActiveX objects, there are a number of properties that define how the object works. Many of these properties are used to supply default values for displaying the HTML document. Others provide useful information about the status of the HTML document's parsing and how the document should be laid out on the form.

BackColor

Format: `HTMLObject.BackColor [= long]`

The `BackColor` property sets or returns a value that contains the default color value to be used for the document background. This value can be overriden by the `<Body BGColor>` construct in the HTML document.

BackImage

Format: `HTMLObject.BackImage [= string]`

The `BackImage` property sets or returns the name of the file that is displayed as the background image of the HTML document (the image is tiled to fill the screen). This property can be overriden when the document includes the `<Body Background=>` construct.

BaseURL

Format: `HTMLObject.BaseURL`

The `BaseURL` property returns a string with the base URL reference from the current document. This information is taken from the `<Base>` construct. If no `<Base>` construct is included in the document, the value from `URL` is returned.

DeferRetrieval

Format: `HTMLObject.DeferRetrieval [= boolean]`

The `DeferRetrieval` property sets or returns a boolean value that is used to turn the inline retrieval of embedded documents on or off.

DocBackColor

Format: `HTMLObject.DocBackColor`

The `DocBackColor` property returns a long with the current value of the document's background color. This value is set using the `<Body BGColor>` construct in the HTML document. If this construct is not included, this value defaults to the `HTMLObject.BackColor` property.

DocForeColor

Format: `HTMLObject.DocForeColor`

The `DocForeColor` property returns a long with the current value of the document's foreground color. This value is set using the `<Body Text>` construct in the HTML document. If this construct is not included, this value defaults to the `HTMLObject.ForeColor` property.

DocInput

Format: `HTMLObject.DocInput`

The `DocInput` property returns a reference to the `DocInput` object associated with the control. It is used primarily to access the various properties of the `DocInput` object.

DocLinkColor

Format: `HTMLObject.DocLinkColor`

The `DocLinkColor` property returns a long with the current value of the document's link color. This value is set using the `<Body Link>` construct in the HTML document. If this construct is not included, this value defaults to the `HTMLObject.LinkColor` property.

DocOutput

Format: `HTMLObject.DocOutput`

The `DocOutput` property returns a reference to the `DocOutput` object associated with the control. It is used primarily to access the various properties of the `DocOutput` object.

DocVisitedColor

Format: `HTMLObject.DocVisitedColor`

The `DocVisitedColor` property returns a long with the current value of the document's link color. This value is set using the `<Body VLink>` construct in the HTML document. If this construct is not included, this value defaults to the `HTMLObject.VisitedColor` property.

ElemNotification

Format: `HTMLObject.ElemNotification [= boolean]`

The `ElemNotification` property sets or returns a boolean value that determines if the `DoNewElement` event is to be triggered while parsing an HTML document.

FixedFont

Format: `HTMLObject.FixedFont [=string]`

The `FixedFont` property sets or returns the name of the font that is used to display fixed width text.

ForeColor

Format: `HTMLObject.ForeColor [= long]`

The `ForeColor` property sets or returns a value that contains the default color value to be used for the document text. This value can be overriden by the `<Body Text>` construct in the HTML document.

Forms

Format: `HTMLObject.Forms`

The `Forms` property returns a reference to the `Forms` object associated with the control. It is used primarily to access the various properties of the `HTMLForms` object.

HeadingFont

Format: `HTMLObject.Heading[level]Font [= string]`

`HeadingFont` is a set of properties that sets or returns the font to be used for the various heading levels available in an HTML document. The level ranges from 1 to 6 and is explicitly included as part of the property (for example, `HTMLObject.Heading1Font` or `HTMLObject.Heading6Font`). The levels correspond to the `<H1>` to `<H6>` HTML constructs.

LayoutDone

Format: `HTMLObject.LayoutDone`

The `LayoutDone` property returns a boolean value that indicates when the document layout phase is complete.

LinkColor

Format: `HTMLObject.LinkColor [= long]`

The `LinkColor` property sets or returns a value that contains the default color value to be used for the document links. This value can be overriden by the `<Body Link>` construct in the HTML document.

Method

Format: `HTTPObject.Method [=integer]`

The `Method` property determines technique that is used to retrieve a document from the server or send the document to the server.

Table 25-1 ***Method*** **Values**

Method Value Name	*Method* Value	Description
`prcGet`	0	Retrieves the entire document.
`prcHead`	1	Retrieves only the document headers.
`prcPost`	2	Sends the entire document using the Post technique.
`prcPut`	3	Sends the entire document using the Put technique.

ParseDone

Format: `HTMLObject.ParseDone`

The `ParseDone` property returns a boolean value that indicates when the HTML parsing phase is complete.

Redraw

Format: `HTMLObject.Redraw [= boolean]`

The `Redraw` property sets or returns a value that indicates whether or not the form should be automatically redrawn as changes are made to the screen. It is a good idea to set `Redraw` to `false` while making many changes, and reset it to `true` when the changes are complete to avoid screen flicker.

RequestURL

Format: `HTMLObject.RequestURL`

The `RequestURL` property returns the name of the new document to be retrieved. This value is set by using the `RequestDoc` method.

RetainSource

Format: `HTMLObject.RetainSource [= boolean]`

The `RetainSource` property sets or returns a value that indicates whether the source code to the HTML document should be retained. You should set this value to `true` if your application needs to keep the source code the HTML document around (because you either want to parse it for information or allow the user to view it). If you do not need the source for the document, you should set the value to `false` to help conserve memory.

RetrieveBytesDone

Format: `HTMLObject.RetrieveBytesDone`

The RetrieveBytesDone property returns a long value with the total number of bytes retrieved during the current transfer. If no transfer is in progress, this property is set to zero.

RetrieveBytesTotal

Format: `HTMLObject.RetrieveBytesTotal`

The RetrieveBytesDone property returns a long value with the total number of bytes in the document being transferred. If no transfer is in progress, this property is set to zero. When used with the RetrieveBytesDone property, you can display a percent completed value or a progress bar to the user. This may be helpful to the user during long document transfers.

SourceText

Format: `HTMLObject.SourceText`

The SourceText property returns a string value with the contents of the document's HTML source code. Note that the RetainSource property must be set to true in order to retain the source code.

TimeOut

Format: `HTMLObject.TimeOut [= long]`

The TimeOut property sets or returns the number of seconds that must pass without receiving a document before the Timeout event occurs. Note that while the TimeOut property applies to all documents, the Timeout event only occurs for the main document.

TotalHeight

Format: `HTMLObject.TotalHeight`

The `TotalHeight` property returns the total height of the formatted document in pixels. While this property returns values during the parsing and layout phases, the final value is only available after the `EndRetrieval` event occurs.

TotalWidth

Format: `HTMLObject.TotalWidth`

The `TotalWidth` property returns the total width of the formatted document in pixels. While this property returns values during the parsing and layout phases, the final value is only available after the `EndRetrieval` event occurs.

UnderlineLinks

Format: `HTMLObject.UnderlineLinks [= boolean]`

The `UnderlineLinks` property sets or returns a value that indicates whether links should be underlined in the displayed document.

URL

Format: `HTMLObject.URL [= string]`

The `URL` property is a string that holds the name of the current document being transferred. The `URL` may be set before using the `SendDoc` or `GetDoc` methods.

URLEncodedBody

Format: `HTMLObject.URLEncodedBody`

The `URL` property returns a string that holds the URL encoded body text before submission to the HTTP control.

UseDocColors

Format: `HTMLObject.UseDocColors [= boolean]`

The `UseDocColors` property sets or returns a value that indicates whether the colors and background image from the retrieved document should override the default values set in the control. If this property is set to `true` and the document does not specify values, the defaults set in the control are used. If this value is set to `false`, the default values are always used. Setting this value to `false` may be useful to prevent downloading large background images, which will speed up the total download time.

ViewSource

Format: `HTMLObject.ViewSource [= boolean]`

The `ViewSource` property sets or returns a value that indicates whether the formatted document should be displayed or just the document source code. If this value is set to `true`, the document source code is displayed. Otherwise, the formatted document is displayed.

VisitedColor

Format: `HTMLObject.VisitedColor [= long]`

The `VisitedColor` property sets or returns a value that contains the default color value to be used for links that have already been visited.

Methods

The HTML ActiveX client control provides several methods that assist with processing an HTML document. These methods take advantage of the HTML control's ability to use the HTTP ActiveX control without the programmer having to explicitly define it.

Cancel

Format: `HTMLObject.Cancel`

The `Cancel` method is used to cancel a pending request. After this method is finished, the `Cancel` event is triggered.

RequestAllEmbedded

Format: `HTMLObject.RequestAllEmbedded`

The `RequestAllEmbedded` method is used retrieve all embedded documents using the `DoRequestEmbedded` event. `DeferRetrieval` must be set to `false` for this method to work.

RequestDoc

Format: `HTMLObject.RequestDoc url`

The `RequestDoc` method retrieves the specified URL as a new main document.

Table 25-2 *RequestDoc* Method Arguments

Argument Name	Argument Type	Description
`url`	string	URL reference for the document to be retrieved.

Events

The HTML events are called in response to various conditions that happen during the execution of a program using the HTML ActiveX control. Some are useful for displaying a progress bar or percent complete status. Others are useful for extracting information from the HTML document.

BeginRetrieval

Format: `HTMLObject_BeginRetrieval`

The `BeginRetrieval` event occurs when the document transfer begins. The `URL` property is copied from the `RequestURL` property immediately before this event. Because this event occurs at the start of the document retrieval process, it is a good time to initialize a progress bar or set the percent completed value to zero.

DocInput

Format: `HTMLObject_DocInput(ByVal docinput as DocInput)`

The `DocInput` event occurs when data has been transferred from this control to the remote host.

Table 25-3 *DocInput* Event Parameters

Parameter Name	Argument Type	Description
`docinput`	DocInput	Object that describes the current input data for this transfer.

DocOutput

Format: `HTMLObject_DocOutput(ByVal docoutput as DocOutput)`

The `DocOutput` event occurs when data has been transferred to this control from the remote host.

Table 25-4 *DocOutput* Event Parameters

Parameter Name	Argument Type	Description
`docoutput`	DocOutput	Object that describes the current output data for this transfer.

DoNewElement

Format: `HTMLObject_DoNewElement(ElemType As String, EndTag As Boolean, Attrs As HTMLAttrs, Text As String, EnableDefault As Boolean)`

The `DoNewElement` event occurs whenever a new tag is found while parsing the HTML document. Some common tags include `a` (for anchor), `font`, and `img` (for image).

Table 25-5 *DoNewElement* Event Parameters

Parameter Name	Argument Type	Description
`ElemType`	string	Element type for tags or an empty string if the type is character data.
`EndTag`	boolean	Indicates end tag has been found.
`Attrs`	HTMLAttrs	Collection of tag attributes.
`Text`	string	Character data if `ElemType` is an empty string, an empty string otherwise.
`EnableDefault`	boolean	Used to overide default processing.

Table 25-6 *EndTag* Values

EndTag Value	Description
`true`	End tag has been encountered for this element.
`false`	End tag has not yet been encountered for this element.

Table 25-7 *EnableDefault* Values

EnableDefault Value	Description
`true`	Use default processing.
`false`	Override default processing, do not store data for this element, continue parsing.

DoRequestDoc

Format: `HTMLObject_DoRequestDoc(URL As String, Element As HTMLElement, DocInput as DocInput, EnableDefault As Boolean)`

The `DoRequestDoc` event occurs in response to a `RequestDoc` method. For HTTP and FILE URLs, the `DoRequestDoc` event creates a `DocInput` object. For all other objects, the `DocInput` object is set during event handling. If the `EnableDefault` processing is set to true, the `URL` parameter value is copied to the `RequestURL` property. The `URL` property is set during later processing.

Table 25-8 *DoRequestDoc* Event Parameters

Parameter Name	Argument Type	Description
`URL`	string	Reference to the requested document.
`Element`	HTMLElement	Identifies the anchor element of the link (unsupported in beta 2).
`DocInput`	DocInput	Reference to the `DocInput` object used to process the request.
`EnableDefault`	boolean	Used to override default processing.

Table 25-9 *EnableDefault* Values

EnableDefault Value	Description
`true`	Use default processing.
`false`	Cancel default processing.

DoRequestEmbedded

Format: `HTMLObject_DoRequestEmbedded(ByVal URL As String, ByVal Element As HTMLElement, ByVal DocInput as DocInput, EnableDefault As Boolean)`

The `DoRequestEmbedded` event occurs when an embedded URL (like an image) in the master document is processed.

Table 25-10 *DoRequestEmbedded* Event Parameters

Parameter Name	Argument Type	Description
`URL`	string	Reference to the requested document.
`Element`	HTMLElement	Identifies the anchor element of the link (unsupported in beta 2).
`DocInput`	DocInput	Reference to the `DocInput` object used to process the request.
`EnableDefault`	boolean	Used to override default processing.

Table 25-11 *EnableDefault* Values

EnableDefault Value	Description
`true`	Use default processing.
`false`	Cancel default processing.

DoRequestSubmit

Format: `HTMLObject_DoRequestSubmit(ByVal URL As String, ByVal Form As HTMLForm, ByVal DocOutput as DocOutput, EnableDefault As Boolean)`

The `DoRequestSubmit` event occurs when a document is submitted to the server. By default, it submits the document to the server using HTTP and receives the response from the server and displays it as the next main document.

Table 25-12 *DoRequestSubmit* Event Parameters

Parameter Name	Argument Type	Description
`URL`	string	Reference to the requested document.
`Form`	HTMLForm	Identifies the form being submitted.
`DocOutput`	DocOutput	Reference to the `DocInput` object used to process the request.
`EnableDefault`	boolean	Used to overide default processing.

Table 25-13 *EnableDefault* Values

EnableDefault Value	Description
`true`	Use default processing.
`false`	Cancel default processing.

EndRetrieval

Format: `HTMLObject_EndRetrieval`

The `EndRetrieval` event occurs when the document transfer, including all embedded documents, ends. If you started a progress bar in the `BeginRetrieval` event, this is the appropriate place to stop it.

LayoutComplete

Format: `HTMLObject_LayoutComplete`

The `LayoutComplete` event occurs when the document layout is finished. Note that all the embedded documents may not have been retrieved, but their space has been allocated on the form.

ParseComplete

Format: `HTMLObject_ParseComplete`

The `ParseComplete` event occurs when the document parsing has been completed. Note that the layout may not be complete, and all of the embedded documents may not have been retrieved.

TimeOut

Format: `HTMLObject_TimeOut(ByVal event as integer, continue as boolean)`

The `TimeOut` event occurs when the specified event does not occur within the interval defined in the `TimeOut` property for that event.

Table 25-14 *TimeOut* Event Parameters

Parameter Name	Argument Type	Description
event	integer	Event to which the timer interval applies.
continue	boolean	Determines if the timer will remain active.

Table 25-15 *event* values

event Name	*event* Value	Description
prcConnectTimeout	1	If a connection is not made within the timeout period, the `TimeOut` event is triggered.
prcReceiveTimeout	2	If no data arrives for a receive process within the timeout period, the `TimeOut` event is triggered.
prcUserTimeout	65	User defined `TimeOut` event.

Table 25-16 *continue* Values

continue Value	Description
true	The timer continues to run.
false	The timer is stopped.

UpdateRetrieval

Format: `HTMLObject_UpdateRetrieval`

The `UpdateRetrieval` event occurs periodically between the `BeginRetrieval` and `EndRetrieval` events. This event is most useful for updating a progress bar or other status display.

Summary

In this chapter we discussed the HTML client control. This control provides methods to interact with a World Wide Web server. It can automatically use the HTTP control to access a Web server without specifically including it in your program. In fact in the next chapter, we build the Five-Minute Web Browser using the HTML control.

In case you want to check your answers to the questions in the Overview section, here are the answers:

- *What other objects are used by this control?*

  `HTMLAttr`

  `HTMLAttrs`

  `HTMLForm`

  `HTMLForms`

Chapter 26

WebRunner

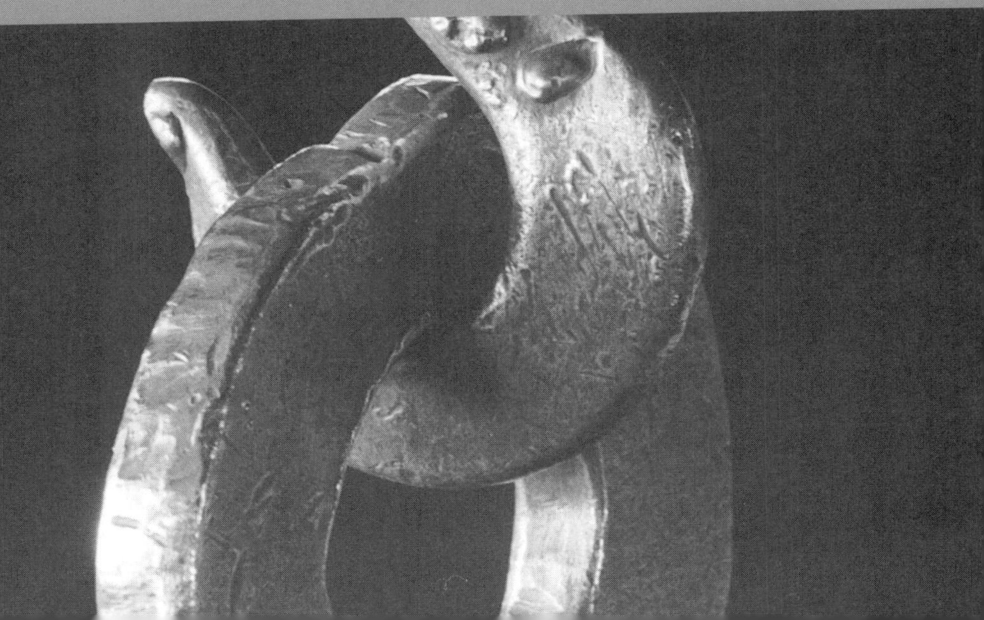

Overview

In this chapter we build two programs that can surf the Internet. One of these programs is a working Web browser that you can build in less than five minutes. The other program is the last member of the Runner family of programs. WebRunner is a fully functional Web browser that is roughly equivalent of some of the earlier versions of Netscape Navigator and Mosaic.

By the end of this chapter, you should be able to answer the following question:

- What is the significance of the `Me` object?

The Five-Minute Web Browser

All the programs we have discussed so far took hours to build and debug. But one of the most enjoyable aspects of programming in Visual Basic is the capability to create functional programs quickly. This is because Visual Basic handles most of the grungy details of Windows programming. While the way it handles some of these details may leave a lot to be desired, the point is that it is good enough to allow you to prototype new ideas.

When I first saw the ActiveX controls, the first thing I did was write a simple Web browser much like the one we are going to write here (well actually, the first thing I did was to install the controls, but you know what I mean). I was impressed with the time and effort that the Microsoft developers took with this product. The fact that it took less than five minutes to make it work was even more impressive. So take this book over to your Windows machine, start Visual Basic, and get ready to build your first Web browser. (If you have not installed the ActiveX Internet Control Pack, see Chapter 5 for installation instructions.)

When Visual Basic first starts, it loads a default form called Form1 (see figure 26-1). We are going to take this form and build the Five-Minute Web Browser. The first thing we need to do is add the HTML ActiveX control Toolbox. We do this by choosing the Tools | Custom Controls option from the menu. This displays the window shown in figure 26-2.

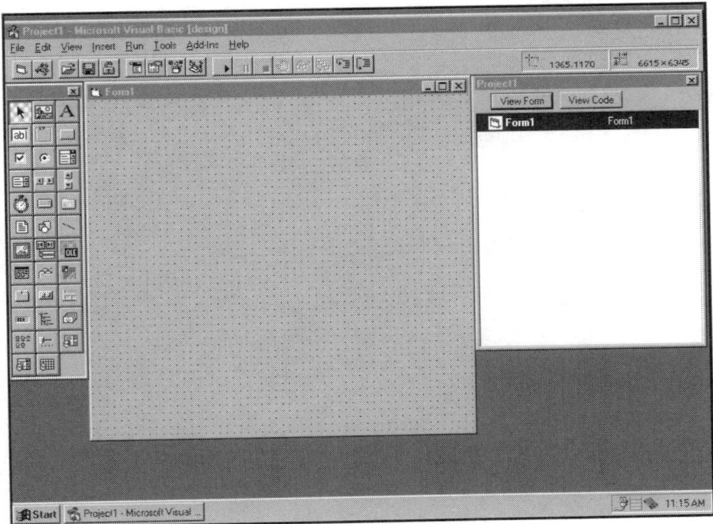

FIGURE 26-1

Starting Visual Basic.

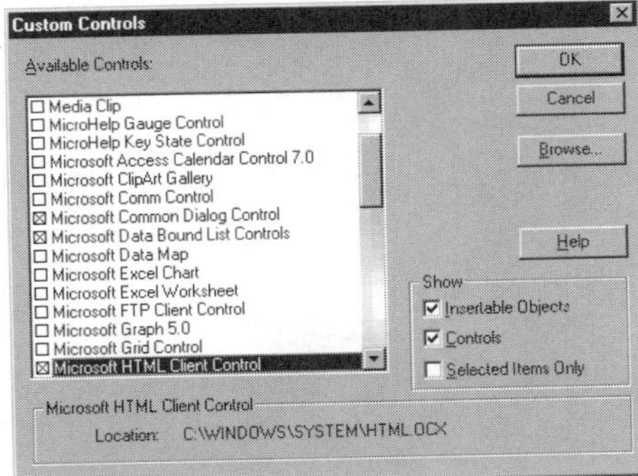

FIGURE 26-2

Adding the HTML control to the Toolbox.

Next, put an X in the Microsoft HTML Client Control check box. When you click OK, the HTML control is added to the toolbox. Note that the other controls will be listed here, and this method should be used to add any of the other controls to the toolbox. The next step is to add the Microsoft Internet Support Objects to the List of Available References for Visual Basic. While they may not always be needed when working with the ActiveX controls, it is probably a good idea to make them available anytime you add a control to the toolbox. To do this, you should go the Visual Basic main menu again and select Tools | References (see figure 26-3).

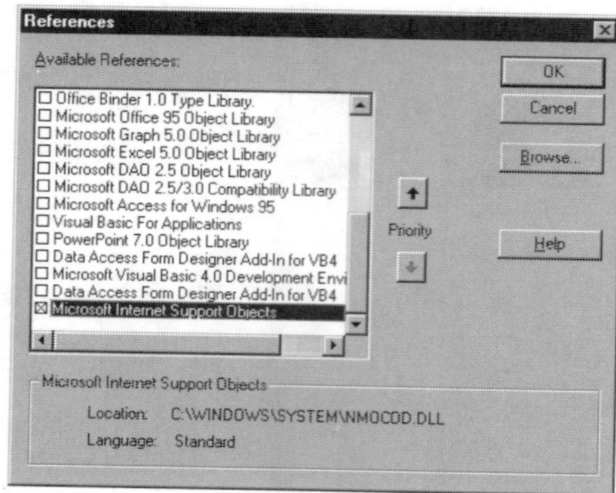

FIGURE 26-3

Adding the Internet Support Objects to the Toolbox.

Put an X in the Microsoft Internet Support Object check box and click OK. Now we are ready to begin putting controls onto the form. In figure 26-4, I began this program by putting a text box on the form. This text box is used to hold the URL that the user wants to see.

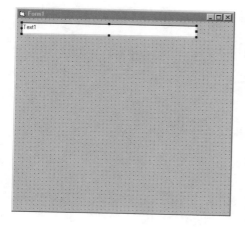

FIGURE 26-4

Adding a text box to hold the URL on the form.

Next, select the HTML control from the toolbox (lower-right corner) and draw a large area on the form (see figure 26-5). This is used to display the Web page when we receive it from the server.

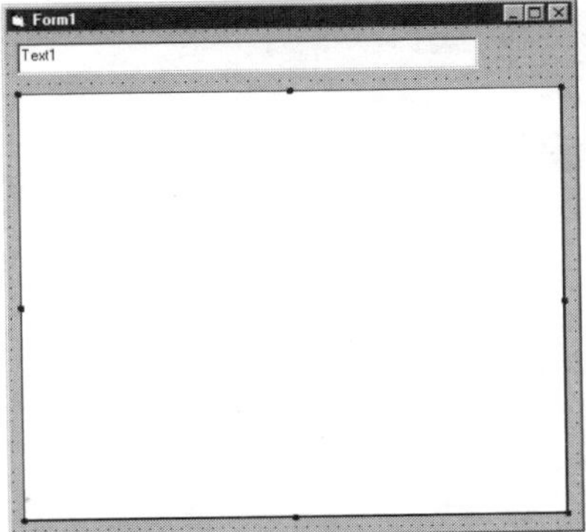

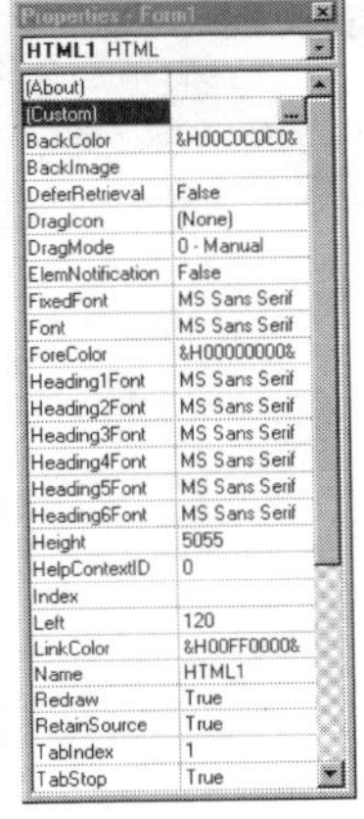

FIGURE 26-5

Putting the HTML display box on the form.

In figure 26-6 you can see that I added a CommandButton on the form. This button is used to instruct the HTML control to retrieve the Web page specified by the URL in the text box. Because I wanted something a little fancier than Command1 displayed on the button, I took a moment to change the caption for the button to *Load*.

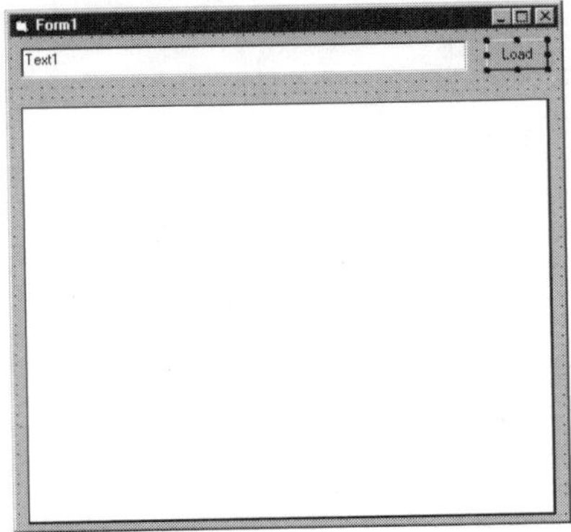

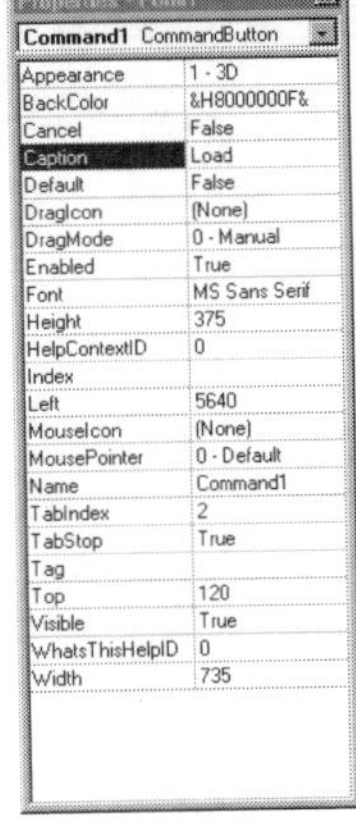

FIGURE 26-6

Putting a CommandButton on the form.

By double-clicking the CommandButton, I display a code window as shown in figure 26-7. Into this window, I add the only line of code that is needed in this program. This line invokes the HTML `RequestDoc` method with the contents of the text box.

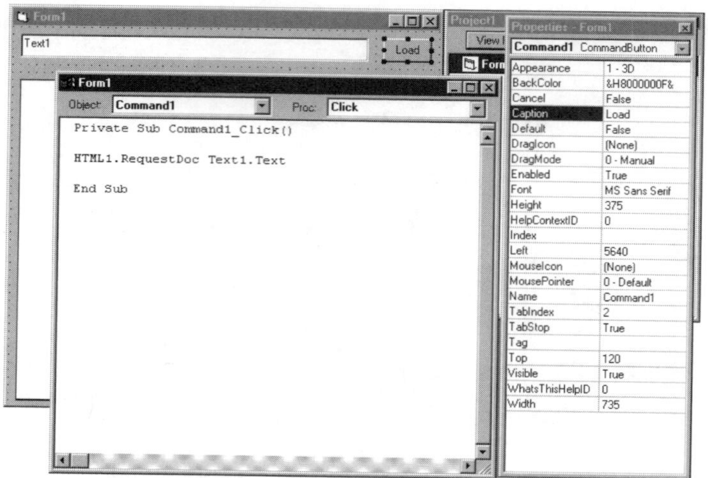

FIGURE 26-7

Entering code for the CommandButton.

At this point, I have written all the code and put in all of the controls that are required to run this program, so the next step is to test it. Test the program by pressing the F5 key and entering a URL into the text box (see figure 26-8).

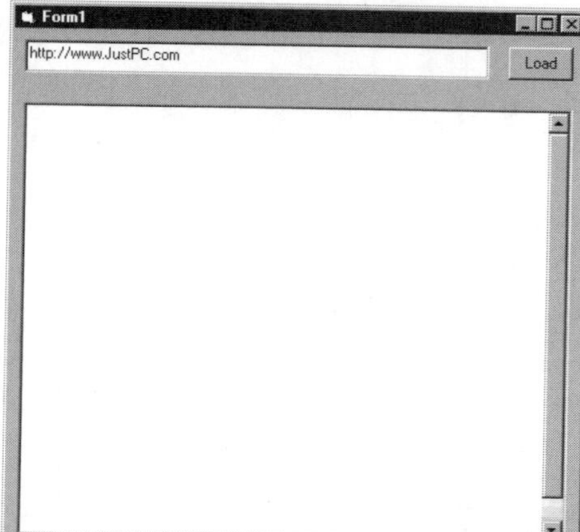

FIGURE 26-8

Starting the program.

After entering the URL, press the command button to execute the `RequestDoc` method. The results are displayed in figure 26-9.

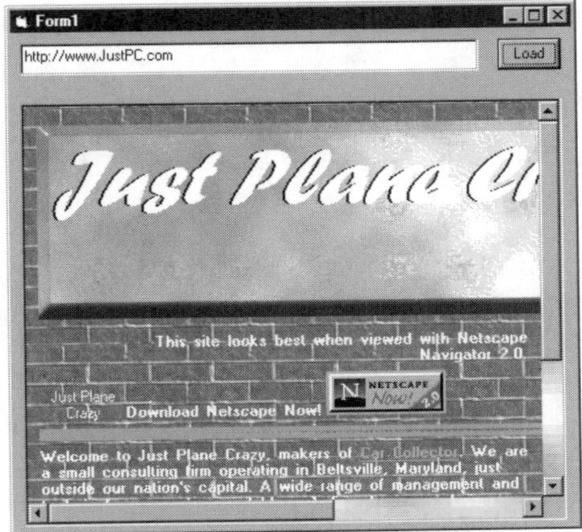

FIGURE 26-9

The results.

As you can see, it works. If you were to compile the program and add it to your Start menu, you could amaze your friends by showing them how you wrote your own Web browser. Just remember to choose a URL that you know will work, and you should be fine.

Obviously this is not a full-featured Web browser, but it does serve to demonstrate the power of Visual Basic and the ActiveX Internet controls. This program can serve as a basis for starting your own browser. It is also possible to take this program and add some code to keep a history of URLs that you have visited, and add some code to help recover from bad URLs and Web pages that use features that are not supported in the Internet Control Pack. This is how WebRunner started, and in the rest of the chapter, we explore the HTTP and HTML ActiveX controls a little more.

How to Use WebRunner

After working with the Five-Minute Web Browser, you will quickly notice that several features are missing. There is no way to move to the previous form or the next form. Also, there is no way to refresh the current form, nor is there a history of previous URLs that have been visited. WebRunner addresses these problems and a few others I have not mentioned.

Basically, WebRunner consists of three forms: the WebRunner Control form, the Document Display form, and the View Information form. The WebRunner form provides the controls and buttons the user needs to select a document for display. The document is displayed on the Document Display form. The reason I display the document separately from the controls is that you can display a larger document without having the controls on the form. With the Windows taskbar at the bottom of the screen, it is easy to shift from the Document form to the WebRunner form, and I feel that this more than compensates for the convenience of having the controls at the top.

The final form I call the View Information form. This is mostly a utility form that is used to display things like the HTML source code or a list of URLs from within the document.

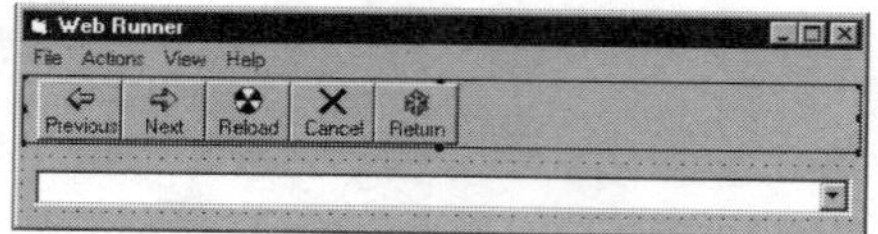

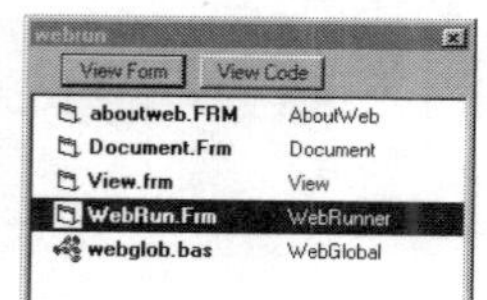

FIGURE 26-10

The WebRunner form.

The WebRunner form contains five buttons: a Previous button to display the last previous document in the history list; a Next document to display the next document in the history list; a Reload button to retrieve a fresh copy of the current document; a Cancel button to cancel the current data transmission; and a Return button that exits the program. It also contains a ComboBox that is used to keep the history of URLs that the user visits.

The menu bar contains all the same functions that are provided by the buttons plus four additional functions. The Help | About command displays the AboutWeb form. The View menu provides three options that can be used to find out internal information about the loaded HTML document in the View form. The View | Source is used to display the HTML source code. The View | URLs displays a list of URL references that are included inside the document. The View | Forms displays information about the methods and URL information associated with the fill-in-the-box fields that are displayed with the document.

The Document form is basically one large HTML document display form. This form can be resized or even made full-screen in order to better see the displayed document.

Much like the Document form is just one large form for displaying HTML documents, the View form is just one large form for displaying text information. When you are finished with the form, simply click the form close button in the upper-right corner. The program will redisplay the form whenever necessary.

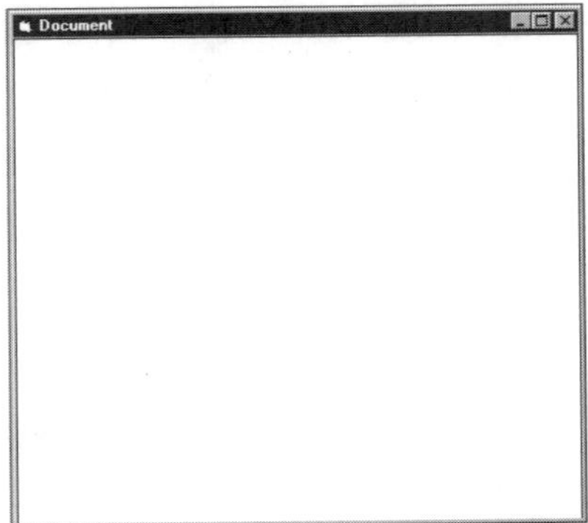

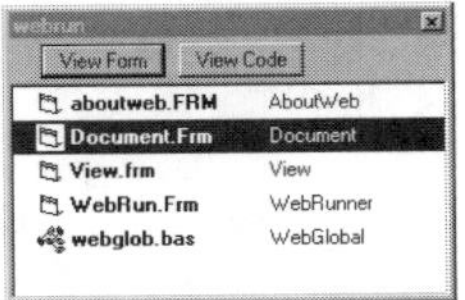

FIGURE 26-11

The Document form.

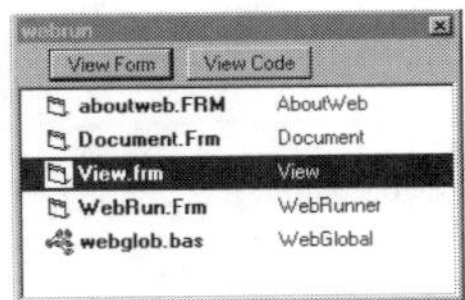

FIGURE 26-12

The View form.

The Program Structure

This program contains one main form (WebRunner) and two display forms (Document and View). It also contains one module (WebGlobal). As I have done with all the other programs, the module contains a `Main` subroutine that is used to launch the program plus whatever global variables are needed. In Listing 26-1, you can see that there are only four global variables and one global constant.

One of the global variables, `WebAddit`, is used to determine whether or not to add a new URL to the history list. Adding items to the history list is a little more complicated than it may first appear because items may be entered from the WebRunner form by typing a new entry, or by selecting one from the drop-down window. Pressing the previous and next keys also changes the current URL. Finally, the user can select a hypertext link from the document itself. So while there are multiple places one can change the URL, as you will see a little later, there is only one place where they can be added to the history list.

The remaining global variables are used to hold information about URL entries that were found while the HTML control was parsing the document. Unlike the `Forms` property, where all the form's information is stored, there is no place to store the equivalent URL information. The constant `WebURLMax` is used to determine the size of the string arrays used to hold the URL information, as well as to provide a variable that the code can use to prevent subscripting errors. `WebURLs` holds the URL references from within the anchor clauses, and the `WebURLText` array holds the text that falls between the anchor tag and the end anchor tag. `WebURLCount` holds the number of items that are stored in the arrays.

Listing 26-1 WebRunner Global Variables

```
' Form/Module:   WebGlobal
' Author:        Wayne S. Freeze
' Version        1.0
' Date Written:  7 August 1996
' Date Revised:  7 August 1996
' Description:
'   This module initialized the global variables
'   and starts the WebRunner form.

Option Explicit

' Define the WebRunner Global Variables
' ==============================================

' True when the Document needs to add the
' web URL to the combo box
Global WebAddit As Boolean

' Holds URL references extracted from the
' current form.
Global Const WebURLMax = 256
```

```
Global WebURLs(WebURLMax) As String
Global WebURLText(WebURLMax) As String
Global WebURLCount As Integer
```

Retrieving a Web Document

Retrieving a Web page is a relatively easy task as we saw in the Five-Minute Web Browser. For WebRunner, I replaced the text box with a combo box that will eventually hold the URL history. For now, however, we are going to treat it as a simple text box. We allow the user to key anything they choose into the ComboBox, and when we receive a carriage return (which has an ASCII value of 13), we attempt to retrieve the document.

Requesting the Document

First we set the `WebAddit` flag to `true`, which says this is a new URL that needs to be added to the history list. Then we check to see that we are already in the process of receiving a new document by checking the caption of the Document form for the word "Loading". (The caption always begins with "Loading" whenever we are loading a new Web page. Just hang on, we discuss how this gets set in a moment.) If we are receiving a document, we assume that the user wants to cancel active action and replace it with the new action. Finally, we use the `HTML.RequestDoc` method to retrieve the new Web page, and then show the Document form to ensure that it is the topmost form on the screen.

Listing 26-2 The WebRunner *Combo1_Keypress* Subroutine

```
Private Sub Combo1_KeyPress(KeyAscii As Integer)

If KeyAscii = 13 Then
   WebAddit = True
   If Left(Document.Caption, 7) = "Loading" Then
      Document.HTML1.Cancel
      DoEvents
```

continues

Listing 26-2 Continued

```
    End If
    Document.HTML1.RequestDoc Combo1.Text
    Document.Show 0
End If

End Sub
```

In the Beginning

The HTML ActiveX control provides three events that are called during the document transfer. The first event is the `BeginRetrieval` event (see Listing 26-3), which is called when the transfer begins. The second event is `UpdateRetrieval` (see Listing 26.4), which is called periodically during the transfer. The third event is `EndRetrieval` (see Listing 26-5), which is called when the transfer ends.

At the beginning of the transfer, we set the caption of the document to indicate three things: that we are loading the document; the URL of the document; and the number of bytes transferred. (This is how we were able to check to see if the document was being loaded in the `Combo1_KeyPress` event.) You should note that I do not refer to the form as Document, but by the word object `Me`. The `Me` object always refers to the current form. (There is a reason I am using Me rather than Document, but you will have read a few more chapters to find out why.) I set the `WebURLCount` to zero because we have yet to begin parsing the document. Finally, we add the URL to the history list if `WebAddit` is `true`. Also, we ensure that the default value for `WebAddit` is `true` because we always want to add the references unless we specifically flag it otherwise.

Listing 26-3 The Document *`HTML1_BeginRetrieval`* Subroutine

```
Private Sub HTML1_BeginRetrieval()

Me.Caption = "Loading: " & HTML1.URL & " (" & Format(HTML1.RetrieveBytesDone) & " bytes
➥loaded)"
```

```
WebURLCount = 0

If WebAddit Then
   WebRunner.Combo1.AddItem HTML1.URL
   WebRunner.Combo1.ListIndex = WebRunner.Combo1.NewIndex
Else
   WebAddit = True
End If

End Sub
```

While We Are Working

During the transfer, the `UpdateRetrieval` (see Listing 26-4) is called from time to time. About all this routine is useful for is updating a progress bar or some other status display.

Listing 26-4 The Document *`HTML1_UpdateRetrieval`* Subroutine

```
Private Sub HTML1_UpdateRetrieval()

Me.Caption = "Loading: " & HTML1.URL & " (" & Format(HTML1.RetrieveBytesDone) & " bytes
➥loaded)"

End Sub
```

And Finally

The `EndRetrieval` event (see Listing 26-5) is called after the transfer is complete. At this point all we need to do is to reset the caption to the current URL.

Listing 26-5 The Document *HTML1_EndRetrieval* Subroutine

```
Private Sub HTML1_EndRetrieval()

Me.Caption = HTML1.URL

End Sub
```

When All Else Fails

While testing WebRunner, I encountered several pages that managed to confuse the HTML control's parser. When this happened, I would get no indication other than a call to this routine. Most of the informational parameters are not very helpful, including the description of the error. But something is better than nothing (at least I think so). Anyway, I simply display the error message using a message box and continue with the program.

Listing 26-6 The Document *HTML1_EndRetrieval* Subroutine

```
Private Sub HTML1_Error(Number As Integer, Description As String, Scode As Long, _
                        Source As String, HelpFile As String, HelpContext As Long, _
                        CancelDisplay As Boolean)

MsgBox "Error: " & Description

End Sub
```

Making History

We have already seen how to add URLs to the history ComboBox, so now it is time to look at how we manage this information.

Choosing a URL from the ComboBox

Choosing a URL is a relatively straightforward process. First, I set the `WebAddit` flag to `false` to ensure that we do not add this URL to the list again because all we are really doing is resetting the history pointer. Next, we check to see if we are in the process of loading a document and if so, we cancel it. Finally, we request the new document and show it on the Document form.

Listing 26-7 The Document *HTML1_EndRetrieval* Subroutine

```
Private Sub Combo1_Click()

WebAddit = False
If Left(Document.Caption, 7) = "Loading" Then
   Document.HTML1.Cancel
   DoEvents
End If

Document.HTML1.RequestDoc Combo1.Text
Document.Show 0

End Sub
```

Reloading a Document

The code to reload a document is identical to the code above, but instead of being triggered by changing the value of the ComboBox, we simply use the current value of the ComboBox.

Listing 26-8 The Document *HTML1_EndRetrieval* Subroutine

```
Sub DoReload()

WebAddit = False
If Left(Document.Caption, 7) = "Loading" Then
   Document.HTML1.Cancel
   DoEvents
End If
Document.HTML1.RequestDoc Combo1.Text
Document.Show 0

End Sub
```

Choosing the Next URL From the History List

The DoNext subroutine (see Listing 26-9) is called whenever the user wants to move to the next item in the history list. First, we check to see if there is a next URL that we can move to by checking to see if the current Combo1.ListIndex is less then the last item in the list (Combo1.ListCount -1). If it is less, we load the document like we did in the two previous routines. Otherwise, we need to let the user know that we are already at the end of the history list.

In a similar fashion, the DoPrevious routine is called when we want to move backward in the list. The only differences are that I check to see if the current Combo1.ListIndex is greater than zero, subtract one from the ListIndex instead of adding one, and then display a message saying that we are at the beginning of the list. I did not include the code for DoPrevious here, so check the CD-ROM if you want to take a look at it.

Listing 26-9 The Document *HTML_DoNext* Subroutine

```
Sub DoNext()

If Combo1.ListIndex < Combo1.ListCount - 1 Then
   Combo1.ListIndex = Combo1.ListIndex + 1
```

```
      WebAddit = False
      If Left(Document.Caption, 7) = "Loading" Then
         Document.HTML1.Cancel
         DoEvents
      End If
      Document.HTML1.RequestDoc Combo1.Text
      Document.Show 0
   Else
      MsgBox "You are at the last entry."
   End If

End Sub
```

View Information

While writing this program, I decided to include a few frills that were relatively easy to implement. All three work with the View form to display information about the Web document. The first routine is the View Source routine, which is used to display the source code for the HTML document. The second routine displays the list of methods, URLs, and `URLEncodedBody`. The last routine displays the list of URL references found inside the document with their associated text information.

All of this information is displayed on the View form. The only interesting part about the View form is that I used a RichTextBox rather than a plain TextBox. For all practical purposes I could use either, but the standard TextBox is limited to 64KB. While there are not many documents that are that large, with my luck, it would be the very document I wanted to see!

Viewing the Source

Viewing the source code is the easiest of the three information displays to generate. The `MenuSource_Click` event (see Listing 26-10) occurs when the user selects the View | Source option from the menu. To capture the document source, we must first, ensure that the `RetainSource` property of the HTML control is `True`. (This can be done at design time.) Then we must copy the source text from the `HTML.SourceText` property to the form to be displayed, and display the form.

Listing 26-10 The WebRunner *MenuSource_Click* Event

```
Private Sub MenuSource_Click()
View.View.Text = Document.HTML1.SourceText
View.Caption = "View Source for " & Document.HTML1.URL
View.Show 0

End Sub
```

Viewing the Forms Information

The forms information is saved as part of the `HTMLForms` object, which is stored as part of the `HTML.Forms` property. So in the `MenuForms_Click` event (see Listing 26-11), I simply step through each `HTMLForm` in the `HTMLForms` collection and append its three properties to the View.Text box on the View form. Then I display the View form.

Listing 26-11 The WebRunner *MenuForms_Click* Event

```
Private Sub MenuForms_Click()

Dim f As HTMLForm

View.View.Text = ""
View.Caption = "View form information for " & Document.HTML1.URL
For Each f In Document.HTML1.Forms
   View.View.Text = View.View.Text & f.Method & vbCrLf & f.URL & vbCrLf & _
                                            f.URLEncodedBody & vbCrLf
Next
```

```
View.Show 0

End Sub
```

URLs and Their Text

Of the three routines, the last is the most complicated. In the previous routines, the information was already saved as part of the normal operation of the control. This time we have to use an event inside the HTML control to capture the information we need. The `DoNewElement` event (see Listing 26-12) is called while the HTML control is parsing the HTML document. In this situation I only want to keep URLs that are included as part of an anchor's href. Then I also want to save all the text that follows, until the end anchor is reached. This information is saved in the `WebURL` series of global variables. A routine similar to the two listed above is used to display this information on the View form.

First, I look for an anchor by testing for an `ElemType` of "a". If I find one, I scan through the `HTMLAttrs` collection looking for hrefs that point to HTTP documents. When I find one, I add it to the `WebURLs` array. This is a little difficult because it is possible to code a URL that is relative to a base URL, so I check to see if there is a leading value of "http://", which I assume will be a complete URL. If it is not, I construct a URL using the `BaseURL` and the `at.Value`. Because the `BaseURL` may or may not end in a slash ("/") and the `at.Value` may or may not begin with a slash, I have to check and handle each case.

After I handle the case of the anchor element itself, I collect the text between the begin anchor tag and the end anchor tag. Because the text comes in one word at a time, I initialize the text field to a null string and set the `FoundA` flag to `true` in the same block of code I use to save the URL. I reset the flag when I receive the next end tag. Then each time the flag is set, I append the word to the `WebURLText` string using the `WebURLCount` subscript.

While the code in this event is a little messy, it is relatively straightforward if you think about the three different conditions. So once I capture this information, I also have a routine called `MenuForms_Click` that displays this information, which is very similar to the `MenuSource_Click` and the `MenuForms_Click` routines that we have discussed above. Because it is so similar, I am not going to discuss it here. If you want to look at it, check the source code on the CD-ROM.

Listing 26-12 The Document *HTML1_DoNewElement* Subroutine

```
Private Sub HTML1_DoNewElement(ByVal ElemType As String, ByVal EndTag As Boolean, _
                    ByVal Attrs As HTMLAttrs, ByVal Text As String, _
                    EnableDefault As Boolean)

Dim at As HTMLAttr

If ElemType = "a" Then
   For Each at In Attrs
      If at.Name = "href" Then
         WebURLCount = WebURLCount + 1
         FoundA = True

         If WebURLCount < WebURLMax Then
            WebURLText(WebURLCount) = ""
            If Left(at.Value, 7) = "http://" Then
               WebURLs(WebURLCount) = at.Value
            ElseIf Right(HTML1.BaseURL, 1) = "/" And Left(at.Value, 1) = "/" Then
               WebURLs(WebURLCount) = Left(HTML1.BaseURL, Len(HTML1.BaseURL) - 1) &
at.Value
            ElseIf Right(HTML1.BaseURL, 1) = "/" And Left(at.Value, 1) = "/" Then
               WebURLs(WebURLCount) = HTML1.BaseURL & "/" & at.Value
            Else
               WebURLs(WebURLCount) = HTML1.BaseURL & at.Value
            End If
         End If
      End If
   Next
End If

If ElemType = "" And FoundA Then
   If WebURLCount < WebURLMax Then
      WebURLText(WebURLCount) = WebURLText(WebURLCount) & " " & Text
   End If
```

```
End If

If EndTag And FoundA Then
   FoundA = False
End If

End Sub
```

Summary

In this chapter we discussed how to create a functional Web browser in five minutes. While this Web browser lacks many functions, it demonstrates the power of Visual Basic and the new ActiveX controls in a way that few other programming tools can claim. We followed up this simple program with WebRunner. WebRunner adds some of the functions that were missing from the Five-Minute Web Browser. We discussed how to create a history list of URLs that we have visited and how to move through the history list. We also discussed how to extract the URLs and their attached text from the source document. Finally, we walked through the code that we use to view the raw HTML source, the form information, and the list of URLs and associated text from the HTML document.

In the next chapter, we to take the WebRunner program and add it to the NetRunner program. This is the last major function we add to NetRunner. While we are working with this, we add a few other interesting features along the way. Then we continue in the next part of the book with some new ideas that take the basic functions that we implemented and add a few off-the-wall ideas.

In case you want to check your answer to the question at the front of the chapter, here is the answer:

- *What is the significance of the* `Me` *object?*

  The `Me` object is used to refer to the current form. This object is especially useful when you create new instances of a form, or you have some standard code that may be used by multiple forms.

Chapter 27

NetRunner—Part Three

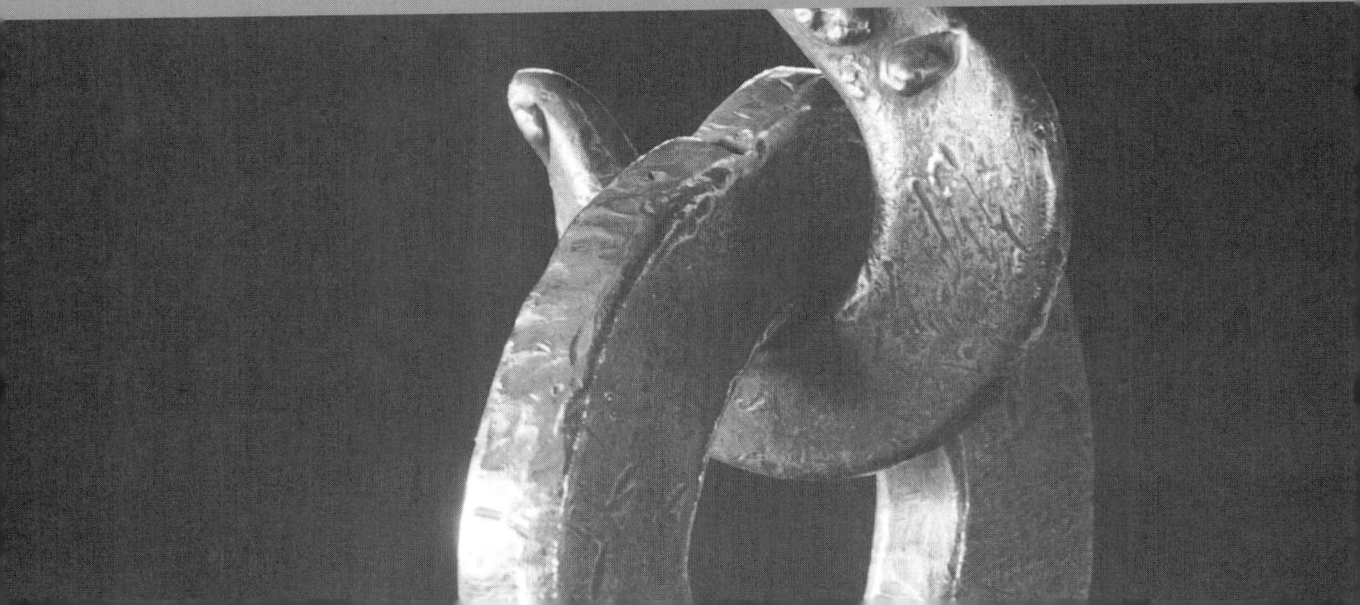

Overview

In previous chapters we combined the FTPRunner, NewsRunner, and MailRunner programs to form a program called NetRunner. In the last chapter we built a program called WebRunner that is used to access the World Wide Web. In this chapter, we add the WebRunner program to the NetRunner program and integrate it into the existing NetRunner program by highlighting all HTTP links in news articles and e-mail notes, starting the Web browser when the highlighted link is clicked, and using the Note form to send a newly discovered URL to someone using e-mail. One additional enhancement to WebRunner itself is also introduced: the capability to access a search engine when an invalid URL is entered.

By the end of this chapter, you should be able to answer the following question:

- What how do you select a specified string in the RichTextBox?

How to Use NetRunner—Part Three

As you can see in figure 27-1, I added some new fields that are used to implement some new functions in WebRunner. One of the new fields is used to hold a default URL value, which is loaded whenever WebRunner is started.

The second set of values is used to enable a feature called auto refresh. As you may guess from its name, auto refresh is used to automatically reload a Web page. While at first this may appear to be a useless feature, there are several sites that provide updated information in real time. For instance, NASCAR has a Web site (http://www.NASCAR.com) that provides real-time information about its auto races. With some browsers you have to click the Refresh button every minute or two to get the updates. The auto refresh feature takes care of this for you.

The third set of values is used to enable one of the most interesting features of WebRunner. If, for some reason, a URL cannot be found, WebRunner will do one of five things. If the Search Lycos radio button is clicked, WebRunner automatically starts a search on Lycos. If present, the “www.” and the “.com” are stripped from the host name and the resulting value is used as a search argument. The same process is followed if either the Search Yahoo or Search Infoseek radio buttons are clicked. If the Goto radio button is clicked, WebRunner automatically loads the specified URL. If no URL is specified, WebRunner simply does nothing.

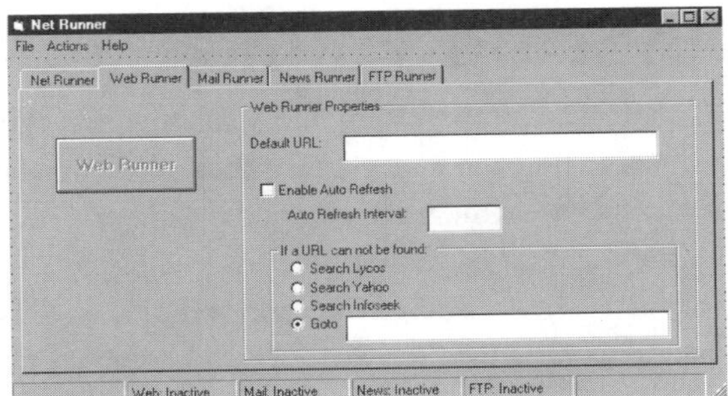

FIGURE 27-1

The NetRunner form, WebRunner tab.

One new button was added to the WebRunner form (see figure 27-2). This button takes the current URL and builds an e-mail note to send to someone on the Internet. Say you stumble onto this really cool new Web site and you want to tell a friend about it—until you see the obnoxiously long URL you have to rekey into an e-mail note for him. NetRunner simplifies this by automatically generating an e-mail note with the complete URL. When this feature is combined with the new feature in MailRunner that displays all URLs that are inside an e-mail note or a news article, exchanging interesting URLs with friends will be a breeze.

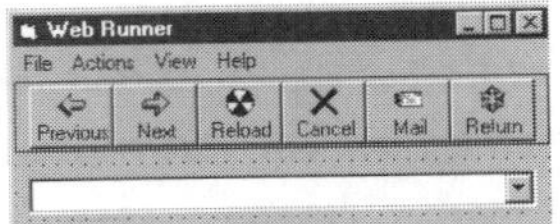

FIGURE 27-2

The WebRunner form.

Merging WebRunner into NetRunner

Because we have already discussed this subject to death in the previous NetRunner chapters, I am not going to go into a lot of detail here. Basically what you need to do is add all the individual forms to the program, and add the global variables to the NetGlobal module (including the code to initialize them in the Initialization routine). Finally, you need to merge the code from WebRunner's timer routine into NetRunner's timer code.

Unlike the previous programs, WebRunner did not have an explicit Connect form to define standard servers that it would access, so there is no need to convert a form that does not exist. Other features such as resizable forms and automatic saving of form size and locations are also added to WebRunner.

When a URL Cannot be Found

What do you do when you cannot find a site on the Internet? Usually the first thing is to go to one of the popular search engines to find some new URLs that may help you find the original site, or some URLs that may have similar information. In either case, you start by entering the URL for a search engine. The thought occurred to me that it may be useful to automatically go to one of these sites whenever you cannot find the URL you are looking for. Because you may not always want to use a search engine each time you cannot find a URL, or may want choose different search engines depending on what type of information you are surfing for, I made this option very configurable.

Handling this is both straightforward and a little tricky at the same time. In the `HTML1_Error` event (seen in Listing 27-1), an error number of 1003 indicates that the control cannot find a URL. Because this is the only event we want to handle by switching to a different URL, we need only test for Number = 1003 to handle this condition. All other errors generate a standard MsgBox with the error description.

However, handling the event is significantly different than you might think. For some reason you cannot switch URLs inside an HTML event. After spending a lot of time trying to work out a more straightforward solution, I chose to take advantage of the `Timer` event in NetRunner to switch to a new URL. I created a new global variable called `WebErrorTick`, which is used as a signal to the `Timer` routine that it needs to handle switching to the new URL. This variable is decremented each time the `Timer` event is invoked, so I can specify the delay between the time I detect the error and when the new URL should be fetched. After a little experimentation, I found that setting `WebErrorTicks` to one for a one second delay was sufficient.

Listing 27-1 ***HTML1_Error* Event**

```
Private Sub HTML1_Error(Number As Integer, Description As String, _
            Scode As Long, Source As String, HelpFile As String, _
            HelpContext As Long, CancelDisplay As Boolean)

If Number = 1003 Then
   Me.Caption = "Can't find: " & Right(Me.Caption, Len(Me.Caption) - 13)
   WebErrorTick = 1
```

```
Else
   Me.Caption = "Error retrieving: " & Right(Me.Caption, Len(Me.Caption) - 13)
   MsgBox "Error: " & Description

End If

End Sub
```

Listing 27-2 shows a fragment of code from the `NetRunner.Timer1_Timer` event that handles the `WebErrorTick`. The first thing we check is to see if the `WebErrorTick` is greater than zero. If it is not, we continue with the rest of the event because we do not have anything to process. If the value is greater than zero, we decrement `WebErrorTick`.

If `WebErrorTick` is equal to zero, choose one of the error actions discussed earlier. Essentially we check each of the radio buttons from the WebRunner tab on the NetRunner form, and begin a search on that particular search engine or load the URL associated with the Goto radio button.

Beginning a search without bringing up the main form for a search engine is an interesting challenge. In order to have something to search on, I created a routine that extracts the name of the host system from the URL. Then I take this value and combine it with some other information and construct a new URL that I request using the `RequestDoc` method. The next Web page displayed on the screen is the response from the search engine.

Listing 27-2 ***NetRunner.Timer1*** **Event**

```
Private Sub Timer1_Timer()

'  There are only a few timers in Windows, so rather than
'  let each ActiveX control use it's own timer, the Net
'  Runner timer will handle all of there events.

Dim h As Long
Dim m As Long
Dim s As Long
Dim X As Long
```

```
.
.
.
If WebErrorTick > 0 Then
   WebErrorTick = WebErrorTick - 1
   If WebErrorTick <= 0 Then
      If WebSearchYahoo.Value Then
         Document.HTML1.RequestDoc "http://www.yahoo.com/bin/search?p=" & _
             GetHostFromURL(Right(Document.Caption, Len(Document.Caption) - 12))
      ElseIf Websearchlycos.Value Then
         Document.HTML1.RequestDoc "http://www.lycos.com/cgi-bin/pursuit?query=" & _
            _GetHostFromURL(Right(Document.Caption, Len(Document.Caption) - 12))
      ElseIf WebSearchInfoseek.Value Then
         Document.HTML1.RequestDoc "http://www.infoseek.com/Titles?qt=" & _
             GetHostFromURL(Right(Document.Caption, Len(Document.Caption) - 12)) &_
             "&col=WW&sv=IS&lk=noframes"
      ElseIf WebSearchDefault.Value Then
         If Len(WebErrorURL.Text) > 0 Then
            Document.HTML1.RequestDoc WebErrorURL.Text
         End If
      End If
   End If
End If
.
.
.
End Sub
```

Automatic Refresh of Web Pages

In the `NetRunner.Timer1` event, we need to put in the code that watches for the time when the URL should be reloaded. In Listing 27-3, I show the fragment of code that manages the refresh process. Each time the `Timer1_Timer` event is called, I check to see if the AutoRefresh function has been turned on by checking the value of the `WebAutoRefresh` checkbox on the NetRunner form.

By adding a global variable called `WebRefreshTick`, we can count the number of timer ticks until the Web page must be reloaded. Each time the timer event is fired, one second has passed. So by decrementing `WebRefreshTick` each time the timer event is fired, we can count the number of seconds remaining until the URL must be reloaded.

Reloading the URL is a relatively straightforward process. Simply use the `RequestDoc` method using the current value for the URL, and then show the document form. Notice that I did not set the `WebAddit` value; I do not want to add the URL to the history list each time the document is refreshed.

Listing 27-3 *NetRunner.Timer1* Event

```
Private Sub Timer1_Timer()

' There are only a few timers in Windows, so rather than
' let each ActiveX control use it's own timer, the Net
' Runner timer will handle all of there events.

Dim h As Long
Dim m As Long
Dim s As Long
Dim X As Long

 .
 .
 .
```

```
    If webautorefresh.Value Then
        WebRefreshTick = WebRefreshTick - 1
        If WebRefreshTick <= 0 Then
            Document.HTML1.RequestDoc Document.HTML1.URL
            Document.Show 0
        End If
    End If

End Sub
```

Now that the document is displayed, we need to reset the `WebRefreshTick` value so that the document can be refreshed at the appropriate time. Originally I reset the value at the same time I used the `RequestDoc` method to retrieve the document. While in most cases this should not cause a problem, it does assume that the document is completely retrieved before the document is refreshed. When testing using short refresh periods and a relatively slow Internet connection, I ran into the problem where the document was being refreshed before it could be entirely loaded. As a result, I chose to reset the `WebRefreshTick` value after the document has been retrieved. You can see this code in Listing 27-4.

Listing 27-4 ***HTML1_EndRetrieval* Event**

```
Private Sub HTML1_EndRetrieval()

Me.Caption = HTML1.URL

If NetRunner.webautorefresh.Value Then
    WebRefreshTick = CInt(NetRunner.webrefreshinterval.Text)
End If

End Sub
```

Displaying Web Pages from Notes and Articles

One of the more useful features in NetRunner is that all HTTP URL references are now highlighted in blue. When you click the reference, the WebRunner function is started and the Web page is automatically displayed. To implement this function requires two steps. The first step is to scan through the e-mail note or news article and mark all the URL references. This is done using the `ScanURL` subroutine found in the `NetGlobal` module. The second step is to include some code in the note or article control to process the `Click` event. Each time the user clicks on the note or article, the `Click` event is called and determines if the spot on the note is marked in blue. If it is, the Web page is displayed.

Scanning for URLs

The `ScanURL` subroutine (shown in Listing 27-5) takes advantage of methods and properties of the `RichTextBox` control to simplify the search and highlight process. Note that I passed the entire control to this routine as an object. This permitted me to use all the properties and events without having to know the specific name of the control.

The first step is to append a space to the end of the RichTextBox. This prevents problems later while trying to find the end of the URL. The next step is to find a reference to the string "http:" by using the `RichTextBox.Find` method. If the string is not found, the method returns a value of -1. Otherwise, the method returns the starting position of the "http:" string.

Assuming that I find a string, I use the `Span` method to find the end of the URL. Because a URL cannot have a space, carriage return, or line feed inside it, I let the `Span` method select characters until any one of these three characters are found. Next, change the color of the selected text to blue. I then start the search for the next URL by starting at the next character after the end of the selected text. I repeat the loop if I find the "http:" string again, or end the loop if I do not find it. Finally, after highlighting all the URLs, I set the select starting point to zero to ensure that there are no blocks of selected text on the screen.

Remember when I added the space to the end of the text? This ensures that the Span method has something to because it is possible that a URL will be the very last part of the text. If I did not use this trick, I would have to add a lot of special code to handle the situation where the URL extends to the end of the text.

Listing 27-5 ***Notebox_Click*** **Event**

```
Sub ScanURL(o As Object)

Dim i As Long

o.Text = o.Text & " "

i = o.Find("http:")
Do While i > -1
   o.Span " " & vbCrLf, True, True
   o.SelColor = &HFF0000  '  turn the selected text blue
   i = i + o.SelLength
   i = o.Find("http:", i)
Loop

o.SelStart = 0
o.SelLength = 0

End Sub
```

Clicking on a Note or Article

With all the URLs in the note or article highlighted in blue, it is a relatively simple matter to determine if the user has clicked a URL. Because clicking the text sets the select properties (`SelColor`, `SelLength`, `SelStart`, `SelText`, among others), all we have to check is to see if `SelColor` is blue (&HFF0000). If it is not, we can exit the routine.

However, knowing that we have a URL is much easier than knowing the exact text of the URL. To determine the text, we need to scan backwards through the text to find the start of the URL. To do this we need to check for a few different conditions. First, we know we have found the start of the URL when the character's color changes from blue to black. We also know we have found the start of the URL if the line number changes. Finally, we know that we have the start of the URL when we look at the first character in the text buffer.

After we find the start, finding the end is easy. We just use the same `Scan` method we used to find the URL in the first place. We do not have to add a space to the end of the text buffer like we did in the `ScanURL` routine because we never deleted it when we finished the `ScanURL` routine. Finally, we can display the Web page by using the Document's `RequestDoc` method and passing the selected text as the value of the URL.

Listing 27-6 ***`Notebox_Click`*** **Event**

```
Private Sub notebox_Click()

Dim done As Boolean
Dim oldline As Long
Dim webwin As Form

If Notebox.SelColor = &HFF0000 Then
   done = False
   oldline = Notebox.GetLineFromChar(Notebox.SelStart)
   Notebox.SelLength = 1
   Do While Not done
      If Notebox.SelStart < 1 Then
         done = True
      ElseIf Notebox.SelColor <> &HFF0000 Then
         done = True
         Notebox.SelStart = Notebox.SelStart + 1
         Notebox.SelLength = 1
      ElseIf Notebox.GetLineFromChar(Notebox.SelStart) <> oldline Then
         done = True
         Notebox.SelLength = 1
```

```
        Else
            Notebox.SelStart = Notebox.SelStart - 1
            Notebox.SelLength = 1
        End If
    Loop
    Notebox.Span " " & vbCrLf, True, True
    WebAddit = True
    Document.HTML1.RequestDoc Notebox.SelText
    Notebox.SelLength = 0

End If

End Sub
```

Summary

In this chapter we continued the process of building NetRunner by incorporating the WebRunner code into the existing NetRunner code. While we were working on the program, we added some new features that integrate WebRunner with the rest of the NetRunner functions. These functions include automatic refresh of Web pages; calling search engines when a Web page cannot be found; e-mailing URLs; and providing a default URL that is used when WebRunner is first started.

This chapter concludes our discussion of the basic ActiveX controls and how they can be incorporated into a program. In the next part of the book, we continue working with the NetRunner program and implement some new functions that demonstrate the full power of Visual Basic and the ActiveX Internet Control Package.

In case you want to check your answer to the question at the front of the chapter, here is the answer:

- *What how do you select a specified string in the RichTextBox?*

  The you can use the `Find` function against the RichTextBox's `Text` property to locate the start an interesting string. Next you use the `Span` method to locate the end of the string. This marks the specified text as selected. Then you can use the `SelColor` property to change the color of the text, the `SelUnderline` property to underline the text, or the `SelText` property to change the text itself.

PART VI

NetRunner

NetRunner

As we have seen so far, NetRunner is a program that uses all the ActiveX controls in the Internet Control Pack. But after writing some relatively standard programs to show how to use the controls, it is time to have a little fun.

One of the problems with the Internet is that there is too much information available. It is very easy to suffer from information overload. One of the goals of this chapter is to enhance the NetRunner program to filter out some of the garbage. The other goal is to experiment with some different techniques to display the filtered information to the user.

After spending a lot of time talking about the ActiveX Internet Control Package and building some sample programs, my work is nearly complete. Now it is up to you to take this information and do something creative. Whether you build the Five-Minute Web Browser into your own application or write your own mail program, the best way to learn how the controls work is to work with the controls.

Chapter Summary

Chapter 28—NetRunner—Part Four

This chapter discusses how to search through the information found in a Usenet newsgroup and display only the subject lines of interesting news articles in a scrolling window. Then the user need only click the subject line as it appears in the window to see the entire article.

- Overview
- How to Use NetRunner—Part Four
- Updates to the Timer
- Interesting Articles
- Changes to NewsRunner
- ScrollBox
- Summary

Chapter 29—NetRunner—Part Five

This chapter discusses how to automatically search through the World Wide Web and find interesting Web pages. But to ensure that the end result is fun to use, we include the capability to display up to 81 different Web pages at the same time.

- Overview
- How to Use NetRunner—Part Five
- Updates to the Timer
- Changes to WebRunner
- Summary

Chapter 30—Now It's Your Turn

This chapter discusses ideas that can be used to improve the sample programs that we built throughout this book. Each of the programs is examined and specific suggestions are made that would significantly improve each program. I also spend a little time discussing why you should use the Internet Control Pack in your Visual Basic programs.

- Overview
- General Improvements
- FTPRunner
- NewsRunner
- MailRunner
- WebRunner
- NetRunner
- A Few Last Words
- Summary

Chapter 28

NetRunner—Part Four

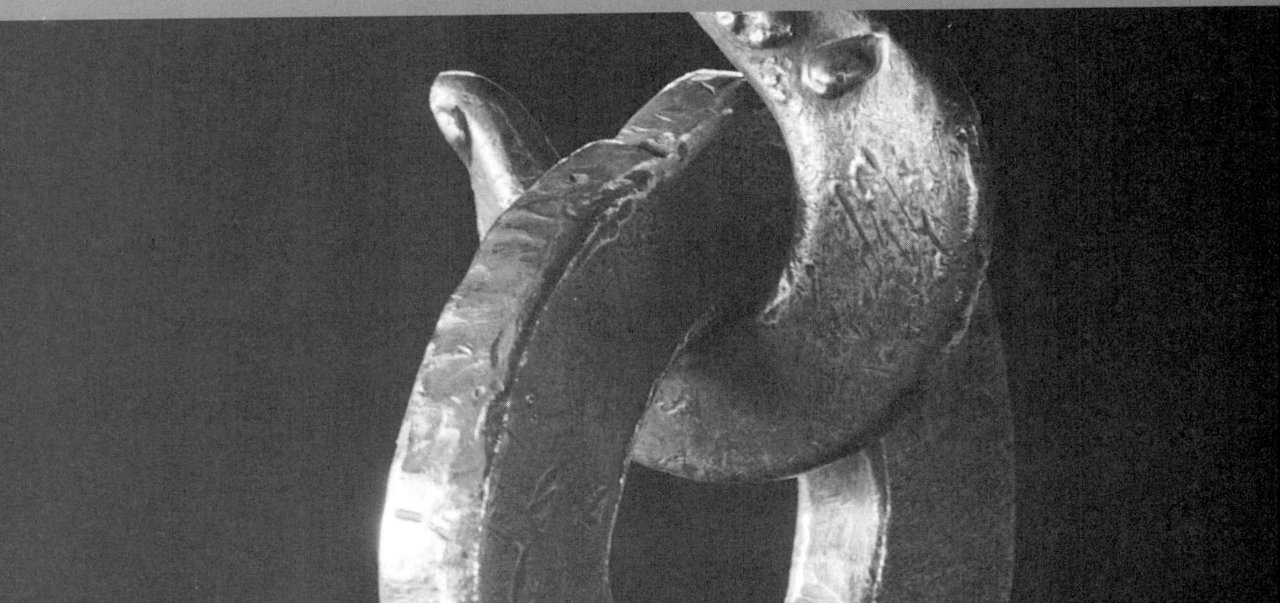

Overview

In previous chapters we created a program called NetRunner. In this chapter we continue to add to the program with the capability to select news articles based on a list of keywords. However, simply displaying the articles as we have done in the past is not nearly as interesting as scrolling the information across the top of the screen.

By the end of this chapter, you should be able to answer the following question:

- How do you change the color of a string inside a RichTextBox?

How to Use NetRunner—Part Four

NetRunner—Part Four goes back to the NewsRunner program and adds two new enhancements. The first enhancement is displaying the subject line of the articles in a newsgroup in a scrolling window across the top of the screen. Clicking one of the subject lines automatically invokes the Article form with the selected article.

The second enhancement works with the first one and is used to select only those articles that have a specified keyword in their subject line. This function hopefully eliminates articles that you do not want to see, and attracts your attention to the keywords in the article by marking them in red.

As you look at the NetRunner form in figure 28-1 you should notice two changes. The first and most obvious is that there is finally something on the NetRunner tab. There is a check box that is used to enable news searching, and an empty text box that is used to hold the name of a newsgroup to be searched. The NetRunner button is used to start the NetRunner function, which starts the scanning process.

This NetRunner tab shown in figure 28-2 contains a text box where you can enter a list of keywords or phrases, one per line. This list is used later to compare against the subject line and text of an article.

The Scroll form in figure 28-3 is a rather uninteresting box is used to display the subject lines from various news articles. The subject lines are displayed as a fixed font character set, and the first character in the display is removed every tenth of a second. Thus the display appears to scroll from right to left from the user's point of view. Clicking any of the subject lines as they scroll past displays the related article using the familiar Article form.

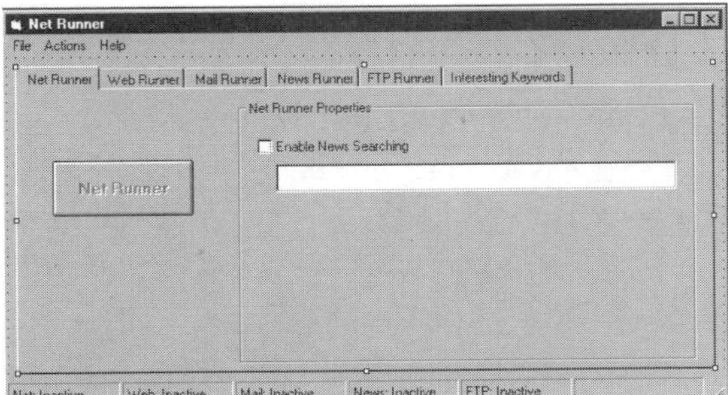

FIGURE 28-1

The NetRunner form, NetRunner tab.

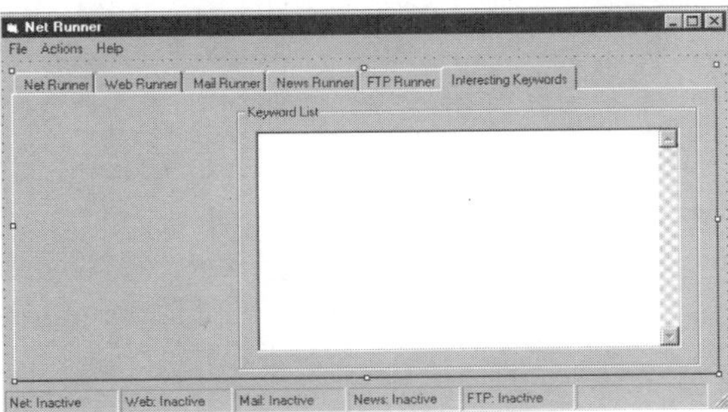

FIGURE 28-2

The NetRunner form, Interesting Keywords.

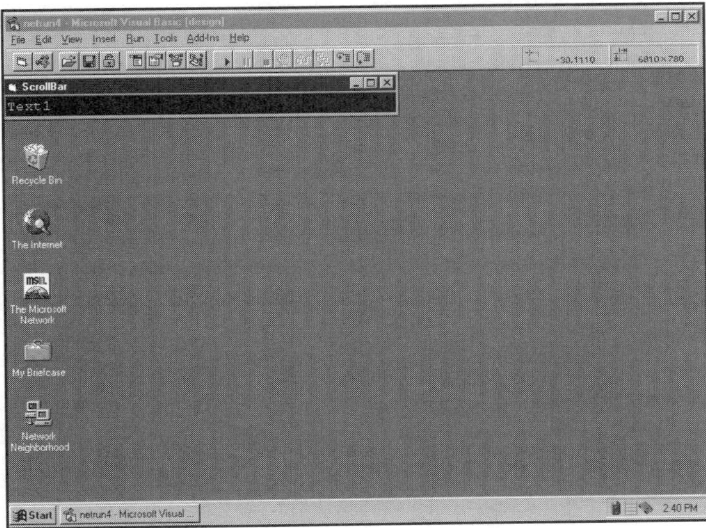

FIGURE 28-3

The Scroll form.

Updates to the Timer

The basic theory of scrolling the text is that periodically you delete a character off one end of the display and append a character to the other. The big trick is to find a way to make these operations occur at a fairly regular interval. When you see the term regular interval, you should begin thinking about clocks and timers. Because we already have a timer, let us begin there.

Our current timer is activated once every 1,000 milliseconds, or once every second. If we were to shift the characters in the display at this speed, the 60-character subject line would take a minute to scroll off the display. This is too slow. The next step is to set the timer to 100 milliseconds. After trying the display, I found this to be too fast. After a few experiments, I finally arrived at a speed of 200 milliseconds.

Now that we know the speed we want for the timer, how do we implement it without making major changes to the program? The easiest way is to use a second timer, but we really do not want to waste another timer when we already have one, so we modify the code for the `NetRunner.Timer1` Timer (see Listing 28-1) to handle the more frequent events.

First, change the `Timer1.Interval` line in the `NetRunner.Form_Load` event from 1,000 milliseconds to 100 milliseconds. Then create a new global variable called `NetTenths`. Each time the `Timer1_Timer` event occurs, we add one to this variable. Ten ticks of the timer means a second has passed and we can let the rest of the code execute.

However, before we let the rest of the code execute, we scroll characters in the ScrollBox every even tick ((NetTenths Mod 2) = 0). Because we let another routine stuff text into the box, we only worry about deleting the text from the box. The first thing we do is save the position of the cursor (`SelStart`) into a temporary variable. Then, if we have more than 100 characters in the buffer, we delete the first character. Then we restore the cursor position. (This is necessary because deleting a character resets the cursor position.)

Now you may wonder why I do not delete any characters if there are less than 100 in the buffer. If I start deleting things from the buffer immediately, it is possible to scroll the text off the window before more characters are added. This is especially true if you have a highly selective set of keywords or when the form is first initialized. The most important factor here is to make the scrolling a little easier for the user.

Listing 28-1 NetRunner.*Timer1_Timer* event

```
Private Sub Timer1_Timer()

'  There are only a few timers in Windows, so rather than
'  let each ActiveX control use it's own timer, the Net
'  Runner timer will handle all of there events.

Dim h As Long
Dim m As Long
Dim s As Long
Dim X As Long

NetTenths = NetTenths + 1

If NetScroll And ((NetTenths Mod 2) = 0) Then
   h = Scroll.scrollbox.SelStart
   m = Len(Scroll.scrollbox.Text)
   If m > 100 Then
      Scroll.scrollbox.Text = Right(Scroll.scrollbox.Text, m - 1)
   End If
   Scroll.scrollbox.SelStart = h
End If

If NetTenths <> 10 Then
   Exit Sub
End If

NetTenths = 0

.
.
.

End Sub
```

Interesting Articles

Filtering out the gems from the garbage is a difficult, time-consuming thing to do. There are hundreds of new news articles added to the comp.lang.basic.visual.misc newsgroup each day. While many of the posts are interesting to someone, not all of them are interesting to me. To help save time, it would be useful to have a function that can scan through the subject lines of a newsgroup and select only those news articles that are of interest.

FindInteresting

There are a number of ways to determine what is interesting. We are going to go with the simplest. Remember the Interesting Keywords tab on the NetRunner form? The `FindInteresting` function compares each of those keywords with the text of the subject line and returns `true` if it finds a match.

The `FindInteresting` function (see Listing 28-2) initially assumes that there is nothing interesting. It uses the variable `i` to keep track of where we are in the InterestingKeywords TextBox, and the `GetText` function to return the string starting at location `i` until the next carriage return. If no keywords are specified, then I assume that all subjects should be selected. Otherwise, I go through the list of keywords and use the `InStr` function to see if the keyword is contained in the subject line. As soon as we see a single match, we assume that the article is Interesting. If there is no match, we get the next item from the InterestingKeyword TextBox and try it again. When we run out of keywords (k is a null string), we exit the routine and assume that the article is not interesting.

Listing 28-2 ***FindInteresting* Subroutine**

```
Function FindInteresting(s As String) As Boolean

Dim i As Long
Dim k As String

FindInteresting = False
i = 1
```

```
k = GetText(NetRunner.interestingkeywords.Text, i)

If Len(k) = 0 Then
   ' if no keywords were specified, then everything is interesting
   FindInteresting = True
End If

Do While Len(k) > 0
   If InStr(LCase(s), LCase(k)) > 0 Then
      FindInteresting = True
      Exit Function
   End If
   i = i + Len(k) + 2
   k = GetText(NetRunner.interestingkeywords.Text, i)
Loop

End Function
```

MarkInteresting

The `MarkInteresting` function in Listing 28-3 is very similar to the `ScanURL` function we saw in Chapter 27. It takes advantage of the RichTextBox ability to handle mixed-font types at the same time. What we are going to do is scan through the RickTextBox that is passed to the routine (as `o` the object) using the same techniques that we used in the `FindInteresting` function. When we get a match, we mark the keyword in red.

Note that this causes a problem with the `ScanURL` function. It is possible that a URL will include a keyword. Because I depend on the URL being blue when I extract the URL, I need to modify that routine slightly. In addition to marking the URL in blue, I also underline it. Thus the `MarkInteresting` routine can safely change a keyword in a URL from blue to red because the `Article.ArticleBox_Click` routine uses the underline property rather than the color to build the URL.

Listing 28-3 *MarkingInteresting* Function

```
Function MarkInteresting(o As Object) As Boolean

' This routine will compare the information in
' in the RichTextBox with the information in
' the interesting keywords box

Dim i As Long
Dim j As Long
Dim k As String

MarkInteresting = False
j = 1
o.TextRTF = o.TextRTF & " "

k = GetText(NetRunner.interestingkeywords.Text, j)

Do While Len(k) <> 0
   i = o.Find(k)
   Do While i > -1
      o.SelLength = Len(k)
      o.SelColor = &HFF  '  turn the selected text red
      MarkInteresting = True
      i = i + o.SelLength
      i = o.Find(k, i)
   Loop
   j = j + Len(k) + 2
   k = GetText(NetRunner.interestingkeywords.Text, j)
Loop
```

```
o.SelStart = 0
o.SelLength = 0

End Function
```

Changes to NewsRunner

I had to add one new subroutine and make a small addition to support the new NetRunner functions.

SearchNewsGroup

The `SearchNewsGroup` subroutine (see Listing 28-4) is based heavily on the `GetNewsGroup` subroutine. While the `GetNewsGroup` subroutine starts with the first article available in the newsgroup and ends with the last, the `SearchNewsGroup` subroutine runs continuously until the `NetScroll` function is stopped.

Listing 28-4 *SearchNewsGroup* Subroutine

```
Function SearchNewsGroup(g As String) As Integer

'  Specify NewsType to retrive a list of articles in the
'  DocOutput routine, for the specified newsgroup.
'  DocOutput will put the information directly onto the
'  Scroll form.

NewsType = 4

If Len(g) = 0 Then
   g = NewsCurrentGroup
```

continues

Listing 28-4 Continued

```
End If

NetArticle = 0
Scroll.scrollbox.Text = ""
NewsCurrentGroup = g

News.SelectGroup g
Do While News.Busy
   DoEvents
Loop

If News.ReplyCode <> 211 Then
   MsgBox "Error in SearchNewsGroup(SelectGroup). Reply text is: " & _
            News.ReplyString
   SearchNewsGroup = News.ReplyCode
   NewsType = 0
   Exit Function
End If

Do While NetScroll
   News.GetArticleByArticleNumber
'   News.GetHeaderByArticleNumber
   Do While News.Busy
      DoEvents
   Loop

   If News.ReplyCode <> 220 Then
'   If News.ReplyCode <> 221 Then
      MsgBox "Error in SearchNewsGroup(GetHeaderByArticleNumber). Reply text is: " & _
               News.ReplyString
      SearchNewsGroup = News.ReplyCode
      NewsType = 0
      Exit Function
```

```
        End If

        Do While Len(Scroll.scrollbox.Text) > 100 And NetArticle = 0
           DoEvents
        Loop

        If NetArticle > 0 Then
           GetArticle (NetArticle)
           Do While News.Busy
              DoEvents
           Loop
           NewsType = 4
           NetArticle = 0
        End If

        News.SetNextArticle
        Do While News.Busy
           DoEvents
        Loop

        If (News.ReplyCode <> 223) And (News.ReplyCode <> 421) Then
           MsgBox "Error in GetNewsGroup(SetNextArticle). Reply text is: " & _
                   News.ReplyString
           SearchNewsGroup = News.ReplyCode
           NewsType = 0
           Exit Function
        ElseIf News.ReplyCode = 421 Then
           News.SelectGroup g
           Do While News.Busy
              DoEvents
           Loop
        End If

     Loop
```

continues

Listing 28-4 Continued

```
NewsType = 0

SearchNewsGroup = News.ReplyCode

End Function
```

DocOutput

For the most part the `DocOutput` routine shown in Listing 28-5 is the same as the old one. Basically all I did was add support for NewsType = 4 processing. I use the `FindInteresting` function to determine if the subject is interesting. If it is, I add it to the ScrollBox and append the article number surrounded by "##". These marks are used later to determine which article should be loaded when the user clicks on the scrollbar.

Listing 28-5 *News_DocOutput* Event

```
Private Sub News_DocOutput(ByVal DocOutput As DocOutput)

'  Check the DocOutput.State value to determine
'  the state of the transmission process (Begin, End,
'  Headers, Data, or Errors). Within each state,
'  choose the appropriate action based on the
'  value of NewsType (1=newsgroup list, 2=article list,
'  3=article header and body, 4=interesting subjects).

Dim hdr As DocHeader
Dim i As Long
Dim j As Long
Dim l As ListItem
Dim s As String
Dim X As Variant
Static Y As Variant
```

```
Select Case DocOutput.State

.

.

.

Case icDocHeaders
    Select Case NewsType

.

.

.

    Case 4
        For Each hdr In DocOutput.Headers
            Select Case LCase(hdr.Name)
            Case "subject"
                If FindInteresting(hdr.Value) Then
                    Scroll.scrollbox.Text = Scroll.scrollbox.Text & hdr.Value & _
                          " ##" & Format(NewsCurrentArticle) & "## "
                End If
            End Select
        Next hdr
    End Select

.

.

.

End Select

End Sub
```

ScrollBox

The code used by the Scroll form is relatively simple. In the `Form_Load` event, the form is moved to the top of the screen. Then the form and the TextBox inside the form are resized so that they take up the full width of the screen.

The only other code in the Scroll form exists to handle the `ScrollBox_Click` event (see Listing 28-6). This event is called when the user clicks a part of the scrolling text. The `SelStart` property of the TextBox is set to the position of the cursor when the mouse is clicked. From this value we can scan forward looking for the "##" that indicates the beginning of the article number. From there it is relatively simple to convert the string value to a Long integer that the search newsgroup displays in between retrieving headers.

Listing 28-6 ***ScrollBox_Click* Event**

```
Private Sub ScrollBox_Click()

Dim i As Long

scrollbox.SelLength = 2
Do While scrollbox.SelText <> "##"
   scrollbox.SelStart = scrollbox.SelStart + 1
   scrollbox.SelLength = 2
Loop
scrollbox.SelStart = scrollbox.SelStart + 2
scrollbox.SelLength = 10

NetArticle = Val(scrollbox.SelText)

scrollbox.SelStart = 0

End Sub
```

Summary

In this chapter, we enhanced the original functions provided by NewsRunner to provide a scrolling window at the top of the user's screen that displays a list of subject lines from interesting news articles. The user may click anywhere on the scrolling window to view the rest of the news article. In the next chapter, we conclude NetRunner by adding a similar function to WebRunner.

In case you want to check your answer to the question at the front of the chapter, here is the answer:

- *How do you change the color of a string inside a RichTextBox?*

  The `SelStart` and `SelLength` properties of a RichTextBox can be used to mark the string you want to change. Then you can use the `SelColor` property to change the color of the text. You also can use other properties like `SelUnderline` to underline the text, `SelFontSize` to change the font size, and `SelFontName` to change the name of the font for the selected text.

Chapter 29

NetRunner—Part Five

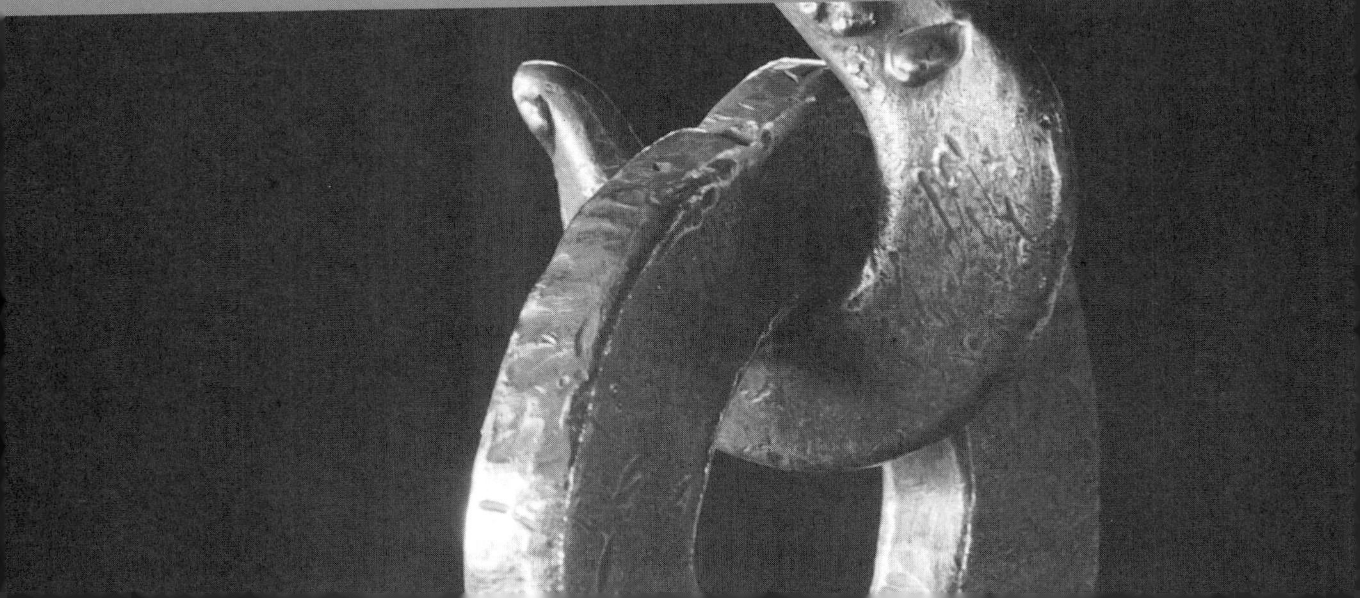

Overview

In the last chapter we discussed how to take a relatively standard program like NewsRunner, make a few changes, and end up with radically different program that is even more interesting to use. In this chapter, we are going to do the same thing with WebRunner. We take some of the components that we worked with in the last chapter and make a few changes to a number of the routines. These enhancements make NetRunner look completely different from WebRunner.

By the end of this chapter, you should be able to answer the following questions:

- What is a queue?
- How do you create a new copy of a form?

How to Use NetRunner—Part Five

NetRunner—Part Five takes advantage of the Document form and the HTML control to display up to 81 separate HTML documents on the screen at one time and automatically refresh them with new documents. I call this feature Net Surfing. The URLs for the new documents are extracted from the HTML documents as they are displayed. This process is repeated until no more URLs are available to be displayed. So for some Web sites like www.yahoo.com or www.news.com, this means that this program runs for quite a while before running out of URLs to display. Other sites may run for shorter amounts of time.

The programming changes are less obvious than NetRunner—Part Four because most of them are buried inside existing subroutines. The only really visible change to the program was made to the NetRunner form's NetRunner tab and is shown in figure 29-1. The new fields on the NetRunner tab control the size of the display and the URL that is used to start the process.

While up to nine rows and nine columns can be selected for up to 81 separate displays, it is probably more practical to have a display of one row and two columns or two rows and one column. Some typical configurations are one row and two columns, three to five rows and one column, and two rows and two columns. The configurations are really affected by the screen resolution. The larger the resolution, the more usable displays can be viewed.

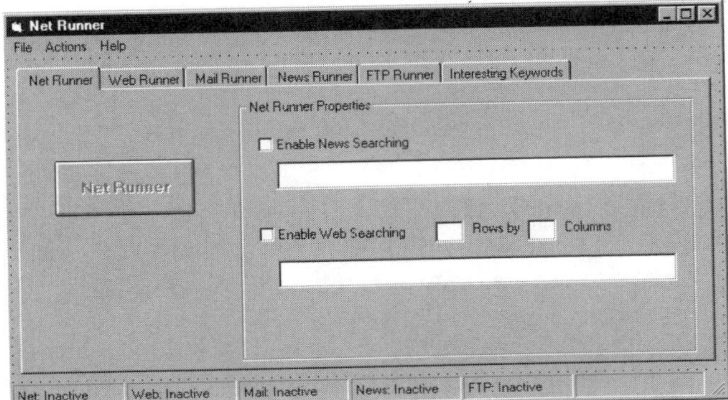

FIGURE 29-1

The NetRunner form, NetRunner tab.

The Web surfing function starts with a single URL. This URL is retrieved and displayed in the first window. While the Web page is loading, all the URL references and their associated text descriptions are saved. After the document is retrieved, the list of text descriptions is scanned for interesting keywords. If a match is found, the URL is added to a queue of URLs that are displayed in subsequent screens. Then the next URL in the queue selected is displayed in the next available screen. This process continues until there are no more URLs to be displayed in the queue.

Because this function is enabled by pressing the NetRunner button, which also activates the news scrolling function, check boxes are included on the NetRunner tab to select either the news scrolling, Web surfing, or both automated functions. Clicking the NetRunner button a second time stops all of the activities.

Global Variables

This time the changes we are going to make are a little more complex than we have made in the past. In Listing 29-1, I show the list of global variables used by the NetRunner component of the program. There are two sets of variables that are key to implementing Net Surfing: `NetDoc` and `NetURL`. The `NetDoc` variables are used to hold information about the individual screens, and the `NetURL` variables are used to hold the queue of URLs.

The `NetDoc` variables consist of `NetDocs`, which is an array of forms. Remember in WebRunner how all the code inside the Document form referred to the form using the `Me` object? That is because I intended to dynamically create multiple copies of the Document form to support NetRunner. If the code inside the form referred to itself as Document, there is the possibility of confusion as to which form is actually being referred to. Using Me eliminates this problem.

The other key NetDoc variable is the NetDocSecs, which is used to count the number of seconds remaining before the timer should move onto the next form. For purposes of identifying the current Document display, the NetDocX and NetDocY variables are used. This ensures that the initialization code and the timer code access only one Document form at a time, which also serves to reduce confusion and problems in the long run.

The NetURL variables are used to form a queue. While I could have created a fancy object to manage a queue, I wanted something easy to debug so I created a simple data structure that consists of an array that stored the queue values (NetURLs) and two pointers—one to the top of the queue where new URLs are added (NetURLTop), and one to the bottom where URLs are removed from the queue (NetURLBottom). To make it relatively easy to use, I created two global subroutines (AddURL and GetURL) that are used to access the queue.

Listing 29-1 Global Variables for NetRunner

```
'  Define the Net Runner Global Variables
'  ==============================================


'  Article number from the scrollbar to be displayed
Global NetArticle As Long


'  Count up to one second
Global NetTenths As Integer


'  News scrolling is active
Global NetScroll As Boolean


'  Reference to the forms that can be displayed on the screen
Global NetDocs(9, 9) As Form


'  Delay before displaying the screen
Global NetDocSecs(9, 9) As Integer
```

```
'  Web surfing active
Global NetWeb As Boolean

'  Current screen location
Global NetDocX As Integer
Global NetDocY As Integer

'  queue of URLs to be displayed
Global Const NetURLsMax = 256
Global NetURLs(NetURLsMax) As String

'  bottom and top queue pointers
Global NetURLBottom As Integer
Global NetURLTop As Integer
```

Managing the URL Queues

We have essentially two parts to NetRunner's Net Surfing function. The first part is where URLs are extracted from Web documents as they are displayed. The second part is where an extracted URL is selected and displayed. Because the URLs are extracted faster than they are displayed, we need a mechanism that can sit between the two parts and hold the information generated by the first part until the second part is ready to use it. The best way to handle this situation is to use a queue.

Queues are a relatively standard data structure that is taught to everyone who has taken a computer science course, but almost no one ever finds a practical application where it should be used. (Queues are occasionally used by systems programmers, but almost never by an applications programmer.) Yet when you think about it, queues can be relatively useful, especially in this program.

A queue works something like the checkout line at the grocery store. People arrive at the end of the line and slowly work their way to the front. When they reach the front, the cashier processes their order. Likewise as new URLs are found, they are added to the end of the line while the `Timer1.Timer` event waits until it is time to grab a new URL and start retrieving this new document.

Adding a URL to the Queue

Listing 29-2 shows the code that adds a URL to the queue. First, we check to see if the top of the queue has overflowed the space available. If it has, we need to determine if there is space at the bottom of the queue. If there is, we can compact the queue by copying each element to the bottom and resetting the top and bottom pointers. If we cannot compress the queue, we discard the URL. (After all, because the queue size is 256 elements, chances are very low that we will run out of information to look at!)

Assuming that there is space for at least one more item in the queue, we check to see if the URL is already in the queue. This prevents the situation where a group of documents all reference a single document. (This might happen if someone includes a link to the home page or to another common page like a search page.) Assuming that it is a new entry, we can add it to the top of the queue.

Listing 29-2 *AddURL* Subroutine

```
Sub AddURL(u As String)

Dim i As Integer
Dim j As Integer

If NetURLTop >= NetURLsMax Then
   If NetURLBottom = 1 Then
      ' the queue has overflowed, so we are
      ' going to discard this URL
      Exit Sub
   End If

   ' compress the queue to get more space at the top
   j = 1
   For i = NetURLBottom To NetURLTop - 1
      NetURLs(j) = NetURLs(i)
      j = j + 1
```

```
      Next i
      NetURLBottom = 1
      NetURLTop = i - 1
   End If

   '  eliminate duplicates

   For i = NetURLBottom To NetURLTop - 1
      If NetURLs(i) = u Then
         Exit Sub
      End If
   Next i

   NetURLs(NetURLTop) = u
   NetURLTop = NetURLTop + 1

End Sub
```

Getting a URL from the Queue

Getting a URL from the queue is relatively easy. In the `GetURL` subroutine (see Listing 29-3), we simply look in the location pointed to by the bottom pointer and return that value. Of course, we also need to increment the bottom pointer so the next time we can retrieve the correct value.

One other thing we need to do is check to see if there is something in the queue before we can return a value. Because the top pointer always points to the next spot in the array to be used, and the bottom pointer always points to the next URL to be retrieved, an empty queue is found when both pointers point to the same cell. In this case, we return a empty string and reset both pointers to the first member of the array. (This may help to avoid a compacting operation later on.)

Listing 29-3 *GetURL* Subroutine

```
Function GetURL() As String

If NetURLBottom = NetURLTop Then
  '  empty queue
  GetURL = ""
  NetURLBottom = 1
  NetURLTop = 1
Else
  GetURL = NetURLs(NetURLBottom)
  NetURLBottom = NetURLBottom + 1
End If

End Function
```

Running NetRunner

Now that we have gone over some of the tools that we use later in this chapter, I want to talk about how to start NetRunner. Starting NetRunner's Net Surfing function is done through the SSCommand5 button (yeah, I know I should use a better name, but have you ever wondered why Microsoft does not automatically use its own standards when creating default names for variables?) and the `Form_Load` event for the Document form.

On the NetRunner Form

In the `SSCommand5_Click` event (see Listing 29-4), we are going to start our Net Surfer. Similar to what we did with the newsgroup scrolling function, we use a global variable called `NetWeb` to start and stop the surfing. When starting up, we examine the two fields `NetDocXMax.Text` and `NetDocYMax.Text` for proper values to set the screen size. If they are okay, we lock those values into place so the user cannot change them and start building all of the forms.

A form is created by doing a `SET NetDocs(NetDocX, NetDocY) = New Document` statement. This statement creates a new occurrence of the Document form and saves a pointer to it in the `NetDocs` array. After the form is created, it is shown and the count-down timer for that form is set to 30 seconds as a default.

After all the forms have been created and shown on the screen, the program selects the first form and sets the count-down time to one second. Then we add the default URL to the queue. When the `Timer1.Timer` event occurs, this value is decremented to zero, and then the next URL from the queue is loaded and the first screen is displayed.

Stopping the program is relatively easy. The next time the NetRunner button is clicked, the forms are unloaded and the fields that hold the number rows and columns are unlocked. When the `NetWeb` value is set to `false`, the timer event stops displaying URLs.

Listing 29-4 ***SSCommand5_Click*** **Event**

```
Private Sub SSCommand5_Click()

If NetScroll Then
   Unload Scroll
   NetScroll = False
   StatusBar.Panels("NetRunner").Text = "Net: Inactive"
Else
   Scroll.scrollbox.Text = ""
   Scroll.Show 0
   NetScroll = True
   StatusBar.Panels("NetRunner").Text = "Net: Active"
   NewsRunner.SearchNewsGroup (NetNewsGroup.Text)
End If

If NetWeb Then
   For NetDocY = 0 To Val(NetDocYmax.Text) - 1
      For NetDocX = 0 To Val(NetDocXmax.Text) - 1
         Unload NetDocs(NetDocX, NetDocY)
      Next NetDocX
```

continues

Listing 29-4 Continued

```
   Next NetDocY
   NetDocXmax.Locked = False
   NetDocYmax.Locked = False
   NetWeb = False
Else
   NetDocX = Val(NetDocXmax.Text)
   If NetDocX < 1 Or NetDocX > 9 Then
      MsgBox "Number of colums must be between 1 and 9"
      Exit Sub
   End If
   NetDocY = Val(NetDocYmax.Text)
   If NetDocY < 1 Or NetDocY > 9 Then
      MsgBox "Number of rows must be between 1 and 9"
      Exit Sub
   End If

   NetDocXmax.Locked = True
   NetDocYmax.Locked = True

   For NetDocY = 0 To Val(NetDocYmax.Text) - 1
      For NetDocX = 0 To Val(NetDocXmax.Text) - 1
         Set NetDocs(NetDocX, NetDocY) = New Document
         NetDocs(NetDocX, NetDocY).Show 0
         NetDocSecs(NetDocX, NetDocY) = 30
      Next NetDocX
   Next NetDocY
   NetDocX = 0
   NetDocY = 0
   NetDocSecs(0, 0) = 1
   AddURL NetWebURL.Text
   NetWeb = True
End If

End Sub
```

On the Document Form

The code for the Document Form_Load (see Listing 29-5) is a little trickier than the others. We need to preserve the capability to let WebRunner use this form without modifying the WebRunner code, while at the same time adding the new code required for Net Surfing. I use NetDocX to indicate when I'm using Net Surfing or WebRunner. A value of -1 means that the Document form is just loading a plain old web document and should use the default settings from the system registry.

The first thing we do is save the NetDocX and NetDocY values into the Tag property associated with the form. This information is important to identify the position in the NetDocs array and the NetDocSecs array. Without this information, we cannot identify which form is actually executing the code. (We see a little more about this later in this chapter.)

For NetRunner, we need to compute the location and size of the form based on the number of forms being displayed. First, I determine if the NetRunner news scroll bar is displayed and adjust the screen top and size available for me to put the individual Document forms. Because I know how many Document forms I want to display in a row, I divide the screen width by that number to set the Width property. Then, I multiply the width of the Document form by the form's position on the row to get the Left property.

Listing 29-5 ***Document.Form_Load*** **Event**

```
Private Sub Form_Load()

Dim TopAt As Single
Dim TopHeight As Single
Dim x As Integer
Dim xmax As Integer
Dim y As Integer
Dim ymax As Integer

hhgap = GetSetting("NetRunner", "Document", "hhgap", Me.Height - HTML1.Height)
hwgap = GetSetting("NetRunner", "Document", "hwgap", Me.Width - HTML1.Width)
```

continues

Listing 29-5 Continued

```
Me.Show 0

If NetDocX = -1 Then
   Me.Top = GetSetting("NetRunner", "Document", "Top", WebRunner.Top + WebRunner.Height)
   Me.Left = GetSetting("NetRunner", "Document", "Top", WebRunner.Left)
   Me.Width = GetSetting("NetRunner", "Document", "Top", WebRunner.Width)
   Me.Height = GetSetting("NetRunner", "Document", "Top", WebRunner.Height * 2)
Else
   Me.Tag = Format(NetDocX) & "," & Format(NetDocY)
   If NetScroll Then
      TopAt = Scroll.Height
      TopHeight = Screen.Height - Scroll.Height
   Else
      TopAt = 0
      TopHeight = Screen.Height
   End If

   Me.Width = Screen.Width / Val(NetRunner.NetDocXmax.Text)
   Me.Left = NetDocX * Me.Width

   Me.Height = TopHeight / Val(NetRunner.NetDocYmax.Text)
   Me.Top = NetDocY * Me.Height + TopAt
   Me.Caption = Me.Tag

End If

FoundA = False

End Sub
```

Displaying New URLs Automatically

Now that we have loaded the screen with document forms and are showing the first Web page in the first form, we need to deal with the code that processes the rest of the Document forms. Each Web page displayed is started by the `Timer1.Timer` event. The `EndRetrieval` and `Error` events in the Document form indicate that this process is complete for this Document form and permit the timer to continue on to the next Document form. The `HTML1_Click` event is triggered whenever a user clicks something on the from. This event is used for adding some time to the count-down timer to prevent the screen from being refreshed before the user is ready.

Changes to the Timer Routine

Changing the timer routine (see Listing 29-6) is a relatively simple process. Essentially we are going to take the value in the `NetDocSecs` and subtract one for each second, and when we reach zero we are going to load the next Document form using the next available URL in the `NetURLs` queue. When we run out of URLs in the queue, we let the user know using a MsgBox statement and then start over again with the starting URL.

Now before you complain that I have not loaded any URLs into the queue, all I am going to say at this point is trust me. Either they will be there when we are ready to use them, or the default URL will be used again. If that happens, the user may be encouraged to use a different URL.

Listing 29-6 ***Timer1.Timer*** **Event**

```
Private Sub Timer1_Timer()

'  There are only a few timers in Windows, so rather than
'  let each ActiveX control use it's own timer, the Net
'  Runner timer will handle all of there events.

.
.
.
```

continues

Listing 29-6 Continued

```
If NetWeb And NetDocX >= 0 Then
   NetDocSecs(NetDocX, NetDocY) = NetDocSecs(NetDocX, NetDocY) - 1
   If NetDocSecs(NetDocX, NetDocY) = 0 Then
      NetDocX = NetDocX + 1
      If NetDocX > Val(NetDocXmax.Text) - 1 Then
         NetDocX = 0
         NetDocY = NetDocY + 1
         If NetDocY > Val(NetDocYmax.Text) - 1 Then
            NetDocY = 0
         End If
      End If
      NetDocSecs(NetDocX, NetDocY) = 30
      u = GetURL
      If Len(u) = 0 Then
         MsgBox "No more URLs to surf"
         u = NetWebURL
      End If
      NetDocs(NetDocX, NetDocY).HTML1.RequestDoc u
   End If
End If

End Sub
```

Changes to the Document Form

There are two events that indicate that loading a Web page has finished loading: the `EndRetrieval` event, which occurs when the Web page is successfully loaded, and the `Error` event, which occurs when the Web page cannot be loaded. In Listing 29-7, the action we take is relatively simple. If we are surfing, we will wait five more seconds before the timer starts displaying the next Web page. This allows a user to continue working with this page before it times out.

In Listing 29-8, we set the count-down timer to three seconds before we starting loading the next Web page. Note that in both the `EndRetrieval` and `Error` events I use the tag value to determine the appropriate countdown timer to update. This is necessary because the `NetDocX` and `NetDocY` values we have used before may not necessarily point to this particular instance of the form.

Finally, in Listing 29-9 you can see that each time the user clicks this form, we set the count down timer to 60 seconds to prevent this particular form from being refreshed. Any subsequent forms that the user may access by clicking a hypertext link only add five seconds to the counter if they are successful, so the page continues to hang around for a while.

Listing 29-7 *HTML1_EndRetrieval* Event

```
Private Sub HTML1_EndRetrieval()

Me.Caption = HTML1.URL
If NetRunner.webautorefresh.Value And Not NetWeb Then
   WebRefreshTick = CInt(NetRunner.webrefreshinterval.Text)
End If

If NetWeb Then
   NetDocSecs(Val(Left(Me.Tag, 1)), Val(Mid(Me.Tag, 3, 1))) = _
            NetDocSecs(Val(Left(Me.Tag, 1)), Val(Mid(Me.Tag, 3, 1))) + 5
End If

End Sub
```

Listing 29-8 *HTML1_Error* Event

```
Private Sub HTML1_Error(Number As Integer, Description As String, Scode As Long, Source
As String, HelpFile As String, HelpContext As Long, CancelDisplay As Boolean)

If Number = 1003 Then
```

continues

Listing 29-8 Continued

```
        Me.Caption = "Can't find: " & Right(Me.Caption, Len(Me.Caption) - 13)
        If NetWeb Then
            NetDocSecs(Val(Left(Me.Tag, 1)), Val(Mid(Me.Tag, 3, 1))) = 3
        End If
    Else
        Me.Caption = "Error retrieving: " & Right(Me.Caption, Len(Me.Caption) - 13)
        MsgBox "Error: " & Description
    End If

End Sub
```

Listing 29-9 *HTML1_Click* Event

```
Private Sub HTML1_Click()

NetDocSecs(Val(Left(Me.Tag, 1)), Val(Mid(Me.Tag, 3, 1))) = 60

End Sub
```

Adding URLs to the Queue

All through this chapter we assumed that the URLs would be around when they are needed, but we never took the time to discuss how they were added to the queue. In the `HTML1.DoNewElement` event (see Listing 29-10), we previously added code to capture all the URL references into the `WebURLs` and `WebURLText` arrays.

After we finish retrieving a URL and its associated text, we check to see if text is interesting by using the same routine we used for news scrolling. If it is interesting and it is an HTTP type URL, we add it to the queue to be displayed later.

Listing 29-10 ***HTML1_DoNewElement*** **Event**

```
Private Sub HTML1_DoNewElement(ByVal ElemType As String, ByVal EndTag As Boolean, _
                                    ByVal Attrs As HTMLAttrs, ByVal Text As String,
➥EnableDefault As Boolean)

Dim at As HTMLAttr
Dim i As Integer

If ElemType = "a" Then
   For Each at In Attrs
      If at.Name = "href" Then
         WebURLCount = WebURLCount + 1
         FoundA = True
         If WebURLCount < WebURLMax Then
            WebURLText(WebURLCount) = ""
            If LCase(Left(at.Value, 7)) = "http://" Or _
               LCase(Left(at.Value, 7)) = "mailto:" Or _
               LCase(Left(at.Value, 7)) = "gopher:" Or _
               LCase(Left(at.Value, 5)) = "news:" Or _
               LCase(Left(at.Value, 5)) = "nntp:" Or _
               LCase(Left(at.Value, 4)) = "ftp:" Then
                  WebURLs(WebURLCount) = at.Value
            ElseIf Left(at.Value, 1) <> "/" Then
               WebURLs(WebURLCount) = GetURLBase(HTML1.URL) & "/" & at.Value
            Else
               WebURLs(WebURLCount) = GetURLBase(HTML1.URL) & at.Value
            End If

         End If
      End If
   Next
End If
```

continues

Listing 29-10 Continued

```
If ElemType = "" And FoundA Then
   If WebURLCount < WebURLMax Then
      WebURLText(WebURLCount) = WebURLText(WebURLCount) & " " & Text
   End If
End If

If EndTag And FoundA Then
   FoundA = False
   If NetWeb And FindInteresting(Text) Then
      If LCase(Left(WebURLs(WebURLCount), 7)) = "http://" Then
         AddURL WebURLs(WebURLCount)
      End If
   End If
End If

End Sub
```

Summary

This is the final chapter about the NetRunner program and this also concludes the last sample program in this book. I hope that you have enjoyed walking through the NetRunner program. In the next and final chapter, we discuss some ideas that can be implemented using each of the controls. In some cases these ideas are merely extensions to the existing Runner family of programs, while in others they are completely different programs. But throughout this chapter one thing will be emphasized—it's your turn.

In case you want to check your answer to the question at the front of the chapter, here is the answer:

- *What is a queue?*

  A queue is a mechanism that holds data. It allows you to add data to it and retrieve the same data in the order it was added. This is extremely useful when you have one process that creates data for a second process to use and both processes run at different speeds.

- *How do you create a new copy of a form?*

  You can create a new copy of a form by using the `Set` statement with the `New` option (see Listing 29-4 for an example). This creates a new copy of a form that is totally independent of the original. This may be useful when you want to display a copy of transient data like the source code to a Web page or in the case of NetRunner, the Web page itself.

Chapter 30

Now It's Your Turn

Overview

In this book we developed a number of programs using the new ActiveX controls. In some cases these programs are not quite complete because they do not have some functions offered by their commercial counterparts. In others, new functions could be added to make the programs more interesting to the user. Theoretically, there is even a possibility that there may be better ways to implement some of the functions we have discussed. There is even a more remote possibility that there may be a bug in one of the programs. (Naw. No way. Never. Could not happen. Imposssible…well, maybe….)

I omitted many of these functions because I didn't want to focus on things you already know how to do. This is not a book on database design and implementation using Visual Basic. This is not a book on how to design good user interfaces. The goal of this book was to provide you with the information you need to add the ActiveX controls to your own programs. You, the reader, have the opportunity to take these programs and perform your own experiments with them. The goal of this chapter is to provide some comments and ideas about how these programs can be changed and enhanced. Sometimes the comments refer to the stand-alone program, and sometimes the comments are directed to the integrated NetRunner program. Often the comments apply to both. The important point is that you should load the programs and make some changes. I have found that actually working with sample programs like these is the best way to learn how to use a new set of programming tools like the ActiveX Internet controls.

By the end of this chapter, you should be able to answer the following question:

- How do I contact the author?
- Why should I leverage Visual Basic with ActiveX?

General Improvements

One possibility that immediately pops into my mind is that none of the text fields that are used to keep passwords are encoded. The easiest way to do this is to change the `PasswordChar` property to an asterisk or "*". This causes any text that is displayed in the text box to appear as a series of asterisks while preserving the actual value of the characters typed in the `Text` property. The main reason I did not set the `PasswordChar` property while developing the programs is that it is easier to test programs when you can see the values in the various fields. You need to ensure that all kinds of improper passwords cause the security logic on the remote servers to return the proper reply codes. (After all, you would never type the wrong password and spend two and a half hours setting traces and breakpoints through the code trying to find out why your last change caused the program not to connect to the remote computer now would you? Stranger things have happened in the wee hours of the morning!)

Another improvement is one that I have worked hard to avoid implementing while writing the programs developed for this book. I'm sure that you have noticed that I do not provide a method to store information like news articles, e-mail notes, and Web bookmarks. The reason for this is that I wanted to focus on the Internet controls rather than develop a database (or worse yet, develop my own specialized file formats) to store this kind of information. I discuss this issue in more detail later in the chapter, but whatever solution you choose, you should make an effort to be consistent across all applications you will be using.

Printing is another area I have totally ignored. With the exception of FTPRunner, all the functions in NetRunner could really benefit from the ability to print the document that is currently being viewed. The `RichTextBox` control makes this relatively easy to do for NewsRunner and MailRunner; however, there is no corresponding function for the HTML control, which makes implementing the capability to print Web pages a little more difficult.

One other area that could be improved is to provide support for multiple servers. While I may not be a typical Internet user, I have access to two different Internet providers, e-mail accounts on at least four different systems, and two different news servers. I use at least six or eight different FTP servers on a regular basis. This often causes problems because some servers can only be accessed only through some connections while others require different userids and passwords to access them. While this is a general problem, I have some specific suggestions for each of the programs in the following sections.

FTPRunner

Of all the programs presented in this book, probably the least expandable is FTPRunner. There are several reasons for this, but perhaps the most basic is that the FTP protocol is the most specialized protocol we discussed. Its sole purpose is to transfer files from one system to another. Because the FTPRunner program already does that fairly well, how can it be improved?

One thing that is lacking is a better status display. We should be able to track the progress of an FTP transfer. While the protocol does not pass along information about the file size, we should be able to display the rate of the data transferred by keeping track of the time that has passed since the transfer began, and the number of bytes received. The best way to do this is by using the `DocInput` and `DocOutput` objects. While we did not include them in FTPRunner, they would be easy to add and could greatly improve the information displayed to the user.

As I mentioned earlier, I use a number of FTP servers. Sometimes I use anonymous FTP to access sources of programs and utilities. Other times I collect and analyze data from multiple computer systems on my PC, and then the results have to be put on yet another computer for others to view them. It would be nice to define all of these systems with their associated userids, passwords, and port information to an FTP Server Repository. Then all I would have to do is merely select the computer I wanted to access, and I would be automatically signed on. This information could be stored in the system registry or in a database table, and then accessed from the FTPConnect form or the NetRunner main form as a drop-down box for host name. This would also allow the user to override the default values and offer an option to save them.

Another area that could benefit from improvement is designing the drop-and-drag interface to interact with the desktop. That way files could be dragged from the desktop (or other window) to the remote system and vice versa. Depending on how you implement it, you could have a desktop icon that would automatically transfer the file to a remote system (using the FTP Server Repository above).

NewsRunner

This program leaves a lot of room for improvement. The most obvious area to improve is the way newsgroups are displayed. While the ListView display does an adequate job of displaying the available newsgroups, a far better way would be to go back to using the TreeView control and find another way to keep track of the information.

One way we could keep track of the newsgroups is to create a database to hold the information. The database would have a table holding the name of each newsgroup, and then the TreeView control would only have to load the information necessary for the display. This would significantly improve the performance of the TreeView control because only a few items would need to be added as each level of the tree structure is loaded by the user.

Another useful database table would be a list of newsgroups to which the user has subscribed. Subscribed in this case means that the user only sees a much shorter list of newsgroups that he or she is interested in reading. (Subscribing to a newsgroup does not involve any interaction with the NNTP server.) Attached to this table would be another table that could be used to track the article numbers of the articles that have been read (or not yet read). This would make it easy to change NewsRunner so that it did not display articles the reader has already seen.

Because it is possible to cross-post articles to multiple newsgroups, it may be useful to record the message-ids of any news articles that have been read. This list can then be used whenever a new newsgroup is accessed to determine whether or not the user has already seen the given article in a different newsgroup. It would work well with the function that keeps track of article numbers that have already been read. You would only need to keep the list of read message-ids until you saved the article number lists. Because article numbers tend to be much smaller than message-ids, you would save a significant amount of disk space. (Especially because you can code a list of article numbers such as 5,6,7,8,9, and 10 as 5-10.)

If you do not want to use a database file, you could implement a flat file similar to the ones used by news programs such as rn (read news) which are found on a UNIX system. These store the newsgroups one per line, followed by a colon (for a subscribed newsgroup) or an exclamation point (for an unsubscribed newsgroup), followed by a list of read article numbers. This method has the advantage of being compatible with other news programs, but may require more processing to parse out the relevant information.

While I am talking about flat files, there is another feature I want to discuss: saving articles onto your local system. Often (well at least occasionally) there is information posted in a newsgroup that you want to keep around for reference. This may be a programming trick or an amusing story. But no matter what is in the article, if you do not make a copy of it on your system, eventually the news server will delete it. Because the RichTextBox includes a `SaveFile` method, this should be a relatively easy task to implement.

Like the multiple FTP server issue I talked about in the previous section, NewsRunner could also benefit from support for multiple news servers. Because many Internet providers permit only people who connect through their modem pool to access their news servers, if you have access to more than one Internet provider, you may have a problem. The same newsgroups may not always be available on all servers. Article numbers are also a problem because they are unique to the server that assigned them, so essentially you need to keep all the information that applies to one server separate from any other. This can be done by having one database for each news server and opening the proper database based on which news server is accessed.

One last function that I omitted from NewsRunner is an option to handle binary documents. Essentially, the document is translated into a text-based file using a utility called UUEncode. Then the document is posted to a newsgroup as a series of one or more news articles. Converting the documents into their original format is done by using a UUDecode utility. While these utilities allow you to post nearly any type of file to a newsgroup, it is most commonly used to post pictures and ZIP'ed files. There are many newsgroups devoted to exchanging this type of information, such as alt.binaries.pictures and comp.binaries.ms-windows.

MailRunner

The mail functions in this program are relatively good, but like the other functions discussed in this book there is room for improvement. Because in many ways MailRunner and NewsRunner provide similar types of functions (both allow you to send and receive RFC-822 formatted documents to and from external servers), it should come as no surprise that many improvements that could be made to NewsRunner could also be made to MailRunner. This covers such areas as saving documents, access to multiple servers, and using UUEncode and UUDecode utilities. If you are going to address these areas for NewsRunner or MailRunner, you should consider an implementation that serves both equally well.

Saving mail is actually a more useful feature for a mail program than a newsreader program. Some would probably even consider it a necessity. This is because there is a greater need to file information in such a way that it is easy to find and retrieve. This implies the need of a hierarchical storage method that would also be able to identify such document information as the subject line, the user who sent it, and the date it was sent. (Note that these fields would be found in a news article too.) This implies that the standard Windows common dialog may not be sufficient for this task.

There are any number of ways to help the user select a document. Perhaps the easiest is to use the Windows hierarchical folder structure to store the documents, and have the form that displays the list of available documents scan each document for the header information. While this may be a little slow (due to the number of files that have to be scanned each time the user wants to save a document), it is probably better than using a set of database tables to accomplish the same thing.

Multiple servers are also a problem because you may want to access more than one mail server at a time. A very clean design would hide the actual mail server from the user and just treat the notes on the server as a special folder as part of the structure we just discussed. That way a user could file a document by dragging a document from one folder to another. With a little creativity, you could also include newsgroups as part of this same structure.

One advantage of many new mail programs is the capability to attach a binary document to an e-mail note. This is typically done using Multipurpose Internet Mail Extensions (MIME). You can attach a large document such as a word processing file or a spreadsheet file and send it to another user. They can extract this file from their mail, and then process it using a compatible application program.

Finally, if you are like me, I can remember people's names but I have difficulty remembering e-mail addresses. To solve this problem, most mail programs include an address book facility. This allows you to keep a virtual little black book on your computer with a list of people and their e-mail addresses. A useful feature in an address book is one where you can assign each person in the address book a nickname and all you have to do is enter the person's nickname on the to (or cc) line of the note, and the proper e-mail address is inserted from the address book.

WebRunner

WebRunner is one of those programs that is very fun to write because there are so many ways you can change it. We have added a number of enhancements in the NetRunner programs such as the auto refresh timer and automatically going to a search engine when you cannot find a URL. But that does not mean that there are no more enhancements to be made.

One area that we totally neglected is to support bookmarks. While there are many ways we could add them to the program, probably the best way is to create a local HTML document with the bookmarks. You can provide the users with the ability to create folders by using a link on one page to link to another Web page. One advantage of this technique is that you can display the bookmarks using the HTML control and it would not require a lot work to implement them.

Another area I did not address is the HTML control's ability to set default values for a lot of properties. Implementing this is a very straightforward task and you can use the same techniques we used to save form size and location to save the these values.

Like MailRunner, WebRunner does not include any MIME functions. This means that WebRunner does not handle any other types of documents except for HTML. This means that I do not support documents like WAV files, AVI files, or any other multimedia files. I also cannot launch an application like Microsoft Word or Excel when I receive a DOC or XLS document. This should not be very difficult to add, but may make WebRunner a lot more interesting to use.

NetRunner

Because NetRunner is really a combination of all of the above programs, all the ideas we have discussed in this chapter could be used to make it even better. But there are a few ideas that could make NetRunner even more unique. It is not that difficult to turn a Visual Basic program into a screen saver. When combined with NetRunner's ability to walk through Web pages and to select interesting news articles, turning these functions into a screen saver would provide an interesting application. A new Web page would be displayed every 15 seconds or so. If the user clicks the display or hits a key, the program would allow the user to view the Web page; and if there has been no activity from the user for a minute or so, the program would resume its walk through the Web.

A Few Last Words

Throughout this book, I have tried to take a very complex technology and make it understandable. In doing this, I have sometimes simplified things by hiding some of the details and by only briefly touching on others. But this is not necessarily bad. Not many people would be able to develop the B-tree data structure that is used to hold a database index, but nearly all programmers today can create an SQL query that uses the index. The same argument applies to the ActiveX controls. You do not need to know all the details of how the Internet works to access an FTP server, but a good knowledge does help.

For those people who are fairly comfortable with technology, I suggest you take a look at the RFCs on the CD-ROM. I have put copies of all the RFCs that I have discussed in this book in both text format and Word 95 format. They are very interesting to read, especially if you are as interested in technology as I am. But if you feel overwhelmed, do not despair. It is not necessary to understand these documents to use the ActiveX controls. They merely help to provide some insight into how the people who developed the ActiveX controls were thinking.

As with most new advances in computer technology, the people who will benefit most from them are the same people who are willing to take the time to work with the new technology. I believe that over the next few years the Internet will become as important as the telephone (and maybe even more important). Understanding how the Internet works is important to those people who want to be able to exploit its power and capabilities. Whether you are an applications programmer who makes your living writing Visual Basic code, or are simply curious about how a Web browser works, you really should take the time to try some of these programs and then go and build your own programs.

When you start to build your own programs, you may want to take advantage of some of the subroutines I have written. Please feel free to include them with your own code. That is why I wrote these programs. Often the best way to understand how to use something is to look at someone else's program. Just send me an e-mail note and let me know how you are using it. I am curious about the kinds of applications and the different ways these controls may be used.

This is my first book. I hope you enjoyed reading it because I had a lot of fun writing it. I am hoping that you will consider this your primary reference for the ActiveX Internet Control Pack. If you have any comments or suggestions about the programs or the book, please let me know. You can send e-mail to me at WFreeze@JustPC.com, or you can visit my Web site at WWW.JustPC.com. If you have your own program that you want to share with others, please send it to me and I will add it to the Web site. In any case, I am sure that you will agree that the ActiveX Internet Control Pack brings the functions of Internet a lot closer for the Visual Basic developer and insures that their applications can remain on the leading edge of technology.

Summary

In this chapter we discussed a number of ways to improve the sample programs included with this book. In fact there are enough ways to improve these programs that you could spend a year or two incorporating all of these suggestions. Of course, by time you complete all of these suggestions, the industry will have moved on to something even more fascinating. These controls are not designed to let you develop a Web browser that will compete with Microsoft's Internet Explorer and Netscape's Navigator, however. They are targeted at helping an applications programmer include some basic capabilities in their programs. I also encourage each of you to spend a little time behind the keyboard to try out the sample programs and to write some of your own.

In case you want to check your answer to the question at the front of the chapter, here is the answer:

- *How do I contact the author?*

  I can be reached by electronic mail at WFreeze@JustPC.com or you can check my Web site at http://WWW.JustPC.com. Please let me know what you think of this book. Also, you should feel free to send me questions and I will do my best to answer them. You can also check the Web site for the latest versions of the sample programs and any other information that I may have about the Internet Control Pack. If you have your own ActiveX program that you would like to share with the rest of the world, please let me know and I will be happy to include it on the Web site.

- *Why should I leverage Visual Basic with ActiveX?*

  If you cannot answer this question by now, you should go back and reread the book. But seriously, I have done my part to ensure that you have the necessary knowledge and materials to incorporate the ActiveX Internet Control Package into your own programs. So my job is complete and now it's your turn.

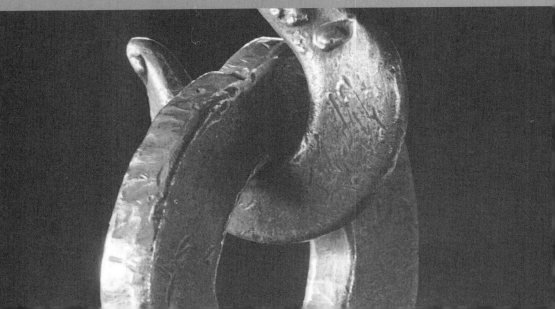

PART VII

Appendices

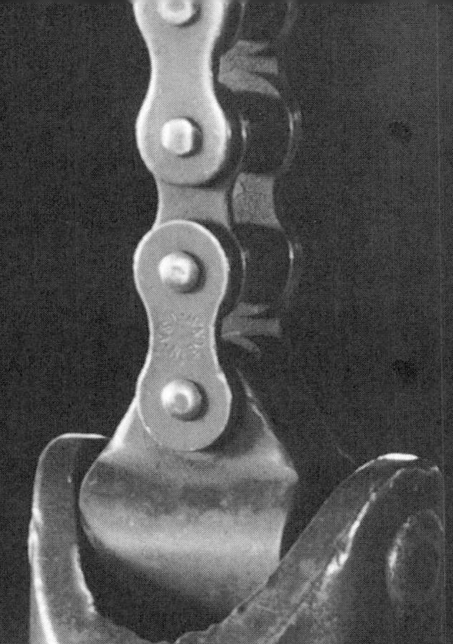

Appendix A

Glossary

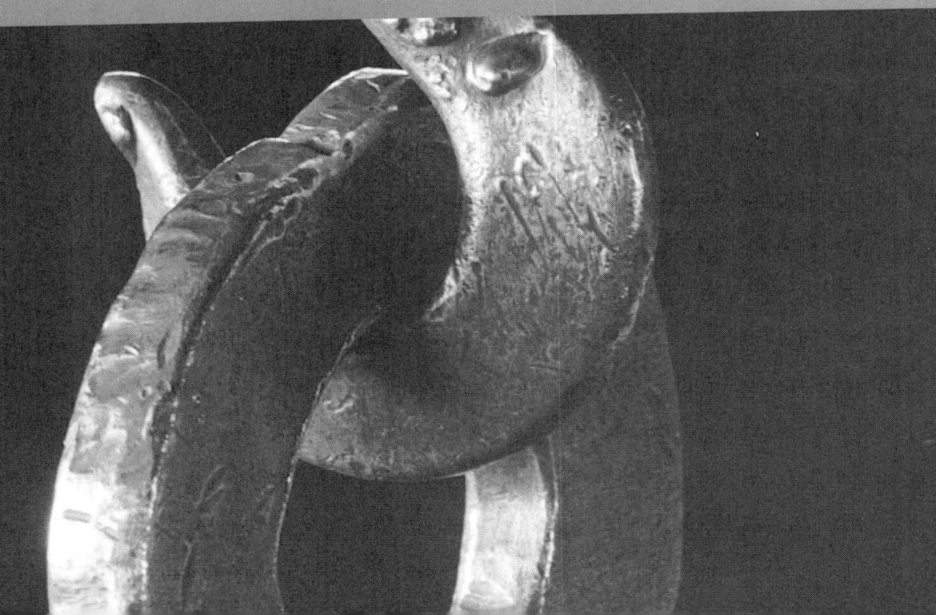

ActiveX The latest generation of tools from Microsoft to help Windows 95 application developers create better applications. These tools are based on the previous generation of tools called OCX.

application Often used instead of application software or application program, this term simply refers to the use of a computer for a specific purpose such as surfing the Net, reading newsgroups, or sending e-mail.

ASCII This acronym (pronounced as-key) stands for the American Standard Code for Information Interchange. In this book, ASCII refers to a standardized character set of 96 upper- and lowercase letters and should be differentiated from binary, which includes .EXE files, word processing documents, .GIFs and the like.

bit Created from the words BInary digiT, a bit is the basic unit of information in a binary numbering system, which is made up of a series of 0s and 1s.

BNF The Backus-Naur form (BNF) is a set of rules describing a program's organization without using a particular programming language. This makes it easier to compare procedures written in different programming languages.

byte A byte equals eight bits and is the fundamental data unit of personal computers.

carriage return This is an ASCII character that causes the cursor to return to the left margin. It is often paired with line feed to indicate the end of a line of text in a file.

client A computer (such as the one you will be working on to write the programs in this book) that can request information from a network server.

client-server An environment where two programs cooperate in order to perform a function. This generally consists of a client program and a server program.

control A dialog box feature in Microsoft Windows 95 that allows a Visual Basic programmer to implement high level functions in a program without having to worry about all the lower level details. This can be a check box, a button, or some other device.

DLL A file extension (.DLL) used in MS-DOS to refer to a collection of library subroutines that are available to a program at run time.

dynamic IP address A changing 32-bit number that uniquely and precisely defines each computer on the Internet. Because computers using SLIP or PPP connections are not always attached to the Internet, their IP address changes each time they log on.

EBCDIC Just as personal computers use ASCII as their standard, IBM mainframes use the Extended Binary Coded Decimal Interchange Code (now we know why they refer to it as EBCDIC!), which contains 256 standardized characters. Naturally networks linking personal computers to an IBM mainframe must equip these computers with some kind of translation device.

electronic mail Messages sent and received with the use of a computer network. Often referred to as an electronic note.

e-mail See *electronic mail.*

EtherNet Developed by Xerox Corporation, EtherNet is a hardware, cabling, and communications standard for Local Area Networks (LANs) that can link up to 1,024 nodes to a bus network.

FDDI Abbreviation for Fiber Distributed Data Interface, which is a standard for high-speed networks connected by fiber-optics.

Finger An Internet utility that allows you to retrieve additional information about a person with an e-mail address. A user's full name and address may be found as well as additional data the user wishes to make available.

firewall A device that separates two computer networks (usually a private network and the Internet) and is used to filter unauthorized transmissions from one side to the other.

FTP Short for File Transfer Protocol, FTP is the Internet standard for exchanging files between various computer systems.

Greenwich Mean Time The standard time for the world and it is usually abbreviated as GMT. All time zones are referred to as many hours before or after GMT. For example Eastern Standard Time is five hours after GMT.

Gopher Developed at the University of Minnesota and named after the school mascot. Gopher is a menu-driven program used by UNIX systems linked to the Internet to help users locate files, programs, or other resources on specified topics. With the advent of the World Wide Web, Gopher has taken a back seat to its graphic counterpart.

HTTP HyperText Transfer Protocol is an Internet standard that dictates how information is exchanged over the World Wide Web.

HTML Stands for HyperText Markup Language, which formats the documents accessed by Web browsers. This language is used to give Web documents a unique appearance.

host Any computer linked to the Internet that can initiate a file transfer, or that other computers can access to download files. Essentially any computer with Internet access has the potential to act as a host.

hypertext A way of preparing and publishing data on the Internet that allows a user to click on a word or phrase, and then be transported to yet another document.

IBM Mainframe Is an IBM-produced multi-user computer intended to meet the computing needs of large organizations. These computers often support hundreds or thousands of concurrent users and usually run a complex operating system like MVS.

IEFT Stands for the Internet Engineering Task Force. This division of the Internet Architecture Board concerns itself with the immediate technical challenges facing the Internet.

Internet A group of computers worldwide that are linked to facilitate communication.

IP Abbreviation for Internet Protocol. It is a standard that defines how data should be broken down to be transferred over the Internet.

IP Address A 32-bit number that uniquely identifies each computer linked to the Internet. This number is typically displayed a series of four numbers ranging from 0 to 255 and separated by periods. (ex: 127.0.0.1)

line feed This is an ASCII character that causes the cursor to move to the next physical line. It is often paired with a carriage return to indicate the end of a line of text in a file.

MIME An acronym for Multipurpose Internet Multimedia Extensions. It is a code that specifies the content type of multimedia files. Examples include .JPEG, .MPEG, .WAV, and so on.

modem A device used to link a computer to the Internet via a telephone line.

MVS (Multiple Virtual Storage) The operating system generally used by a large IBM Mainframe. It is optimized for high volume transaction processing and batch processing.

name server The computer that translates the alphabetical domain name to the IP address.

object An object is a high level package that contains code and/or data that can be accessed through a well defined interface. Thus the lower level details of the actual work required to perform a specific task can be hidden from the program that uses the object.

object oriented A programming discipline that uses objects in the development process.

OCX This is a second generation Visual Basic control that is based on OLE technology. These tools support 32-bit programming.

OLE Object Linking and Embedding allows you to create dynamic and automatically updated links between documents. The set of standards also enables you to embed a document created by one application into that of another. The ActiveX Controls we discuss in this book are basically new and improved OLE controls. Both were created by Microsoft Corporation.

Ping One of the less well-known Internet utilities used for checking to see if a computer is properly connected to the Internet. PING stands for Packet Internet Groper.

POP3 Is the third version of the Post Office Protocol, which is a standard that defines how a computer with a part time connection to the Internet can receive mail.

port An address on a computer that can be used to access a TCP/IP server. When combined with an IP address, the pair can be used to indicate a specific server anywhere on the Internet. (See also *well-known ports*).

protocol A standard for transferring information from one computer to another. In this book we discuss the following protocols: TCP/IP, PPP, NNTP, SMTP, FTP, and HTTP.

PPP Stands for point-to-point protocol. This is a standard used to connect computers to the Internet via telephone line.

queue A programming device that allows data to be saved in a First In First Out method. The first value stored into the queue will be the first value retrieved from a queue.

RFC Request for Comments (RFC) is an Internet publication that communicates various standards. The Internet Architecture Board-controlled RFC has over a thousand articles available, several of which are included on the CD-ROM with this book.

server A computer that holds data other computers can access.

SLIP The second standard of connecting a computer to the Internet via telephone line. Older than its PPP counterpart, SLIP (Serial Line Internet Protocol) was the first improvement of the text-only shell account that enabled a user to use any Internet applications they wanted, including graphical Web browsers. SLIP connections also allowed one to have multiple sessions going at once (i.e., executing an FTP transfer while surfing the Web).

SMTP This stands for Simple Mail Transport Protocol. It is used to send and receive electronic mail. However, receiving mail requires a full-time connection to the Internet. POP3 is used to receive mail when the client computer system only has a part time connection to the Internet.

socket A Internet address that combines an IP address with one of those well-known port numbers used to specify certain Internet applications.

static IP address A computer with a non-changing IP address. Servers and other computers constantly linked to the Internet are the most common holders of a static IP address.

T-1 A high-bandwidth telephone line with the capability to transfer up to 1.544 megabits (Mbp) of data per second.

T-3 Nearly 30 times faster than the T-1 link, the T-3 connection can transfer up to 44.21 megabits per second.

Talk An Internet application allowing users to communicate in real time. The screen is divided in two, and both users' text is displayed simultaneously for comment by the other.

Telnet Another Internet protocol enabling people on the Internet to link to other computers on the Internet. This protocol allows users to connect to computers incapable of communicating with the TCP/IP protocols (SLIP and PPP).

third-party vendor A firm that markets accessories (hardware or software) for a given brand of computer or computer software.

Traceroute An Internet utility that allows a user to see the path taken by a document sent over the Internet. This can be useful for identifying network problems and the like.

UNIX A flexible operating system used on computers ranging in size from personal computers to mainframes. Well-suited to the needs of advanced computer users, UNIX supports multitasking as well as multiuser applications.

V.34 A protocol for transmitting and receiving data at 28,800 bits per second (bps). V.34 modems adjust to changing conditions to get the fastest possible transfer rate.

VBX Stands for Visual Basic extension. This is a first generation Visual Basic control and limited to only 16-bit programs.

Visual Basic A high-level programming language used to develop applications for Microsoft Windows, Windows 95 and Windows NT.

well-known ports An Internet port address that is permanently linked to a certain application by the Internet Assigned Numbers Authority.

Winsock A growing standard that dictates how a dynamic link library (DLL) should be written to provide TCP/IP support for computers using Microsoft Windows 95.

World Wide Web Abbreviated WWW, the World Wide Web uses hypertext documents with hyperlinks on the Internet so the user can simply point and click his way around the world.

Appendix B

What's on the CD?

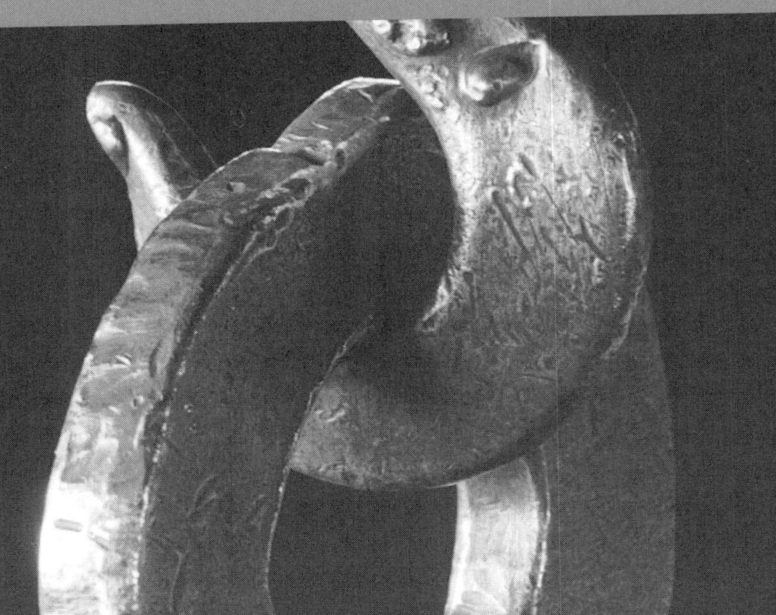

The CD that accompanies this book contains numerous tools and utilities to assist the Visual Basic programmer in implementing Internet functionality into applications. There are links to downloadable ActiveX control sites, HTML editors, Windows utilities, and more. Examples and source code from the book are included as well.

Running the CD

To make the CD more user friendly and take up less of your disk space, you don't have to install the CD, which means that the only files transferred to your hard disk are the ones you choose to copy.

> **CAUTION:** Significant differences between the various Windows operating systems (Windows 3.1, Windows 95, and Windows NT) sometimes render files that work in one Windows environment inoperable in another. 32-bit programs that run in Windows 95 and Windows NT cannot run in Windows 3.1, which is a 16-bit operating system. In addition, the length and case of file names can make files invisible to one operating system or the other.
>
> Prima has made every effort to ensure that this problem is minimized. However, it is not possible to eliminate it entirely. Therefore, you may find that some files or directories appear to be missing from the CD. Those files are, in reality, on the CD, but remain hidden from the operating system. To confirm this, view the CD using a different Windows operating system.

Windows 3.1

To run the CD under Windows 3.1, follow these steps:

1. Insert the CD in the CD-ROM drive.
2. From File Manager, choose File, Run to open the Run window.
3. In the Command Line text box type **D:\primacd.exe** (where D:\ is the CD-ROM drive).
4. Click OK.

Windows 95

Because there is no install routine, running the CD in Windows 95 is breeze, especially if you have autorun enabled. Simply insert the CD in the CD-ROM drive, close the tray, and wait for the CD to load.

If you have disabled autorun, place the CD in the drive and follow these steps:

1. From the Start menu select Run.
2. Type **D:\primacd.exe** (where D:\ is the CD-ROM drive).
3. Click OK.

The Prima User Interface

Prima's user interface is designed to make viewing and using the CD contents quick and easy. It contains six category buttons, four options buttons, and a display window. Click a category button to show a list of available titles in the display window. Highlight a title in the window and click an option button to perform the desired action.

Category Buttons

- *Examples.* Examples and source code from the book.
- *ActiveX.* Links to Internet sites with downloadable ActiveX controls.
- *HTMLTools.* A large collection of HTML editors, templates, and add-ons to help you create sophisticated Web pages.
- *Multimedia.* A variety of graphics and WAV editors.
- *Net Tools.* Internet plug-ins and add-ons.
- *Utilities.* File and system utilities to help manage your system and improve its performance.

Options Buttons

- *Install/Run.* If the highlighted title contains an install routine, choosing this option begins the installation process. If the title has no install procedure but contains an executable file, the executable is run. If neither an install nor an executable file is present (as in the case of a graphics library), the folder containing the information is shown. In the event that an application contains an executable file that does not run from the CD, the entire application is placed in a compressed zip file, which can be accessed by installing WinZip (included on the CD).

> **NOTE:** You can install some of the shareware programs that do not have installation routines by copying the program files from the CD to your hard drive and running the executable (.EXE) file.

- *Information.* Data about the selection is shown, if available. This information is usually in the form of a readme or help file.
- *Explore.* This option allows you to view the folder containing the program files.
- *Exit.* When you're finished and ready to move on, choose exit.

The Software

This section gives you a brief description of some of the software you find on the CD. This is just a sampling. As you browse the CD you will find much more.

- *Cool Edit.* A full-featured wave editor for Windows.
- *Cute FTP.* Simple and straightforward FTP software for beginner and pro, alike.
- *Drag and View Gold.* A handy utility that lets you drag, drop, and view word processing, spreadsheet, database, and graphics files without opening the parent application.
- *Frame-IT!.* A feature-packed HTML frame generator, which allows you to generate complex HTML frames using only your mouse.

- *Gomer.* An easy-to-use HTML editor.
- *HotDog.* A stand-alone HTML editor that supports extensions from Microsoft and Netscape as well as proposed HTML 3 elements.
- *HTML Assistant.* A simple Web publishing tool for creating HTML Web pages.
- *Kenn Nesbitt's Webedit.* The popular HTML editor for novice and pro alike.
- *Live Markup.* It's as close as you can get to a WYSIWYG HTML editor.
- *Lview Pro.* A versatile Windows graphics editor.
- *Mapedit.* A WYSIWYG editor for imagemap files.
- *Paint Shop Pro.* The popular bitmap image editor from JASC, Inc.
- *PolyView.* A multi-threaded, 32-bit Microsoft Windows 95 and Windows NT application that provides viewing, file conversion, and image manipulation support for most popular graphics image file formats.
- *Webber.* A fast, flexible HTML editor from Cerebral Systems Development.
- *Web Weaver.* An easy-to-use HTML text editor.
- *WinZip.* One of the leading file-compression utilities for Windows 95, NT, and Windows 3.1.

INDEX

Notes

Notes

Notes

Notes

Notes

Notes

Notes

Notes

To Order Books

Please send me the following items:

Quantity	Title	Unit Price	Total
______	______________________________	$ ______	$ ______
______	______________________________	$ ______	$ ______
______	______________________________	$ ______	$ ______
______	______________________________	$ ______	$ ______
______	______________________________	$ ______	$ ______

Shipping and Handling depend on Subtotal.

Subtotal	Shipping/Handling
$0.00–$14.99	$3.00
$15.00–$29.99	$4.00
$30.00–$49.99	$6.00
$50.00–$99.99	$10.00
$100.00–$199.99	$13.50
$200.00+	Call for Quote

Foreign and all Priority Request orders:
Call Order Entry department
for price quote at 916/632-4400

This chart represents the total retail price of books only (before applicable discounts are taken).

Subtotal $ ______

Deduct 10% when ordering 3-5 books $ ______

7.25% Sales Tax (CA only) $ ______

8.25% Sales Tax (TN only) $ ______

5.0% Sales Tax (MD and IN only) $ ______

Shipping and Handling* $ ______

Total Order $ ______

By Telephone: With MC or Visa, call 800-632-8676, 916-632-4400. Mon-Fri, 8:30-4:30.

WWW {http://www.primapublishing.com}

Orders Placed Via Internet E-mail {sales@primapub.com}

By Mail: Just fill out the information below and send with your remittance to:

Prima Publishing
P.O. Box 1260BK
Rocklin, CA 95677

My name is ______________________________

I live at ______________________________

City ____________________ State ______ Zip ______

MC/Visa# ____________________ Exp. ______

Check/Money Order enclosed for $ ____________ Payable to Prima Publishing

Daytime Telephone ______________________________

Signature ______________________________

Other books from Prima Publishing, Computer Products Division

ISBN	Title	Price	Release Date
0-7615-0801-5	ActiveX	$40.00	Available Now
0-7615-0680-2	America Online Complete Handbook and Membership Kit	$24.99	Available Now
0-7615-0915-1	Building Intranets with Internet Information Server and FrontPage	$45.00	Available Now
0-7615-0417-6	CompuServe Complete Handbook and Membership Kit	$24.95	Available Now
0-7615-0849-X	Corporate Intranet Development	$45.00	Fall '96
0-7615-0692-6	Create Your First Web Page in a Weekend	$24.99	Available Now
0-7615-0503-2	Discover What's Online!	$24.95	Available Now
0-7615-0693-4	Internet Information Server	$40.00	Available Now
0-7615-0815-5	Introduction to ABAP/4 Programming for SAP	$45.00	Available Now
0-7615-0678-0	Java Applet Powerpack	$30.00	Available Now
0-7615-0685-3	Javascript	$35.00	Available Now
0-7615-0901-1	Leveraging Visual Basic with ActiveX Controls	$45.00	Available Now
0-7615-0682-9	LiveWire Pro Master's Handbook	$45.00	Fall '96
0-7615-0755-8	Moving Worlds	$35.00	Available Now
0-7615-0690-X	Netscape Enterprise Server	$40.00	Available Now
0-7615-0691-8	Netscape FastTrack Server	$40.00	Available Now
0-7615-0852-X	Netscape Navigator 3 Complete Handbook	$24.99	Available Now
0-7615-0733-7	Netscape Navigator Gold Master's Handbook	$40.00	Fall '96
0-7615-0751-5	NT Server Administrator's Guide	$50.00	Available Now
0-7615-0759-0	Professional Web Design	$40.00	Available Now
0-7615-0773-6	Programming Internet Controls	$45.00	Available Now
0-7615-0780-9	Programming Web Server Applications	$40.00	Available Now
0-7615-0063-4	Researching on the Internet	$29.95	Available Now
0-7615-0686-1	Researching on the World Wide Web	$24.99	Available Now
0-7615-0695-0	The Essential Photoshop Book	$35.00	Available Now
0-7615-0752-3	The Essential Windows NT Book	$27.99	Available Now
0-7615-0689-6	The Microsoft Exchange Productivity Guide	$24.99	Available Now
0-7615-0769-8	Vbscript Master's Handbook	$45.00	Available Now
0-7615-0684-5	Vbscript Web Page Interactivity	$40.00	Available Now
0-7615-0903-8	Visual FoxPro 5 Enterprise Development	$45.00	Available Now
0-7615-0814-7	Visual J++	$35.00	Available Now
0-7615-0383-8	Web Advertising and Marketing	$34.95	Available Now
0-7615-0726-4	Webmaster's Handbook	$40.00	Available Now

License Agreement/Notice of Limited Warranty

By opening the sealed disk container in this book, you agree to the following terms and conditions. If, upon reading the following license agreement and notice of limited warranty, you cannot agree to the terms and conditions set forth, return the unused book with unopened disk to the place where you purchased it for a refund.

License:

The enclosed software is copyrighted by the copyright holder(s) indicated on the software disk. You are licensed to copy the software onto a single computer for use by a single concurrent user and to a backup disk. You may not reproduce, make copies, or distribute copies or rent or lease the software in whole or in part, except with written permission of the copyright holder(s). You may transfer the enclosed disk only together with this license, and only if you destroy all other copies of the software and the transferee agrees to the terms of the license. You may not decompile, reverse assemble, or reverse engineer the software.

Notice of Limited Warranty:

The enclosed disk is warranted by Prima Publishing to be free of physical defects in materials and workmanship for a period of sixty (60) days from end user's purchase of the book/disk combination. During the sixty-day term of the limited warranty, Prima will provide a replacement disk upon the return of a defective disk.

Limited Liability:

THE SOLE REMEDY FOR BREACH OF THIS LIMITED WARRANTY SHALL CONSIST ENTIRELY OF REPLACEMENT OF THE DEFECTIVE DISK. IN NO EVENT SHALL PRIMA OR THE AUTHORS BE LIABLE FOR ANY OTHER DAMAGES, INCLUDING LOSS OR CORRUPTION OF DATA, CHANGES IN THE FUNCTIONAL CHARACTERISTICS OF THE HARDWARE OR OPERATING SYSTEM, DELETERIOUS INTERACTION WITH OTHER SOFTWARE, OR ANY OTHER SPECIAL, INCIDENTAL, OR CONSEQUENTIAL DAMAGES THAT MAY ARISE, EVEN IF PRIMA AND/OR THE AUTHORS HAVE PREVIOUSLY BEEN NOTIFIED THAT THE POSSIBILITY OF SUCH DAMAGES EXISTS.

Disclaimer of Warranties:

PRIMA AND THE AUTHORS SPECIFICALLY DISCLAIM ANY AND ALL OTHER WARRANTIES, EITHER EXPRESS OR IMPLIED, INCLUDING WARRANTIES OF MERCHANTABILITY, SUITABILITY TO A PARTICULAR TASK OR PURPOSE, OR FREEDOM FROM ERRORS. SOME STATES DO NOT ALLOW FOR EXCLUSION OF IMPLIED WARRANTIES OR LIMITATION OF INCIDENTAL OR CONSEQUENTIAL DAMAGES, SO THESE LIMITATIONS MAY NOT APPLY TO YOU.

Other:

This Agreement is governed by the laws of the State of California without regard to choice of law principles. The United Convention of Contracts for the International Sale of Goods is specifically disclaimed. This Agreement constitutes the entire agreement between you and Prima Publishing regarding use of the software.